AF082109

Age of the Spirit

John Maiden is a Senior Lecturer in Religious Studies at The Open University in the United Kingdom. He is also the non-residential Director of the Evangelical Studies Program at Baylor Institute for Studies of Religion, Texas. He lives in Manchester, England.

'John Maiden's *Age of the Spirit* is by far the best study of Anglophone charismatic renewal in global context. Not only is this beautifully written book abundant with meticulous new research from diverse archival sources, it is also theoretically sophisticated, offering new interpretive paradigms for understanding the global impact of this crucial movement. Maiden's book is instantly essential reading for anyone seeking to understand contemporary manifestations of charismatic-style Christianity, from Hillsong to Pope Francis and all points between.'

Rev Dr Caleb Maskell, Associate National Director, Vineyard USA

'John Maiden's magisterial *Age of the Spirit* is essential reading for those seeking to understand the connections between the Catholic charismatic renewal and the evolving Christian landscape in the years after the Second Vatican Council (1962–65). Every page yields surprising details, unappreciated personal connections and rich theological debates across seemingly distinctive forms of denominational identity and ecclesial expression. In charting the theological intricacies of these dynamic and vibrant 'Spiritscapes' of renewal, we encounter global networks and transnational currents linking suburban churches in Brisbane and Guildford to charismatic and pentecostal hubs in South Bend and Toronto. It powerfully intervenes, with closely sketched case studies, into longstanding debates about secularisation and post-Sixties ecclesiological experimentation while also offering new framings of contemporary expressive spirituality and practical ecumenical exchanges. It will become a staple on all modern religious history reading lists.'

Dr Alana Harris, Director of Liberal Arts and Reader in Modern British Social, Cultural, and Gender History, King's College London

'The charismatic renewal changed everything, including if this book is any guide, how history might be written. Spiritscape calls for a spirited account, a disciplined focus on often unrestrained phenomena [...] The resulting map is richly complex: the Spirit is clearly brilliant at multi-tasking, harvesting seekers from an astonishing array of mystical esoterica as well as the struggling orthodox in need of reviving and marginalised poor and migrants in need of survival rations. Local developments become global movements; Anglophone Christianity flows into the spiritualities of Asia, Africa, Europe, and South America; the apparently haphazard morphs into the organic while maintaining uniqueness; the thematic and chronological are happily married; sympathetic treatment of the novelties of renewal increases the credibility of critical discernment; the weight of massive scholarship is worn lightly in sparkling prose. This book is a miracle and, as such, a worthy account of probably the most significant movement in twentieth-century Christianity.'

Associate Professor Stuart Piggin, Director, Centre for the History of Christian Thought and Experience, Macquarie University, NSW, Australia

'[...] the volume succeeds in explaining the complex nature of the charismatic renewal in its denominational and non-denominational forms and above all its significance as a global spiritual enterprise in the long 1960s. It has laid the groundwork for future research regarding the post-history of the charismatic renewal, the nature of the interrelationship (or not) with non Anglo-World Pentecostal movements, the significance of social class and the gendered nature of the charismatic renewal.'

Carmen M. Mangion, *British Catholic History*

'[...] a highly readable, compellingly argued account of one of the most significant ecclesial phenomena of the 20th and 21st centuries. It will be an essential reading for those interested in the impact of charismatic renewal on mission and evangelism, particularly church growth theories, in Pentecostalism and global Christianity in contemporary times.'

Alison Ruth Kolosova, *Mission Studies*

'[...] Maiden's naming and framing of the charismatic movement will remain essential reading for years to come. John Maiden has delivered a major contribution on the central importance of spirituality to the globality of Christianity worldwide.'

Dana L. Robert, *Journal of Presbyterian History*

Age of the Spirit

Charismatic Renewal, the Anglo-World, and Global Christianity, 1945–1980

JOHN MAIDEN

OXFORD
UNIVERSITY PRESS

Great Clarendon Street, Oxford, OX2 6DP,
United Kingdom

Oxford University Press is a department of the University of Oxford.
It furthers the University's objective of excellence in research, scholarship,
and education by publishing worldwide. Oxford is a registered trade mark of
Oxford University Press in the UK and in certain other countries

© John Maiden 2023

The moral rights of the author have been asserted

First published 2023
First published in paperback 2025

All rights reserved. No part of this publication may be reproduced, stored in a retrieval system, or transmitted, in any form or by any means, without the prior permission in writing of Oxford University Press, or as expressly permitted by law, by licence or under terms agreed with the appropriate reprographics rights organization. Enquiries concerning reproduction outside the scope of the above should be sent to the Rights Department, Oxford University Press, at the address above

You must not circulate this work in any other form
and you must impose this same condition on any acquirer

Published in the United States of America by Oxford University Press
198 Madison Avenue, New York, NY 10016, United States of America

British Library Cataloguing in Publication Data
Data available

Library of Congress Cataloging in Publication Data
Data available

ISBN 978–0–19–884749–6 (Hbk.)
ISBN 978–0–19–897192–4 (Pbk.)

DOI: 10.1093/oso/9780198847496.001.0001

Links to third party websites are provided by Oxford in good faith and
for information only. Oxford disclaims any responsibility for the materials
contained in any third party website referenced in this work.

For

David Bebbington and Mark Hutchinson—giants

and

Hannah, Esmé, Jacob, Max, Miriam, and Rachel

Preface

> The Holy Spirit is the power – God's atomic power, the power that can change a lot of things.[1]

In the sphere of North America, the British Isles, South Africa, and Australasia, the 1950s to the 1970s were marked by social, cultural, economic, technological, and political transformations. Against this backdrop there was an effort to renew—to reanimate—Christianity. In an age of rapid scientific advancement, some of which presented an awful and existential threat, many Christians imagined an *age of the Spirit*.

'Those who like their religion straight from the fridge would be thoroughly put off', said one observer of a charismatic conference in 1971.[2] It would appear some historians of religion have had some aversion to the study of charismatic Christianity. There is some scholarship on the drift towards charismatic Christianity within the Anglo-world during these decades, but the literature is not extensive. Given the degree to which charismatics have changed the face of contemporary Christianity, and in some cases (if the reader will forgive the cliché) appeared to 'buck the trend' of secularisation, this is surprising. It is worth pausing to ask why this has been so. Does it say something about the Academy, some avoidance of 'irrational' forms of contemporary Western culture? Or does it say something about the field of religious history? Has there been an inclination to avoid charismatic Christianity and prefer the study of cerebral forms of religion with proper ideas or structures to consider? When I set out on a doctorate in religious history in 2003, it never occurred to me I might eventually research charismatics, even though I attended a charismatic congregation at the time.

How should we go about writing the history of charismatic Christianity? For many of its practitioners, understandably, charismatic renewal is understood largely or solely with reference to God's inbreaking work in the world. This assumption has also been evident in some scholarship. One of the influential chroniclers of charismatic renewal, the Catholic historian Peter Hocken, offers a superb account of lineages behind British charismatic origins in *Streams of Renewal* (1986). However, he also puts forward the prophecy given by Smith Wigglesworth, the British pentecostal evangelist, to David du Plessis in 1936

[1] David du Plessis, 'Acts 29: Where we are NOW in the continuing Acts of the Holy Spirit', *Episcopalian Charismatic Fellowship Newsletter*, November 1973, 20–21.

[2] DGC, Fountain Trust, photo album, 'The fellowship of the Holy Spirit', conference programme.

('There is a revival coming that at present the world knows nothing about. It will come through the churches') as 'a possible framework within which to interpret the movement not only in Britain but throughout the world'.[3] The issue here is not whether the charismatic renewal was the work of the Holy Spirit. That question is above my pay grade as a historian. Rather my point is that singularly religious explanations have sometimes resulted in a cursory engagement with historical context. This approach to history is theologically unsatisfactory anyway, given that the central drama of the Christian story is the incarnation of God *in* history. Whether from a secular or religious perspective, the history of charismatic Christianity deserves to be taken seriously. It should be written using all the tools of critical scholarship which are available to the historian.

A distinctive feature of this book is that the primary arena of study is the Anglo-world nations of the United States, Canada, the United Kingdom, the Republic of Ireland, South Africa, Australia, and New Zealand. However, at every step this English-speaking sphere is placed in a wider global frame to include sub-Saharan Africa, Latin America, continental Western Europe, South-East Asia and even the Soviet bloc. I am interested in interconnections. The very idea of 'Pentecost' has globalising implications. I will argue that eschatology, mediated by text, audio, and audio-visual, fostered an imagined community, or 'imaginary', of charismatic renewal. I also assume the importance of *translocality*. This refers to the multi-directional flows of people, media, prayer letters, prayers, air mail, practices, and money etc., but also pinpoints on the map of the charismatic geography of the Spirit the localities—including inner cities, suburbs, small towns, and remote rural locations—which contributed to the wider nexus.

A colleague once shared something about the writing of global religious history which he had been told by another scholar: 'you can only do your best with an impossible job'. Perhaps never truer words were spoken on the topic. I will get my excuses in early, therefore, and readily admit that this book has limitations. There will be absences of places, persons, or events to irritate almost every reader. For these limitations and omissions, I apologise in advance, but I trust this endeavour will still have been worthwhile. I have also referred to the Spirit in the feminine, in line with the Hebrew, Aramaic, and Syriac languages. I realise this will be controversial to some and accept there is no consensus amongst biblical scholars on this point. The outdated term "Third World" is used in the study only to reflect its contemporary usage in the period covered by this book.

Some people mentioned in the hardback version of *Age of the Spirit*—including Mike Pilavachi and Mike Bickle—have since been the subject of investigations into

[3] Peter Hocken, *Streams of renewal: the origins and early development of the charismatic movement in Great Britain* (Carlisle: Paternoster Press, 1986), 19, 20. Connie Ho Yan Au, in a similar vein, has explicitly affirmed the view that from the 1950s to the 1970s 'the Spirit renewed the Church worldwide'. See *Grassroots unity in the charismatic renewal* (Eugene: Wipf & Stock, 2011), 1.

serious allegations of abusive behaviour. The relationship between charismatic Christianity and the abuse of power is a theme of this book.

A privilege in writing this book has been visiting so many libraries and archives and meeting fascinating and generous people in various parts of the world. In order of distance from my home in Manchester, England, I would like to thank the staff of the Nazarene Theological College, Didsbury; the Donald Gee Library, Mattersey; the British Library, London; Lambeth Palace Library, London; Chicago Public Library; Billy Graham Centre Archives, Wheaton College, Chicago; University of Notre Dame Archive, South Bend; Library of Congress, Washington DC; Regent University Library and Special Collections, Virginia Beach; David Allan Hubbard Library, Pasadena; James Wallace Memorial Library, Alphacrucis College, Sydney; Veech Library, Catholic Institute of Sydney; and John Kinder Theological Library, Auckland. Images are reproduced with permission. I am particularly grateful to the trustees of the Donald Gee Library and Archive (and subsequently the Institute for Pentecostal Theology at Regents Theological College, Malvern, where the Fountain Trust archive moved), for their generosity in allowing the reproduction of images, and to the Faculty of Arts and Social Science at the Open University for providing funds for the same purpose.

I am sincerely grateful to my interviewees. I am thankful also for the collegiality (and very good humour) of the Religious Studies department at the Open University, and the 'regulars' at the Modern Religious History seminar at the Institute of Historical Research, London, which I have the pleasure of co-convening. My editor at Oxford University Press, Tom Perridge and his team—Karen Raith and Katie Bishop—has been unfailing helpful and professional. The book would never have been completed without the intellectual input, encouragement, and occasional rebuke of various scholars and archivists: Andrew Atherstone, Uta Balbier, David Bebbington, David Bundy, Valentina Ciciliot, Dave Emmett, Larry Eskridge, Sally Gibbs, Geordan Hammond, Mark Hutchinson, Bill Jacob, Tim Larsen, Peter Lineham, Caleb Maskell, Melanie McAllister, Mark Noll, Kendrick Oliver, Amber Thomas Reynolds, Tom Schwanda, Stefanie Sinclair, Brian Stanley, Steven Sutcliffe, Vinson Synan, and John Wolffe. Closer to home, thanks to Ron and Sue Stout for their boundless generosity and to Chris Bullivant, Tom and Cathy Cox, Simon and Sue Cook, the Revd. Jamie and Amy Kidd, Lois and Clarence Lindblom, Gill Maiden, Richard and Jennifer McCormick, Rachel Welsby-Maiden, Ali Welsby, Chris, Esther, Andrew and Natalie Lane, and Paul Sheriffs for taking an interest in 'this book I'm writing'. I am thankful, more than I can ever say, to my parents for their love and encouragement.

The book is written in loving memory of Peter Maiden – 'there must be more than this'.

Contents

List of Illustrations

List of Abbreviations

Archives

APCSA	Alan Paton Centre and Struggle Archives, Durban (online)
DAHL	David Allan Hubbard Library, Pasadena
DGC	Donald Gee Centre, Mattersey
JKTL	John Kinder Theological Library, Auckland
LPL	Lambeth Palace Library, London
RUSCA	Regent University Special Collections and Archives, Virginia Beach
SiS	Sword in the Spirit archive (online)
UNDA	University of Notre Dame Archive, South Bend

Biographical collections

ADPCM	*Australasian Dictionary of Pentecostal and Charismatic Movements* (online)

Service agencies

BTS	Blessed Trinity Society (United States)
CAM	Christian Action Ministries (New Zealand)
CCRSC	Catholic Charismatic Renewal Service Committee (United States)
CFO	Camps Farthest Out
CGM	Christian Growth Ministries (United States)
CIF	Christian Interdenominational Fellowship (South Africa)
FT	Fountain Trust (United Kingdom)

All Scripture references are taken from the *New International Version* (NIV)

Now the earth was formless and empty,
darkness was over the surface of the deep,
and the Spirit of God was hovering
over the waters

Genesis 1:2

1
Introduction

...wait for the gift my Father promised
Acts 1:4

'Veni, Creator, Spiritus' is a prayer found throughout Guildford's Cathedral of the Holy Spirit. Consecrated in 1961, it was the first Anglican cathedral built on a new site in south England since the Reformation. The design of the architect Edward Maufe displayed a subtly neo-gothic fabric with a progressive edge, becoming known as 'the motorist's cathedral' because of the distinctive road approach. The design implied both continuity with the past and a Christianity for the present.[1] Ten years later, the venue carried a powerful symbolism for the first international conference of the Fountain Trust (Fig. 1.1), a service agency for a growing translocal Christian subculture which coalesced around the label of 'charismatic renewal'. The choice of Guildford, just beyond the London commuter belt, as the location reflected the suburban middle-class demographic of many participants, 650 of whom assembled for five days of lectures at the University of Surrey and nightly meetings in the Anglican sanctuary.[2] A panoply of charismatic manifestations were said to have been in evidence: singing in the Spirit, tongues with interpretation, prophecy, words of wisdom or knowledge, healings, conversions and 'glorious baptisms in the Spirit'.[3] Photographs showed a cathedral filled with worshippers, many raising one or both hands.[4] A pentecostal speaker, the South African-born ecumenist David du Plessis, claimed 'There were so many charismatic manifestations that one sometimes felt like saying that it was really a Pentecostal conference.'[5]

It was a cosmopolitan affair. The press release spoke of drawing together 'Christians from various church traditions and countries to learn more about the Holy Spirit and enjoy fellowship and worship together in Him'.[6] The ecumenical diversity was striking. The conference theme 'the fellowship of the Holy Spirit' had been suggested by a Roman Catholic member of the organising committee, and there was Mass for Catholic delegates each afternoon.[7] Alongside speakers

[1] See David Pepin, *Cathedrals of Britain* (London: Bloomsbury, 2016), 122–23.
[2] DGC, Fountain Trust, photo album, 'The fellowship of the Holy Spirit', conference programme.
[3] David du Plessis, 'Unity breaks down barriers', *Renewal*, 34 (1971), 4–6, quote at 6.
[4] See front cover, *Renewal*, 34 (1971).
[5] Du Plessis, 'Unity', 6
[6] DGC, Fountain Trust, box 2, Press release, International conference 2.
[7] Bob Balkam, 'Charism and institution: 1968–1978', unpublished.

Age of the Spirit: Charismatic Renewal, the Anglo-World, and Global Christianity, 1945–1980. John Maiden, Oxford University Press. © John Maiden 2023. DOI: 10.1093/oso/9780198847496.003.0001

Fig. 1.1 The 1971 international Fountain Trust conference at Guildford Cathedral.

from mainline churches like the distinguished Methodist Dr Leslie Davison were independent evangelicals such as Arthur Wallis of the inchoate house church movement. 'Protestants, Catholics and Pentecostals enjoyed each other's company', remarked du Plessis (omitting to mention a group of pentecostals who had protested outside because of Catholic involvement).[8] A global dimension was evident, with visitors from around twenty countries, including the Republic of Ireland, United States and Canada, South Africa, Australia and New Zealand, and northern Europe (France, Norway, Denmark, Sweden, West Germany, and Holland).[9] The worship had an international flavour, with Toronto's guitar duo Merv and Merla Watson and a choir from Anaheim, California, participating; and speakers included American non-denominational leaders Robert Frost and Ralph

[8] Du Plessis, 'Unity', 4–5. On the public protest, see Michael Harper, 'The coming-of-age', *Renewal*, 34 (1971), 2–4, at 3. In advance it was estimated representatives of 14 denominations had booked, including over 100 Anglicans, 45 Methodists, 35 Roman Catholics, and 26 Baptists—see: Press release, International conference 2.

[9] International conference 2; DGC, Fountain Trust, box 2, Guest list.

Wilkerson, and J. Rodman Williams, Professor of Systematic Theology and Philosophy at Austin Presbyterian Theological Seminary, Texas. The conference obtained media coverage across the wider Christian community. One observer for the British evangelical *Crusade* magazine commented: 'Whatever view one holds of it, this is now unquestionably the most important single development in British church life since the War; possibly this century. Its potential for good or ill is incalculable.'[10]

* * *

This book concerns charismatic renewal during the period c.1945 to c.1980. The 'renewal' saw Christianity in various of its existing mainline, independent, and pentecostal forms undergo a process of reanimation through awareness of the presence and power of the Spirit, the rediscovery of *charisms*, the restoration of 'primitive' patterns of ministry, authority, and community, and the re-enchantment of everyday piety through the lens of the supernatural world of the Bible, in particular the Acts of the Apostles. The focus will be a distinctive religious subculture and patterns of exchange which mapped largely onto the Anglo-world settings of North America, the British Isles, South Africa, and Australasia, but which were in their emergence and development connected with a global nexus of charismatic, pentecostal, and holiness movements. A central argument is that during these years, participants in charismatic renewal in the Anglo-world imagined themselves to be living in a particular eschatological moment—a 'new Pentecost'—the contexts of which were the crises of the 'long 1960s'. For many who became involved, it seemed they were living in an age of the Spirit.

For the historian of global Christianity, the long-term influence of charismatic renewal is remarkable. Within Anglicanism, for example, Holy Trinity Brompton, the west London birthplace of the *Alpha* evangelistic course (and former stomping ground of the 105th Archbishop of Canterbury, Justin Welby), became a driving force in England and then globally. Further afield, the character of entire Anglican Provinces, for example Singapore and Nigeria, has been reshaped by charismatic influences, with Jesse Zink observing the 'Anglocostalism' of the latter.[11] Charismatic renewal is now integrated with the institutional life of the Roman Catholic Church. It has contributed to the emergence of countless independent congregations and networks, variously labelled the 'new paradigm churches', the 'New Apostolic Reformation', and 'Independent Network Christianity'.[12] Some

[10] David Winter, *Crusade*, September 1971.

[11] Jesse Zink, '"Anglocostalism" in Nigeria: neo-Pentecostals and obstacles to Anglican unity', *Journal of Anglican Studies*, 10/2 (2013), 231–50.

[12] Donald E. Miller, *Reinventing American Protestantism: Christianity in a new millennium* (Berkeley: University of California Press, 1997); John Weaver, *The New Apostolic Reformation: history of a modern charismatic movement* (Jefferson: McFarland and Co, 2016); Brad Christerson and Richard Flory, *The rise of network Christianity: how independent leaders are changing the religious landscape* (New York: Oxford University Press, 2017).

within the existing pentecostal denominations, too, have been charismaticised, notably in their approaches to worship and apostolic authority. Charismatics dominate religious television and are the driving force behind contemporary Christian music. Their sounds and practices have also penetrated non-charismatic circles—as, for example, Sunday visitors to many conservative evangelical congregations would now observe. Yet if charismatic Christianity is now part of the 'mainstream', it was not always thus. This book explains how it became so.

Charismatic Renewal: Spiritscape(s) and Imaginary

One person not in the South African contingent at Guildford, but who became a prominent participant in Fountain Trust events in future years, was the Right Revd. Bill Burnett, the Bishop of Grahamstown. Burnett had been vaguely aware of charismatic developments in South Africa and elsewhere, but on 13 March 1972 had an experience of the Spirit, quite independently, while praying before lunch in his private chapel. He felt the Lord was saying: 'I want you to offer your body to Me'. The bishop began to list parts of his body in response. As he did so, he recalled, 'the Holy Spirit simply fell on me'. He explained in the Fountain Trust magazine *Renewal*:

> I can only speak of it in terms of a mighty rushing wind. I did not really know what was happening then because I wasn't expecting anything very much. But there was a wonderful tingling and a sense of the love of God, and an overpowering sense of His presence. Presently I found myself being pressed to the ground, and simply submitting to Him in joy, saying the one word "yes" and not able to say any other word, and not wanting to say any other word, but "yes, yes and yes again, and yes again yes".

Burnett then looked at his watch and saw it was lunch time—'you see how British I am!', he told readers.[13] His story provides a helpful point of departure for consideration of the category charismatic renewal. What can it mean? In the Christian tradition, 'charismatic' experiences and practices have been reported amongst individuals and groups from the beginning. Burnett in 1972 therefore found himself in the company of many others in church history (if I wanted to underline the point, I would call this experience 'small c' charismatic). It was only later after this experience that Burnett found himself enter into what Karla Poewe describes as a 'global culture' of charismatic Christianity, and more specifically

[13] Bill Burnett, 'The Holy Spirit simply fell on me', *Renewal*, 48 (December 1973–January 1974), 2–4, quote at 3.

still, came to identify with charismatic renewal (capital 'CR', if you like).[14] Soon after his experience, when Burnett preached at the local Community of the Resurrection he realised one of the Revered Mothers, Joanna Mary, was in fact the daughter of Alexander Boddy, the Anglican vicar who led early twentieth-century English pentecostalism. 'She had been charismatic all her life', Burnett realised, surprised to find an antecedent in his own denomination for the charismatic renewal of which he now found himself a part.[15]

How might we begin to make sense of this diverse, translocal subculture? Something of this scope requires a theoretical framework on which to build. I will draw on a cluster of theoretical approaches which trace intellectual lineages to Benedict Anderson's notion of 'imagined communities'.[16] To understand the production of the imagined community or 'imaginary' of charismatic renewal it is helpful to turn to Arjun Appadurai's theory of changing—homogenising and heterogenising—cultural 'landscapes'. He describes these ethnoscapes, technoscapes, financescapes, mediascapes, and ideoscapes as the 'building blocks of [. . .] imagined worlds'. The products of transnational cultural 'flows' (e.g. people, machinery, money, images, and ideas), these landscapes 'are not objectively given relations that look the same from every angle of vision but, rather, they are deeply perspectival constructs, inflected by the historical, linguistic, and political situatedness of different sorts of actors'.[17] Following Appadurai, other scholars have proposed adding to his list 'sacriscapes' or 'religioscapes'.[18] This book maps out the relations and exchanges which constituted a *Spiritscape of charismatic renewal*. The opening vignette of the Guildford conference is one 'sighting' of this—but countless others could have been selected.

The term Spiritscape in the singular denotes some coherence to the subculture of charismatic renewal. It is not meant, however, to infer homogeneity. In a similar vein to Victor Roudometof (in his work on the 'Orthodox religioscape'), I use Spiritscape as an agile heuristic device to describe a complex, changeable transnational and translocal terrain and the multidirectional cultural flows which shaped it.[19] In fact, it was always a 'Spiritscape of Spiritscapes' with varying understandings of eschatology, ecclesiology, and pneumatology—but which in mutual recognition and exchange were part of a larger whole. With colleagues

[14] Karla Poewe, 'Preface', in Poewe (ed.), *Charismatic Christianity as a global culture* (Columbia: University of South Carolina Press, 1994), xi–xii.

[15] Bill Burnett, 'Evidence on the fringe', *Renewal*, 49 (February–March 1974), 10–13, quote at 11.

[16] Benedict Anderson, *Imagined communities: reflections on the origin and spread of nationalism* (London: Verso, 1983).

[17] Arjun Appadurai, *Modernity at large: cultural dimensions of globalization* (Minneapolis: University of Minnesota Press, 1996), 33, 37.

[18] Malcolm Waters, *Globalization* (London: Routledge, 1995); Rachel Dwyer, 'The Swaminarayan movement', in Knut Jacobsen and P. Patap Kumar (eds.), *South Asians in the diaspora: histories and religious traditions* (Leiden: Brill, 2004), 180–99.

[19] Victor Roudometof, 'Orthodox Christianity as transnational religion: theoretical, historical and comparative considerations', *Religion, State and Society*, 43/3 (2015), 211–27, at 212.

Mark Hutchinson and Andrew Atherstone, the author has previously described the renewal as an 'emerging global sacriscape'.[20] The slightly different terminology adopted in the present study—with the emphasis on *Spirit*—attempts to highlight even further distinctive dynamics of the renewal. There was an underpinning sense of eschatological certainty that God was doing something 'new' in a particular cultural moment (or series of moments), which helped bind this translocal charismatic community. The script for this imaginary, as with many historic, primitivist Christian movements, was the Lukan account of the Book of Acts. Charismatic subculture transposed the biblical 'Pentecost' to a context of contemporary religious, social, cultural, political, and geo-political crises. The *new* Pentecost was the unfolding of the Old Testament prophecy of Joel which Peter had referred to in Jerusalem: 'I will pour out My Spirit on all people. Your sons and daughters will prophesy, your young men will see visions, your old men will dream dreams' (Acts 2: 17). 'Spiritscape' also recognises that spiritual practices had a translocal dimension; and the Spirit, too, was understood to be involved in—and working through—technologies and media which charismatics adopted.

Several scholars have addressed the global dimensions of charismatic renewal. A recent collection of essays edited by Atherstone, Hutchinson, and Maiden looked closely at the transatlantic sphere.[21] Before this, Hutchinson, a pre-eminent historian of global pentecostalism, explored the global flows—multidirectional and reflexive—which shaped post-1945 pentecostal and charismatic Christianity in Australia and New Zealand.[22] His decentred approach, from the position of Oceania, is a signal contribution which provides a valuable signpost for this study. The anthropologist Thomas J. Csordas' work on Catholic charismatic renewal has perhaps the widest geographical scope, giving attention to numerous global North and South locations.[23] In each of these studies, there is recognition of the local-global dynamic in cultural processes. Csordas adopts the term 'transnational transcendence', referring to the bi- and multidirectional mobilities of 'religious phenomena – symbols, ideas, practices, moods, motivations'.[24]

[20] Andrew Atherstone, Mark Hutchinson, and John Maiden, 'The evidence of things unseen: the transatlantic Charismatic Movement in the postwar period', in Atherstone et al. (eds.), *Charismatic renewal in Europe and the United States since 1950* (Leiden: Brill, 2020), 1–18 at 22.

[21] Atherstone et al., *Charismatic renewal.*

[22] See, for example, Mark Hutchinson, 'Australasian charismatic movements and the "New Reformation" of the 20th century?', *Australasian Pentecostal Studies*, 19 (2017), 24–53; 'The Latter Rain movement and the phenomenon of global return', in Michael Wilkinson and Peter Althouse (eds.), *Winds from the north: Canadian contributions to the Pentecostal movement* (Leiden: Brill, 2010), 265–84. See also Atherstone et al., 'The evidence'.

[23] See for example, *Language, charismatic and creativity: the ritual life of a religious movement* (Berkeley: University of California Press, 1997), 39.

[24] Thomas J. Csordas, 'Modalities of transnational transcendence', in Csordas (ed.), *Transnational transcendence: essays on religion and globalization* (Berkeley: University of California Press, 2009), 1–30, at 3.

The sociologist Peggy Levitt writes 'Rather than assuming that religious life stays primarily within contained spaces (be they religious traditions, congregations, or nations), I start from the assumption of circulation and linkages.'[25] The orientation of what follows is the same. To organise our thinking about the charismatic Spiritscape, we will consider flows and both places and spaces. What flows are we addressing? We will see that charismatic renewal was a convergence of existing pieties—for example, the Latter Rain, *Cursillos de Cristiandad* (Cursillo), and Higher Life evangelicalism—and their mobilities of people, including missionaries, clergy, and migrants, travelling through denominational, para-church, and apostolic channels. As the new charismatic subculture took shape in the 1960s, mobilities continued to define it. Affordable jet air travel allowed middle-class clergy and laity to see 'what the Spirit was doing' elsewhere, perhaps combining their journey with a stop-off pilgrimage to the Holy Land or tourism (Melodyland, a flagship non-denominational charismatic ministry in Anaheim, California, was only a stone's throw from Disneyland). These connections provided a basis for a translocal community of affect: connections of feeling (often maintained by airmail) cultivated by shared experiences of the Spirit. Spiritual practices like prayer, intercession, fasting, discipleship, and prophecy also served this imaginary, maintaining at a distance the bonds of the charismatic community.

The important hubs for charismatic flows were local and national 'service agencies'. The Fountain Trust was one of these. These facilitated the production and movement of media. Charismatic renewal is a powerful case study for David Morgan's assertion that mediation is 'a domain of religious activity' and that '"media logic"' has powerful influence 'over the social practices, community formation and the operation of power and social organisation'.[26] In Christianity this was nothing new. Morgan discusses how eighteenth- and nineteenth-century evangelicalism might be seen as a 'global communication network'.[27] We will explore charismatics' reliance on the circulation of texts (magazines, books, pamphlets, newsletters, and prayer letters) and the utilisation of recent technologies, such as radio and records, and the 'new media' of tape recordings (reel to reel and cassette), video and television, in the formation of ideas, practices, and sentiments. The impact of the new media on the 'global' long Sixties is widely recognised in historical scholarship.[28] The immediacy which media technologies

[25] Peggy Levitt, 'Religion on the move: mapping global cultural production and consumption', in Courtney Bender, Wendy Cadge, Peggy Levitt, and David Smilde (eds.), *Religion on the edge: de-centering and re-centering the sociology of religion* (New York: Oxford University Press, 2013), 159–78, at 160.

[26] David Morgan, 'Mediation or mediatisation: the history of media in the study of religion', *Culture and Religion*, 12/2 (2011), 137–52, at 140 and 151.

[27] Ibid., 142.

[28] See, for example, Anne E. Gorsuch and Diane P. Koenker, 'The socialist 1960s in global perspective', in Koenker and Gorsuch (eds.), *The socialist Sixties: crossing borders in the Second World* (Bloomington: Indiana University Press, 2013), 1–24, at 7.

offered produced the 'sensational forms' (to borrow Birgit Meyer's insight on contemporary pentecostalism) of the charismatic renewal.[29] The heightening of sensory experiences of spiritual power or even the extent to which sound and image conveyed or invoked 'anointings' in teaching, healing, or musical worship, in many ways defined the charismatic Spiritscape.

As we follow these flows, we will recognise, too, the significance of places and spaces—sites invested with meanings created by experiences, and where religious phenomena were translated and negotiated. One space to constitute the charismatic Spiritscape was the suburban living room, where mid-week prayer meetings gathered for teaching and sharing in the gifts of the Spirit. We will also encounter charismatic renewal in manses and vicarages, 'community' houses and communes, churches and church halls, coffee shops, concert halls, and stadia—some of which obtained a kind of 'flagship' reputational status. A classic example is Teen Challenge in Brooklyn, New York City, the ministry associated with the charismatic bestseller *The Cross and the Switchblade* (1963), which drew visitors from across America and the world eager to learn the secrets of urban evangelism. Places and spaces were the charismatic mental map of the world.

This book's primary focus on the United States, Canada, United Kingdom, Republic of Ireland, South Africa, Australia, and New Zealand is justified by the distinctiveness of what Levitt describes as 'geographies of circulation': the ease with which charismatic Christianity moved through the social fields of this sphere.[30] These seven nations had in common their English-speaking culture, as well as significant migrant diasporas—including English, Welsh, Scots and Ulster Scots, Irish, as well as mainland European such as Swedish, Norwegian, and German. The North Atlantic world had a long history of English-speaking cultural and religious interaction and became an important zone of charismatic exchange. The Revd. Dennis Bennett, an Episcopalian priest in California who became a leading figure in the American charismatic scene from 1960, was originally from London, and spoke to English charismatics of visiting the 'old country'.[31] One of the first American charismatics to visit England, in 1963, the Revd. Frank Maguire, another Episcopalian from the Los Angeles area, did so while visiting family in Northern Ireland. In the decades after the Second World War, the Anglo-world sphere was rapidly being reconfigured. We will see that charismatic exchanges overlaid the United States' growing economic, military, and cultural influence. After all, transnational religion, as Robert Wuthnow and Stephen Offutt remind us, does not mean a level playing field, and the United States has been a

[29] Birgit Meyer, 'Mediation and immediacy: sensational forms, semiotic ideologies and the question of the medium', *Social Anthropology*, 1/19 (2011), 23–39.

[30] Levitt, 'Religion on the move', 164.

[31] LPL, Michael Harper papers, 1967/1, Dennis Bennett to Michael Harper, 10 January 1967.

'dominant player'.[32] However, although the networks of 'Greater Britain' were loosening during this period, aspects of the economic and cultural ties of 'Britonism' were resilient in Canada, Australia, and New Zealand into the 1960s (the United Kingdom joining the European Economic Community in 1973 was widely felt as a decisive blow).[33] Kinship and religion moved through these channels. This was evident, for example, in the case of the Scottish Brethren preacher Campbell McAlpine, who worked in South Africa for Youth for Christ, where he was baptised in the Spirit, before in 1959 moving to New Zealand where he became a proponent for this experience. The United Kingdom, furthermore, sometimes played gatekeeper for the entrance of American charismatic influences into the old Commonwealth world.

The direction of travel for charismatic influences, however, was not only north to the south of the equator. New Zealand, for instance, was to have a remarkable global impact on song-writing (as Australia would later). American and British charismatics were aware of the intensity of the renewal in that country. A 1973 editorial of the *Episcopal Charismatic Fellowship Newsletter* in the United States commented, 'Per capita, New Zealand has more Spirit filled people than any other country and the activities and manifestations of the Holy Spirit there are the same as here, so we have a confirmation of the guidance the Lord is giving us all over the world.'[34] South African connections, too, would prove extensive, as they were previously with pentecostal and holiness movements. The country provided two of the most influential international leaders of charismatic renewal: David du Plessis and Bill Burnett.

However, in the Anglo-world there were also diverse cultural identifications at play. In Canada, the province where Catholic charismatic renewal was strongest was French-speaking Quebec. In 1970s South Africa, charismatic subculture included both the 'neo-British' and dominant Afrikaner groupings; however, the political situation was such that despite some efforts to bring a prophetic challenge to racial segregation—including from the Black Anglican *Iviyo Lofakazi BakaKristu* (Legion of Christ's Witnesses), who had been moving in the charismatic gifts in Natal and Zululand years before they appeared in the largely white South African 'renewal' movement—there was little interaction.[35] White charismatic renewal in South Africa, specifically, has been charged with lacking a political critique of apartheid; and elsewhere, too, charismatics often failed to challenge barriers of race, culture, and class. In the United States, few Black Church congregations became involved in the charismatic renewal and there

[32] Robert Wuthnow and Stephen Offutt, 'Transnational religious connections', *Sociology of Religion*, 69/2 (2008), 209–32.

[33] See James Belich, *Replenishing the earth: the settler revolution and the rise of the Angloworld* (Oxford: Oxford University Press, 2011), 472–73.

[34] R. H. Hawn, editorial, *Episcopal Charismatic Fellowship Newsletter*, August 1973, 1.

[35] Stephen Hayes, *Black charismatic Anglicans* (Pretoria: University of South Africa, 1990).

was remarkably little commentary in charismatic media on civil rights. In the United Kingdom, since the mid-1950s migration had produced an 'urban evangelical explosion' of pentecostal and holiness African-Caribbean congregations and denominations.[36] However, rarely were there cross-fertilisations between charismatic renewal and this 'new Nonconformity' of Black, Spirit-filled, and working-class Christians.[37] Charismatic renewal, as constituted in this study, was very largely the preserve of white and 'white settler' middle-class Christianity.

While we will primarily examine the Spiritscape of charismatic renewal in the Anglo-world—where service agencies constructed or 'packaged' the charismatic renewal—what follows is always interested in the wider global setting. There was, we shall see, interpenetration with mainland Western Europe; for example, with the Protestant ecumenical Sisterhood of Mary (*Ökumenische Marienschwesternschaft*) in Darmstadt, West Germany. The threat of communism, which charismatics often imagined in eschatological terms, fostered links between English-speaking and continental European charismatic groups. Furthermore, by the mid-1970s the leadership of Roman Catholic renewal began to shift from America towards Europe as the Vatican integrated the movement into its ecclesiological structures. There was interaction, too, with Third World charismatic, pentecostal, and holiness Christianity. During the 1950s in the Anglo-world, there was some dissatisfaction about the ostensibly overly cerebral or bureaucratised aspects of church life. Some looked to examples of Christianity in the Third World, which in some societies, K. K. Yeo reminds us, emerged from a 'common "shamanic underlay"' which saw 'spirits and principalities very much at work in all dimensions of life'. They saw the potential of reanimated faith.[38] In the 1970s, places such as St Andrew's Anglican Cathedral, Singapore, *El Minuto de Dios*, a Catholic community in Bogotá, and *El Tabernáculo de la Fe*, the pentecostal congregation of Juan Carlos Ortiz in Buenos Aires, became imprinted in the imagined geography of Western charismatics.

'The Holy Ghost Is a Ghost No Longer': The Scope of Renewal

The eclecticism of charismatic renewal, so evident at Guildford, displayed the qualities of what Kees de Groot describes as 'liquid religion'.[39] It had no discernible

[36] Clifford Hill, *Black churches: West Indian and African sects in Britain* (London: British Council of Churches, 1971).

[37] John Maiden, 'A new Nonconformity: ethnicity, evangelicalism and ecumenism, c. 1952–1985', in David Bebbington and David Ceri Jones (eds.), *Evangelicalism and dissent in modern England and Wales* (London: Routledge, 2020), 176–96; John Maiden, '"Race", black majority churches and the rise of ecumenical multiculturalism in the 1970s', *Twentieth Century British History*, 30/4 (2019), 531–56.

[38] K. K. Yeo, 'Biblical interpretation in the majority world', in Mark P. Hutchinson (ed.), *The Oxford history of Protestant dissenting traditions*, vol. 5: *The twentieth century: themes and variations in a global context* (Oxford: Oxford University Press, 2019), 131–69, at 155.

[39] Kees de Groot, 'Three types of liquid religion', *Implicit Religion*, 11/3 (2008), 277–96.

starting place. As a grassroots phenomenon, the use of media—particularly stories and testimonies—allowed it to flow easily back and forth through ecclesiastical barriers, including between Protestant and Roman Catholic. Charismatics found commonality in their experiences (chiefly baptism in the Spirit), embodiments (hand-raising, hugging, etc.), practices (singing in tongues, prophecy, etc.), and words ('Praise the Lord!'). From their point of view there was a reason for this fluidity. The radical hope 'I will pour out My Spirit on all people' implied spontaneous expansion and unity, not boundary making and exclusivity. A 1970 statement by the American Bob Mumford, formerly of the Assemblies of God, is telling: 'Charismatic renewal, restoration, or Divine intervention are only adjectives which seek to describe the indescribable—a spiritual revolution which is taking place universally.'[40]

In some existing scholarship 'renewal' refers only to developments in the mainline churches and a sharp distinction is made with non-denominational 'neo-pentecostalism' or 'restorationism'. While there may be valid theological reasons for this, and studies distinguishing between these constituencies can have significant value, they also risk obscuring the overlaps between them. The extent to which all swam in a wider charismatic subculture is evident in some studies. Peter Hocken's pioneering study of British charismatics observed that in the mid-1960s there was 'one discernible movement'.[41] When reading William L. De Arteaga's study of Camps Farthest Out, the 'schoolhouse of charismatic renewal' in the United States, one is struck by the seamless interaction between mainliner (including some Catholics), pentecostal, New Thought, and conservative evangelical Christians.[42] Michael Reid's doctoral study of charismatic renewal in Christchurch, New Zealand, demonstrates fluidity at the grassroots level.[43] I will repeat: to recognise the coherence of the Spiritscape of charismatic renewal does not imply homogeneity. There were multiple charismatic identities, and matters of pneumatology, ecclesiology, and eschatology often required negotiation. Therefore, in this book the 'renewal'—the reanimation of all Christianity—is organised into three broad varieties.

Mainline charismatics were those who engaged in parachurch charismatic subculture (attending, for example, prayer groups and conferences) while remaining committed to furthering the Spirit's impact on their own denominations.[44]

[40] Bob Mumford, 'Editorial', *New Wine*, August 1970, 2.

[41] *Streams of renewal: the origins and early development of the charismatic movement in Great Britain* (Carlisle: Paternoster Press, 1986), ch. 20. See also Roger Shuff, *Searching for the true Church: Brethren and evangelicals in mid-twentieth-century England* (Milton Keynes: Paternoster Press, 2005).

[42] William L. De Arteaga, 'Glenn Clark's Camps Furthest Out: the schoolhouse of charismatic renewal', *Pneuma*, 25/2 (2003), 256–88.

[43] Michael Andrew Reid, 'But by my Spirit: a history of the charismatic renewal in Christchurch, 1960–1985', University of Canterbury, PhD thesis (2003).

[44] On mainline expressions, see: Valentina Ciciliot, 'The origins of the Catholic Charismatic Renewal in the United States: early developments in Indiana and Michigan and the reactions of the

The Fountain Trust, which was largely Anglican led, was a service agency with this aim. Mainliners often initially drew heavily on pentecostal influences, but over time sought to legitimise their experiences of the Spirit within their own denominational traditions and theologies of Christian initiation. These mainline charismatics were as diverse as the denominations (they were to be found, even, amongst the Quakers, Mennonites, and Orthodox), but were also often representative of the variety *within* them. Catholics represented a variety of different emphases within their denominational setting. Amongst Anglicans and Episcopalians were charismatics who were evangelical and Anglo-Catholic—constituencies which had shared a historical animus. There could be a continuum, too, from conservative Biblicists to what Pamela E. Klassen calls the 'supernatural liberal'—charismatics who drew on therapeutic approaches, such as Jungian theory and New Thought. We shall see also some blurring of boundaries with the inchoate New Age movement.[45]

Independent charismatics were situated outside of the mainline and pentecostal denominations. They included those who were 'put out' of these churches (often due to tongues speaking) and those who left them in search of 'pure' New Testament Christianity. This constituency was diverse, drawing on influences as various as the post-1945 healing evangelism revival, the 1948 Latter Rain movement, the Plymouth Brethren, and Baptist/Baptistic traditions.[46] The impulse for independents was restorationism. This combined a selection of various ideas and practices such as the victory of a powerful Church before the return of Christ, teachings on 'the church in the home', the Ephesians 4 ministries of apostles, prophets, evangelists, pastors, and teachers, the unity of the local church, and radical discipleship and submission. One constituency to whom this primitivism appealed was the Jesus People, the hippie Christian milieu which Larry Eskridge describes as 'awash in a Pentecostal ethos'. These seekers were drawn to the New

ecclesiastical authorities', *Studies in World Christianity*, 25/3 (2019), 250–73; John Maiden, 'The emergence of Catholic Charismatic Renewal "in a country": Australia and transnational Catholic Charismatic Renewal', same issue, 274–96; Donald S. Swenson, 'The Canadian Catholic Charismatic renewal', in Michael Wilkinson (ed.), *Canadian Pentecostalism: transition and transformation* (Montreal: McGill-Queen's University Press, 2009), 214–32; David A. Reed, 'Denominational charismatics – where have they all gone? A Canadian Anglican case study', in Wilkinson, *Canadian Pentecostalism*, 197–213; Carter Lindberg, *Charismatic movements and the Lutheran tradition* (Macon: Mercer University Press, 1983); Ian Randall, 'Baptist revival and renewal in the 1960s', in Kate Cooper and Jeremy Gregory (eds.), *Revival and resurgence in Christian history* (Woodbridge: Boydell Press, 2008), 341–53; Paul Barreira and David Hilliard, 'Filled with terrific joy! The beginnings of charismatic renewal in South Australian Methodism', *Church Heritage*, 8/2 (1993), 61–83.

[45] Pamela E. Klassen, *Spirits of Protestantism: medicine, healing and liberal Christianity* (Berkeley: University of California Press, 2011), 3.

[46] On independent restorationism, see, for example: William K. Kay, *Apostolic networks in Britain: new ways of being church* (Milton Keynes: Paternoster Press, 2007); Andrew Walker, *Restoring the Kingdom: the radical Christianity of the house church movement* (Guildford: Eagle, 1998); S. David Moore, *The shepherding movement: controversy and charismatic ecclesiology* (London: T&T Clark, 2003); Brett Knowles, *New Life: a history of the New Life Churches in New Zealand, 1942–1979* (Dunedin: Third Millennium, 1999).

Testament experience of the supernatural and community (Eskridge's remarkable, and sometimes hilarious, oral history includes a member of a commune claiming to have witnessed the feeding of thirty young people from one can of tuna).[47] We shall see how—very often in the context of ecumenical prayer groups—the question of whether to 'stay in' or 'come out' of the denominations was a slow-burning tension. Another impulse for some independents (though some dismissed the teachings as unbiblical) was the search for the 'abundant life'. The global healing evangelism ministries of Oral Roberts, T. L. Osborn, and others orientated many towards God's physical and material blessings during the post-war decades. The teachings of 'word of faith' ministries (based on the idea that God's covenant with the individual believer is realised through their speaking out the promises of Scripture) found some fertile ground on the edges of charismatic renewal, and in particularly its non-denominational varieties.

Charismaticised pentecostals are the third main constituency. Pentecostal denominations such as the Assemblies of God and Elim are often presented as distinct from the 'new move' of the charismatic renewal. Charismatic renewal tended to appeal to a different demographic—the middle-class or the universities and the suburbs. Theologically, charismatics tended not to insist, at least in theory, on tongues as the 'initial evidence'. However, another dynamic was at work. What Shane Clifton has observed of the Australian scene was sometimes true more widely: charismatic renewal could have 'as much impact on Pentecostalism as Pentecostals were to have on Charismatic movements'.[48] The routes these influences took could be circuitous. The radical pentecostals of the Latter Rain revival of 1948 were dedicated to the restoration of a primitive version of pentecostalism.[49] Many who became independent were later drawn towards the charismatic renewal. Here, they laundered some of the traits of early pentecostalism—ecumenicity, 'singing in the Spirit', and laying on of hands. Later, these reanimating practices flowed back into the pentecostal denominations. The scope of the 'New Pentecost' was far reaching and pervasive.

Age of the Spirit: Secularisation, Cosmopolitanism, and Authenticity

For the American Presbyterian theologian J. Rodman Williams, the Guildford conference was indicative of the 'emergence of an era of the Spirit such as has not

[47] Larry Eskridge, *God's forever family: the Jesus People movement in America* (New York: Oxford University Press, 2013), quote at 78, tuna reference at 81.

[48] Shane Clifton, *Pentecostal churches in transition: analysing the developing ecclesiology of the Assemblies of God in Australia* (Leiden: Brill, 2009), 139.

[49] This is a point made well in David Edwin Harrell Jr., *Oral Roberts: an American life* (Bloomington: Indiana University Press, 1985), 152–55.

been seen since New Testament times'.[50] Religious, social, and political uncertainties in the decades after 1945, and particularly the long Sixties, heightened eschatological interest and produced movements for renewal or reformation in or on the edges of the churches. These were years of scientific advancement—for example, nuclear power and space travel (with the launch of Sputnik in 1957)—rising affluence, and an increasingly dominant cultural narrative of secularisation. The English historian Sam Brewitt-Taylor observes how the eschatological emphases of liberal movements in the Protestant churches were shaped by the Cold War's 'years of maximum danger', 1958–62. At the 1958 Lambeth Conference, for example, there was a conviction that the 'world's confusion' made it 'the urgent duty of the Church to be the channel of God's reconciling power'.[51] In the preceding years, as liberals reimagined the Church they often did so with reference to the Holy Spirit. The radical pioneer John Wren-Lewis spoke of making 'all the old familiar formulae become suddenly alive with new meaning, like the dry bones of Ezekial's vision'.[52] By the time the Anglican Bishop John Robinson began to articulate a secular Christianity for a 'new era' it was the language of a 'new Reformation'.[53] In the Roman Catholic Church similar themes were evident in the Vatican II promise of a 'New Pentecost'. Pope John XXIII's description, one scholar argues, 'invited attention primarily to the origin of the church, not to 20 intervening councils including Vatican I, and connoted a reawakening of what the church is in all ages and contexts'.[54] The notion of the Council bringing the effusion of the Holy Spirit was widely held. On the edge of the churches, others were drawn towards metaphysical religion and the New Age.[55] *A Faith for the New Age* (1967), published by Anglican lay author David Vaughan on the 450th anniversary year of Luther's Reformation, called for a 'supernaturalistic' Christianity that would 'open up vast new continents of mind and soul for mankind to explore in a truly New Renaissance and a truly New Reformation in a truly New Age'.[56] For Steven Sutcliffe, the New Age was an 'eschatological emblem'.[57] A vector for these movements of reformation and renewal was the hope of reanimation by God's Spirit.

Charismatic renewal was an eschatological response to a series of cultural and political moments. The early pentecostal eschatology of the 'latter rain' was

[50] J. Rodman Williams, 'Genuine concern for Pentecostal theology', *Renewal*, 34 (1971), 6–9, quote at 9.

[51] On this see Sam Brewitt-Taylor, *Christian radicalism in the Church of England and the invention of the British sixties, 1957–1970* (Oxford: Oxford University Press, 2019), 113–15, quote at 114.

[52] Ibid., 157.

[53] John T. Robinson, *The new Reformation?* (London: SCM, 1965).

[54] Thomas Hughson, 'Interpreting Vatican II: "A new Pentecost"', *Theological Studies*, 69 (2008), 3–37, at 10.

[55] Steven Sutcliffe, *Children of the New Age: a history of spiritual practices* (London: Routledge, 2003).

[56] David Vaughan, *A faith for the New Age* (London: Regency Press, 1967), quoted in Sutcliffe, *Children*, 27.

[57] Sutcliffe, *Children*, 4.

resurgent amongst charismatics. This was the notion that a 'former rain' was the Pentecost of the Book of Acts; God pouring out his Spirit on the Church with the accompanying sign of tongues. Following centuries of apostasy, in which the Church lacked power, the Reformation signalled the beginnings of the preparation of the Church for a latter rain outpouring. This would restore the church in apostolic power as preparation for global revival and Christ's imminent return. In the 1930s the pentecostal denominations took on the fundamentalist scheme of a pre-tribulation 'secret' rapture. However, after the war, Latter Rain pentecostals, as well as many independent evangelicals, revived the optimism of the Church empowered before Christ's return.[58] This idea permeated what became charismatic renewal. Even as cautious an Anglican as Michael Harper, although he refused to be drawn on definitive predictions, still asserted 'there are signs that this well may be the last final, latter rain outpouring of the Spirit before the return of Christ'.[59] For many, we shall see, the expansion of 'Pentecost' was also linked with a fulfilment of biblical prophecy: the establishment of the State of Israel in 1948 and the Six-Day War of 1967.[60]

Obviously, Catholic charismatics tended not to use latter rain terminology because of its implications for interpreting the pre-Reformation Church. However, their message of a resurgence of the supernatural gifts in the Church carried a similar sense of climactic eschatological drama.[61] Although Catholics searched for evidence of supernatural gifts throughout the history of the Church, they narrated the putative antecedents to the Catholic renewal as parallel to the turn of the century pentecostal outpouring. According to this narrative, Sr. Elena Guerra (1833–1914), the founder of the Oblate Sisters of the Holy Spirit, Lucca, Italy, had between 1895 and 1903 sent letters to Pope Leo XIII urging renewed preaching on the Holy Spirit. Guerra predicted God would grant 'a long-awaiting renewal of the face of the earth'. Pope Leo issued *Provida Matris Caritate* (1895), which called for a novena to the Holy Spirit preceding the feast of Pentecost; and he then published his encyclical on the Holy Spirit, *Divinum Illud Munus* (1897). On the first day of 1901 the Pope sang '*Veni Creator Spiritus*' in front of the Holy Spirit window of St Peter's Basilica. Guerra also began prayer groups—'permanent cenacles' (cenacle refers to the 'upper room' where the disciples received the last supper and waited for the Spirit after Christ's death). She called for ceaseless prayer to the Holy Spirit in the Church, a 'Universal Cenacle'. Pope John XXIII beatified Guerra, and early Catholic

[58] Peter Althouse, *Spirit in the last days: pentecostal eschatology in conversation with Jügen Moltmann* (London: T&T Clark, 2003), ch. 1.

[59] 'Michael Harper "views the church"', *Charismatic Contact*, 4/1 (1975), n.p.

[60] Alan Langstaff, 'A new wave's about to break', *Vision*, 30 (January–February 1979), 5–8.

[61] Peter Hocken, 'What challenges do Pentecostals pose to Catholics?', *Journal of the European Pentecostal Theological Association*, 35/1 (2015), 48–57.

charismatics described her as a 'forerunner' of the charismatic renewal. Her dream of a 'Universal Cenacle', they asserted, was realised in charismatic prayer groups. Arguably, though, the key point of the narrative was this: on the day that Pope Leo sang '*Veni Creator Spiritus*', hadn't Agnes Ozman received the Spirit in Topeka, Kansas?[62]

Against this backdrop of heightened eschatology, this book relates charismatic renewal to three key themes in scholarly work on these decades: secularisation, cosmopolitanism, and authenticity. The scholarly debate about secularisation is fraught with assertions and counter-assertions; but notwithstanding national and often significant regional variations, recent histories of religious and social change in settings across the Anglo-world have tended to assume a 'religious crisis of the Sixties'.[63] For contemporary Protestants and Catholics there was a perception of the rise of the 'secular' (a narrative, as Sam Brewitt-Taylor shows in the case of England, largely constructed *within* the churches), which was in fact more dramatic than actual quantitative trends indicate.[64] In fact, statistics on the popularity of marriage amongst the young suggest moral change during the 1960s was initially quite gradual. However, the narrative within the churches was one of crisis, particularly, for Catholics, with the legalisation of the pill. Two broad responses of the laity to *Humanae Vitae*—either not participating in Church life or selective observation of its teaching—were each challenging for clergy.[65] There was also a profound sense that the churches lacked capacity, strategy, and confidence to respond to the crisis around them; a view expressed, for example, in the Church of England's *The Deployment and Payment of Clergy: a Report* (1964). Early in the next decade the Anglican Diocese Council of Grahamstown, South Africa (whose Bishop, as we saw earlier, had recently experienced baptism in the Spirit) put the situation bluntly: 'our problems stem from a lack of personal experience of our Lord Jesus Christ and the power of his Holy Spirit within Christian fellowship. We are neither hot nor cold. Something has to happen.'[66] The desire to see the churches reanimated by the Spirit came in a context of secularisation, real and imagined.

[62] See for example, Fr. Val Gaudet, 'A woman and the Pope', *New Covenant*, 3/4 (1973), 4–7.

[63] The following list is only indicative. For international studies, see Callum Brown, *Religion and the demographic revolution: women and secularization in Canada, Ireland, UK and USA since the 1960s* (Woodbridge: Boydell Press, 2012); Hugh McLeod, *The religious crisis of the 1960s* (Oxford: Oxford University Press, 2007). National studies include: Callum Brown, *The death of Christian Britain: understanding secularisation, 1800–2000* (London: Routledge, 2001); David Hilliard, 'The religious crisis of the 1960s: the experience of the Australian Churches', *Journal of Religious History*, 21 (1997), 209–27; Kevin Ward, *Losing our religion? Changing patterns of believing and belonging in secular Western societies* (Eugene: Wipf & Stock, 2013); S. Macdonald, 'Death of Christian Canada? Do Canadian church statistics support Callum Brown's timing of church decline?' *Historical Papers: Canadian Society of Church History*, 2006, 135–56.

[64] Brewitt-Taylor, *Christian radicalism.*

[65] See, for example, McLeod, *Religious crisis*, 168–69; Hilliard, *Religious crisis.*

[66] DAHL, DDP, Box 10, file 6, Letter from Diocesan Council of Grahamstown.

Second, charismatic renewal reflected the cosmopolitanism of the long Sixties and after. There was an intensification of transnational exchange, not only within the West but also with movement of cultural products—fashion, sounds, and literature—technologies, and ideologies between the West, the Soviet bloc, and Third World.[67] Charismatic cosmopolitanism found its script in the Book of Acts, where the Pentecost in Jerusalem had established bonds of the Spirit across national, ethnic, and ecclesiological boundaries.[68] While most sections of charismatic renewal were theologically exclusivist, its subculture corresponds with Nina Glick Schiller et al.'s notion of 'cosmopolitan sociability' in its ecumenical idealism and translocal mobilities and exchange.[69] In the Anglo- and wider Western world, this was a cosmopolitanism of the middle-classes and religious professionals; those with the resources to travel and consume books, music, and magazines orienting them to the wider world. Research on the radical Left in post-war decades indicates the growing reputation of the 'heroic Third World freedom fighter', leaders such as Ché Guevára and Amílcar Cabral.[70] Christians in the Anglo-world were also turning their gaze towards the Third World, for very different reasons. In the mid-1950s, Henry Van Dusen, President of New York's Union Theological Seminary, spoke of pentecostal, adventist, and holiness groups as the 'third mighty arm of Christian outreach' bearing the marks of 'the most vital and dynamic expressions of the sixteenth century Reformation'.[71] Charismatics were looking to the Third World, desirous for what American historian David R. Swartz describes as the 'enchantment of the West'.[72]

Finally, this book relates charismatic renewal to authenticity. New understandings of the Self—a privileging of self-expression and the emotions—had been evolving since the late nineteenth century. The cultural historian T. J. Jackson Lears, for example, describes a feeling of 'weightlessness' amongst wealthier Americans during the Progressive era, as they became disorientated by modern social and economic conditions and urban, consumer society.[73] During the inter-war years a therapeutic ethos was increasingly apparent and after 1945 widespread amongst the middle-classes.[74] This was evident in the search for 'real' love in

[67] See, for example, Samantha Christiansen and Zachary Scarlett (eds.), *The Third World in the global 1960s* (New York: Berghahn Books, 2013).

[68] On this, see also Mark Porter, 'Charismatic worship and cosmopolitan movement(s)', *Liturgy*, 33/3 (2018), 4–11.

[69] Nina Glick Schiller, Tsypylma Darieva, and Sandra Gruner-Domic, 'Defining cosmopolitan sociability in a transnational age: an introduction', *Ethnic and Racial Studies*, 34/3 (2011), 399–418.

[70] Carole Fink, Philipp Gassert, and Detlef Junker, 'Introduction', in Fink, Gassert, and Junker (eds.), *1968: the world transformed* (Cambridge: Cambridge University Press, 1998), 1–30, quote at 25.

[71] Henry Van Dusen, 'Caribbean holiday', *Christian Century*, 72 (August 1955), 946–47.

[72] David R. Swartz, *Facing west: American evangelicals in an age of world Christianity* (New York: Oxford University Press, 2020), ch. 6.

[73] T. J. Jackson Lears, *No place for grace: antimodernism and the transformation of American culture, 1880–1920* (New York: Pantheon, 1981), 41.

[74] For one interpretation, see Nikolas Rose, 'Assembling the modern self', in Roy Porter (ed.), *Rewriting the self: histories from the renaissance to the present* (London: Routledge, 1997), 224–48.

marriage, the popularity of psychotherapy, and the shift from 'cognitive rationality' towards self-expression in universities.[75] Charismatic renewal took shape in a period of social change and existential anxiety, and in spaces such as universities and suburbs where middle-classes negotiated new disorientations. As an expression of Christian authenticity, it had been predicted by the German sociologist Georg Simmel (whom Max Weber described as 'musical' in his understanding of religion). Simmel argued at the turn of the century that in the face of modernity, religion would need to emphasise subjectivity. Francesca Montemaggi's study of Simmel asserts that he 'foresaw the emergence of a more mystical form of religion through which the individual could express their own religious sentiment'.[76]

Charismatic authenticity was of a particular type: finding the Self—and 'reality'—in self-surrender. The central, subjective experience was baptism in the Spirit. This was a moment which often, as Mark Hutchinson perceptively asserts, followed 'a combination of personal, social and ecclesiological crises'.[77] For clergy who entered the renewal, the 'weightlessness' which prompted a search for spiritual reality was often dissatisfaction with ministry. 'The Charismatic Renewal emphasises religion as an *experienced* reality', argued Catholic theologian Donal Dorr in *Remove the Heart of Stone* (1978).[78] Spirit baptism narratives commonly described a new commitment to holiness and witness, as well as a feeling of joy, freedom, and love. This new, spiritually authentic Self was expressed in embodied practices, for example, 'new freedom in worship, accompanied by such manifestations as clapping during songs, raising hands in praise, and outward expressions of love between the church members'.[79] The subjective Self was placed in the framework of community. The body charismatic, as this book describes these expressions of community, took many different forms. Just as the Christian New Left, Doug Rossinow shows, elevated community, so charismatics found authenticity in the experience of the Body of Christ.[80] The expression of the Body could be found variously in radical ecumenicity, co-ministry of the gifts (famously, the notice board of the charismatic Anglican parish of St Paul's, Darien, Connecticut, said 'Ministers: the whole congregation'),[81] the making of 'covenant' community vows, submission to a 'shepherd', and the giving up of autonomy of finances and possessions. As one American asserted in the

[75] Claire Langhamer, 'Love, self-hood and authenticity in post-war Britain', *Cultural and Social History*, 9/2 (2012), 277–97; Hera Cook, 'From controlling emotion to expressing feelings in mid-century England', *Journal of Social History*, 47/3 (2014), 627–46; Talcott Parsons and Gerald M. Platt, *The American university* (Cambridge, MA: Harvard University Press, 1973).

[76] Francesca E. S. Montemaggi, *Authenticity and religion in a pluralistic age: a Simmelian study of Christian evangelicals and new monastics* (Lanham: Rowman & Littlefield, 2019), 79.

[77] Hutchinson, 'Charismatic movements'.

[78] Donal Dorr, *Remove the heart of stone* (Indianapolis: Paulist Press, 1978), 55.

[79] Jamie Buckingham, 'Charismatic renewal', *Logos Journal*, 3/5 (September–October 1973), 7–9.

[80] Doug Rossinow, *The politics of authenticity: liberalism, Christianity, and the New Left in America* (New York: Columbia University Press, 1998).

[81] Michael Barling, 'Life in the body', *Renewal*, 77 (October–November 1978), 13–14.

magazine *New Wine*: 'God does not deal with us only as individuals. His will is a "corporate man" – single unified body made up of multiplied individuals!'[82]

This was not an unbridled, existentialist break with the past. Charismatic authenticity often sought rootedness in tradition. There was normally a strong commitment to the authority of Scripture and conservative theological interpretations. The New Zealand youth evangelist Winkie Pratney warned against experience-centred Christianity, describing this as a 'grave danger'. 'IF faith is not based on FACT, but only experience', he argued, 'how can you know whether the Christ a man has an experience with IS the Christ of the Bible, instead of a "christ" of his own imagination or a Satanic counterfeit?'[83] Charismatics sought to appropriate the primitivism of the early Church. 'The truth is that, where we do not see and experience the supernatural, we have no right to speak of New Testament Christianity. New Testament Christianity can never be separated from the supernatural, or experienced in isolation from it', asserted Bible teacher Derek Prince in his *Foundations* series.[84] Here again, where scholars make sharp distinctions between 'renewal' and 'restorationism', they risk obscuring the considerable common ground between them. The American Catholic Ralph Martin asserted 'I think God is moving to *restore* New Testament Christianity to all his people—that is more than renewal.'[85]

Authenticity, too, often went hand in hand with attempts to historicise charismatic devotion within a Church tradition. Methodists turned to their founders. Donald H. Kelly, a Sunday school superintendent at First Methodist, North Platte, Nebraska, claimed that one of 'the many glories' since his baptism in the Spirit in the early 1960s was 'the discovery of and identity with the great outpouring of the Spirit from which sprung "the people called Methodists"'. Wesley's 'Aldersgate' experience took on a new significance, as did his insistence that miracles did not cease with the Apostolic age.[86] Presbyterians looked to the early nineteenth-century Scotsman Edward Irving; a man who was convinced that the supernatural gifts were 'substantial and permanent forms of operation proper to the Holy Ghost, and in no wise to be separated from Him or from the Church'.[87] When the Presbyterian minister Douglas Watt went 'public' with his Spirit baptism, he announced in the *New Zealand Herald*: 'I have to take my stand beside my fellow townsman Edward Irving (I was born in Annan, Dumfriesshire) and state my belief that the use of tongues in the form of ecstatic utterance or as an expression of communion with God is perfectly Scriptural. Nor should it be

82 Charles P. Schmitt, 'New wine in new wineskins', *New Wine*, 1/1 (1969), 1, 5, 6, 14, 15; quote at 5.
83 Winkie Pratney, 'Truth or consequence', *New Wine*, September 1971, 4–7, 19.
84 Derek Prince, *Purposes of Pentecost* (Charlotte: Derek Prince Ministries International, 1966), 31.
85 Ralph Martin, 'God is restoring his people', *New Covenant*, 4/3 (1974), 3–6.
86 Donald H. Kelly, 'A Methodist and the charismata', *Trinity*, 3/2 (1964), 6–7, at 7.
87 Edward Irving, 'Facts connected with recent manifestations of spiritual gifts', *Fraser's Magazine*, January 1832, 754.

looked upon as an emotional extravagance.'[88] In Scotland, another Presbyterian, Gordon Strachan, imagined a pentecostal genealogy whereby pneumatic emphases appeared in his Church through Irving, after 'rejection, and long exile' reappeared (outside the Church of Scotland) at the turn of the twentieth century, before a 'return to the Kirk' in the form of charismatic renewal.[89] Catholics, too, looked to their tradition. As Brian Smith, an Australian layman explained in 1973, Spirit baptism was the 'awakening response to God's ever abiding love in the soul' in the tradition of St Francis of Assisi, St Teresa of Avila, St Vincent de Paul and St Peter Damien.[90] In Pecos, New Mexico, charismatic Benedictine monks revisited the Pope Gregory I biography of St Benedict of Nursia, finding stories of supernatural ministry and claiming affinity with the founder of their Order.[91] Charismatic authenticity often involved a claim to historic deep-rootedness.

* * *

The following chapters are primarily thematic but ordered to give the reader some sense of chronological development. Chapter 2, *Potential*, looks at antecedents and 'follows the flows' which would eventually produce a distinctive new subculture in the Anglo-world. Chapter 3, *Pentecost*, analyses the coming together of these influences as a Spiritscape of charismatic renewal amidst the geo-political, cultural, and religious flux of the long Sixties. Chapter 4, *Mediation*, examines how service agencies and circulations of text, audio, and visual media shaped the various formations of the charismatic subculture. Chapter 5, *Body*, assesses charismatic models and practices of gathering, ministry, and communal life, and key issues such as the negotiation of authority and gender. Chapter 6, *Imagination*, concerns the Spiritscape as it reached its most kinetic phase in the 1970s. How did charismatics imagine what God was doing, and how was this contested? Chapter 7, *World*, stands back and situates renewal in the Anglo-world within global Christianity and makes the case for a charismatic 'global reflex' in the 1970s.[92] Finally, *Legacy* shows how after 1980 the Spiritscape of charismatic renewal was increasingly subject to diversification, diffusion, and institutionalisation, as it also grew increasingly integrated with the wider charismatic/pentecostal world.

[88] Quoted in Douglas Watt, 'Editorial', *Logos* (NZ), 1/4 (1967), 1–2, at 2.

[89] Gordon Strachan, 'Pentecostal worship in the Church of Scotland, part 1', *Liturgical Review*, November 1972, 16–27, at 16; part 2, November 1973, 34–47.

[90] Brian Smith, 'Charismatic renewal in the Catholic Church', *Newsletter (for the Catholic Charismatic Renewal)*, August 1973, pp. 5–7, at 5.

[91] Tape recording quoted in Kody Sherman Jackson, 'Jesus, Jung and the charismatics: the Pecos Benedictines and visions of religious renewal', MA thesis, University of Texas, 2016, 102.

[92] On evangelicals and the 'global reflex' or 'reverse influence', see for example: David R. Swartz, *Moral minority: the evangelical Left in the age of conservatism* (Pittsburgh: University of Pennsylvania Press, 2012), esp. ch. 6; Brian Stanley, *The global diffusion of evangelicalism* (Downers Grove: Intervarsity Press, 2013), esp. ch. 6.

2
Potential

> ...but you will receive power when the Holy Spirit comes on you.
>
> Acts 1:8

In 1969, Donald A. Schmit set foot in a Protestant church building for the first time. A former US Marine, now an employee of the Internal Revenue Service, Schmit had recently relocated with his wife Genevieve (Jenny) and children to Kansas City, to take a post at the Midwest Region Data Processing Centre. They bought a house in the Catholic parish of St Elizabeth's, where their children attended school.[1] Soon after, Schmit committed his life to Jesus through a Cursillo group. Shortly after this he walked through the door of the Protestant congregation. Its pastor, A. J. Rowden, was formerly of the Evangelical United Brethren, but had been expelled after his baptism in the Spirit through a pentecostal evangelist. Rowden started a non-denominational church which became Evangelistic Centre Church. At the meeting which Schmit attended, the visiting speaker was a Catholic priest from Buffalo, New York. Schmit went forward at the altar call and Rowden prayed that he be filled. After his experience, Schmit and his wife, along with a local priest, established an interdenominational charismatic small group in their home.[2]

It is worth pausing at the moment of Schmit's baptism in the Spirit. At this point there was a crossing of religious flows. He would never have visited the charismatic church if his nominal religiosity had not been awakened by Cursillo, a Catholic lay apostolate founded in Spain by Eduardo Bonnín Aguiló decades earlier (Fig. 2.1). As Schmit was prayed for by Rowden, he encountered Spirit filled non-denominationalism—and the entwined influences of holiness evangelicalism and pentecostalism. There is nothing—and everything—special about Schmit's story. We might have drawn on countless other individual testimonies, each unique, to indicate the entangled spiritual lineages which contributed to charismatic beginnings. As Pam Klassen argued in relation to 'supernatural' liberal Protestantism, the established 'myths of origin' of charismatic renewal, which we will discuss in the next chapter, 'do the simultaneous work of

[1] Marty Denzer, 'Revd. Mr Donald Schmit'. https://catholickey.org/2014/10/10/rev-mr-donald-schmit/ (accessed 7 November 2020).

[2] Donald Schmit, 'An RC's story of renewal', *Christian Life* (July 1974), 16–18, 39–41. On Rowden, see Henry Lunn, 'The charismatic church', *Logos Journal* (March–April 1972), 12–14.

Age of the Spirit: Charismatic Renewal, the Anglo-World, and Global Christianity, 1945–1980. John Maiden, Oxford University Press. © John Maiden 2023. DOI: 10.1093/oso/9780198847496.003.0002

Fig. 2.1 The Spanish founder of Cursillos de Cristiandad, Eduardo Bonnín Aguiló.

simplifying and mythologizing complex influences, contributing a sense of inevitability, or even divine intervention to these phenomena'.[3] Klassen is right. This chapter presents a richer pre-history of charismatic potential evident in highly mobile early and mid-century experiential religious milieus. It follows the flows of mainline healing, Catholic apostolates, empowered evangelicalism, and pentecostal revivalism towards what became, in the 1960s, charismatic renewal.

'An Increased Flow of Energy': Ritual, Subconscious, and Mainline Protestant Healing

In 1925, in the wake of global war and the influenza epidemic, Hensley Henson, the Anglican Bishop of Durham, observed that spiritual healing had 'invaded the religious world'.[4] In mainline Protestant circles, particularly amongst Anglicans

[3] Pam Klassen, *Spirits of Protestantism: medicine, healing and liberal Christianity* (Berkeley: University of California Press, 2011), 143.

[4] Hensley Henson, *Notes on spiritual healing* (London: Williams and Norgate, 1925), xxiv.

and Episcopalians, healing techniques varied between the sacramental, thaumaturgical, and experimental. These were also combined; for example, the Revd. Percy Dearmer, the first President of the Guild of Health (1904), advocated the restoration of healing rites as part of a project to rediscover the 'English tradition' of liturgy; but (along with his wife, Nancy) he was also fascinated by psychic research.[5] At the sacramental end of the spectrum, Mark Hutchinson has drawn attention to the significance of the 'Worcester circle' and its central theological figure, Charles Gore, the bishop of the English diocese from 1902 (and later Bishop of Oxford). Gore's Anglo-Catholicism was rooted in a socially aware incarnationalism and the promise of a future disestablished Church, empowered not by State privilege but the 'presence and activity of the Holy Spirit of God'.[6] The Community of the Resurrection (later based in Mirfield, Yorkshire), of which Gore was the first Principal, became a hub of healing practice. When, for example, Mirfield's J. C. Fitzgerald gave evidence to a Royal College of Physicians' committee of inquiry on divine healing, he related this to incarnation ('the extension of the Incarnate Life of the Church' through clergy and 'Charismatic people, laymen and women') and the restoration of the Apostolic church.[7] This combination of presence and power spread with the Community. Indeed, if we look forward momentarily, in South Africa the Community of the Resurrection contributed to the shaping of *Iviyo Lofakazi BakaKristu* from 1948.[8] This was over two decades before the mainline Anglican hierarchy in the country recognised a charismatic renewal in the Church.

An Australian became the most impactful member of the Worcester circle. James Moore Hickson was raised in rural Victoria, where he may well have encountered—and been influenced by—aboriginal healing practices before he moved to England in 1899.[9] Here he joined the 'circle' and became President of the Society of Emmanuel (later the Divine Healing Mission). After a successful tour of the United States in 1919, Hickson embarked on a worldwide healing ministry through which—drawing on Gore's incarnationalism—he aimed 'to tell

[5] J. Barrington Bates, 'Extremely beautiful, but eminently unsatisfactory: Percy Dearmer and the healing rites of the Church, 1909–1928', *Anglican and Episcopal History*, 73/2 (2004), 196–207; Klassen, *Spirits*, 118–20.

[6] Mark Hutchinson, 'The Worcester circle'. https://www.academia.edu/345662/The_Worcester_Circle_An_Anglo_Catholic_attempt_at_Renewal_in_the_1920s (accessed 16 June 2021). Gore quoted in Hutchinson.

[7] 'Appendix C', *Spiritual healing: report of the clerical and medical committee of inquiry into spiritual, faith and mental healing* (London: Macmillan and Co., 1914), 37–38.

[8] See this book, p. 9.

[9] See Mark Hutchinson, 'Introduction: Australian charismatic movements as a space of flows', in Cristina Rocha, Mark Hutchinson, and Kathleen Openshaw (eds.), *Australian Pentecostal and Charismatic movements: arguments from the margins* (Leiden: Brill, 2020), 1–24, at 11. The significance of Australia in sacramental healing movements is marked: for example, Revd. F. L. Wyman in New York City, the Revd. William Wood in London, and H. A. Madge in Dorset, England, and later Scotland, came also from Australia.

the sick of Christ, to preach the Gospel message of healing and to bring them to Christ who is present with us now'.[10] The ministry operated in ritual, sacramental environs, sponsored by Anglo-Catholics; but as James Robinson has shown, Hickson's approach was thaumaturgic, not dissimilar to contemporary pentecostal healers.[11] One New South Wales mining town newspaper described his ministry as follows: 'Some smiled and others quietly wept but, as each rose from the foot of the altar rails, after being prayed for by the missioner, they seemed to be imbued with a new life.'[12] The response could be dramatic. An English newspaper spoke of church healing mission as 'reminiscent of a casualty clearing station behind the front line of a Flanders battlefield'. Indeed, stretcher bearers sometimes followed behind Hickson as he ministered.[13]

Hickson left a powerful legacy in the United States. From the 1930s it was here, rather than in England, that mainline healing gathered most momentum. The Episcopalian priest John Gayner Banks and his wife Ethel Tulloch Banks founded in 1932 the Fellowship of Saint Luke, later the International Order of St Luke the Physician (OSL). Its teachings and practices flowed internationally, taking root in places such as the London Healing Mission and the Revd. John Hope's Christ Church St Laurence, Sydney.[14] Charismatic testimony narratives in the 1960s indicate that OSL was often a gateway for mainliners towards awareness of a New Testament 'dynamis'. This was the case for Larry Christenson, an OSL member in San Pedro, California, who later pioneered charismatic activity amongst American Lutherans.[15] Despite the ambivalent and sometimes critical position of OSL on baptism in the Spirit and *glossolalia*, its most influential figure became an advocate for the experience. The Episcopalian Agnes Sanford, who worked extensively with OSL and (from 1958) through her School of Pastoral Prayer, witnessed privately to Spirit baptism and tongues. The Revd. William Wood, the Warden of the London Healing Mission from 1949 and later a Chaplain to the OSL, heard of the experience through Sanford while attending a conference in America in 1956. Two years later during another visit, he and twenty-five others received prayer for the experience. Wood did not speak in tongues but had a powerful encounter. London Healing Mission became sympathetic to the emerging charismatic movement.[16]

[10] James Moore Hickson, *The healing of Christ in his Church* (New York: Edwin S. Gorham, 1919), 26.

[11] James Robinson, *Divine healing: the years of expansion: theological variation in the transatlantic world* (Eugene: Wipf & Stock, 2014), 106–09.

[12] 'Spiritual healing', *The Barrier Miner* (Broken Hill), 16 July 1923, 1.

[13] Quoted in Robinson, *Divine healing*, 109. On stretchers, see A. Fay Farley, 'A Spiritual healing mission remembered: James Moore Hickson's Christian healing mission at Palmerston North, New Zealand, 1923', *Journal of Religious History*, 34/1 (2010), 1–19, at 14.

[14] On Hope, See Mark Hutchinson, 'John Hope', *ADPCM*.

[15] Christenson, 'A Lutheran pastor speaks', *Trinity*, 1/4 (1962).

[16] Peter Hocken, *Streams of renewal: the origins and early development of the charismatic movement in Great Britain* (Carlisle: Paternoster Press, 1986), 67.

In Australia, it was during Sanford's visit to Christ Church St Laurence in 1961 that Jim Glennon, a Precentor at St Andrew's Cathedral, Sydney, was 'immersed in the Holy Spirit'.[17] He went on to lead charismatic healing ministry at the Cathedral. Flows of mainline healing sometimes crossed with those of pentecostal practices. This was evident in the story of the Revd. Douglas Watts, a New Zealand Presbyterian who came out as a charismatic in the *New Zealand Herald* in 1967. He heard of Spirit baptism through Sanford—and then met David du Plessis at a School of Pastoral Prayer in Holland.[18] As Hickson's legacy was carried forward by his Anglican and Episcopalian successors, the impact on early charismatics was significant. They, too, encouraged the gift of healing amongst lay people through the laying on of hands. The 'prayer circles' which Hickson encouraged in churches had parallels with later charismatic small groups.[19] Indeed, congregational memories of Hickson's ministry were sometimes powerful enough to shape responses to charismatic renewal. All Saints, Palmerston North, New Zealand, was amongst the country's first Anglican churches to be impacted by renewal in the mid-1960s. When the outbreak amongst young people, encouraged by the curate and university chaplain, Ray Muller, was discussed at a church meeting, elderly parishioners related these happenings to their own lasting experience of Christ's presence following Hickson's visit in 1923.[20]

The rediscovery of healing in mainline Protestantism was a response to the popularity of alternative spiritualities. The 1920 Lambeth Conference called for a renewal of healing to counter the contemporary interest in Theosophy and other practices. Nevertheless, the ritual and thaumaturgic techniques which some mainline churches adopted often overlapped with alternative and experimental approaches focused on the subconscious. Agnes Sanford, for example, drew on New Thought visualisation and meditation techniques.[21] Her teaching on energy was like that of an early century pioneer of experimental healing, Revd. F. H. Du Vernet, the Archbishop of Caledonia, Canada.[22] Sanford argued in *The Healing Light* (1949):

> The very chemicals contained in the body – the "dust of the earth" – live by the Breath of God, by the primal Energy, the original force that we call God. This being so, it is not strange at all that when we establish a closer

[17] Jim Glennon, *Your healing is within you* (London: Hodder & Stoughton, 1978), 100.
[18] Douglas Watt, Editorial, *Logos*, 1/4 (1967), 1–2.
[19] Robinson, *Divine healing*, 107; Farley, 'Spiritual', 14.
[20] Farley, 'Spiritual', 17–19. DAHL, Jean Stone and Rick Willians collection, box 5, Ray Muller to Jean Stone, n.d.
[21] New Thought is difficult to classify, but broadly refers to a cluster of mind-cure movements which emerged in the United States in the nineteenth century.
[22] Klassen, *Spirits*, 145–48.

> connection with God in prayer, we would receive more abundant life – an increased flow of energy.[23]

For Sanford and others, the subconscious was the human control centre for mind, body, and soul.

Sanford developed synergies with Camps Farthest Out (CFO), an organisation founded in the United States by Presbyterian mystic Glenn Clark in 1930. CFO was modelled on the intensity of sports training (Clark used the term 'athletes of the Spirit') and camps attracted not only Protestant mainliners but Catholics and Jews.[24] In its early years, Clark's CFO integrated New Thought practices and teachings—including an individual's entitlement to abundance in family, health, and materiality—with Christian mysticism. Clark's publishing house, Macalester Park, produced Sanford's early work on inner healing and she was a regular CFO speaker. However, increasingly the camps became spaces where metaphysical influences crossed with pentecostalism—the latter being the direction in which, before his death in 1957, Clark, like Sanford, had moved decisively.[25] Many mainliners who later came to identify with charismatic renewal had a CFO background; indeed, some were baptised in the Spirit on the camps. William Sherwood, who later became a leading Episcopalian charismatic, was baptised in the Spirit at CFO in 1959 after a pentecostal brother enquired if he desired 'a certain unusual experience'.[26] The American Dominican Fr. Francis MacNutt first encountered Sanford at a CFO retreat in 1967, before embarking on an international charismatic healing ministry.[27] By the early 1960s, CFO was expanding internationally, running retreats in various Australian states, New Zealand, South Africa, England, and Canada. Creative practices continued; for example, the uses of creative art to 'open up the gates of the subconscious' and creative motion so 'a perfectly aligned body can be made into a radar station helping to make the souls sensitized to the infinite harmonies of the spirit'.[28] CFO grew charismatic in emphasis but the metaphysical dimension was not entirely lost.

Sanford influenced other ministries which became associated with charismatic renewal. In Toronto, she was admired by the Revd. G. Moore W. Smith of St. Matthias Church, which became an Anglo-Catholic healing centre. Here, however, divine healing took a dark turn. In 1967, violent practices of exorcism and sexual abuse were revealed following the death of Kathy Globe, a young woman with meningitis.[29] Sanford also influenced Morton Kelsey, a Jungian therapist

[23] Agnes Sanford, *The healing light*, English edition (Evesham: Arthur James, 1949), 29.

[24] Miles Clark, *Glenn Clark: his life and writings* (Nashville: Abingdon Press, 1975), 43.

[25] On Clark's spiritual development, see William L. De Arteaga, 'Glenn Clark's Camps Furthest Out: the schoolhouse of charismatic renewal', *Pneuma*, 25/2 (2003), 256–88. Clark was influenced in a pentecostal direction by Rufus Mosely, who had in fact been taught by William James at Harvard.

[26] William Sherwood, 'And it came to pass', *Acts 29 Newsletter*, March 1971, 1.

[27] De Arteaga, 'Camps Furthest Out', 284–85.

[28] *CFO*, 11.

[29] Klassen, *Spirits*, ch. 4.

whose ministry at St Luke's Episcopal Church, Monrovia, Los Angeles, brought together Christianity and psychology. Her son, John Sanford, was a curate at St Luke's during the 1950s (Agnes, in fact, joined the congregation in the mid-1960s). The parish became an early outpost of Episcopalian renewal in autumn 1959, when a small prayer group of parishioners prayed to receive 'the many gifts of the Spirit and know the Holy Spirit as an experience and a possession'. St Luke's combined the experience of Pentecost with Jungian influences, emphasising the realisation and healing of the inner Self. 'There has been', another St Luke's curate explained, 'a unique blending of the sacramental and prayer life of the Church with the truths of psychology and the outpouring of the Holy Spirit'.[30] Though not a tongues speaker, Kelsey authored a scholarly work *Tongue Speaking: an Experiment in Religious Experience* (1964) and came to regard the experience as an expression of the collective subconscious. This variation on Sanford's approach, although controversial to some charismatics, was influential on others. Kelsey later encouraged the Roman Catholic priest David Geraets to explore depth psychology and inner healing techniques such as praying dreams and visualisation.[31] Geraets was Abbot of a Benedictine monastery in Pecos, New Mexico, which became a centre for experimental mainline charismatic approaches. Agnes Sanford made a powerful therapeutic contribution to charismatic renewal.

'A New Descent of the Holy Ghost': Catholic Apostolate Networks

That Catholic charismatic renewal emerged just over a year after Vatican II might suggest the Council was *the* decisive factor. However, historical continuities with developments in Catholic devotionalism were at least as important. The first half of the century saw new stirrings of Catholic apostolates which incorporated the lay faithful into the mission of the Church. The work of Catholic Action reflected the emphasis of Pius XI on laity participating in the apostolate of the hierarchy. His successor, Pius XII shifted emphasis towards lay collaboration with the hierarchy and impetus in mission.[32] The theologian Yves Congar made the case for this development in primitivist terms; to 'rediscover the Church, and, in a sense, to re-enter and renew her from below'.[33]

30 Revd. Stuart G. Fitch, 'When the Spirit fell on St. Lukes', *Trinity*, 3/3 (1964), 32–33, quotes at 33.

31 Kody S. Jackson, 'Jesus, Jung and the charismatics: the Pecos Benedictines and visions of religious renewal', MA, University of Texas (2016), 155–60.

32 This distinction is explained in Brendan Leahy, *Ecclesial movements and communities: origins, significance and issues* (Hyde Park: New City Press, 2011), 28.

33 Quoted in ibid., 30.

A context for these new apostolates was a resurgence of Marian spirituality. This had a pneumatic dimension, as evident in French Jesuit theologian Jean Daniélou's *Advent* (translated and published in English in 1950):

> there is much to be hoped from the emphasis on Mary in our century, that in the same measure as we return towards such great mysteries as her Mediation and Assumption, God will, in His own mysterious way, prepare a new Descent of the Holy Ghost, a new Pentecost. There again the presence of Mary is an earnest and a promise that the Holy Spirit is coming soon, that the infidels will be converted, and – I am most profoundly convinced – that there will be a unity among Christians.[34]

A pre-eminent figure in the flourishing of Marian devotionalism was Belgian Cardinal Desiré Félicien François Joseph Mercier (1851–1926). The symbiosis with pneumatic spirituality was evident in his prayer, 'Holy Spirit, soul of my soul, I worship you. Enlighten me, guide me, strengthen and comfort me! Tell me what I must do and command me to do it!'[35] Mercier's mysticism achieved a legacy in some circles. In Sydney in 1969, Alex Reichel, a layman, sought permission from the local hierarchy to start the first Catholic charismatic group in the city (and, indeed, the country). The respect which Archbishop Gilroy had for Mercier's theology, obtained whilst studying in Rome years earlier, predisposed him to support the initiative.[36]

The Legion of Mary, established in Ireland in 1921, was a key network for Marian piety. Participants were required to take an oath of allegiance to the Holy Spirit on entry. Continuities can be traced forward to charismatic developments, particularly in the cases of Cardinal Léon Joseph Suenens, Mercier's protégé (and successor-but-one as Archbishop of Malines-Brussels), and the Irish laywoman Veronica O'Brien. The Belgian became patron of the Legion and was later author of *Theology of the Apostolate of the Legion of Mary* (1964). O'Brien, his secretary, and confidant introduced the Legion to France and Belgium during the war. In 1972, she urged Suenens to visit a charismatic prayer group in New York. He was persuaded and became an advocate for the renewal. At a charismatic conference at the University of Notre Dame the year after, he asserted: 'I will tell you a secret which will help you to welcome the Holy Spirit: it has a name; it is union with Mary.'[37] The ecumenism of early Catholic charismatic prayer groups meant that Marian spirituality was often discouraged. Nevertheless, scratching the surface of

[34] Jean Daniélou, *Advent* (London: Sheed and Ward, 1950), 120–21.

[35] Quoted in *Open the frontiers: a spiritual testimony from Cardinal Suenens* (London: Darton, Longman and Todd, 1980), 8.

[36] Mark Hutchinson, 'Reichel, Alex (1927–2012)', *ADPCM.*

[37] Léon Joseph Suenens, *Memories and hopes* (Dublin: Veritas, 1992), 273.

the renewal often reveals an underlayer of Legionary spirituality. In Brisbane, Brian Smith, a pre-eminent figure in Australian renewal in the 1970s, had years earlier as a Legionary experienced a mystical encounter with Mary while saying the Rosary.[38] At a national conference for English Catholic charismatics in 1974, it is notable that there was a special meeting for Legionaries in attendance. They used the Magnificat as 'their own personal canticle of praise'.[39]

The wider culture of lay Marian devotionalism cultivated charismatic potential in mid-century Catholicism. The cults of Lourdes and Fatima remained influential. In 1958, the centenary of the apparition of Mary at Lourdes fostered renewed and widespread interest—for example, as many as 700 Australians led by Cardinal Gilroy visited the French town that year.[40] Other devotions, 'unsanctioned' by the hierarchy, were remarkably popular. The Marian cult of Necedah, Wisconsin, drew a remarkable 100,000 visitors in the summer of 1950.[41] Visions and healings remained plausible in the post-war worldview of many Catholics. As within Protestantism, there were indications of a shift of emphasis from physical healing to self-actualising 'inner' healing and experience. Alana Harris' work on Lourdes shows how it began to be represented as a place of personal spiritual experience and renewed purpose. In 1956 a laywoman visiting the grotto at a time of personal crisis found 'A feeling of peace such as I had never known, not even as a child, filled my heart and I knew from that moment that I had changed.'[42] A decade or so later, echoes of this language were evident in Spirit baptism narratives.

Marian piety of a very localised variety was one stimulus for a lay apostolate established on the Spanish island of Mallorca in 1944. The principal founder of *Cursillos de Cristiandad*, Eduardo Bonnín Aguiló, established the small group course to intensify the piety of men.[43] Spanish-speaking groups for young men of Mexican descent began in the United States, in Waco, Texas, in 1957. With Bonnín's support women soon became involved. Four years later, English-language Cursillo was adopted. Cursillo gatherings were characterised by lay empowerment, spontaneity, and intimacy; and involved singing, prayer, and the reading of Scripture. It established strong roots in two upper Midwest dioceses, Fort Wayne-South Bend and Lansing. These were the homes of the University of

[38] Brian Smith, *Streams of living water: autobiography of a charismatic leader* (Melbourne: Comsoda Communications, 2000), 3–4.

[39] *Day of Renewal*, November 1974, n.p.

[40] Mark Hutchinson, 'Windows on the world: sources for the Catholic Charismatic Renewal in Sydney, Australia', paper given at University of Venezia, 14 June 2019.

[41] Thomas A. Kselman and Steven Avella, 'Marian piety and the Cold War in the United States', *The Catholic Historical Review*, 72/3 (1986), 403–24.

[42] Alana Harris, 'Lourdes and holistic spirituality: contemporary Catholicism, the therapeutic and religious thermalism', *Culture and Religion*, 14/1 (2013), 23–43.

[43] See Kristy Nabhan-Warren, *The Cursillo movement in America: Catholics, Protestants and fourth day spirituality* (Chapel Hill: University of North Carolina Press, 2013).

Notre Dame, Michigan State, and the University of Michigan, where in 1967 'Catholic pentecostalism' would spread like wildfire through these existing Cursillo networks.[44] Two prominent charismatics, Steve Clark, of The Word of God community in Ann Arbor, and Ralph Martin, editor of charismatic magazine *New Covenant*, were on the National Cursillo Secretariat. For Clark, the mentality of the *cursillistas* meant they were likely 'to find all the good that was in the "new thing"' where pentecostal practices were concerned.[45] There were continuities between the small group dynamics of Cursillo and charismatic prayer groups. Cursillo reached Australia by 1969; and here, too, the pentecostal experience took hold in its networks.[46] Cursillo, Martin argued, was the 'seed-bed out of which the Charismatic Renewal blossomed'.[47]

Marian devotion and the mystical relationship with Christ were key components of Bonnín's Mallorquin spirituality, but a third was the experience of the fire of the Spirit.[48] While not 'pentecostal', there was potential for some overlap with a Pentecost paradigm. Clark heard of Cursillo through an American priest who described the movement in Mexico City in 'Pentecostal terms' – as men 'filled with the Holy Spirit' empowered to become effective apostles. Later Clark met Mexican *cursillistas* and came to think of the movement as 'something that would probably be good for Americans too'.[49] At the University of Notre Dame, Cursillo cultivated a New Testament atmosphere. During a meeting in 1965 there was even a case of tongues.[50] Ralph Martin, who had a reputation as the argumentative atheist on campus, was converted through Cursillo, an experience which he later recalled as being an 'overwhelming flood of God's love'. Months later, before he was pursuing any pentecostal experience, Martin manifested tongues, but without understanding this at the time.[51] There was an affinity between Cursillo and what emerged as the charismatic movement. At the International Conference on the Charismatic Renewal in the Catholic Church in 1978, Eduardo Bonnín was an invited speaker.[52] Cursillo's communitarian form and experiential piety, flowing from Spain to the United States, was a Hispanic contributor to charismatic origins.

[44] Jim Manney, 'Before Duquesne: sources of renewal', *New Covenant*, February 1973, 12–17. Martin and Clark both joined the National Cursillo Secretariat.

[45] RUSCA, Dennis J. Bennett papers, Box 4, Steve Clark, 'Renewal in the Catholic Church', *Pastoral Newsletter*, June 1970.

[46] John Maiden, 'City, portal and hub: Brisbane and Catholic Charismatic Renewal', in Rocha et al., *Australasian Pentecostal and Charismatic movements*. On Cursillo in Australia, see 'Cursillo success', *Catholic Weekly*, 23 October 1969, 3.

[47] Quoted in: Patti Gallagher Mansfield, *As by a new Pentecost: the dramatic beginning of the Catholic Charismatic Renewal* (Phoenix: Amor Deus, 2016), 194.

[48] Nabhan-Warren, *The Cursillo movement*, 3; 38; 47.

[49] Manney, 'Before Duquesne', 15.

[50] Ibid., 17.

[51] Mansfield, *New Pentecost*, 195.

[52] Louise Bourassa, 'You shall be my witnesses', *New Covenant*, 8/3 (September 1978), 4–8.

'A World-Sweeping Revival Now in Progress': Empowered Evangelicalism and Its Global Feedback

An important genealogy behind charismatic renewal began with John Wesley's teaching on the possibility of a late-in-life attainment of 'perfect love' or 'Christian perfection'. This was taken further by his colleague John Fletcher, who foregrounded crisis—an experience of 'entire sanctification'—over process. Instead of Wesley's Christological emphasis on sanctification and the 'mind of Christ', Fletcher adopted a Pentecost paradigm and the language of 'baptism of the Holy Spirit'.[53] In the 1830s, the notion of instantaneous experience—sanctification by faith—developed popularity within American Wesleyanism, notably through Phoebe Palmer's ministry in New York City. It established synergies with Oberlin College and Charles Finney, Asa Mahan, and others, and this produced a subtle shift of emphasis towards a second blessing of 'enduement of power'. In the 1870s, the Keswick movement became a channel for a 'higher life' expression of this radical evangelicalism, consolidating 'power'—following an act of 'surrender' and consecration—as the leitmotif of the second blessing (along with victory over sin, 'abiding in Christ', and various other benefits). Higher life evangelicals were often open to the gift of divine healing, both as a manifestation of the second blessing and of New Testament power in a modern age.[54] John Alexander Dowie and his International Divine Healing Association, established in Melbourne in 1886, and later his Christian Catholic Church in Chicago, were influential throughout the English-speaking world.[55] Dowie was one of many radical evangelicals who taught that Christ's death bore human sins *and* sicknesses—and in London, 1885, an International Conference on Divine Healing and True Holiness demonstrated the wider popularity of this teaching.[56] The language of 'baptism in the Spirit' was utilised by higher life teachers such as R. A. Torrey of the Moody Bible Institute, Chicago, A. B. Simpson, the Canadian founder of the Christian and Missionary Alliance, the British Baptist F. B. Meyer, and others.[57] In South Africa, the Dutch Reformed teacher Andrew Murray was

[53] Donald W. Dayton, 'Methodism and Pentecostalism', in James Kirby and William Abraham (eds.), *The Oxford handbook of Methodist studies* (Oxford: Oxford University Press, 2010), 171–87, at 173–75.

[54] Heather D. Curtis, 'A sane gospel: radical Evangelicals, psychology, and Pentecostal revival in the early twentieth century', *Religion and American Culture*, 21/2 (2011), 195–226, at 199.

[55] See Grant Wacker, 'Marching to Zion: religion in a modern Utopian community', *Church History*, 54/4 (1985), 496–511.

[56] Heather D. Curtis, 'The global character of nineteenth-century divine healing', in Candy Gunther Brown (ed.), *Global Pentecostal and Charismatic healing* (New York: Oxford University Press, 2011), 29–45, at 34; Donald Dayton, 'The rise of the Evangelical healing movement in nineteenth century America', *Pneuma*, 4/1 (1982), 1–18.

[57] On higher life, see George Marsden, *Fundamentalism and American culture: the shaping of twentieth-century evangelicalism, 1870–1925* (New York: Oxford University Press, 1980), 72–80.

another advocate. His *The Full Blessing of Pentecost* (1908) described the experience of the Spirit as 'the one needful thing for the Church'.[58] By the late nineteenth century, many radical evangelicals had adopted the Pentecost paradigm advocated by John Fletcher.

At the beginning of the next century, a cluster of revival movements, combining local cultural influences and missionary endeavour, appeared in locations as various as North America, Wales, India, Korea, and Chile. Eschatologically, they drew on a particular strand of radical evangelical thinking. The latter rain had been espoused by teachers such as William Boardman, A. T. Pierson, and A. B. Simpson.[59] God was pouring out his Spirit, almost two millennia after the former rain of the day of Pentecost, as a prelude to global revival in the last days. However, what soon distinguished emerging 'pentecostals' was their emphasis on tongues.[60] For many of their radical evangelical brethren, *glossolalia* was problematic. In the higher life tradition, consecration was considered as a mental act rather than an embodied manifestation.[61] Furthermore, radical evangelicals who did not reject tongues (and may even have sought the gift), such as A. B. Simpson, objected to the teaching that it was the evidence, or initial evidence, of baptism of the Spirit. Despite Simpson's efforts to maintain unity in the Christian and Missionary Alliance, it became bitterly divided, with many leaders joining the Assemblies of God. The relationship between radical evangelicals and pentecostals descended to internecine conflict. It was, in Grant Wacker's words, 'a brawl fought without rules, in the mud'. Outside the United States, anti-pentecostalism could go hand in hand with anti-Americanism—one London evangelical pastor said the teachings came from 'the land of wonder-meetings and freak religions'.[62] The rift within evangelicalism was now severe.

The controversy dampened charismatic impulses within evangelicalism. One casualty was divine healing, with suspicion now of the anti-medicine stance of some pentecostals, as well as teachings on demonology.[63] There was a fundamentalist, cessationist backlash. The Princeton theologian Benjamin Warfield claimed in *Counterfeit Miracles* (1918) that medical evidence for healing 'melts away'

Torrey and Meyer used the terminology of baptism of the Spirit and Pentecost. See R. A. Torrey, *The baptism with the Holy Spirit* (New York: Fleming H. Reveal, 1895); F. B. Meyer, *Back to Bethel: separation from sin, and fellowship with God* (Chicago: Fleming R. Revell, 1901).

[58] Andrew Murray, *The full blessing of Pentecost: the one thing needful* (London: James Nisbet and Co., 1908), 9.

[59] See, for example, Edith L. Blumhofer, *Restoring the faith: the Assemblies of God, Pentecostalism and American culture* (Urbana: University of Illinois Press, 1993), 95–96.

[60] We can divide these 'pentecostal' radical evangelicals into two main groups: those with a Wesleyan-Holiness background who decided to adopt the empowerment of Spirit baptism as a third stage after conversion and entire sanctification, and those who took a Reformed two-stage view.

[61] On the higher life suspicion of embodied manifestations, see Curtis, 'A sane gospel', 199–203.

[62] Grant Wacker, 'Travail of a broken family: evangelical responses to Pentecostalism in America, 1906–1916', *Journal of Ecclesiastical History*, 47/3 (1996), 505–28, quotes at 506, 511.

[63] Dayton, 'Evangelical healing', 17.

before the eyes.[64] The charismatic gifts, he argued, were 'the characterizing peculiarity of specifically the Apostolic Church'.[65] With notable exceptions, for example the British theologian Samuel Chadwick's *The Way to Pentecost* (1932, published in the United States 1937), evangelical attachment to any Pentecost paradigm was weakened. The Belfast-born revivalist and scholar of revivalism, J. Edwin Orr, later called the period 1908 to 1948 'forty years of the wilderness experience' due to the dearth of teaching on the filling of the Spirit.[66] Under the leadership of Graham Scroggie, the emphasis of the Keswick Convention in England shifted from crisis towards process. In 1956, the Scotsman claimed the search for a baptism in the Spirit was 'bringing large numbers into bondage and darkness'.[67] For Scroggie, too, the Spirit was to be experienced through engagement with the Word of God, not in the empowerment of a single experience.[68] The foregrounding of the text of Scripture in the conflict evangelicals waged on liberal theology also came at the expense of experience. The *modus operandi* of Keswick became, decisively, the expositional preaching of the Word. The missionary Reuben Archer Torrey III later recalled how mid-century American evangelicals recoiled from his grandfather's teaching on crisis experience: 'There were a lot of people who didn't want to settle for supernatural power, they wanted to settle for academic power. Study the Bible enough and you'll be okay.'[69]

An organisation which continued to cultivate a distinctive variety of evangelical experientialism, albeit with little explicit reference to the Pentecost paradigm, was the pan-denominational Oxford Group.[70] 'The Group', as it was known, fostered 'the realization of the power of the Holy Spirit as a force for spiritual and material stability and betterment of the world'. 'Sin is the frustration of God's Plan for us all', was the positive spin on a grave dogma.[71] A distinctive practice was listening to the Spirit's guidance—or 'luminous thoughts'.[72] Malcom Muggeridge observed that the Group attracted 'enthusiastic teams of young men and women mostly belonging to middle and upper classes' eager for a more subjective expression of Christianity.[73] The founder, a Pennsylvanian Lutheran, Frank Buchman, drew on the higher life teaching on 'surrender', Christian mystic writers, and the 'personal

[64] Benjamin Warfield, *Counterfeit miracles* (New York: Charles Scribner's Sons, 1918).

[65] Ibid. [66] J. Edwin Orr, *Full surrender* (London: Marshall, Morgan and Scott, 1951), 72.

[67] W. Graham Scroggie, *The Baptism of the Spirit and speaking with tongues* (London: Pickering and Inglis, 1956), 14.

[68] See, for example, Alisdair Black, 'Pour out your Spirit: experiences of the Holy Spirit amongst Scottish Baptists in the twentieth century', in Brian R. Talbot, *A distinctive people: a thematic study of aspects of the witness of Baptists in Scotland in the twentieth century* (Milton Keynes: Paternoster Press, 2014), 166–77, at 163. On Scroggie, see also Ian Randall, 'Graham Scroggie and evangelical spirituality', *Scottish Bulletin of Evangelical Theology*, 18/1 (2000), 71–86.

[69] Wheaton College, Collection 331, Tape 1, interview with Reuben Archer Torrey III, 14 May 1986.

[70] The organisation began life as the First Century Christian Fellowship in the 1920s and later became Moral Rearmament.

[71] L. W. Grensted, *What is the Oxford Group?* (Oxford: Oxford University Press, 1933), 6.

[72] Ibid., 8–9.

[73] Malcolm Muggeridge, *The thirties, 1930–1940, in Great Britain* (London: H. Hamilton, 1940), 37.

work' model of Henry Wright (1877–1925).[74] Although charismatic renewal came decades later, there were some continuities with the Group. For example, the Revd. William Sherwood, mentioned above, had decades before his baptism 'with the Holy Ghost and with fire' known the Group's 'surrendered life' and guidance by the Spirit.[75] Some fellow travellers with the charismatics had a Group background. Cuthbert Bardsley, the Bishop of Coventry, was involved in Buchman's ministry in the 1930s and this likely predisposed him to become the first English bishop to actively support charismatic renewal (reassuring colleagues that emotionalism could not be regarded as the chief peril of Anglican clergy.[76] In the United States, the Revd. Samuel Shoemaker, the Rector of Calvary Episcopal Church, the New York headquarters of the Oxford Group until 1941, continued to advocate for spiritual empowerment of clergy in the diocese of Pittsburgh. When news emerged of charismatic awakenings amongst Episcopalians in the 1960s, Shoemaker defended tongues speakers as having experienced 'a new power they did not have before'.[77]

Although the Oxford Group fostered a charismatic potential amongst evangelicals, it was after the Second World War that there was a larger resurgence of the Pentecost paradigm. It came with the renewed hope for spiritual awakening. The year 1949 was a landmark for two examples of revivalism with a historic evangelical pedigree. On the periphery of the Anglo-world there was a 'spontaneous' awakening on the Isle of Lewis in the Scottish Outer Hebrides; while in the metropolis of Los Angeles, Billy Graham arrived with his sophisticated evangelistic machine.[78] 'Praise God for a world-sweeping revival now in progress', wrote Robert Walker in *Christian Life*, a leading higher life magazine, in September that year.[79] Graham toured widely, visiting Britain in 1954/55, Canada in 1955, and Australia and New Zealand in 1959. There were numerous other initiatives for revival. The Methodist Sir Alan Walker's Mission to the Nation in Australia from 1953–54 ('The wind is in the gum trees! The wind is in the gum trees!' he was convinced) was hailed a success.[80] Later, the anniversaries of the 1857 awakening in the United States and the 1859 revival in Britain boosted hopes of divine intervention. During 1959, Martin Lloyd-Jones, the revered London-based Welsh nonconformist, spoke every Sunday on revival at Westminster Chapel.[81]

[74] On Buchman and origins, see: Philip Boobbyer, *The spiritual vision of Frank Buchman* (University Park: Pennsylvania State University Press, 2013), 11–13.

[75] William Sherwood, 'The Lord called me out of retirement', *Trinity*, 1/1 (1961), 8–9; William Sherwood, 'And it came to pass', *Acts 29 Newsletter* (March 1971), 1.

[76] David Bebbington, *Evangelicalism in modern Britain: a history from the 1730s to the 1980s* (London: Unwin Hyman, 1989), 240.

[77] Samuel M. Shoemaker. 'Can our church change our kind of world…?', *Trinity*, 3/1 (1963), 3.

[78] 'Revival sweeps islands off Scottish coast', *Christian Life*, March 1951, 27.

[79] Editorial, 'Formula for revival', *Christian Life*, September 1949, 6.

[80] Alan Walker, *Breakthrough: rediscovering the Holy Spirit* (Nashville: Abingdon Press, 1969), 53.

[81] 'Revival sweeps islands off Scottish coast', *Christian Life*, March 1951, 27; Ian Randall, 'Lloyd-Jones and revival', in Andrew Atherstone and David Ceri Jones (eds.), *Engaging with Martyn Lloyd-Jones* (Leicester: Inter-Varsity Press, 2011), 91–113.

Prayer for revival vented domestic concerns about youth delinquency and irreligion, with the release of *Rebel Without a Cause* (1955) and 'Rock Around the Clock' (1956) a double-blow to evangelical moralists. It was also an outlet for existential uncertainties about the Soviet Union's acquisition of the atomic bomb. It was '4 minutes to midnight', asserted one writer in *Christian Life*, in a reference to the 'doomsday clock' of the *Bulletin of the Atomic Scientists.*[82] News from the Third World appeared to confirm the hope of global awakening. A 1956 article in the same magazine asked, 'can revival scenes from the 19th century be duplicated in our modern, atomic-age world?' It mapped contemporary awakenings on every continent, including in Brazil, East Africa, the Belgian Congo, Korea, and Japan. The correspondent Don Hoke argued, 'The prophecy of Joel was not exhausted but rather only initiated by Pentecost. I believe that we can expect from God in the last days a gracious outpouring of His Holy Spirit in revival.'[83]

Revivalism brought heightened expectation of manifestations of the Spirit. Nights of Prayer for World-wide Revival (NOPFWR), the transnational network which supported Billy Graham's evangelism (established during the 1954 London crusade), prayed for 'nothing less than a sweep of God's Spirit throughout the world, a breaking through of the powers of the realm of the invisible'.[84] *Christian Life* desired a revived church to resemble the empowered Christianity of the Book of Acts. A 1950 editorial, 'Signs and Wonders' spoke of a 'small but growing circle of men and women in the very heart of conservative Christianity restudying the account of the visible demonstration of the power of the Holy Spirit in the Acts of the Apostles'. Pointing towards the 'remarkable growth of the much-maligned pentecostal movement', it urged readers 'in this late hour' to be open to the powerful works of the Spirit.[85] An increasing number of articles and letters asserted similar views. A minister of an English Baptist church asked, 'is there a possibility that I – together with evangelical Christians as a whole – am to blame for this lack of the power of God being manifested today'.[86] Another Baptist from Tennessee spoke of 'The great discrepancy' between what evangelicals preached and what the Scriptures said of Spirit-empowered ministry.[87] A. W. Tozer of the Christian and Missionary Alliance urged *Christian Life* readers to seek a crisis experience of the Spirit; while other articles critiqued cessationism, testified to

[82] On geopolitical and nuclear anxieties, see for example, William W. Gothard, '4 Minutes to 12', *Christian Life*, January 1950, 11–13, 35. On youth delinquency, see David Hilliard, 'Church, family and sexuality in Australia in the 1950s', *Australian Historical Studies*, 27/109 (1997), 133–46.

[83] 'Revival today', *Christian Life*, February 1968, 18–20; 45; quote at 45.

[84] 'How to hold revival prayer meetings', *Christian Life*, July 1956, 44–45.

[85] Robert Walker, editorial, 'Signs and wonders', *Christian Life*, November 1950, 8. On *Christian Life*, see also Amber Thomas Reynolds, 'Robert Walker's Christian Life magazine: a missing link between mainstream American evangelicalism and charismatic renewal', in Andrew Atherstone, Mark P. Hutchinson and John Maiden, *Transatlantic charismatic renewal c. 1950–2000* (Leiden: Brill, 2021), 37–60.

[86] Myrddin Lewis, 'Are we missing something?', *Christian Life*, April 1953, 28–29.

[87] Donald W. Wells, 'The great discrepancy', *Christian Life*, August 1953, 26–27.

healing, or discussed spiritual warfare.[88] The empowerment of the Spirit, the magazine asserted in 1956, was the 'need of the hour', explaining: 'Terminology doesn't matter. You may call it victorious life of Keswick Conference fame, fullness of the Spirit, sanctification, deeper life experience, baptism in the Spirit, the life that wins of Charles G. Trumbull or the exchanged life of Hudson Taylor. Essentially they all mean the same.'[89] As articles appeared also on the ministry of the Assemblies of God, it was clear the early century divide between radical evangelical and pentecostal was narrowing.[90]

In his global ministry, the Revd. J. Edwin Orr played an important role reinvigorating an 'advanced' version of the Keswick higher life. This provided a gateway for some towards a charismatic experience. In New Zealand, after the Anglican clergyman Cecil Marshall (who, also, in 1954 had been the first person in the country to join the Order of St Luke) heard Orr in 1956, he was left feeling 'hungry for more'. Through the witness of pentecostals he moved towards an experience of the Spirit before taking a leading role in the charismatic renewal from the mid-1960s.[91] At this point Marshall developed a close connection with the English charismatics Michael and Jeanne Harper. Michael Harper had also become attentive to revivalism through reading Orr and in the 1950s had some interest in a definite experience of the Spirit (he was apparently reported to the Inter-Varsity Fellowship for suspect teachings on this). In 1962, while a curate at All Souls, Langham Place—the preaching flagship of the Revd. John R. W. Stott—he and his wife had powerful experiences of the Spirit which bore the marks of a Keswick second blessing.[92] Soon they moved in a more pentecostal direction; however, Michael Harper continued to draw on the terminology of empowered evangelicalism. Baptism in the Spirit, he said, brought 'victorious Christian living'.[93] Harper, as Chaplain to the Stores, helped organise All Souls' mid-week services, which began regularly to attract fellow travellers, such as William Wood, of London Healing Mission, the Revd. G. H. Forester of St Paul's, Beckenham, and the Revd. M. C. Peppiatt, another of Stott's curates, among the speakers. Revivalism was also to be found in the *Work and Worship* newssheet, which claimed there was 'overwhelming evidence that He is at this time reviving many,

[88] A. W. Tozer, 'How to be filled with the Spirit', *Christian Life*, December 1957, 14–15. On the supernatural, see, for example: William H. Good MD, 'I saw a miracle', *Christian Life*, 21, 68–70; W. Douglas Roe, 'I clashed with the Spirit world', *Christian Life*, January 1952, 21, 64, 66; Samuel Shoemaker, 'Healing prayer', *Christian Life*, August 1959, 16–17.

[89] 'Need of the hour', *Christian Life*, December 1956, 18–20, quote at 19.

[90] 'Fifty years of sign and wonders', *Christian Life*, July 1951, 22–24, 28.

[91] Dale Williamson, 'An uncomfortable engagement: the charismatic renewal in the New Zealand Anglican Church, 1965–85'. PhD University of Otago, 2007, 42–44.

[92] On this, see Martin Robinson, 'The charismatic Anglican: historical and contemporary. A comparison of the life and work of Alexander Boddy (1854–1930) and Michael C. Harper', M.Litt thesis, University of Birmingham, 1976, 131–37.

[93] Michael Harper, *Power for the body of Christ* (London: Fountain Trust, 1969), 8.

even members of the most unspiritual churches'.[94] Arthur Wallis, the independent evangelical discussed below, was amongst those to feature, with his piece 'The laws of the Kingdom' (based on Robert William Service's 'The law of the Yukon') saying of revival-minded Christians:

> With instinct of wrestling Jacob they plead for the Spirit's power, Praying and fasting and waiting till clothed with the tongue of fire.[95]

As Chapter 4 describes, the heightened spiritual atmosphere around All Souls helped birth the charismatic Fountain Trust.

Another speaker at these All Souls services in June 1964 was the Ugandan evangelist Festo Kivengere.[96] A decisive influence on the reanimation of higher life piety was reverse flows of radical evangelicalism. The recent historiography of the East Africa Revival shows how Keswick theology was indigenised in the 1930s—the practice of public confession of sin displayed close parallels with elements of traditional religions.[97] While downplaying the specificities of the local contribution in its 'African Keswick' narrative, the Worldwide Evangelisation Crusade (WEC)—founded in 1913 by C. T. Studd of the 'Cambridge seven'—and its publishing arm, Christian Literature Crusade, mediated the work of the Spirit in the East Africa Revival to the Anglo-world audience. Roy and Revel Hession's *The Calvary Road* (1950) and Norman P. Grubb's *Continuous Revival* (1952) described a phenomenon in central and eastern Africa of 'continuous revival' and 'cups running over' as normative daily experience. In 1953 the WEC sponsored a United States tour by Grubb, Roy Hession, and two representatives of the Ruanda Mission, Joe Church and William Nagenda. Accounts could be dramatic. Grubb's *Spirit of Revival* (1954) included testimonies, such as the following, from the Congo:

> Then, as I led in prayer, the Spirit came down in mighty power, sweeping through the congregation. My whole body trembled with the power. We then saw a marvellous sight, people literally filled and drunk with the Spirit. Never have we seen anything like this. The power and presence of the Lord were awful indeed. Elders and evangelists were swept to their feet, reeling around like drunken men, shouting out, "I am filled! I am filled!"[98]

94 Michael Harper, 'What Jesus said about the Church', *Work and Worship*, 32 (Autumn 1963).

95 Arthur Wallis, 'The laws of the Kingdom', *Work and Worship*, 34 (1964).

96 List of speakers, *Work and Worship*, 36 (1964).

97 Jason Bruner, 'Keswick and the East African Revival: an historiographical reappraisal', *Religion Compass*, 5/9 (2011), 477–89.

98 Norman Grubb, *Spirit of Revival: a first-hand account of the Congo revival of the 1950s* (Gerrards Cross: WEC, 1954), ch. 2.

Such reports stirred desires for an intensification of the spiritual context at home. At St Mark's Anglican church, Gillingham, there was discussion of whether the revivalism described by Hession might be transplanted to the English evangelical parish. It was not attempted—it was recognised that public confession would jar with English pastoral sensibilities—but the parish was amongst the first to move into charismatic renewal early the next decade.[99] After experiencing the baptism in the Spirit, its vicar, the Revd. John Collins, wrote Michael Harper 'apart from extravagancies, God was previously trying to say something to the Church throughout the world in the Ruanda Movement'. The message had not spread sufficiently, but the latest move of God had taken hold.[100]

WEC missionaries noticed a contrast returning home. In 1952, after arriving in Britain from Ruanda, one missionary described coming 'face to face again with the desperate need for revival in the English-speaking world'.[101] Some attempted to encourage revival fires in the churches. In New Zealand, the former WEC workers W. Ivor Davies and Kiwi Thorne spoke of their experiences.[102] Owen Woodfield, the Chair of the Methodist Revival Fellowship in Christchurch, was enthused by Davies' account of the Congo awakening. Some years later Woodfield was baptised in the Spirit—and tellingly, he at first compared the experience to the Keswick 'blessing'.[103] In Australia, Geoff Bingham, the Anglican Principal of the Bible College of South Australia, had experienced a spiritual breakthrough at the Katoomba (Keswick) Convention, before leaving to serve in Pakistan with the Christian Missionary Society in 1956. Here he witnessed repentance, healings, prophecy, and spontaneous singing during revival meetings. He brought reports back to Australia.[104] After returning home in 1966, although Bingham could be critical of aspects of the inchoate charismatic movement—particularly pitfalls of 'human pride' and supernaturalism for its own sake—his testimony of the Spirit's work contributed to the openness of some Australians towards the renewal.[105]

Strains of resurgent radical evangelicalism had a sharper restorationist quality. In England, this was evident in the teaching of Arthur Wallis, an independent of Brethren stock. During the early 1950s, Wallis experienced a 'filling' through the influence of a friend who had discovered R. A. Torrey. Wallis longed for revival, inspired by events on the Isle of Lewis, where he visited in 1951. *In the Day of Thy Power* (1956) looked for a latter rain of global awakening, supernatural

[99] Teddy Saunders and Hugh Samson, *David Watson* (London: Hodder & Stoughton, 1992), 71–72.

[100] LPL, Michael Harper papers, 1964/8, John Collins to Michael Harper, 30 July 1964, 3.

[101] F. C. Renich, 'The wind of God in Africa', *Christian Life*, November 1952, 36.

[102] Peter Lineham, 'Tongues must cease: the Brethren and the charismatic movement in New Zealand', *Christian Brethren Review*, 34 (1983), 1–48, at 17; 19.

[103] George Bryant, 'Four leaders in the Methodist Revival Fellowship, Aldersgate Fellowship and Affirm', *Wesley Historical Journal* (New Zealand), 65 (1997), 36–37; W. J. Clifford, 'The Evangelical/Charismatic aspect of Methodism in New Zealand', *Wesley Historical Journal*, 65 (1997), 11.

[104] Jae Kook Kim, 'Bingham, Geoffrey Cyril (1919-2009)', *ADPCM*.

[105] LPL, Michael Harper papers, 1966/9, Geoff Bingham to Michael Harper, 15 October 1966.

manifestations of apostolic power, and the restoration of the primitive church.[106] It later became a key charismatic text, particularly amongst independents. From 1958, Wallis and David Lillie (who had been ejected from the Brethren in the late 1930s) led a series of seminal conferences in south-east England. Alongside their primary emphases of revival and the restoration of New Testament patterns, there was soon a third, largely through the influence of Cecil Cousen, an independent of Apostolic Church background: explicit teaching of the Pentecost paradigm. Brethren influences moved through old Commonwealth family and church networks. In South Africa, Denis G. Clark, a Brethren from Johannesburg, was filled with the Spirit in around 1953 while working as director of Youth for Christ; Campbell McAlpine, a Scotsman working in South Africa, soon after had the same experience, but with tongues. Both moved to Britain in 1955 and witnessed discretely to Spirit baptism. In 1959, McAlpine went to be with relatives in New Zealand, where he included charismatic emphases while teaching at Brethren cottage meetings.[107] Wallis, who by this point was speaking in tongues, arrived in 1963. Together they advocated a second stage experience with *glossolalia*.[108] A distinctive, independent charismatic milieu became evident in Britain, New Zealand, and South Africa *before* the United States, and the primary reason for this was Brethren influence.

Restorationism was also shaped by 'reverse' global flows. In China, higher life piety had been fostered by the work of the China Inland Mission, founded in 1865 by James Hudson Taylor. Various Brethren had worked for the mission, and later more arrived with their own organisation, Echoes of Service. These influences were apparent in the theology of Ni Doushen, or Watchman Nee, the leader of the indigenous Little Flock movement. The best-selling collection of his teachings, *The Normal Christian Life* (1957) drew on Finney, Moody, and Torrey to underline a second crisis experience. The book generated great enthusiasm. One youth group in St Leonards-on-Sea, England, for instance, took turns reading aloud Nee around a circle and became aware of lacking the 'powerful, Spirit-filled, boldly witnessing lives' of the early Christians.[109] Radical ecclesiological teachings were evident in Nee's teaching. During a 1938 visit to Britain, Nee spent time at the Honor Oak Fellowship, London, which had a conception of the local church like the Brethren. The next year, their imprint published Nee's *Concerning Our Missions*. The message was that the church must 'return to the beginning'—a biblical model which assumed that locality was the only basis for the division of churches. In 1962 this was republished in Los Angeles as *The Normal Christian*

[106] Arthur Wallis, *In the day of thy Power: the scriptural principles of revival* (London: Christian Literature Crusade, 1956), ch. 3.
[107] Lineham, 'Tongues', 23–25.
[108] Lineham, 'Tongues', 29; 40.
[109] Tom Walker, *Renew us by your Spirit* (London: Hodder & Stoughton, 1982), 13.

Church. Nee's teachings on primitive Christianity flowed into independent charismatic understandings of ecclesiology and authority.

The post-war resurgence of radical evangelicalism—a delayed backlash to Warfieldian cessationism—was a precursor for charismatic origins. Alongside the ministries of Orr, Tozer, Grubb, Nee, and others, was a flourishing interest in historic evangelical divines—such as Meyer, Torrey, and Murray—and their testimonies to a post-conversion spiritual experience.[110] The next decade a similar appetite for these texts was evident amongst the pioneers of charismatic renewal. A transatlantic airmail exchange between Larry Christenson and Michael Harper in 1963 referred to Andrew Murray as 'Our great friend'. The American joked he might regard Murray as his patron saint.[111] Charismatic service agencies would publicise these holiness luminaries; in a kind of historical *ressourcement* amongst evangelicals seeking to orientate a 'pentecostal' experience to their tradition. Non-Protestant charismatics, too, discovered these writings. In Brisbane in 1973, one Catholic charismatic newsletter recommended Andrew Murray's *The Prayer Life* (1914) as a 'gem'. 'We strongly recommend this book', it added.[112] No doubt the long-deceased author would have been surprised at the breadth of his new readership.

'In This Day I Am Visiting Hungry Hearts Everywhere': Revivalistic Pentecostalism

The 1940s enhanced the visibility and reputation of pentecostalism. Various factors contributed, including the consolidation of denominational structures (with some joining the National Association of Evangelicals in the United States), intra-pentecostal unity, notably the establishment of the Pentecostal World Fellowship in 1947, and upwards trends in the social mobility of adherents.[113] The Oklahoman healing evangelist—and reputedly the man with the world's largest tent—Oral Roberts made a notable contribution. His media empire broadcast on hundreds of television and radio stations in North America, employed representatives in Australasia, South Africa, and Britain, and soon claimed weekly distribution of one million literature units across 105 nations.[114] In Australia, twenty-five radio stations broadcast his 'Healing Waters' show by 1956, the same year in which he visited there and New Zealand.[115] He toured

[110] For example, in Scotland, in the wake of the Lewis revival—see Black, 'Pour out your Spirit', 164.

[111] LPL, Michael Harper papers, 1963/4, Larry Christenson to Michael Harper, 20 December 1963.

[112] *Newsletter* (Bardon Catholic Charismatic Renewal), March 1973, 4.

[113] David E. Harrell Jr., *Oral Roberts: an American life* (Bloomington: Indiana University Press, 1985), 146–47.

[114] Ibid., 138; 276.

[115] Ibid., 123; Revd. J. E. Worsfold, *A history of the charismatic movements in New Zealand* (Bradford: Puritan Press, 1974), 316; Lineham, 'Tongues', 14.

South Africa in 1955 and 1957. Roberts' crusades impacted mainline Christians. In 1951, during a crusade in Tampa, Florida, reportedly over half of those who went forward were from these denominations.[116] A feature film, *Venture into Faith* (1952), captured Roberts' aim to transcend existing barriers. It told the story of a churchgoing wife and irreligious husband with a young boy, who (like Roberts as a child) had tuberculosis. Roberts' 'tent Cathedral' came to town. The parents were drawn to a pentecostal message which asked the crowd to put aside their prejudices and traditions, but which also urged converts to attend the churches of their choice. The couple's minister, although at first ambivalent about Roberts' ministry, was soon persuaded by the sick boy that God might heal him (he did, of course). Roberts' global reputation was symbolic of a post-war pentecostal achievement.

However, the success of Roberts and a new generation of independent healing evangelists was also indicative of instabilities and tensions within pentecostalism. Some, as in the case of Jack Coe and the Assemblies of God, found they were now at odds with their denominational leaderships. Although Roberts remained with the Pentecostal Holiness Church until 1968, when he joined the United Methodists, relations were sometimes strained.[117] The popularity of healing evangelists—including William Branham and Kathryn Kuhlman, who operated outside the fold of denominational pentecostalism—brought into question whether the existing pentecostal churches had responded adequately to a resurgent cultural interest in divine cures. Various healing evangelists threw their weight behind an organisation which challenged the pentecostal status quo: the Full Gospel Business Men's Fellowship International (FGBMFI). Founded by Demos Shakarian, a California dairy farmer, in 1951, the organisation embodied the social mobility of a younger pentecostal generation as well as the post-war boom in lay-led 'faith at work' initiatives.[118] In North America, local chapters and the magazine *Voice* spread the 'basic doctrine' of Spirit baptism with tongues as initial evidence. As David Harrell has argued, if the rise of independent healing evangelists was 'an uprising in the ranks of the aspiring clergy', the emergence of the FGBMFI was a 'layman's rebellion in pentecostal ranks'.[119] It sought to recover the revivalism and 'missionary' impetus of pre-denominational pentecostalism. Rotary Club-style interdenominational events presented 'Testimonies of outstanding businessmen and Spirit filled ministers'.[120] Denominational 'full gospel' converts, such as Gerald Derstine, a Mennonite minister baptised in the Spirit in 1954 (and removed from ministry in 1956), the Houston independent Baptist

116 Harrell, *Roberts*, 102. 117 Ibid., 159.

118 David Miller, *God at work: the history and promise of the Faith at Work Movement* (New York: Oxford University Press, 2007), 39–61.

119 Harrell, *Roberts*, 153.

120 DAHL, David du Plessis papers, box 53, file 29, Poster for FGBMFI International Convention, Houston, July 1963.

John H. Osteen, baptised in the Spirit in 1958, and the Revd. James Brown, of Upper Octorara Presbyterian Church, Parkesburg, Pennsylvania, were on a roster of popular speakers. When the Black South African Assemblies of God leader and evangelist Nicholas B. H. Bhengu encountered the FGBMFI at a worldwide convention in Los Angeles, he observed:

> Anglican bishops, Roman Catholic priests, nuns and university professors of theology, Doctors of Divinity, judges, attorneys and celebrities from all walks of life. These all have had a touch of Charismatic revival with real experience of glossolalia (speaking in tongues), no sophist or sceptic could easily dismiss this from such learned men and women of our modern times.[121]

FGBMFI was a space for interaction between different social and religious worlds.

The healing evangelist Kenneth E. Hagin was a favourite of the organisation. In 1962, he had a vision which reflected the missionary zeal of the new pentecostalism; a 'river of people' singing praises to God, which the Lord told him were 'denominational people'—'for in this day I am visiting hungry hearts everywhere'.[122] However, the FGBMFI was not, formally at least, in the business of stealing 'full gospel' converts. One English pentecostal evangelist visiting the 1959 FGBMFI annual international conference at the Ambassador Hotel, Los Angeles, encountered a message which resonated with his own convictions: '"Pentecost" is for ALL, irrespective of denomination or creed. It is not "Being in Pentecost" it is "PENTECOST BEING IN YOU" that counts!'[123] By 1963, it was claimed over half of new FGBMFI members in the United States were mainliners.[124] The pan-denominational message of Pentecost was transported worldwide. There was a Chapter in London, England, by 1955, in Toronto by 1958, and soon after in Australia, in Adelaide, Brisbane, Toowoomba, Sydney, and Melbourne; while in South Africa, the Christian Business Men's Fellowship International was an affiliate organisation.[125] FGBMFI became a recruiting ground for what became charismatic renewal. When Michael Harper visited the United States in 1965, at the invitation of FGBMFI, he was surprised to find even Roman Catholics attending their events. It would often play an important role in helping local

[121] Quoted in Daniel Simon Billie Lephoko, *Nicholas Bhekinkosi Hepworth Bhengu's lasting legacy: world's best Black soul crusader* (Cape Town: AOSIS, 2018), 288.

[122] Quoted in Paul Hejzlar, *Two paradigms of divine healing: Fred F. Bosworth, Kenneth E. Hagin, Agnes Sanford and Francis MacNutt in dialogue* (Leiden: Brill 2009), 28.

[123] Fred Squire, 'My most terrific Pentecostal meeting', *Pentecost*, December 1959, 5.

[124] See DAHL, David du Plessis, box 53, file 29, *The New Testament charismatic revival seminar report* (1963).

[125] *Redemption Tidings*, 2 September 1955, 4; DAHL, David du Plessis, box 29, file 4, E. H. Seidel to du Plessis, 20 September 1965.

Catholic charismatic prayer groups get off the ground.[126] The support of FGBMFI for charismatic students, alumni, and Faculty at Notre Dame University was likely a factor in them adopting the label 'Catholic Pentecostal'. The inclusive 'Pentecost in you' message contributed to the grassroots ecumenism which continued to pervade charismatic renewal.

A South African-born 'ecumaniac' (as he called himself), now living in California, saw these post-war full gospel mainline inroads as the fulfilment of prophecy. In 1936 David du Plessis had encountered the British Pentecostal Smith Wigglesworth, who pushed him against the wall of his office and foretold a mainline revival to 'eclipse the present-day twentieth century Pentecostal revival'. 'You will have a prominent part', he told the staggered du Plessis.[127] After pioneering intra-Pentecostal ecumenism as General Secretary of the World Pentecostal Conferences, from the mid-1950s du Plessis began operating as an 'observer' in the World Council of Churches, developing wider ecumenical connections, notably with the Presbyterian John Mackay, President of Princeton Theological Seminary.[128] Du Plessis utilised ecumenical networks and became an indefatigable publiciser of a latter-day revival. His message was not a call to doctrinal purity, but of the renewal of these churches as they were incorporated into Pentecost. His guest editorial for the British *Pentecost* magazine in 1957 spoke of a 'revolution' of latter-day outpouring in the denominational churches. Many were becoming pentecostal 'because of their experience and not because of membership in a full Gospel church'.[129] After attending Vatican II as an observer, he began to testify to the signs of a new Pentecost in the Catholic Church, and claimed from personal conversations with members of the Catholic hierarchy that some wished to see 'Pentecostal Fire' brought into 'the cold formalism of the Church'.[130] The ecumenical message did not always ingratiate him to his own denomination and by 1962 du Plessis and the Assemblies of God had cut ties.

Alongside an extensive ministry in North America, from the end of the 1950s du Plessis visited Britain almost annually. In 1966 he travelled to Australia and then New Zealand. A selection of engagements in the latter indicate his ecumenical reach: in Dunedin he spoke at the church of the Moderator of the Presbyterian Assembly; in Christchurch, at a meeting of the National Council of Churches; and

[126] Michael Harper mentions this in a review of his visit to the United States in 1965. See: 'The new Pentecostalism: after five years', *Crusade*, October 1965: RUSCA, Dennis J. Bennett Papers, box 1, vol. 1. On Brisbane and Canada, see Maiden, 'City"; James Hanrahan, 'The nature and history of the Catholic Charismatic renewal in Canada', *Bilan de l'Histoire religieuse au Canada*, 50/1 (1983), 307–24, at 316; Kevin Ranaghan and Dorothy Ranaghan, *Catholic Pentecostals* (New York: Paulist Press, 1969), 42.

[127] David du Plessis and Bob Slosser, *A man called Mr Pentecost* (Plainfield: Logos, 1977), 2–3.

[128] Joshua Zeifle, *David du Plessis and the Assemblies of God: the struggle for the soul of a movement* (Leiden: Brill, 2011), ch. 2

[129] David du Plessis, 'Pentecostal revival and revolution, 1947–1957', *Pentecost*, November 1957.

[130] DAHL, David du Plessis papers, box 39, file 29, 'The Second Vatican Ecumenical Council from the point of view of a Pentecostal'.

in Auckland, at the Divine Healing Fellowship and to students at Trinity Methodist College.[131] He also spoke in the home of the Roman Catholic auxiliary Bishop of Auckland, Reginald Delargey, where one observer argued that compared to some Protestant clergy 'the Romans were more open and talked about experience'.[132] Clergy, across the Anglo-American world and beyond, 'received' through du Plessis' public ministry and private counsel. The Revd. William Hughes, an Ulster Presbyterian, was urged by du Plessis: 'Ask the Lord! Believe Him! Obey Him! Never mind your intellectual difficulties—set them aside! Believe the Lord!'[133] When du Plessis visited South Africa in 1968, publicity described his 'many contacts throughout Christendom' as being such that 'perhaps no other person has been more used of God in proclaiming the message of the Holy Spirit.'[134] As one study of du Plessis asserts, his 'fingerprints are all over the [charismatic] revival'.[135] His one-man ministry, the ballroom gatherings of full gospel businessmen, and the church, tent, and stadia meetings of independent healing evangelists overlapped significantly. As we see in the next chapter, their collective contribution to charismatic origins was underlined by the prominence of tongues in Spirit baptism narratives.

A further post-war expression of revivalistic pentecostalism was more determinedly radical in its ecclesiology. The New Order of the Latter Rain began as a revival movement in North Battleford, Saskatchewan, in 1948. Its pioneer, George Hawtin, founder of the Sharon Bible College, sought to address the spiritual aridity of contemporary pentecostalism after being inspired to seek a greater move of God during a William Branham crusade in Vancouver.[136] The primary focus of Hawtin's revivalism was the latter-day restoration of the gifts of the Spirit through the laying on of hands. To attend a Latter Rain revival meeting, he claimed, was like 'living in another Chapter of the Acts of the Apostles'.[137] The movement ground to a halt in the mid-1950s but its legacy of local ministries had a profound impact on the renewal.

In North America, various congregations with Latter Rain pedigree, such as Bethesda Missionary Temple, Detroit, John Poole's Gospel Temple, Philadelphia, and Winston Nunes' Broadview Faith Temple in Toronto, became independent charismatic ministries. The Englishman Cecil Cousen encountered the Latter Rain movement in Hamilton, Ontario, in 1949, before returning to Bradford, England,

131 DAHL, David du Plessis papers, box 80, file 1, Itinerary for du Plessis visit to Auckland, 1966.

132 DAHL, David du Plessis papers, box 14, file 21, Betty and Dave Edmonds prayer letter, 15 March 1966, 1–2.

133 Rev William J. Hughes, 'The God of all sufficiency', *Renewal*, December–January 1968/9, 17–19.

134 DAHL, David du Plessis papers, box 108, file 18, Newssheet for Christian Business Men's Fellowship International, 5 November 1968.

135 Ziefle, *David du Plessis*, 104.

136 See D. William Faupel, 'The New Order of the Latter Rain: restoration or renewal', in Michael Wilkinson and Peter Althouse (eds.), *Winds from the north: Canadian contributions to the Pentecostal movement* (Leiden: Brill, 2010), 247–93.

137 Quoted in Faupel, 'Latter Rain', 246.

where after expulsion from the Apostolic Church, he established Dean House Christian Fellowship. Unlike some Latter Rain types, Cousen was not stridently anti-denominational and his *A Voice of Faith* magazine influenced mainline charismatics.[138] In Australasia, the Latter Rain arrived through, amongst others, Ray Jackson, formerly of Bethel Temple (Seattle). In Sydney in 1951, Jackson's 'Bible School' was formative for future independent pentecostal leaders like the Australian Peter Morrow and the New Zealander Rob Wheeler. The impact of Latter Rain teaching was strongest across the Tasman Sea, particularly through the planting of autonomous independent fellowships, 'Indigenous Churches of New Zealand' (indigenous referred to their local independency)—later known as 'New Life Churches'—to nurture mainline converts.[139] Through these networks the Latter Rain made a vital contribution to charismatic renewal in New Zealand and Australia. Whereas pentecostals such as du Plessis sought the renewal of the mainline churches, leaders with a Latter Rain background were more likely to funnel full gospel converts into believer's fellowships. In their insistence, too, on the Ascension Gift ministries of apostle, prophet, evangelist, pastor, and teacher, as well as submission to spiritual authority, Latter Rain teachers also informed the ecclesiology of independent charismatics.

Seekership, Small Groups, and the Self: Mid-Century Proto-Charismatic Flux

The mid-century religious flux in the Anglo-world was one of charismatic potential. Indeed, continuities between earlier decades and the long Sixties provoke questions about the periodisation of religious history and a tendency to 'silo' certain phases. Charismatic origins can be mapped onto this complex pre-history of translocal experiential flows, moving through time and space, inside and outside the Anglo-world. These continuities and the crossings of flows, when comprehended, help us to make sense of the diversity of what became charismatic renewal and the formation of its mainline, independent, and charismaticised pentecostal assemblages. The continuities with mid-century pieties also explain the wide age demographic of the charismatic movement. Researchers at the School of Medicine at the University of California, Los Angeles, in the mid-1960s found a broad age representation.[140] As the Jesus People were integrated into the movement this began to change, but renewal was never merely a 'youth' movement. In

[138] Hocken, *Streams*, 25–28.

[139] Brett Knowles, *New Life: a history of the New Life Churches in New Zealand, 1942–1979* (Dunedin: Third Millennium, 1999), 72–102.

[140] McCandlish Phillips, 'Glossolalia wins new adherents: speaking in strange tongues gains in Protestantism', *New York Times*, 17 May 1964, 86–87.

Auckland in 1973, for example, over one quarter of those attending Catholic or Catholic-ecumenical charismatic prayer meetings were over the age of forty.[141]

Many of those who were caught up in this mid-century religious flux might be regarded as 'seekers'. Although the term is often applied to post-war baby boomers, 'seekership' has a longer history. The inter-war years saw reconfigurations of what Colin Campbell describes as a cultic milieu.[142] This was evident in author and journalist Rom Landau's *God is my Adventure* (1935). As he travelled through Europe, America, and the Far East during the inter-war years, Landau often heard it said 'there must somewhere be a greater reality.'[143] Spiritual restlessness prepared the way for the underground experimentation of the 1950s, where the subculture of seekership produced works such as Aldous Huxley's *The Doors of Perception* (1954) and Jack Kerouac's *The Dharma Bums* (1959). There was a coalescence of popular occulture, older traditions like Theosophy, Spiritualism, and New Thought, the 'exotic' teachings and practices of the Greek-Armenian George Gurdjieff, eastern spiritualities such as Zen Buddhism, and inchoate forms of what became neo-pagan and New Age practice.[144] Some Christian seekers were drawn into this milieu. Founders of the Findhorn New Age community in the north of Scotland, for example, had backgrounds in the Oxford Group and Faith Mission.[145] However, other Christian seekers instead sought more authentic versions of their religion. Interestingly, while Landau's 1935 book included profiles such as the esoteric Rudolf Steiner, Occultist Peter Ouspensky, and Indian spiritual master Shri Meher Baba, it also included George Jeffreys, the British Elim pentecostal, and Frank Buchman, the founder of the Oxford Group.[146] It is difficult to imagine Jeffreys or Buchman in the company of the other modern mystics, but Landau, at least, perceived underlying commonalities.

There were resonances and continuities between 'orthodox' Christian seekerships and charismatic renewal. The Oxford Group was one antecedent. Camps Farthest Out was another—indeed it was quintessentially seeker-friendly, attracting many 'who had lost sight of their religious beginnings but wanted a spiritual home'.[147] When Cursillo arrived in the United States, it appealed initially to first generation and often marginalised Mexican Americans, but non-Hispanic groups were soon established, attracting a middle-class, urban and suburban

[141] JKTL, ANG 016/1/2, Allen G. Neil, 'The origins, development and present extent of the Charismatic Renewal in the Church in New Zealand', Provincial Commission on the Charismatic Renewal, 1973.

[142] 'The cult, the cultic milieu and secularization', in Jeffrey Kaplan and Heléne Lööw (eds.), *The cultic milieu: oppositional subcultures in an age of globalization* (Walnut Creek: Altamira Press, 2002), 12–25, at 14.

[143] Rom Landau, *God is my adventure: a book on modern mystics, masters and teachers* (London: Nicholson and Watson, 1935). Quote at 17; reference to 'seekers' in preface. I am grateful to Dr Steven Sutcliffe for steering me towards Landau.

[144] Steven Sutcliffe, *Children of the New Age: a history of spiritual practices* (London: Routledge, 2003), 35–37.

[145] Ibid., 56–59. [146] Landau, *God is my adventure.* [147] Clark, *Glenn Clark*, 43.

demographic of seekers.[148] The emotional and experiential dimension of the early Mexican-background Cursillo groups were critiqued by some white American Catholics as excessive; but for other Catholics, such as Don Schmit, this authenticity was to be precisely what made it appealing.[149] For *cursillista* seekers such as Schmit, the baptism in the Spirit would be another step towards spiritual reality.

An important setting for the experience of this mid-century religious flux was the small group. This was a broad phenomenon. Amongst American Catholics, for example, the 'pedagogy of participation' described by Joseph P. Chinnici, which included initiatives such as neighbourhood groups for religious instruction and discussion, preceded Vatican II.[150] Protestantism was again moving towards intimate and lay-friendly settings in the 1930s, a resurgence of communal piety with historic evangelical precedents. The experiential flows described in this chapter moved through small group environments, making and remaking them. In 1958, *Christian Life* magazine described cell groups as 'a miracle of our day'. 'If you scratch the surface of virtually any community deeply enough you will discover such a group', it claimed.[151] In the south-east United States, Oklahoman oilman-turned-evangelical spiritual director Keith Miller believed that as churches erected new buildings and parking lots in the 1950s, 'something of the wholeness of Christ' had 'slipped through our [the laity's] fingers'.[152] The answer, which he eventually put into practice with the small group retreats of Laity Lodge, Texas, was holistic 'living Christianity'. The popularity of small groups was also evident beyond the evangelical domain. An early precedent, we have seen, was James Moore Hickson's 'prayer circles' for healing. During the Second World War, an Advisory Group for Christian Cells was formed with the approval of the Archbishop of Canterbury to channel the energies of initiatives such as the Servants of Christ the King. It defined Christian cells as 'small groups of friends who gather together at one another's houses'. Importantly, it added they often involved 'a movement of the Holy Spirit' and were usually 'free and spontaneous'.[153] Lay participation was also cultivated by the liturgical movement. Before any signs of charismatic stirrings at St Mark's, Van Nuys, in southern

[148] Kristy Nabhan-Warren, '"We are the Church": The Cursillo movement and the reinvention of Catholic identities in postwar America and beyond', *US Catholic Historian*, 33/1 (2015), 81–98.

[149] Kristy Nabhan-Warren, '"Blooming where we're planted": Mexican-descent Catholics living out *Cursillo de Cristiandad*', *U.S. Catholic Historian*, 28/4 (2010), 99–125. On Schmit, see pp. 22–3.

[150] Joseph P. Chinnici, 'The Catholic community at prayer, 1926–1976', in James M. O'Toole (ed.), *Habits of devotion: Catholic religious practice in twentieth-century America* (Ithaca: Cornell University Press, 2004), 9–88, at 48–49.

[151] 'Miracle of neighborhood Bible study groups', *Christian Life*, March 1958, 12–16, quotes at 12–13.

[152] Keith Miller, *A taste of new wine* (Waco: Word, 1965), 15.

[153] *Life and power: the "Christian cell" or group* (London: The Advisory Group for Christian Cells, 1945), 2, 4. The Servants of Christ the King was established in 1942 by Church of England clergy inspired by T. S. Eliot's *The idea of the Christian society* (1939). Its autonomous small groups practised silent discernment of the Spirit and interpersonal sharing. See Olive Parker, 'The Servants of Christ the King', *Contact*, 21/1 (1967), 13–17. At St John's Anglican Theological College, Auckland, some students

California—an Episcopalian parish which, as the next chapter describes, in 1960 became a focus in media reports of mainline tongues speaking—there was already a structure of seventy 'key family area' groups for Eucharist and fellowship. The priest celebrated with bread and 'the fruit of the vine' of the host household, demonstrating 'that simple things can be made holy and that *the home is also holy*'.[154] Christianity was moving into the 'New Testament' home environment. This was a space in which, soon, charismatic renewal would flourish.

As proto-charismatic flows moved through these small group settings, they became contexts for the exploration of the inner Self. Parallels were to be evident in the rise of alternative spiritualities such as the New Age movement.[155] There were, too, comparisons with the 'experimental learning environment'—self-realisation in small interpersonal groups—promoted by the secular T-group movement, formed in Maine in 1947.[156] We have seen how healing networks such as OSL and CFO explored the role of the subconscious in emotional and physical health. The rising cases of psychological illness with the return of troops after the Second World War had contributed to greater public awareness of mental health. In 1955 an article 'Mental sickness and the Christian' in *Christian Life* reported that half of the hospital beds in the United States were occupied by mental health patients.[157] Ten years later, the evangelical Fuller Theological Seminary in Pasadena, California, established a graduate school of psychology. Congregational ministry on the ground was impacted. In 1956 the Episcopalian diocese of Pittsburgh had seventy-five home prayer groups, all reading Agnes Sanford's *The Healing Light*.[158] Cursillo, too, had been designed by a psychologist—Eduardo Bonnín—to help men release emotions and discover spiritual freedom. Bonnín later described the environment as one 'conducive to deep penetration of the soul by his truth'.[159] The role of the mind in abundant Christian life was also being popularised by Norman Vincent Peale in his *The Power of Positive Thinking* (1952). Joseph Williams describes a 'growing preoccupation with the power of words' in mid-century pentecostalism as the 'positive confession' teachings of E. W. Kenyon were popularised by Kenneth E. Hagin, F. F. Bosworth, and T. L. Osborne. Some proponents of charismatic renewal

identified the beginnings of a journey towards charismatic renewal in participation in SCK meetings. See D. H. Battley, 'Charismatic renewal: a view from the inside', *The Ecumenical Review*, 31/1 (January 1986), 48–56.

154 'What did happen at St Mark's Church Episcopal', *Trinity*, 1/2 (1961–2), 2–5, quote at 3 (my italics).

155 Sutcliffe, *Children*.

156 Alfred J. Marrow, *The T-group experience: an encounter among people for greater self-fulfillment* (New York: Paul S. Eriksson, 1975), 15.

157 'Mental sickness and the Christian', *Christian Life*, May 1955, 15–17.

158 Jeremy Bonner, *Called out of darkness into marvellous light: a history of the Episcopal Diocese of Pittsburgh, 1750–2006* (Eugene: Wipf & Stock, 2009), 213.

159 Eduardo Bonnín, *The how and the why* (Dallas: National Ultreya Publications, 1981), 34.

would ride the crest of this metaphysical wave. The turning inwards to the Self was a context for charismatic renewal.

* * *

In 1962, David du Plessis wrote to a chaplain at Yale University that in the previous *six years* he had encountered 'hundreds of ministers in all confessions that are enjoying the same experience that the disciples had on and after the day of Pentecost in Jerusalem'. The search for the origins of charismatic renewal requires that we look carefully at a mid-century religious flux. The multiplicity of these antecedents strongly suggests that the idea that charismatic renewal was simply a 'pentecostalisation' of the churches, risks being misleading, even if pentecostalism was one important contributor. As we shall now see, it was the 1960s which saw the convergence of these antecedent sources into an imaginary. Du Plessis' same letter asserted with confidence: 'I believe we are witnessing the beginning of the eschatological fulfilment of Joel 2: 28.'[160] Charismatic potential was about to become 'charismatic renewal'.

[160] DAHL, David du Plessis papers, file 10, box 11, David du Plessis to William Coffin Jr., 13 November 1962.

3
Pentecost

> Suddenly a sound like the blowing of a violent wind came from heaven and filled the whole house where they were sitting.
>
> Acts 2:2

A protagonist of the new Pentecost combined high Episcopalian apparel with an all-American crew cut. At the end of the 1950s, the Revd. Dennis Bennett's ministry at St Mark's, Van Nuys, near Los Angeles, seemed to exemplify the church boom of the decade. The membership grew to two and a half thousand, with 700 communicants on any Sunday and a major building project underway.[1] The church was progressive, at the forefront of the liturgical movement. Yet Bennett felt something was missing. 'For most of us', he would later explain at an FGBMFI meeting, 'religion is a plodding thing, resting on the grim determination of man, rather than the power of God'.[2] Although a man of capable intellect, Bennett was wary of the possible pitfalls of cerebral Christianity. Episcopalians, he thought, often seemed interested in the 'facts' of religion, but he was looking for something more actualised.[3] Bennett (Fig. 3.1) received the fullness of the Spirit in 1959 through an Episcopalian couple who had come into the experience. He spoke in tongues, a kind of 'quasi-Slavonic language'.[4] Around seventy others in the parish also received, including another St Mark's clergyman, although two colleagues were opposed. As rumours circulated (e.g. of tongue speakers rolling on the floor, or with a flower growing in their mouth), at a 9 a.m. service on Passion Sunday 1960, Bennett made his experience public. A controversy erupted—one assistant clergyman removed his vestments and walked out. At the 11 o'clock service, Bennett offered to resign.[5] Soon after, a supporter of Bennett, Jean Stone, offered the story to *Time* and *Newsweek*. Stone, who was to establish the charismatic magazine *Trinity*, reached out to the Anglican Reformed evangelical, the Revd. Dr Philip Edgcumbe Hughes, when he visited the United States in 1962. He wrote an editorial for the *Churchman* in England witnessing to a movement of the

[1] See: RUSCA, Dennis J. Bennett papers, box 3, Notes on Dennis Bennett, 'The recovery of the Holy Spirit in the church', St Mark's, Riverside, Rhode Island, 26 November 1963; box 1, vol. 1, 'St. Mark's Episcopal sets ground-breaking ceremony', *Van Nuys News*, 20 February 1958.

[2] RUSCA, Dennis J. Bennett papers, box 1, vol. 1, Dennis Bennett, 'They spake with tongues and magnified God!', *Full Gospel Men's Voice*, 8/9 (1960), 6–8, at 6.

[3] 'The recovery of the Holy Spirit'. [4] Ibid.

[5] 'What did happen at St Mark's Episcopal Church?', *Trinity*, 1/2 (1961), 3–6.

Age of the Spirit: Charismatic Renewal, the Anglo-World, and Global Christianity, 1945–1980. John Maiden, Oxford University Press. © John Maiden 2023. DOI: 10.1093/oso/9780198847496.003.0003

Fig. 3.1 Dennis and Rita Bennett visiting England in 1967.

Spirit amongst Anglo-Catholics and others, and urging readers to 'pray earnestly and expectantly that the Acts of the Holy Spirit may be powerfully manifested once again in the Church of our day'.[6] News spread of what appeared to be a movement of Pentecost outside of pentecostalism.[7]

Histories of movements both religious and secular often construct origins accounts of their spark to life. For Protestant charismatics, the drama of Passion Sunday 1960 has been described as a 'Wittenburg' or 'Aldersgate' moment.[8] The narrative achieved acceptance outside of the United States. Michael Harper's *As at the Beginning* (1965), one of the first 'company' histories of charismatic renewal, begins with the evocative words, 'It is not far from Azusa Street in Los Angeles to the fashionable suburb of Van Nuys.'[9] As they appeared, scholarly analyses, such as Martin E. Marty's *A Nation of Behavers* (1976), tended to confirm the Van Nuys account.[10] However, the Bennett myth has limitations as a genesis story. Its linear, American-centric account obscured the complex and decentred nature of charismatic origins. Nevertheless, moments such as 'Van Nuys', and others like it,

[6] Philip E. Hughes, 'Editorial', *Churchman*, 76/3 (1962), 113–35.

[7] See, e.g., Philip Hughes, 'A new work of the Holy Spirit – are we ready?', *Australian Church Record*, 4 June 1964, 2, 7.

[8] Larry Christenson, 'The charismatic movement: an historical and theological perspective' at http://www.lutheranrenewal.org/wp-content/uploads/2016/05/The_Charismatic_Movement2.pdf (accessed 18 June 2021).

[9] Michael Harper, *As at the beginning* (Atlanta: Society of Stephen, 1994), 13.

[10] Martin E. Marty, *A nation of behavers* (Chicago: University of Chicago Press, 1976), 107.

were a powerful contribution to the making of the Spiritscape of charismatic renewal.

The emergence of charismatic renewal at a confluence of flows—mainline healing, Catholic apostolates, empowered evangelicalism, and pentecostal revivalism—is the focus of this chapter. We begin by examining moments of emergence similar to that of Van Nuys, and the ways in which their narratives collectively constructed a translocal, eschatological imaginary of the Spirit being poured out. We then survey the appearance of renewal on the ground in the long Sixties. Finally, we return to the eschatological imagination, examining a repertoire of narratives of spiritual power; each a response to a sense of 'crisis' which provided authentic scripts for others to follow.

Moments of Emergence

Just over two years after the Van Nuys drama, Harald Bredesen, a Spirit baptised pastor of Mount Vernon Dutch Reformed Church in New York City, visited Yale. The background to his invitation was a growing interest amongst some members of the Yale Inter-Varsity Christian Fellowship (IVCF), arising from their involvement in healing ministry and encounters with mainline charismatics, in the work of the Spirit. They reached out to Jean Stone, who is mentioned above and whose ministry is discussed further in Chapter 4. She suggested Bredesen visit.[11] During his engagements, various IVCF members received. As Bredesen later described: 'As in the upper room 2,000 years ago, the Spirit fell' and 'men "began to speak with tongues as the Spirit gave utterance"'. The auspicious setting and the social status and mainline affiliations of the participants were a publicity boon for Stone. Her magazine reported the details—that five of those to 'receive' were deacons of the Battell Chapel; that one, David W. Wills, was a Carnegie Teaching Fellow in History; and that scholars had even discussed their experiences with Bishop Lesslie Newbigin.[12] The Pentecost at Yale seemed potent with significance—not least because the Spirit baptisms took place in the Dwight Memorial Chapel, the sanctuary named after Timothy Dwight, a key actor in the Second Great Awakening. Bredesen further reflected: 'Political revolutions start in universities. Why not spiritual ones?'[13] Tapes of testimonies from Yale circulated the United States and beyond.[14]

[11] DAHL, David du Plessis papers, box 5, Robert V. Morris to Jean Stone, 25 September 1962.

[12] Harald Bredesen, 'The Yale story', *Trinity*, 2/2 (1962–63), 2–16, at 3. [13] Ibid., 5.

[14] It was influential, for example, on the Anglican curate Ray Muller, one of the first New Zealand Anglican clergy to enter the renewal. See Dale Williamson, 'An uncomfortable engagement: the charismatic renewal in the New Zealand Anglican Church, 1965–85', PhD University of Otago, 2007. On Muller see this book, pp. 63 and 104.

If the Yale awakening indicated the Spirit was moving in mainline circles, in 1964–65 there were seminal independent charismatic emergences in New Zealand and England. In 1964 a conference 'I will build my church' took place on the campus of Massey University, Palmerston North. It drew largely on the ministry of Brethren and ex-Brethren teachers, such as G. Milton Smith, and from Britain, Arthur Wallis and Campbell McAlpine; although testimonies were presented by independent pentecostals such as Rob Wheeler of Tauranga, and another leader influenced by the Latter Rain movement, Frank Houston, the Assemblies of God pastor of Lower Hutt.[15] A restorationist message was foregrounded in the conference prayer:

> Bound by tradition,
> Chained by her own volition
> Her ancient birthright sold
> Her early fires cold,
> The church, in self-made bondage lies,
> Powerless, beneath Time's threat'ning skies.[16]

Alongside the message of a Church awaiting release from bondage was the call to experience New Testament Christianity in the power of the Spirit. McAlpine asked those present: 'Do you realise you need to be filled with the Holy Ghost? Then rejoice because the promise is unto YOU.'[17] The Massey conference was regarded as the beginning of the charismatic movement in New Zealand, and its restorationist emphasis influenced the orientation of renewal in the country. The following year, McAlpine and Wallis were amongst those to speak at a conference at Herne Bay, south-east England. This was attended by independent evangelicals and pentecostals who later played roles setting up non-denominational house church networks. The two conferences occurred before any comparable independent charismatic gatherings took place in the United States. Importantly, both the New Zealand and British conferences were integrated into inchoate charismatic scenes which included mainliners. Michael Harper and various Baptist leaders, such as Barney Coombs, were at Herne Bay; while the publicity for Massey identified a wider movement of the Spirit. One report read: 'For the first time in the history of New Zealand, we saw Christians and ministers from the BAPTIST-ANGLICAN - PRESBYTERIAN - BRETHREN - S.A., of whom many had received the baptism of the Holy Ghost, also many from the PENTECOSTAL churches all gathered together to worship the Lord under one roof.'[18]

[15] JKTL, ANG 016/12, *Massey conference report: I will build my church* (1964).
[16] Ibid., 1.
[17] Campbell McAlpine, 'The equipment of the Spirit-filled believer', *Massey conference*, 15–18, at 17.
[18] 'The most unique convention in the history of NZ', *The Gospel Truth*, 2/3 (1964), 6.

In London in 1965, an ambitious, large-scale conference brought together Spirit-filled Christians from the United States and Britain. Over a decade after the Western Allies had flown critical supplies to Berlin, the FGBMFI World Convention was described as a 'spiritual airlift' of North American businessmen, wives, and church leaders in especially chartered airplanes ('three jet plane loads of Spirit-filled men and women') to a spiritually impoverished Europe. The purpose was to fulfil a vision to 'send out to the four corners of the world' news of a latter-day spiritual outpouring.[19] London's Hilton Hotel was the base of operations. The secular press, somewhat bemused, described sharply dressed Americans sharing Christ with Soho beatniks in the hotel lobby. *The Sun* tabloid described the 'millionaire' FGBMFI leader, Demos Shakarian, 'dispensing the love of God from his suite'.[20] Assisted by a British organising committee of mainline evangelicals and pentecostals, venues such as the Anglican Church House and the Baptist Metropolitan Tabernacle were booked. At the Royal Albert Hall, Nicky Cruz, the former New York gang leader described in *The Cross and the Switchblade*, spoke to young people, and Oral Roberts preached to adults. Some British charismatics were uneasy with the pentecostal approach, particularly the heavy reliance on testimonies. However, Michael Harper suggested that simple testimonial accounts were in some ways 'a better answer to *Honest to God* than many a theological dissertation'.[21] The conference announced the coming of charismatic Christianity in the British religious scene. It also drew together mainliners and independents. When, weeks later, British participants gathered at High Leigh, Hertfordshire, to take stock, the speakers included Arthur Wallis on 'Tongues as a mark of revival' and Campbell McAlpine on 'The Spirit in the local church'. Both would have participated in a Holy Communion conducted according to the Book of Common Prayer and accompanied by 'unusually long periods of spontaneous prayer and praise'.[22]

'Cleric finds "gift of tongues"'.[23] On 5 December 1965, the *Sydney Morning Herald* published the story of the Revd. Barry Schofield and his Anglican congregation of St Mark's, Picton, in the south-west of Sydney. There were familiar parallels with the Van Nuys story—disputes in the parish following the reception of the Spirit by Schofield and various laity.[24] For some Australian mainline Protestants, 'Picton' was the 'birth of the new Pentecost in this country'.[25] The parish attracted attention again the following year when David du Plessis visited

[19] See DAHL, David du Plessis papers, box 53, file 29, *Airlift to London* (1965), 3.

[20] Quoted in Peter Hocken, *Streams of renewal: the origins and early development of the charismatic movement in Great Britain* (Carlisle: Paternoster Press, 1986), 148.

[21] 'A new breath of life', *Renewal*, 1/1 (1966), 4–10, at 6.

[22] John Watson, 'Teaching weekend follows big meetings', *Renewal*, 1/2 (1966), 4–5.

[23] Headline, *Sydney Morning Herald*, 5 December 1965, 9.

[24] Details of this are also described in Barry Schofield, 'Church renewal: examples', in Geoff Waugh (ed.), *Church on fire* (Melbourne: Joint Board of Christian Education, 2012), ch. 11.

[25] LPL, Michael Harper papers, 1967/14, David Evans to Michael Harper, 15 March 1967, 1–2.

its annual missionary conference. His contribution included the invitation to receive the baptism in the Spirit. '"Tongues" spoken at Picton convention' was the front-page headline in the *Australian Church Record*. The outrage of evangelical sceptics over '"tongues"' (scare quotes underlining cynicism) was made abundantly clear.[26] As with media reports elsewhere the focus was *glossolalia*.

It was not until 1967 that Catholics had their own 'moment'. The background was developments within Cursillo circles in Indiana and Michigan. In January, two instructors at Duquesne University attended an interdenominational prayer group and experienced Spirit baptism and tongues. Other Faculty members followed them into the experience. At a retreat in February 1967—which became known as the 'Duquesne weekend'—students discussed the Book of Acts and a whole group received. News spread through Cursillo networks to the university cities of Sound Bend, East Lansing, and Ann Arbor. In April, around eighty from Notre Dame and Michigan State University, including many now baptised in the Spirit, met together (at what became known as the 'Michigan State weekend').[27] The campus press was intrigued, if confused. One headline read 'Spiritualists claim gift of tongues at exorcism rites'.[28] 'Notre Dame priests and students hold Pentecostal prayer meetings', reported the *National Catholic Reporter*.[29] Notre Dame's position as a global hub for Catholic education meant news travelled worldwide through priests, religious, and laity. The university became synonymous with renewal. Many Catholics in other countries took their cue from South Bend and Ann Arbor in the coming years. In Canada, for example, the 'birth' of Catholic renewal is often tied to the visit by Steve Clark and Jim Cavnar, from Ann Arbor, to the Madonna House apostolate, Combermere, in August 1968. Its foundress, the Russian-Canadian Catherine Doherty (born Ekaterina Fyodorovna Kolyschkine) had grown interested in the work of the Spirit because of her Russian Orthodox background, and after the Americans' visit her community became a centre for those seeking the experience.[30]

These moments of exposure—Yale 1962, Massey University 1964, Herne Bay 1965, London 1965, Picton 1965, and Notre Dame 1967—brought into picture the coming together of the mid-century experiential flows described in the previous chapter. The liquidity of renewal, both in its translocality and the permeations between mainline and independent expressions, is striking. There was a sense of unity in the Spirit. As Arthur Wallis said at the Massey conference, 'Despite what we hear from some quarters, this conference has *not* been convened to call any

[26] *Australian Church Record*, 24 March 1966, 1.

[27] Kevin and Dorothy Ranaghan, *Catholic Pentecostals* (New York: Paulist Press, 1969), 6–49; Jim Manney, 'Before Duquesne: sources of the renewal', *New Covenant*, 2/8 (1973), 12–17.

[28] Ranaghans, *Catholic Pentecostals*, 45.

[29] Mary Papa, 'Notre Dame priests and students hold Pentecostal prayer meetings', *National Catholic Reporter*, 19 April 1967, 3.

[30] James Hanrahan, 'The nature and history of the Catholic Charismatic renewal in Canada', *Bilan de l'Histoire religieuse au Canada*, 50/1 (1983), 307–24, at 308–09.

individual to leave his denomination, church, assembly or fellowship.'[31] The embodied experiences of charismatics contributed to this unity. A report in the *National Catholic Reporter* said of Notre Dame:

> It would be convenient to say that these Catholic Pentecostals were underfed, high-strung, groping intellectuals, misfits, in a wholesome atmosphere of all-American footballhood. It would be convenient, but it would also be quite untrue. There seems to be no one level of conformity in this group except a common experience.[32]

The accounts of these moments were important to the coming together of a translocal charismatic imaginary. We return to the importance of narratives later in this chapter. However, first we will pause to ascertain patterns and trajectories of charismatic growth.

'Sizing Up an Iceberg': Charismatic Growth in the Long Sixties

The calculus for the expansion of the new Pentecost were numbers of baptisms in the Spirit, usually with tongues as the first manifestation. However, as a correspondent for *Christianity Today* commented in 1967, 'Trying to count tongues-speakers within non-Pentecostal churches is like sizing up an iceberg by observing the part above water.'[33] The challenge in mapping charismatic growth is that initially it was largely invisible. A 1968 study by anthropologists at the University of Minnesota observed there were two main contexts for what they called 'neo-pentecostalism'. The first (relating broadly to the independent charismatic assemblage) was independent churches. Some, such as Evangelistic Centre Church in Kansas City, discussed in Chapter 2, pre-existed the renewal and now attracted greater numbers, including mainline Christians. Others, recently established, were organic and less observable, situated in homes or other secular spaces. The second context was 'enclaves of "Spirit-filled" mainline charismatics'. These usually remained active in their denominational churches, but also met regularly, often on weeknights, in homes or on campuses with likeminded Christians. The number of these 'hidden Pentecostals', as the anthropologists called them, is difficult to gauge.[34] Often, it was clergy rather than laity who were visible. With these limitations in mind, what follows offers a broad survey of charismatic expansion.

[31] Arthur Wallis, 'Opening address', *Massey conference*, 2–3, at 2.

[32] Mary Papa, 'People having a good time praying', *National Catholic Reporter*, 17 May 1967.

[33] Russell Chandler, 'Fanning the charismatic fire', *Christianity Today*, 24 November 1967, 39.

[34] Luther P. Gerlach and Virginia H. Hine, 'Five factors crucial to the growth and spread of a modern religious movement', *Journal for the Scientific Study of Religion*, 7/1 (1968), 23–40, at 25.

In the United States, the pan-denominational activities of FGBMFI, CFO, and Inter-Church Team Ministries (ICTMs) (known for 'trying to get ministers to go with the Spirit without using the words Pentecostal or Full-Gospel') were catalysts, largely amongst Protestants.[35] The influence of the healing movement meant Episcopalians were the mainliners who were initially the most impacted. By 1963 there were reportedly two thousand Episcopalian tongues speakers in southern California.[36] Episcopalian hotspots also included the Diocese of Montana, whose bishop, Chandler W. Sterling, was sympathetic, and Louisiana, where in Baton Rouge in 1962 the leadership became aware of parishes 'especially interested in the Third Person of the Blessed Trinity, and particularly in glossolalia'.[37] In the same year, the House of Bishops estimated twenty dioceses were affected.[38] Five years later, *Christianity Today* reported 10 per cent of Episcopalian clergy nationwide had 'received'.[39]

Episcopalians, often because of their role in setting up ecumenical prayer groups, contributed to wider denominational diffusions.[40] In southern California, 'Holy Ghost prayer meetings' involved mainliners and pentecostals.[41] In Fort Lauderdale, Florida, an Episcopalian layman, Eldon D. Purvis, pioneered ecumenical gatherings and founded the influential Holy Spirit Teaching Mission, discussed in the next chapter.[42] Spirit baptisms were reported amongst Presbyterians and Lutherans, some of whom came into charismatic renewal through higher life influences. In Los Angeles, at First Presbyterian Church of Hollywood, the largest congregation of that denomination in the country, there were apparently hundreds of tongues speakers by 1963, and charismatic gifts were also practised at Bel Air Presbyterian.[43] By early 1967, around eighty Presbyterian ministers nationwide had associated themselves with Charismatic Communion, a denominational group organised by pastor Brick Bradford, of First Presbyterian of El Reno, Oklahoma. These came from at least twenty-eight states, including seven in California, Texas, and Virginia; five in Missouri, Ohio, and Oklahoma; and four in both Connecticut and New Jersey.[44] Within Lutheranism, the American Lutheran Church (ALC) was initially most affected, particularly in southern

[35] Chandler, 'Fanning the charismatic fire'. On ICTM see DAHL, David du Plessis papers, box 9, file 9, *Charismatic Communion*, no. 2, March 1967, 6.

[36] Frank Farrell, 'Outburst of tongues: the new penetration', *Christianity Today*, 13 September 1963, 3–6, at 3.

[37] Morton T. Kelsey, 'Tongues in the traditional churches', *Trinity*, 3/4 (1964), 11–36, at 16. DAHL, David du Plessis papers, box 30, file 20, Revd. Warren J. Steele (St James' Church, Memphis) to the clergy of Baton Rouge, Louisiana.

[38] Hazel Barnes, 'Episcopal leader voices gratitude', *Spokane Daily Chronicle*, 10 November 1962, 6.

[39] Chandler, 'Fanning the charismatic fire', 39–40.

[40] DAHL, David du Plessis papers, box 37, file 22, 'God is blessing Anglicans and Episcopalians', n.d.

[41] 'The Holy Spirit and the ecumenical movement', *Trinity*, 1/2 (1961–2), 50–51, at 50.

[42] Eldon D. Purvis, 'Birth of a mission', *New Wine*, April 1970, 12–16.

[43] Farrell, 'Outburst of tongues', 3.

[44] DAHL, David du Plessis papers, box 9, file 9, *Charismatic Communion*, 2 (March 1967), 1.

California, Minneapolis, Montana, and North Dakota. By 1972, reportedly 300 ALC pastors had received, and from 1967 inroads were being made into the Missouri Synod.[45] Christians in all other major Protestant denominations were drawn into the renewal, and various evangelical and independent pentecostal churches also began to identify with it. When the *New York Times* reporter McCandlish Phillips surveyed the charismatic scene in 1964 he described it as 'a random but pervasive movement'.[46]

In 1967, Roman Catholics provided further momentum. The universities of Notre Dame, Michigan State, and University of Michigan were initial hubs for the experience of the Spirit. Through their witness, prayer groups appeared at Iowa State, University of Colorado, and University of Portland. Then from 1969 'Days of Renewal' (modelled on gatherings of the same name in Michigan) were held in Cleveland, New York City, Albuquerque, and New Orleans. Testimonies from South Bend and Ann Arbor circulated widely; for example, a recording of the Notre Dame professor of theology Fr. Edward D. O'Connor at an FGBMFI meeting prompted the formation of a prayer meeting amongst Benedictine monks at Benet Lake, Wisconsin.[47] By mid-1971, 700 American Catholic and Catholic-ecumenical prayer groups were listed in a directory published in Notre Dame.[48] The renewal secured notable successes amongst Protestants and Catholics in the United States during the 1960s.

Americans were onecontribution to charismatic growth in Canada. Episcopalians in southern California developed contact with Anglicans in British Columbia, where the Revd. Dr George T. Pattison, the Dean of St Andrew's Cathedral, Prince Rupert, received with other clergy.[49] In Vancouver, largely through the work of the Revd. Bernice Gerard, a pentecostal chaplain at the University of British Columbia, ministers of mainline denominations were receiving by the end of the decade.[50] In Victoria, John Vickers, a businessman, ordained aged sixty, was influenced through Dennis Bennett's ministry and by the early 1970s the city was a renewal centre. The FGBMFI had some success in Canada, including a mission in Calgary involving Dennis Bennett in 1966.[51] Toronto became an important hub. In the suburb of Etobicoke, prayer groups emerged at St Elizabeth's Anglican Church and at Alderwood United Church.[52] In 1964, the Revd. G. Moore-Smith of St Matthias' parish (discussed in the previous chapter), described 'rich

[45] Larry Christenson, 'Lutheran renewal', *New Covenant*, 1/11 (May 1972), 12–13.

[46] McCandlish Phillips, 'Glossolalia wins new adherents: speaking in strange tongue gains in Protestantism', *New York Times*, 17 May 1964, 86–87.

[47] James Connelly, 'The charismatic movement 1967–1970', in Kevin and Dorothy Ranaghan (eds.), *As the Spirit leads us* (New York: Paulist Press, 1971), 211–32, at 218–25.

[48] 'Sixth international conference', *New Covenant*, 2/1 (July 1971), 1–5, at 1.

[49] George T. Pattison, 'An Anglican Dean and the Holy Spirit, *Trinity*, 3/1 (1963), 2–5.

[50] Michael Harper, 'Michael Harper reports from North America', *Renewal*, 23 (1969), 5–9, at 9.

[51] LPL, Michael Harper papers, 1967/1, Dennis Bennett to Michael Harper, 10 January 1967, 1–2.

[52] Al Reimer, *God's country* (Toronto: G. R. Welch, 1979), 105.

blessings' in the diocese and an 'overflow of love' between Christians of different denominations.[53] In the same year, Bennett visited. There was cross-fertilisation between mainliners, independent pentecostals, and Jesus People. In 1968 an interdenominational group, The Catacombs Club, was formed, meeting in homes, then at Bathurst Street United Church, and finally at St Paul's Anglican Church. Merv and Merla Watson, gifted musicians and songwriters, nurtured the Catacombs' artsy reputation. Attendances reached one thousand and were said to include Jesus People and 'straight kids from every church and every part of town'.[54] Catholic renewal permeated into Canada from its upper Midwest bases. The meeting established at Madonna House, Combermere, following a 1968 visit by Ann Arbor charismatics assisted in the planting of prayer groups, such as at the Marian Centre in Saskatchewan. Another group in Sault Ste. Marie, Ontario, originated from a meeting in its sister city across the St Mary's River in Michigan. Catholic renewal in the west of the country was given impetus in 1968 when Bernice Gerard arranged the visit of South Bend's Kevin Ranaghan to Vancouver.[55]

In Britain, the mainline Protestants initially most affected were Anglican conservative evangelicals. Parishes influenced included St Paul's, Beckenham, St John's, Burslem, and St Mark's, Gillingham. Spirit baptisms were reported at Oak Hill theological college in north London and Liskeard Lodge, a Church Missionary Society centre in Kent. The work of the Spirit infiltrated the 'Vatican' of Anglican evangelicalism, the Revd. John Stott's All Souls, London; although following tensions, the charismatics, including Michael Harper, left. Some Anglo-Catholics, warming to the high churchmanship of Bennett and Jean Stone, were influenced; with a prominent example being the diocese of St Alban's, where the Revd. Michael Meakin, the Rural Dean of Woburn, became an advocate. In 1966 the diocese carried a motion 'giving thanks for the many signs of renewal in the life of the church through the power of the Holy Spirit'.[56] From 1964, primarily through the influence of Anglicans, the Fountain Trust became a catalyst for denominational renewal. That year Michael and Jean Harper drove David du Plessis 1,500 miles around the country to speak to hundreds of ministers of most denominations.[57] Some Baptist congregations, like David Pawson's Gold Hill Baptist, Buckinghamshire, and Farnborough Baptist, were influenced. A few London Baptist ministers began to meet regularly at the

[53] LPL, Michael Harper papers, 1964/36, Revd. G. Moore-Smith to Michael Harper, n.d., 6.

[54] See Bruce Douville, '"And we've got to get ourselves back to the Garden": the Jesus People movement in Toronto', Historical Papers 2006, *Canadian Society of Church History*, 5–24 at 13–14. Douville quotes Merv Watson.

[55] Hanrahan, 'Catholic Charismatic renewal'.

[56] Quoted in DGC, Fountain Trust papers, box 12, 22–32, John Richards, 'A factual presentation of the history of the present movement within the Church of England and a survey of its present extent'. See also, RUSCA, Dennis J. Bennett papers, box 1, vol. 1, 'Programme'.

[57] LPL, Michael Harper papers, 1964/10, David du Plessis prayer letter, July 1964, 2.

Metropolitan Tabernacle.[58] In Scotland, early centres of renewal were Motherwell, through the Presbyterian ministry of the Revd. Brian Casebow, and Edinburgh, amongst students at New College.[59]

Independent groups became associated with the movement, drawing in mainliners and pentecostals who had become disaffected or had been 'turned out' of their denominations. An existing fellowship in South Chard, Somerset, led by former Brethren 'uncle' Sid and 'aunty' Mill Purse, became a national node—and indeed, as we shall see, an unlikely global influencer. Another independent network was the 'North Circuit' group, which gathered around the leadership of G. W. 'Wally' North. This had a distinctly Wesleyan holiness orientation. A key congregation, Devonshire Road Christian Fellowship, was formed in Toxteth, Liverpool, in the mid-1960s and drew Baptists and Calvinistic Baptists as well as local Anglicans—indeed the main leader, Norman Meeten, had left a Church of England curacy.[60] Various independent fellowships in the Glasgow area of Scotland, such as Struthers Memorial Church, Greenock, and Scottish Gospel Outreach in Clydebank, also had connections with North.[61] Another gathering was Bradford's Dean House Christian Fellowship, established in 1953 by the ex-Apostolic Cecil Cousen. This 'New Testament' assembly aimed to function as a centre for renewal in all churches.[62] Following this initial wave, as Chapter 5 explains, a larger house church movement gathered momentum at the beginning of the 1970s.

Protestants witnessed to a few British Catholics. Heythrop College was included in Dennis Bennett's 1965 visit itinerary (his driver, Michael Harper, recalled 'Here was I, a good Protestant driving another good Protestant to the heart of the Jesuit lair, for the purpose of passing on a blessing of the Holy Spirit'). The meeting was well attended and some asked Bennett to pray for the 'blessing'.[63] Local pentecostal witness was also a factor, contributing, notably, to the experience of Catholic laywoman Gabrielle Twomey, who set up a prayer group in Birmingham, and Fr. Simon Tugwell, who with other Oxford Dominicans experienced the Spirit, with tongues, in 1970.[64] These English cases occurred with no connection to—or even predated—the Duquesne moment of 1967. However, soon

[58] LPL, Michael Harper papers, 1969/43, Michael J. Pusey to Michael Harper, 7 June 1969, 2. On Pawson, see same collection, 1964/38, David Pawson to Michael Harper, 26 May 1964, 1.

[59] Hocken, *Streams*, 95.

[60] Mark Rudall, 'The house church in Britain . . . a cursory glance', *The Fraternal*, 212 (1985), 15–24.

[61] Alisdair Black, 'Pour out your Spirit: experiences of the Holy Spirit amongst Scottish Baptists in the twentieth century', in Brian R. Talbot (ed.), *A distinctive people: a thematic study of aspects of the witness of Baptists in Scotland in the twentieth century* (Milton Keynes: Paternoster, 2014), 165.

[62] Jeanne Hinton, 'Church with a lift', *Renewal*, 22 (1969), 20–25.

[63] Michael Harper, *None can guess* (London: Hodder & Stoughton, 1971), 121.

[64] Bob Balkam, 'Charism and Institution, 1968–1978' (unpublished); Peter Hocken, 'Baptism in the Holy Spirit: a spiritual and theological journey', in Eric Nelson Newberg and Lois E. Olena (eds.), *Children of the calling: essays in honor of Stanley M. Burgess and Ruth V. Burgess* (Eugene: Wipf & Stock, 2014), 298–310.

American renewalists began to influence British Catholics. In London, Gill Davies was inspired by Kevin and Dorothy Ranaghan's *Catholic Pentecostals* (1969) to establish a prayer group and 'Day of Renewal' (drawing on the American model) in Marylebone.[65] Fr. Ian Petit OSB encountered the Spirit while visiting the United States and then established a group in Preston, north-west England.[66] In Scotland, developments came slightly later; with one of the earliest prayer meetings established in Aberdeen, at the Sacred Heart convent, from 1973.[67]

On the island of Ireland, the first emergences were amongst revivalistic Presbyterians in the North. By 1968, clergymen John L. Wynne in Ballysillan, Belfast, and William J. Hughes in Enniskillen, were advocates of renewal; and the next year, James Brown, an American Presbyterian, toured these congregations and visited others in Lurgan, Bangor, and Newtownabbey. The FGBMFI were active in Belfast by this point.[68] In the South, Catholic students at University College Dublin established a group in January 1972 through the influence of American literature and the witness of a priest, Fr. Joseph McGreedy, who had visited Ann Arbor. By July there were at least two groups in the city, involving around 150; mostly Catholics but also Anglicans, Presbyterians, and Quakers.[69] Groups were soon established in places such as Cork and Limerick. Against the backdrop of the Troubles in the early 1970s, prayer meetings were established in Belfast, including larger gatherings, averaging around fifty—involving both Protestant and Catholic—in the New Lodge, Falls Road, and Queen's University areas.[70] The renewal on the island arguably had its own moment of emergence on Pentecost Sunday 1973, when prayer groups from the South and North gathered at the Hill of Slane.[71]

In New Zealand the Brethren were charismatic pioneers. By the mid-1960s, some assemblies had already divided over Spirit baptism. Charismatic congregations which were essentially splits from Brethren assemblies appeared. These included Northcote Christian Fellowship, Christchurch, and Strathmore Fellowship and Upper Hutt Christian Fellowship in the Wellington area.[72] Other Brethren along with mainliners drifted into independent pentecostal

[65] Gill Davies, 'One of the organisers of the first London Days of Renewal shares her memories', *Goodnews*, 146 (2000), 22–23.

[66] 'Harrogate day of renewal', *Day of Renewal* (London, n.d.), 5–7.

[67] 'Scotland', *Goodnews*, 1992 (no edn.), 71.

[68] John L. Wynne, Ballysillan Presbyterian, Belfast, 'Aware of the supernatural', *Renewal*, 15 (1968), 15–18, at 15; 'Fountain Trust notes', *Renewal*, 18 (1969), 15; 'Stirrings in Northern Ireland', *Renewal*, 18 (1969), 20–22.

[69] Ray Reynolds, 'Report from Ireland – the Spirit is breaking down old walls', *New Covenant*, 2/1 (July 1972), 22–23.

[70] John Cooney, 'The charismatic movement in the North', *The Furrow*, 25/3 (March 1974), 163–66.

[71] Jerome McCarthy, 'The charismatic renewal and reconciliation in Northern Ireland', *One in Christ*, 10/1 (1974), 31–43.

[72] Peter Lineham, 'Tongues must cease: the Brethren and the charismatic movement in New Zealand', *Christian Brethren Review*, 34 (1983), 1–48, at 41–42.

fellowships rooted in Ray Jackson's Latter Rain teaching. These included Rob Wheeler and Ron Coady's Upper Room Fellowship, Tauranga, and Peter Morrow's Revival Fellowship (New Life Centre from 1970), Christchurch. Morrow's midweek meetings—which from 1965 were in a venue called 'Adullam's Cave'—were popular. Unlike many independent pentecostals, he was relaxed about the continuation of denominational loyalties on Sundays.[73] One observer wrote to David du Plessis in 1965: 'at present God is forming many independent fellowships all over the country [...] Many different types of people from different backgrounds and fellowships are coming together.'[74]

Although independents had the upper hand in New Zealand, mainline groups were slowly impacted. Those most affected were Anglicans and Catholics. A 1973 survey estimated over one thousand Catholics attended twenty-three prayer groups in the country.[75] In Palmerston North, the Anglican Ray Muller coordinated charismatic growth. By 1967, there was a large mid-week group made up mostly of Massey students.[76] Again, Protestant witness brought in some Roman Catholics.[77] Christchurch and Auckland were the main charismatic centres. By 1973, between forty and sixty Anglicans had received through Morrow's ministry in the South Island city.[78] Adullam's Cave was attracting Roman Catholics by at least 1968 (a tape from Notre Dame passed through hands in the city).[79] Morrow built further links, inviting two local Redemptorist priests to lead a meeting at his church in February 1972, where apparently thirty Catholics came forward to experience the Spirit. Catholic-ecumenical prayer groups were established from 1971, led by the same Redemptorists. A group in Papanui, later called the Bread of Life Community, grew to one hundred members by 1973.[80] In Auckland, by 1971 there were five Catholic-led prayer groups, one of these at the university.[81] Anglo-Catholic Archdeacon K. R. Prebble's parish of St Paul's became a hive of activity—and it was soon the largest Anglican congregation in the country.

In Australia, charismatic growth was steady, but slower. In 1966, a Baptist minister, who now worked independently with the FGBMFI, informed Jean Stone that he was aware of home meetings in Victoria, South Australia, New South Wales, and Queensland.[82] A list of Spirit-filled and 'interested' ministers collated by David du Plessis that year indicates Methodists were the mainliners most

[73] Michael Andrew Reid, 'But by my Spirit: a history of the charismatic renewal in Christchurch, 1960–1985', University of Canterbury, PhD thesis, 2003, 107–11.

[74] DAHL, David du Plessis papers, box 8, file 64, Colin J. Bevan to David du Plessis, 10 May 1965.

[75] JKTL, ANG 016/1/2, Allen G. Neil, 'The origins, development and present extent of the Charismatic Renewal in the Church in New Zealand', Provincial Commission on the Charismatic Renewal, 1973, 31.

[76] LPL, Michael Harper papers, 1967/32, Muller to M. and J. Harper, 18 October 1967, 24.

[77] Interview with Ken and Raewyn Harrison; JKTL, Cecil T. Marshall papers, ANG178, series 1, item 15; JKTL, Cecil T. Marshall papers, ANG178, series 1, item 14, Ray Muller to Marshall, 27 June 1966.

[78] Neil, 'Origins', 47.

[79] Reid, 'But by my Spirit', 112.

[80] Neil, 'Origins', 23.

[81] Ibid., 13.

[82] DAHL, Jean Stone and Rick Willans papers, box 4, David Evans to Jean Stone, 5 November 1966.

affected, followed by Anglicans.[83] In South Australia a network emerged around the Revd. Neil Usher in Alberton, which included around twenty Methodists alongside clergy from other denominations.[84] Inroads were made into Anglicanism. In Melbourne in 1964, the Revd. Harry Broadly drew the attention of the *Australian Church Record*, and in Sydney, Jim Glennon's healing ministry at the cathedral and Barry Schofield's Picton congregation were early centres.[85] St Michael's College, Sydney, was the location of the first Catholic prayer group in the country, which was established in 1969 following the return of mathematician Alex Reichel from the University of Colorado.[86] He was joined by another returning Australian, Fr. Gerald Hawkins, a Cistercian who became Archbishop Cardinal Gilroy's liaison with charismatic groups and also travelled around the country. Another key location was the Bardon area of Brisbane. Here, the assistant priest, Fr. Vincent Hobbs, became interested in Spirit baptism after meeting, through Cursillo, another priest who had witnessed *glossolalia* in the United States (including a woman unknowingly praying the Hail Mary in German, in which he was fluent). Prayer groups were established in Adelaide, where again *cursillistas* were early participants, and in Canberra, Perth, and in Melbourne, where a meeting, led by Fr. Humphrey O'Leary, began at the Redemptorist seminary in 1972.[87] Around this time, too, independent Latter Rain influences percolated back from New Zealand—notably through a former Methodist, Paul Collins, at Christian Faith Centre, Sydney, from 1969, and in Brisbane through the ex-Baptist Trevor Chandler at Windsor Full Gospel Church. These became early examples of the mega-churches which later dominated the Australian Christian scene.

In South Africa, in the Transvaal a group of ministers associated with Dennis A. Scott, a Spirit baptised Methodist minister in Nigel who had left the denomination but continued to seek awakening in the mainline churches. A disused mining village was acquired to start a Bible school and further the renewal. Partly through their influence, by 1968 there were prayer groups involving Protestant mainliners and some Roman Catholics in Johannesburg, Pretoria, and Boksburg.[88] In Pretoria, Hatfield Baptist Church, led by Ed Roebert, embarked on a charismatic journey after various elders were filled through the Nigel circle.[89] Roebert jotted down the names of congregants who spoke in tongues in the back

[83] DAHL, David du Plessis papers, box 80, file 1, New Zealand and Australian addresses 1966.

[84] LPL, Michael Harper papers, 1967/14, David Evans to Harper, 15 March 1967, 1–2.

[85] 'Pentecostal outpouring?', *Australian Church Record*, 4 June 1964, 1.

[86] Brian Smith, *Streams of living water: autobiography of a charismatic leader* (Melbourne: Comsoda Communications, 2000), 9.

[87] John Maiden, 'The emergence of Catholic charismatic renewal "in a country": Australia and transnational charismatic renewal', *Studies in World Christianity*, 25/3 (2019), 274–96.

[88] 'South Africa's move of the Spirit', *Renewal*, 17 (1968), 5–6.

[89] Richard M. Ngomane, 'Leadership mentoring and succession in charismatic churches in Bushbuckridge: a critical assessment in the light of 2 Timothy 2: 1–3', University of Pretoria, PhD thesis, 2013, 43.

of his bible—over eighty were listed even before he began to exercise the gift. A growing number of Afrikaans students from the University of Pretoria began to attend.[90] In Natal, the Full Gospel Businessmen were active in Durban and able to influence mainline congregations such as St Elizabeth's Anglican church, in the suburbs.[91] The renewal made ground amongst the white, English-speaking population of Cape Province. A Methodist superintendent, Derek Crumpton, was filled through the witness of an Assemblies of God pastor around 1968. He established a prayer group of around seventy in Queenstown. Later he resigned from the District due to opposition and moved to East London, where he started the Caring Centre, a community which became a catalyst for local charismatic growth. In 1972, David du Plessis was informed that the entirety of the eastern Cape was experiencing the Spirit to some degree.[92] That information came from Bill Burnett, the Bishop of Grahamstown, who as described in Chapter 1 had by now experienced the Spirit with tongues.[93] Not having his own parish, Burnett began a prayer meeting in his home which was soon attended by over one hundred.[94] Four years later, as many as 80 per cent of the trainees for ministry at the Anglo-Catholic St Paul's College were involved in the renewal.[95] By this time, Burnett was the Archbishop of Cape Town, an appointment which assisted the spread and acceptability of renewal in the Church of the Province of Southern Africa.

This was the 'tip of the iceberg' of the new Pentecost during the long Sixties. What general patterns can be observed? Certainly, universities and theological colleges were important settings for renewal. This was an afterglow of the 1950s' resurgence of campus religion. In England, John Collins, an Anglican clergyman, had good reason to pray in 1963, 'Lord, give us Cambridge'.[96] It should be remembered that at the turn of the decade, 40 per cent of students at Liverpool, Edinburgh, and Cambridge still claimed weekly or frequent church attendance. There had been rising evangelical commitment from which charismatic renewal benefited. One British university Vice-Chancellor observed 'young people... becoming fossilized in their development in a naïve form of Christian belief which appears to have been revived in the past few years'.[97] However, the significance of universities—and the role of the young—should not be overstated. Charismatic emergences occurred in a range of settings. The renewal maps on to

[90] Joep de Wit and Jacques Theron, 'From Hatfield Baptist Church to Hatfield Christian Church: perspectives on some historical developments during the ministry of Pastor Ed Roebert' (online).

[91] APCSA, Interview with Dave Philips (by Glen Thompson), 15 December 1995 (online).

[92] DAHL, David du Plessis papers, box 10, file 6, Bill Burnett to David du Plessis, 24 November 1972.

[93] DAHL, David du Plessis papers, box 10, file 6, Bill Burnett to David du Plessis, 23 November 1972.

[94] Bill Burnett, 'Evidence on the fringe', *Renewal*, 49 (February–March 1974), 10–13.

[95] Henry H. Mbaya, *Resistance to and acquiescence in apartheid: St Paul's Theological College, Grahamstown, 1965–92* (Stellenbosch: Sun Press 2018), 80.

[96] LPL, Michael Harper papers, 1963/4, John Collins to Harper, 7 February 1963, 7.

[97] Quoted in: Simon Green, *The passing of Protestant England: secularisation and social change, c.1920–1960* (Cambridge: Cambridge University Press, 2010), 266.

antecedent experiential flows of previous decades, and it would therefore appear haphazard, emerging organically across different religious contexts and locations which had already been influenced by healing movements, lay apostolates, empowered evangelicals, and revivalistic pentecostals. The renewal took hold in larger conurbations but also provincial settings—for example, Palmerston North in New Zealand, East Lansing and South Bend in the American upper Midwest, South Chard in south-west England, and Nigel, Transvaal, which each became nodes for the movement. In each locality, of course, charismatic emergences resulted from unique combinations of global flows and contextual factors. However, while the local particularities of charismatic renewal must be recognised, we can also relate these 'Pentecosts' to a larger context of crisis in the long Sixties.

'Who Will Save Us from This Hour?': Crises, Eschatology, and Empowerment

The long Sixties were experienced by some as an era of eschatological heaviness. As Chapter 1 outlined, radical liberal Protestantism, the Second Vatican Council, and the New Age movement each had eschatological dimensions. In this ferment of uncertainty, the meta-narrative of a new era of the Spirit—falling on 'all flesh' before the return of Christ—fired up the charismatic imagination.

In June 1969, the first editorial of the American charismatic magazine *New Wine* remarked: 'Man has amassed such knowledge and achieved such sophistication that outwardly he pretends to ignore spiritual truth and reality. And because of this spiritual neglect, the world teeters on the edge of disaster.' It added: 'We have vastly increased the power to bring destruction upon ourselves without diminishing the willingness to inflict such destruction.'[98] It is significant that charismatic renewal first gained ground during the Cold War's 'years of maximum danger' of 1958 to 1962. An Episcopalian charismatic pamphlet *What Happened to the Trinity?* was unequivocal: 'In these latter days, when men have designed weapons which may well explode the world into fragments, can the Church be content to exist without the fullness of God?'[99] In Whangaroa, on New Zealand's North Island, in 1966, one Spirit-filled Methodist felt it necessary to preach on 'Guided missiles or guided men', seemingly a charismatic spin on Dr Martin Luther King Jr's 'The man who was a fool' sermon ('Our scientific power has outrun our spiritual power. We have guided missiles and

[98] Don Basham, 'Editorial', *New Wine*, 1/1 (June 1969), 2.

[99] DAHL, Jean Stone and Rick Willans papers, box 1, file 11, *What has happened to the Trinity?* (Van Nuys, 1961), 2.

misguided man').[100] Geopolitical concerns were by no means limited to the northern hemisphere: across the Anglo-world Christians were grasping for religious answers to the existential questions raised by dreadful scientific potential.

Charismatics adopted the language of *power*, a word which a 1963 article in the FGBMFI magazine *Voice* speculated was now amongst the most used words in the English language. 'This is an age of power. We have water, steam, diesel, electric, jet, rocket, man, air, naval, and political power; and not being satisfied with fire power, we have atomic, hydrogen, cobalt, and thermonuclear power', readers were told. Such power had been proved insufficient; the world was still 'desperately ill'.[101] In this febrile atmosphere, charismatic tropes of power and unity in the Spirit were often expressed through imagery which juxtaposed technological developments.[102] For example, in 1969 the cover for a new impression for Michael Harper's *Power for the Body of Christ* showed an Apollo rocket leaving its launchpad. As stockpiles of atomic weapons increased 'the danger of being consumed "with fire"', so 'spiritual weapons' were essential for the last days.[103]

Alongside these technology-driven, global existential anxieties, there were also developments in the Middle East. The establishment of the State of Israel in 1948 had stirred interest from healing evangelists to neo-evangelicals. David du Plessis was one of various pentecostals who believed, as Joseph Williams describes, a 'new wave' of revival would sweep through the churches following the establishment of the State of Israel in 1948. Some asked, furthermore, whether it coincidence that the Catholic charismatic renewal was birthed in the same year as the Six-Day War?[104] Derek Prince, a pre-millennialist, was a close observer of these developments. In 1970 he argued the replacement of 'churchianity' with 'New Testament Fellowship' and the joining together of a fragmented Christendom by charismatic renewal, could well contribute to a change in Israel's assessment of Jesus.[105] As we shall examine fully in Chapter 6, the events in the Middle East charged the eschatological atmosphere in which the charismatic imagination was to take shape.

So did specific national concerns. The often-quoted words of church historian Sydney E. Ahlstrom in 1970, surveying the United States in the previous decade, described 'a time... when the old grounds of national confidence, patriotic idealism, moral traditionalism, and even of historic Judaeo-Christian theism, were

[100] DAHL, David du Plessis papers, box 14, file 21, Betty and Dave Edmonds, Prayer letter, 19 February 1966. For 'The man who was a fool', see Dr Martin Luther King Jr., *A Gift of love: sermons from strength to love and other preachings* (Boston: Beacon Press, 2012).

[101] Bennie Tripplet, 'Power for this hour', *Voice*, February 1963, 24–27, at 24.

[102] Some such language had been used also by post-war healing evangelists, e.g. Franklin Hall, *Atomic power with God through prayer and fasting* (1946).

[103] 'Spiritual weapons in the last days', *New Wine*, June 1970, 13–14, at 13.

[104] Joseph Williams, 'The pentecostalization of Christian Zionism', *Church History*, 84/1 (2015), 159–94, at 181.

[105] Derek Prince, 'Israel report', *New Wine*, February 1970, 22–24, at 24.

awash'.[106] A sense of national crisis was apparent in early issues of Jean Stone's *Trinity* magazine: 'Signs, symptoms and symbols are appearing in such magnitude as to cause a thinking person to take inventory.' A real concern was materialism and consumerism: 'What will happen to a people who have exchanged faith in God for faith in material success?'[107] In the fast-changing American context, evidence of national decay was not difficult to find for those seeking it. A 1964 article by Stone, for example, mentioned the imprisonment of two Episcopalian bishops' wives for participating in a civil rights demonstration in Florida; atheist Madalyn Murray O'Hair's battle against prayers in public schools; and 'anti-Christ' teenage idols (a reference to the Beatles, who visited that year).[108] In Britain, the Suez Crisis of 1956 had left a sense of reduced national confidence.[109] In the Greater British world, also, some identified the need of a new age of spiritual power with the passing of the old order, notably Winston Churchill's death in 1965. The New Zealand Anglican cleric Robert Firebrace wrote to Michael Harper that year that an era of Spirit-filled leadership should end 'human' leadership.[110] Firebrace was one of a number of early charismatics, including the Englishmen Bill Grant and Ben Allen, with a British Israelite background.[111] With the decline of imperialism, the notion of a global era of the Spirit—with Greater Britain playing a leading role—appealed to some. Firebrace maintained the conviction that in the present divine move, the 'English-speaking peoples' would lead the nations into God's kingdom.[112]

Many of those who discovered baptism in the Spirit did so alongside an acute sense of a religious crisis. Amongst Protestants the early 1960s were a hinge point. The 1950s had seen, in Callum Brown's words, 'a period of booming religious culture' in the post-war Anglo-world.[113] Benjamin E. Zeller insightfully characterises this in the United States as 'big religion': an era of church growth and building projects against a backdrop of the bureaucratisation and professionalisation of ecumenical organisations and revival crusades.[114] In North America, New Zealand, and Australia, suburbia was the context for much religious activity. In Britain, although church attendance was weaker, Billy Graham could still cause a

[106] Sydney E. Ahlstrom, 'The radical turn in theology and ethics: why it occurred in the 1960s', *The Annals of the American Academy of Political and Social Science*, 387 (1970), 1–13.

[107] Editorial, *Trinity*, 1/4 (1962), 7.

[108] Jean Stone, 'By my Spirit, saith the Lord', *Trinity*, 3/4 (1964), 54–55, at 55.

[109] Alister Chapman, 'The international context of secularization in England: the end of empire, immigration, and the decline of Christian national identity, 1945–1970', *Journal of British Studies*, 54 (2015), 163–89, at 177.

[110] LPL, Michael Harper papers, 1965/20, R. C. Firebrace to Michael Harper, 28 January 1965, 1.

[111] A Christian movement which identified white British (and white British heritage) as descendants of the lost tribes of Israel.

[112] LPL, Michael Harper papers, 1968/12, R. C. Firebrace to Michael Harper, 18 January 1968, 2.

[113] Callum Brown, *Religion and the demographic revolution: women and secularization in Canada, Ireland, UK and USA since the 1960s* (Woodbridge: Boydell Press, 2012), 52.

[114] Benjamin E. Zeller, 'American postwar "Big Religion": reconceptualizing twentieth-century American religion using big science as a model', *Church History*, 80/2 (2011), 321–51, at 330.

stir and Christianity maintained a cultural dominance. At the coronation of the monarch in 1953, *The Times* had hoped for a new Elizabethan age of 'Christian values re-established, morals reasserted, conscientiousness revived, energy renewed, and national unity restored'.[115] By the beginning of the next decade—and slightly earlier in Britain—Protestant optimism was wavering. There had been doubters before this; alternative narratives about 'spectator-worshippers'.[116] In the 1960s, however, across different national contexts a questioning of the authenticity of mainline piety intensified. In *The Suburban Captivity of the Churches* (1961), Chicago Divinity School's Gibson Winter denounced the churches' complacency and lack of prophetic power. Four years later, the Canadian Pierre Berton's *The Comfortable Pew* (1965) described a church 'shackled by its institutional chains'. '"Religion", as we know it today in all its organizational manifestations, is something quite different from the Christianity of Galilee', he argued.[117] The early charismatics displayed similar concerns. Jean Stone asked her readers in 1962, 'What happens to the Church when its hierarchy rejects the work of the Holy Spirit and sets as its success symbol large attendance records?'[118] The 'before' of Spirit baptism narratives was often characterised by observations like those of Winter and Berton. The latter's work became recommended reading by the Fountain Trust.[119] As a Presbyterian minister in Enniskillen, Northern Ireland, recently filled with the Spirit, testified: before this, *The Comfortable Pew* had 'produced, to say the least, an uncomfortable pulpit!'[120]

In terms of religious decline based on metrics such as participation, affiliation, and attendance, the levee began to seriously leak—or even break—in the 1960s, although the timing of this varied considerably. Britain displayed the first indications of substantial decline. In England, Wales, and Scotland, churchgoing had been in gradual decline since the nineteenth century, but 1956–63 saw a collapse of affiliation. In Canada, New Zealand, and Australia, the onset of decline in churchgoing and affiliation came more suddenly between the early and the mid-1960s.[121] In the United States, a fall in churchgoing and affiliation was less marked: claimed church attendance in the last seven days fell from 47 per cent to 44 per cent between 1957 and 1965, compared to Canada where the decline was from 61 per cent to 55 per cent between 1956 and 1965.[122] In South Africa, decline

[115] 'And after?,' *The Times*, 3 June 1953, 13.

[116] Charles H. Page, 'Bureaucracy in the liberal Church', *Review of Religion*, 14/3 (July 1951), 149–50.

[117] Pierre Berton, *The comfortable pew: a critical look at Christianity and the religious establishment in the new age* (Toronto: McLelland and Stewart, 1965), 115.

[118] Editorial, *Trinity*, 1/4 (1962).

[119] 'Bookshop', *Renewal*, February–March 1967, 23.

[120] Revd. William J. Hughes, 'The God of all sufficiency', *Renewal*, December–January 1968/9, 17–19.

[121] See Brown, *Religion*, ch. 3; Kevin Ward, *Losing our religion? Changing patterns of believing and belonging in secular Western societies* (Eugene: Wipf & Stock, 2013), 9; David Hilliard, 'The religious crisis of the 1960s: the experience of the Australian Churches

[122] Brown, *Religion*, 75.

amongst mainline Protestants was less evident, but the overall trend was downwards as a proportion of the population.[123] Christian socialisation is vital to the sustenance of church participation, and reduced involvement of youth in church activities during the 1960s heightened the sense of crisis.[124] In countries where the seepage was later, there were warning signs from elsewhere of things to come. In 1966, for instance, the *Australian Church Record* reported declining confirmations in England (191,000 in 1961 to 156,000 three years later).[125] There was a sense that old methods were failing, that building projects and more 'scientific' approaches to church growth and organisation were insufficient. Charismatics, furthermore, were amongst those who questioned existing methods of evangelism. By the mid-1960s in Britain there was a sense that post-war revivalism had failed to deliver. One editorial in *Renewal* magazine stated in 1966, 'Billy Graham himself said that he thought Britain was on the edge of a great movement of God's Spirit. But the pundits were wrong. Exactly the opposite was about to take place.'[126]

As we saw in Chapter 1, although some of the data on religiosity were indeed pointing towards decline, Christian anxieties over secularisation were not always proportional to the actual situation on the ground. The idea of the 'secular society' was constructed *before* rapid social and cultural changes took place—and most influentially by Christian leaders rather than social scientists.[127] As Alister Chapman has shown in a case study of All Souls, Langham Place, London, the parish was still thriving, relatively speaking, at the beginning of the decade. However, in 1960 the vicar John Stott still asserted in the parish magazine that only revival could prevent the country 'from lapsing into complete paganism'.[128] Stott's sense of crisis reflected the religious discourse around him and contributed to the atmosphere in which some church staff—ultimately to his dissatisfaction—began to seek the pentecostal blessing. In the United States, too, a perception of Christian decline was being powerfully shaped. Whereas in 1957 only 14 per cent of Americans thought religion was losing its influence in society, in 1965 45 per cent did, and by 1970 the figure was 75 per cent.[129] Secularisation narratives were prominent everywhere.

[123] David Goodhew, 'Church growth and decline in South Africa's churches, 1960–91', *Journal of Religion in Africa*, 30/3 (2000), 344–69.

[124] See, for example, Hilliard, 'Religious crisis', 220–21.

[125] 'English church numbers decline', *Australian Church Record*, 27 January 1966, 3.

[126] 'Editorial', *Renewal*, 1/3 (May–June 1966), 2–3, at 2.

[127] Sam Brewitt-Taylor, *Christian radicalism in the Church of England and the invention of the British sixties, 1957–1970* (Oxford: Oxford University Press, 2019).

[128] Quoted in Alister Chapman, *Godly ambition: John Stott and the evangelical movement* (Oxford: Oxford University Press, 2011), 73.

[129] Brown, *Religion*, 35. On the United States, see also: Robert S. Ellwood, *The Sixties spiritual awakening: American religion moving from modern to postmodern* (New Brunswick: Rutgers University Press, 1994); Leonard I. Sweet, 'The 1960s: the crises of liberal Christianity and the public emergence of evangelicalism', in George Marsden (ed.), *Evangelicalism and modern America* (Grand Rapids: Eerdmans, 1984), 29–45; Slavica Jakelic, 'The sixties: secularization and the prophesies of freedom',

What was the answer? Radical liberals proposed a recalibration of theological and moral teaching. The idea that Christianity needed to be reimagined was presented in English bishop John Robinson's *Honest to God* (1963) and the American Harvey Cox's *The Secular City* (1965). Robinson's book was an international phenomenon: after four months 350,000 copies were sold in Britain, America, and Australia (where alone 15,000 copies were sold within a fortnight of its arrival).[130] The media disseminated these theological debates; for example, in the famous 'Is God Dead?' cover of *Time* in 1965 and, in New Zealand two years later, the coverage of the 'heresy' trial of Professor Lloyd Geering by the General Assembly of the Presbyterian Church. In fact, some astute charismatics recognised parallels between the questions both they and radical liberals were asking. Michael Harper believed both wanted to start again and revitalise the faith for the new age, but that charismatics rightly reasserted 'the truth of the old theology and morality—reanimated by the power of the Holy Spirit'.[131] The renunciation of orthodoxy was regarded as a terrible error. 'We hear much today about the "Death of God" Theology and the time is right for Christians to witness with bold assurance that God is very much alive', contested the first editorial of the New Zealand charismatic magazine *Logos* in 1966.[132] The pneumatic dimension to this witness was essential to the viability of an alternative to demythologised Christianity. An article by an anonymous charismatic Presbyterian minister on the Geering trial argued: 'The question which crops up is: what do our people want? Legalistically correct doctrine, or a reductionism by which Christ has been rendered virtually powerless? – A growing number of people reject both these solutions.'[133] Mere conservative objective acceptance of doctrine was insufficient without the empowering reality of the Spirit. A new Pentecost was the hope for the Church.

Declining church attendances were primarily a Protestant problem, with Catholic weekly Mass more resilient (attendance in Ireland was far and away the strongest at a remarkable 91 per cent in 1974).[134] However, despite expectations surrounding the Second Vatican Council, Catholics were still coming to terms with what they experienced as a secularising society. When Steve Clark returned to the United States from Germany in 1963, he remembered a Church 'in the first stages of a nervous breakdown. Nothing really worked. There were only

in Charles Mathewes and Christopher McKnight Nichols (eds.), *Prophesies of godlessness: predictions of America's imminent secularization from the Puritans to postmodernity* (Oxford: Oxford University Press, 2008).

[130] David L. Edwards, *The Honest to God debate* (London: Hymns Ancient and Modern, 1963), 7; Hilliard, 'Religious crisis', 213.

[131] Harper, *As at the beginning*, 96; quote at 18.

[132] David W. Edmonds, 'Editorial', *Logos*, 1/1 (August 1966), 1.

[133] Anon., 'Theologian's topic', *Logos*, 2/2 (November 1967), 23–24.

[134] Brown, *Religion*, 78–82; Hugh McLeod, *The religious crisis of the 1960s* (Oxford: Oxford University Press, 2007), 201.

piecemeal solutions instead of effective plans.' At Notre Dame he encountered students disillusioned with traditionalist Catholicism.[135] Soon after the Council, there was a sense that its renewal of the Church had been 'sidetracked', as one divinity student at Maynooth College, Ireland, understood it, by 'divisive and often acrimonious disputes over authority and dissent, organizational and structural problems, celibacy, birth control, priestly defections'.[136] Before entering charismatic renewal, many lay Catholics had already explored alternative ways of expressing their faith—in particular through social justice. Various *cursillistas* at Notre Dame had been involved in civil rights movements in nearby Chicago, with some marching at Selma. Similarly, before a charismatic group formed in Dublin in 1971, a few had tried various forms of civil rights activism.[137]

The priestly profession came under great strain. The vocation was increasingly isolated and challenging. This was partly due to changing patterns of lay religious practice; between 1963 and 1974, for example, the proportion of American Catholics claiming to attend confession once a month declined from 38 to 17 per cent.[138] To many, furthermore, the Church seemed ill-equipped and ill-run.[139] Before Frank McGrath, a priest in training at St Mary's seminary, Baltimore, was baptised in the Spirit at Ann Arbor in 1970, he was ready to join Catholics preparing to raid draft boards and was 'rapidly losing faith in a Church unable to cope with the problems of society'. 'I wondered', he said, 'if Christianity, which offered a solution in love of God and love of neighbour, could make real its ideals.'[140] Ordinations began to fall (in the United States this was underway by 1965) and many priests and religious 'opted out', which in turn impacted socialisation.[141] One Australian charismatic priest in Hunter's Hill, New South Wales, recalled from the late 1960s a 'blight' in society and Church: 'All of us had friends who had left—many of them generous, gifted, hard-working people. Why had they left? A chill entered one's soul with the next question: If they left will I last.'[142] The sexual ferment was significant. The furore over *Humanae Vitae* (1968) was traumatic for laity and clergy, conservative and liberal.[143] As charismatic priest Fr. Edward O'Connor wrote from the perspective of his academic post at Notre Dame in 1972, 'Even those who hold to their beliefs and remain in the Church have suffered such a loss of confidence that this itself amounts to a kind of loss of

[135] Manney, 'Before Duquesne', 14.

[136] John V. McHale, 'The charismatic renewal movement', *The Furrow*, 24/5 (May 1973), 259–71, at 261.

[137] Manney, 'Before Duquesne', 17; Reynolds, 'Report from Ireland'.

[138] McLeod, *Religious crisis*, 194. [139] Ibid., 191–92.

[140] Frank McGrath, 'God is saving his people', *New Covenant*, 1/12 (June 1972), 14–17.

[141] Wim Damberg, 'Is there an American exceptionalism? American and German Catholics in comparison', in David Hempton and Hugh McLeod (eds.), *Secularization and religious innovation in the North Atlantic world* (Oxford: Oxford University Press, 2017), 255–70, at 265.

[142] P. Glynn, 'A testimony by Paul Glynn S.M.', *Newsletter for the Catholic Charismatic Renewal*, December 1974, 11.

[143] McLeod, *Religious crisis*, 182.

faith. Those who by profession are destined to be the religious leaders—clergymen and theologians—are often the very ones who claim most stridently that religion has ceased to matter and are anxiously asking, "Who will save us from this hour?"'[144]

For Protestants and Catholics—clergy, religious, and laity—a sense of crisis ran through the long Sixties. David W. Wills, a Carnegie Teaching Fellow in history at Yale who was baptised in the Spirit in 1962, expressed this anxiety. He believed 'Christian' America was going the way of Europe, 'threatened by strong powers from without and by spiritual loss of nerve from within'.[145] Similar concerns were characteristic across the Anglo-world; however, we now turn to the specificities of both a regional and national context for closer analysis.

Particularities of Crisis: South Africa and Quebec

In the Anglo-world, South Africa and Quebec stood out in their ethnic, linguistic, and cultural diversity and their experiences of the 'global' Sixties. Quebec's 'quiet revolution' (*la révolution tranquille*) saw the collapse of the social and political dominance of the Roman Catholic hierarchy as the provincial government challenged its functional role in education, healthcare, welfare, and other aspects of public life, which had been upheld by the premier, Maurice Duplessis, up to 1959. This dominance had already shown signs of vulnerability. Mass attendance in Montreal was declining in the 1940s, and there had been some calls within the Church for a more democratic and pluralistic society. When the liberal government took office in 1960, many Quebecers were pleased to see traditional society challenged while also remaining resistant to the loss of Francophone distinctiveness to a popular cultural wave. Recognition of the autonomy of secular institutions and the desirability for greater openness were aspects of the package of reforms offered in Vatican II. Most Catholics accepted Quebec's new secular self-definition; however, in terms of belief and practice there was no seamless transition to modernity. In the words of Gregory Baum, the quiet revolution had 'due to its effervescent character, transformed the consciousness of the generation involved in it'.[146] Many rejected the Church on its coercive record in the province. Mass attendance collapsed, from 61 per cent of the population in 1961 to 30 per cent ten years later. There was new interest in alternative religiosity—in the early 1960s, for example, the first Spiritualist church opened in the province.[147]

[144] Edward D. O'Connor, *Pentecost and the modern world* (Notre Dame: Ave Maria Press, 1972), 7.

[145] Bredesen, 'The Yale story', 9.

[146] Gregory Baum, 'Catholicism and secularization in Quebec', in David Lyon and Marguerite Van Die (eds.), *Church, state and modernity: Canada between Europe and America* (Toronto: University of Toronto Press, 2000), 149–65, quote at 164. The preceding analysis is drawn from the same study.

[147] Deirdre Meintel and Guillaume Boucher, 'Doing battle with the forces of darkness in a secularized society', in Giuseppe Giordan and Adam Possamai (eds.), *The social scientific study of exorcism in Christianity* (Cham: Springer, 2020), 111–37.

Flore Crête, a Sister of Providence, was baptised in the Spirit at Notre Dame in 1967. She began Quebec's first charismatic home prayer group two years later.[148] A first English-language group started in 1970 and this was followed by a French-Canadian group at Granby, established by Fr. Jean-Paul Régimbal, a priest who encountered the Spirit through an Anglican woman while visiting Arizona.[149] The growth of renewal was slower than in other parts of Canada; but the impact of the cultural revolution was preparing the ground for charismatic expansion. At Madonna House in Ontario, Fr. Eugene Cullinane was informed by charismatic Quebecers: 'There's a revolt and an anticlericism in many places. It's not so much the old anticlericism. It's more of a disdain for the priests and the Church structure, considering them as antiquated and finished. And there's a great crisis of faith at the bottom of all this.'[150] As some rejected the Church and others were perplexed by its post-Vatican II role, many clergy were disoriented.[151] One priest who was baptised in the Spirit later reflected: 'This society has crumbled away. People are turning to whatever is strange, occult, oriental – or at least different from the old belief.'[152] There was a vacuum for something new.

In March 1971, Régimbal, David du Plessis, and others organised a 'Rally for Christ' at the Montreal Canadiens arena. However, the decisive moment for the province came with the breaking of the language barrier. English-language media and speakers were suspect to French-Canadians, but in 1972, Paul Grégoire, the Archbishop of Montreal, was persuaded (according to one report, by a local pentecostal minister) to hold an information day. Attended by over 300 priests and religious, all the talks—including one by Kevin Ranaghan—were translated into French. Significant growth followed, with more priestly input than elsewhere in Canada. In 1973, there was a bilingual conference at the Loyola University campus in Montreal, where half of the 3,000 participants were French speaking. The year after, an event at Laval University, Quebec City, was attended by 8,000 French-Canadians.[153] Ronald Chagnon in 1979 explained this success as being due to a paradigmatic shift in Quebec society: 'the charismatic conversion, working within a framework in which the Church has lost a major part of its power to control and to constrain, enabled a body, which had been held down, to pull itself together, recognize its own reality and become free.'[154] Charismatic experientialism, although it was relatively speaking adopted by only a small proportion of Quebecers, offered an alternative to traditionalism without a

[148] Hanrahan, 'Catholic Charismatic renewal'.

[149] Louisa Bourassa, 'Canada's "Charismatique Province"', *New Covenant*, 5/11 (May 1976), 27–31, at 28.

[150] Quoted in 'The Canadian renewal', *New Covenant*, 2/7 (January 1973), 11–15.

[151] Bourassa, 'Canada's "Charismatique Province"', 28.

[152] Fr. Cornelius Boekema (diocese of Hull), quoted in ibid.

[153] Bourassa, 'Canada's "Charismatique Province"'.

[154] Ronald Chagnon, *Les Charismatiques au Québec* (Montreal: Quebec/Amérique, 1979), 103. Quoted in Hanrahan, 'Catholic charismatic renewal', 20.

rejection of Catholicism. The extent of the religious crisis of the 1960s in Quebec contributed to its expansion and character. By 1976, *New Covenant* described Quebec as 'Canada's "Charismatique Province"'.[155]

In South Africa, outside of the Dutch Reformed churches the Protestant mainline denominations faced some of the pressures evident elsewhere in the Anglo-world. During the 1960s, their numbers increased but as a proportion of the population each denomination's strength was static or declining. Radical liberal theology made inroads as questions were also asked about the role and function of the churches and clergy. In 1973, the Anglican Diocese Council of Grahamstown asserted: 'There is a crisis in our Church. This is seen in our failure to witness to Christ, a growing shortage of priests, lack of dedicated giving and above all a neglect of Bible reading and prayer.' The call was to authenticity, rather than reorganisation and new programmes: 'We must each discover the reality of Jesus' presence and the power of his Spirit.'[156] The Bishop, Bill Burnett, had been baptised in the Spirit the previous year; however, the willingness of the Council to issue the statement indicated a wider perception of ecclesiastical crisis.

However, the prevailing crisis in South Africa was the system of apartheid. The injustices and challenges of this system were, of course, felt most significantly by Black and coloured mainliners. However, since the Sharpeville massacre in 1960 and the referendum on the South African republic, apartheid had in different ways also dominated English-speaking mainliners' considerations of society, church, and state. A 1963 editorial in the anti-apartheid ecumenical magazine *Pro-Veritate* described the need for 'a spiritual force which will save our country from destruction and lead the Church to a renewal of its message and its service to the world'.[157] One of those to publicly criticise the 'false faith' of the apartheid system was Bill Burnett, who became General Secretary of the South African Council of Churches (SACC). He and others involved in the SACC were in the words of John W. De Gruchy, 'Often regarded as not radical enough by overseas ecumenical bodies and some blacks, and always regarded as too radical by the South African authorities and most whites'.[158] In 1970, when the World Council of Churches offered humanitarian support to liberation movements in Southern Africa, the SACC was left uncomfortable with an external policy decision which appeared to offer international support for violent resistance to the state.

While it is difficult to know whether Burnett's experience in 1972 was prompted primarily by such pressures, it surely cannot be detached from them. His encounter with the Spirit came shortly after a clergy retreat where he had prayed about the need 'to witness in the church politically and socially on matters

[155] Goodhew, 'Church growth and decline'.

[156] DAHL, David du Plessis papers, box 10, file 6, Letter from Diocesan Council of Grahamstown.

[157] Editorial, 'The church in times of crisis', *Pro Veritate*, 15 April 1963.

[158] John W. De Gruchy, *The church struggle in South Africa: 25th Anniversary edition* (Minneapolis: Fortress Press, 2005), 123.

of unity'.[159] Two years later, shortly after the SACC passed a resolution supporting conscientious objection as a valid response for those called by the state to fight liberation movements, Burnett was enthroned Archbishop of Cape Town. His cathedral sermon called for a 'New Pentecost' in South Africa. In the presence of the president, it was taken as a spiritual and political cry of the heart. A collaborator with Burnett in the eastern Cape and later nationally was Derek Crumpton. Before his own charismatic experience, Crumpton was a Methodist superintendent in a district north of Queenstown which included white, coloured, and Black congregations; and was also a representative of the Methodist's Christian Citizenship Department. The spiritual and political crisis which Crumpton observed in the churches was confirmed for him by a vision in the late 1960s of a 'huge, bloated corpse'. He described it as follows: 'Most of it was stinking, festering and decaying but wherever a breath blew, the flesh came together – pink, healthy and alive.' The Lord said to him, 'This is the state of the church in this land and it is a stench in my nostrils.'[160] For some white South Africans, charismatic renewal offered a measure of spiritual empowerment in a challenging social and political context. However, the relationship between renewal and apartheid was complex. At a congregational level, there had been tensions over whether to speak and act against apartheid. Those wishing to do so often found a majority preferring silence and the status quo.[161] For those maintaining silence, charismatic experiences and prayer groups could offer a pietistic turning inward—a withdrawal from the demands of Christian discipleship in a racist situation. As we will discuss in Chapter 6, the notion of unity in the Spirit may ultimately have weakened the impulse for a prophetic challenge to systematic injustices.[162]

Back to the Beginning: Five Narratives of Charismatic Empowerment

Amidst the uncertainties of the long Sixties, charismatic renewal offered the eschatological hope of empowerment in the Spirit: a rediscovery of authentic, empowered New Testament Christianity. The Acts of the Apostles shaped the charismatic thought world; however, the new Pentecost was also mediated by

159 See Bill Burnett, 'The Holy Spirit simply fell on me', *Renewal*, 48 (December–January 1974), 3–5.

160 Dot Mitchell, *He said yes! The story of Derek A. Crumpton* (Self-published, 2018), 190.

161 See K. Nyamayaro Mufuka, 'The Christian Church under stress in Southern Africa since 1960', *Historical Papers: Canadian Society of Church History* (1979), 1–18.

162 On these issues, see Glen Thompson, '"Transported away": the spirituality and piety of charismatic Christianity in South Africa (1976–1994)', *Journal of Theology for Southern Africa*, 128 (2004), 128–45.

various deterritorialising narratives—stories and testimonies of what God was doing, elsewhere and everywhere, in the world.

The same year that *Honest to God* came onto the scene, there was another publishing sensation. *The Cross and the Switchblade* (1963) was the story of David Wilkerson, a preacher from rural Pennsylvania who began to evangelise gangs in New York City. The pivotal moment in the story was a rally where Wilkerson, faced with an intimidating crowd, prayed 'Come, Holy Spirit'. Amongst those to respond with repentance, 'snorting and blinking and angry with himself for crying', was the Mau Mau gang leader Nicky Cruz.[163] A message of the book was that the baptism in the Holy Spirit could break addictions. Amongst the stories was that of a young drug addict:

> I cried to God for help, and that's when He came around. He took over my lips and tongue and I was speaking in a new language. At first I thought I was crazy, but all of a sudden I knew I couldn't be, because something was happening too. I wasn't lonely anymore. I didn't want any more drugs. I loved everybody. For the first time in my life I felt clean.[164]

There was a message of unity in the Spirit. 'The baptism of the Holy Spirit is not a denominational experience', Wilkerson explained to a Jesuit priest, showing him references to the experience in the Douay Bible.[165] In the United States the book was read widely, including in Cursillo circles. It was a set text ahead of the Duquesne weekend of 1967.[166] A movie, distributed by 20th Century Fox and starring Pat Boone as Wilkerson, was released in 1970. It achieved worldwide circulation; shown, for example, in Ipswich, Queensland, in 1973 (in the wake of the Box Flat mine disaster), when the FGBMFI arranged a drive-in cinema showing over four days, apparently attended by over four thousand.[167]

The allure of the book was its representation of divine intervention in a traditional location of evangelical anxiety: the 'unholy' city. In the year of publication, Wilkerson explained in Jean Stone's *Trinity* magazine: 'In this rock and roll, twisting, bopping age of juvenile delinquency, crime and debauchery, God has seen fit to raise up a might army of youth who are beginning to frighten the very gates of hell.'[168] If God could work miracles amongst the toughest teens in New York City, then anything seemed possible. 'In *The Cross and the Switchblade*', wrote one English evangelical, 'we breathe the same atmosphere as exists in the

[163] David Wilkerson and John Sherrill, *The cross and the switchblade* (Old Tappan: F. H. Revell, 1963), 78–79.

[164] Ibid., 160. [165] Ibid., 156. [166] Ranaghans, *Catholic Pentecostals*, 9–10, 20–35.

[167] 'The Holy Spirit at work in Ipswich', *Charismatic Contact*, 2/3 (1973), 7.

[168] David R. Wilkerson, 'On the sidewalks of New York', *Trinity*, 1/3 (1962), 12–13, at 12.

New Testament.'[169] A New Zealand leader described being 'completely shattered' by the book after realising the contrast between the power of Wilkerson's ministry and his own.[170] A female English reader said:

> When *The Cross and the Switchblade* was first published, it quickly spread through the Christian world, making a deep impression as it travelled. Here was a story of God at work today, superseding medicine and psychology in a particular field with the simple Gospel message and the power of the Holy Spirit, breaking down strongholds in satanic territory. It made exciting and sobering reading.[171]

The story brought to life the supernaturalism of New Testament Christianity on the streets of the city.

Another narrative originated on the west coast of America. Dennis Bennett's was the charismatic testimony *par excellence*. This chapter began with an account of the Van Nuys controversy. Bennett came to explain his spiritual searching as follows: 'I found myself hungry for more immediate reality—more experiential knowledge of God. I needed it for myself and I knew I needed to show others how to find God personally.'[172] His appeal was to Protestant mainliners. Bennett's understanding of Spirit baptism and *glossolalia* as the usual first manifestation was marked by the absence of emotionalism. He claimed to be in control whenever he spoke in tongues. As important to his wider acceptability, perhaps, was his style. Ian Ogilvie, the curate of Great St Mary's, Cambridge, wrote in the local newspaper during his English tour in 1965, 'What kind of man is Bennett? A bible puncher? A fire-eater? No, he is quiet, sincere, with a great sense of humour, and a very balanced view of life. And he is a High Churchman. But his faith makes me echo that comment: "That man has got something, and I want it".'[173] He appealed not only to Anglo-Catholics, but to evangelicals surprised to find a high Episcopalian so committed to evangelism, piety, and Scripture. In a Greater British world where church 'party' controversy was a long-standing feature of Anglican life, Bennett contributed to a thawing of evangelical-Anglo-Catholic relations.

There was a second part to Bennett's testimony: his relocation to St Luke's mission in Ballard, Seattle. This became a test case for the possibility of

169 Gavin Read, 'How did it become a bestseller?', *Renewal*, 1/6 (December–January 1966/7), 6–9, quote at 9.

170 *Logos*, 1/1 (August 1966), 7.

171 Carol Acworth, 'David Wilkerson at the Albert Hall', *Renewal*, 1/6 (December–January 1966/7), 5–7.

172 RUSCA, Dennis J. Bennett papers, box 1, vol. 3: 'I was praying with my Spirit', *Canadian Churchman*, 100/11 (December 1974), 1–3.

173 RUSCA, Dennis J. Bennett papers, box 1, vol. 1. Ian Oglivie: 'Weekend thought', *Cambridge News*, 3 October 1965.

congregational resurgence. A dying parish came to life. The budget increased five-fold in three years and Bennett claimed his own ministry was transformed with a greater desire to praise God, spontaneity in preaching, and effectiveness in healing ministry.[174] In 1968, a visiting journalist contrasted St Luke's vibrancy with the Protestant mainline scene where 'Everywhere, worried clergy are visibly shaken by church decline' as they tried 'Socio-religious endeavours, discussion groups, contemporary worship and sacramental services and modernized Sunday school materials, anything to reverse the emptying, darkening edifice trend'.[175] The story of Ballard was attractive to clergy. Michael Meakin, an English Anglo-Catholic, had felt he had 'no Gospel to give to others' before he heard a tape by Bennett—after which he exclaimed to his wife 'this is it!'[176] 'No wonder his story was received with great respect and interest by Christians in England who are tired of gimmicky churchianity – and longing wistfully for something that really works and looks reasonably like the real thing', the Fountain Trust's *Renewal* magazine claimed.[177] This was a re-sacralisation narrative based upon church re-empowerment.

A third charismatic script, from a very different ecclesiastical stable, was Arthur Wallis' *In the Day of Thy Power.* As mentioned in Chapter 2, this 1956 work was imbued with the spirit-empowered evangelical revivalism of that decade; indeed, the Foreword was written by Duncan Campbell of Scottish Outer Hebrides revival fame. The book's message of a 'latter rain of promise' as the world approached its hour of crisis continued to appear relevant in the next decade. 'The nations are lining up for the last great conflagration', Wallis had warned. The revival would be accompanied by supernatural manifestations and a restoration of 'the simplicity of apostolic church order'. Embedded in the text was also a criticism of 'ecclesiasticism, formalism and tradition' and a warning that without the renewal of old churches, 'new wineskins' would be required.[178] It became a foundation text for independent charismatics, including many in Britain and New Zealand for whom Wallis became a spiritual 'father'. However, his description of the 'new thing' God was doing also resonated with mainline Protestants involved in interdenominational prayer groups.

> Can we find those with a deep consciousness of the holiness of God and the sinfulness of sin, with a readiness to confess the sin and put things right? Are

[174] RUSCA, Dennis J. Bennett papers, box 3: Notes on Dennis Bennet, 'The recovery of the Holy Spirit in the church', St Mark's, Riverside, Rhode Island, 26 November 1963.

[175] RUSCA, Dennis J. Bennett papers, box 1, vol. 1: Earl Hansen, 'A phenomenon in Ballard: St Luke's Episcopal Church Pastor defies the times and packs in the crowds', *Seattle Post-Intelligencer*, 22 September 1968.

[176] Quoted in Michael Harper, *Power for the body of Christ* (London: Fountain Trust, 1964), 53–54.

[177] 'Unilateral declaration of independence', *Renewal*, 1/1 (January 1966).

[178] Arthur Wallis, *In the day of thy Power: the scriptural principles of revival* (London: Christian Literature Crusade, 1956), ch. 3; ch. 6; quote at 96.

> there those with a deep and tender concern for the state of the church and the need of the world? Can we discern a spirit of expectancy, a conviction or premonition that God is about to do a new thing? Do we find anywhere a new spirit of unity among the people of God, a breaking down of sectarian barriers, and a meeting together on common ground to seek after God? Is there a new spirit of prayer appearing among believers, that cannot be limited to the weekly prayer-meeting, but which is seen in groups of Christians on bended knee in cottage or mansion, in school or business premises? Are some seizing for prayer the hurried moments of the lunch hour, praying on into the night, or wakening the dawn with their cries?[179]

Wallis' teaching on a latter rain outpouring of the Spirit gained wider traction. He became involved with the Fountain Trust and his emphasis on end-times revivalism likely informed one of the three main aims of the organisation: to 'encourage Church to expect and pray for world-wide revival'. For Wallis and the Fountain Trust denominationalists, the problem of ecclesiology could be kicked down the road for now.

The key Roman Catholic script of empowerment was Kevin and Dorothy Ranaghan's *Catholic Pentecostals* (1969). Combined with testimonies and a theological defence of Spirit baptism, this told the story of the beginnings of renewal amongst upper Midwest Catholics. It was erudite, too, as the authors (leaders of a prayer group in South Bend which had morphed into a charismatic prayer meeting in 1967) both had Masters degrees in theology from Notre Dame. They presented the post-Vatican II American Church as one of potential, but also desperation. 'The Christian', they wrote, 'looks within and around himself and sees only sin and weakness, an ineffective apostolate, and he hears only the pounding roar of God's silence'.[180] The book demonstrated, too, the extent to which theories of secularisation had pervaded Catholic thinking:

> The rapid spread of what is usually termed "secularity" among men in contemporary society is by now a fact. It is alarming to some, understandable to many. Its cause is debated quite regularly in academic circles. But one thing seems clear: There has been a remarkable failure on the part of institutional Christianity, Catholic and Protestant alike, to speak a relevant word of salvation to modern man.

The answer, the Ranaghans stated simply, was Christ himself and the inbreaking power of the Spirit. 'We believe the baptism in the Holy Spirit with these dynamic gifts and fruit speaks radically to the secular man', they contended.[181] *Catholic Pentecostals* offered detailed instructions on receiving the baptism in the Spirit

[179] Ibid., 212–13. [180] Ranaghans, *Catholic Pentecostals*, 3. [181] Ibid., 188–89.

and yielding to tongues. This was presented within a framework of Christian initiation and a history of proto-pentecostal Catholicism.

> The answer lies in the fact that baptism in the Holy Spirit, as we use the term, has been poured out in the Church since Pentecost Sunday and through every complete baptismal celebration still today. The Church is filled with the Holy Spirit; as the Body of Christ, it has already received all the gifts and fruits of the Spirit. What this new pentecostal movement seeks to do through faithful prayer, and by trusting in the Word of God, is to ask the Lord to actualize in a concrete living way what the Christian people have already received.[182]

The baptism described by the Ranaghans brought intimate experience of Christ, greater expression of Christian love, supernaturally empowered life, and ecumenism with Christians ('our very dear brothers and sisters in Christ') who shared in Pentecost.[183] The eschatological significance of the moment was implicit. 'From the embers of the Christian past we are witness now to the fire of a new Pentecost', the Ranaghans asserted.[184] This was God's action at a critical time:

> Today the Church and the world are both in a time of severe crises, of religious, political, and economic revolutions. The relevance of Christianity to the world is severely challenged on all sides. The past sins of Christian people are bearing bad fruit while waves of bitterness rise up from young people and young nations in reaction to the old order. In this situation, Jesus along with the life of the Spirit is renewing the dramatic charisms of the Spirit – not only to build up the Church but to call attention and communicate the good news of salvation.[185]

As the wind of the Spirit was renewing the institutional Church through the Second Vatican Council, it was also empowering clergy, religious, and laity for discipleship.

The final script—a series of texts by the prolific author Basilea (Klara) Schlink—came from Darmstadt in West Germany; however, as Chapter 7 explains in more detail, it had a profound influence in the Anglo-world. The Protestant ecumenical Sisterhood of Mary was established in 1947 in the aftermath of the city's destruction by the Royal Air Force. The community and Schlink, its Lutheran founder, emphasised repentance for the sins of the Nazi regime; accepting guilt, as she believed all Germans should, for the Third Reich's treatment of Jews.[186] Schlink's teachings juxtaposed contemporary political events—the establishment of Israel and the threat of nuclear war—and the global outpouring of the Spirit. The

[182] Ibid., 141. [183] See for example, ibid., 189–225 (quote at 225).
[184] Ibid., 5. [185] Ibid., 155–56.
[186] For a close analysis of the Sisterhood's understanding of repentance and reconciliation, see George Faithful, *Mothering the Fatherland: a Protestant sisterhood repents for the Holocaust* (New York: Oxford University Press, 2014).

re-established nation of Israel heralded a new stage in the Jewish story which would end with repentance 'brought on by grief at the Messiah's appearing'. To hasten this coming the Church must repent and prepare for the tribulation, 'For we are living in the atomic age, the beginning of the end-time.'[187] In *The World in Revolt* (1969), Schlink explained that the final days ('Antichristianity is on the march!') would involve nuclear war:

> We know that an atomic war will bring with it pestilence and famine to an extent that the world has never known. The nuclear fall-out will destroy all plants and radioactive material; biological and chemical warfare will cause dreadful diseases to break out. Yes, mankind will have to suffer horrible things, like never before.[188]

It was in this age of apostasy where 'God is declared to be dead' and of nuclear threat that Schlink saw signs of the Spirit's readiness to empower the Church.[189] In the Book of Acts, she reminded readers, the Spirit's work had been 'a breath-taking pageant of continuous all-conquering power'.[190] Schlink's teachings moved through charismatic networks outside of West Germany. By 1971 an estimated 2,000 of her cassettes were in circulation in the United States. When the Order celebrated its twenty-fifth anniversary, guests visited from seventeen countries, including Australia and Canada.[191] Schlink fostered apocalyptic urgency in the charismatic search for empowerment.

While other prominent texts also testified to a resurgent New Testament Christianity in the long Sixties, these five 'scripts' made a powerful contribution to a translocal coalescence of believers around the themes of authentic empowerment and unity in the Spirit. While the precise meaning of Joel 2:28/Acts 2:17 ('I will pour out my Spirit upon all people') was interpreted variously, there was an overriding conviction that Christians were witness to the eschatological fulfilment of a new Pentecost.

'If Not an "Evidence" Certainly as a "Consequence"': Spirit Baptism Narratives and Tongues as Identity Marker

As Chapter 1 discussed, evolving ideas of the Self, which were widely evident in social and church contexts, are implicated in charismatic emergences. In

187 Basilea Schlink, *Repentance: the joy-filled life* (London: Lakeland, 1972), 55–56. First published 1969. On the tribulation, see Basilea Schlink, *Praying our way through life* (London: Marshall, Morgan and Scott, 1970), first published 1969.

188 Basilea Schlink, *The world in revolt* (Minneapolis: Bethany House, 1969), 5; 22.

189 Basilea Schlink, *Ruled by the Spirit*, translated by John and Mary Foote and Michael Harper (London: Oliphants, 1969), 9.

190 Ibid., 29.

191 UNDA, Louis Rogge collection, ROG 3/43: *Into the world: 25th anniversary* (1972), 1, 16.

preceding decades, understandings of marriage had become more marked by self-actualisation, emotional intimacy, and inner fulfilment.[192] In mainline American Protestantism during the inter-war years there had been a shift—reflecting wider cultural trends—from a prizing of 'character' towards emphasis on personality, receptivity, and the emotions.[193] Harry Emerson Fosdick's *On Being a Real Person* (1943) spoke of religion as something which could 'recreate and empower us' through 'inward and spiritual' processes.[194] In the middle-class environments where the charismatic renewal tended to take root, the ground had been prepared by developing notions of the Selfhood which rendered forms of Christianity that relied on externally found knowledge, habit and behaviour, and the organisational, marketing, and technological strategies of 'big religion' less satisfactory.

Authenticity was in demand. Spirit-baptism narratives, while unique to the individual, were patterned with spiritual intensification and actualisation. As a New Zealand Anglo-Catholic explained, 'the gift of the Holy Spirit was not something one just believed about intellectually but something one KNEW about, it was REAL. The reality being that, as promised, the gift brought POWER with it.'[195] The experience was described in unequivocal terms. The immediate results often included a new feeling of love for God and others, the Scriptures coming alive in new ways, greater sensitivity and resistance towards sin, heightened awareness of the supernatural world and spiritual warfare, new spiritual liberty, and a desire to evangelise. As Mary Spradley, a Baptist attending the evangelical Wheaton College near Chicago, testified: 'I had a new joy, a spontaneous love for others, and many new insights into God's Word. I had a new freedom in prayer, in the "liberty of the Spirit." And I began to understand what intercession was, "for we wrestle not against flesh and blood, but against principalities and powers".'[196] The experience could accent denominational backgrounds. One Lutheran pastor explained, 'I *felt* justified and righteous—never *felt* that before. I *knew* it but I hadn't *felt* it.'[197] A Catholic who attended the Duquesne weekend testified, 'Our faith has come alive, our believing has become a kind of knowing', Jesus had become a 'real' person, prayer and sacraments were now 'truly our daily bread', there was a new love of the Scriptures and Church, a 'transformation of our relationships with others', and a 'need and a power to witness'.[198] For Catholic religious, the baptism might transform their ordered life. Fr. Daniel Scully, an American Benedictine, found 'Everything we had believed in,

[192] Claire Langhamer, 'Love, selfhood and authenticity in post-war Britain', *Cultural and Social History*, 9/2 (2012), 277–97.

[193] Heather A. Warren, 'The shift from character to personality in mainline Protestant Thought, 1935–45', *Church History*, 67/3 (1998), 537–55.

[194] Quoted in ibid., 554.

[195] David Balfour, 'Testimony', *Logos*, 1/1 (August 1966), 6–7.

[196] Mary Spradley, 'Awakening at Wheaton', *Trinity*, 2/3 (1963), 12–13, quote at 13.

[197] Quoted in Erling Jorstad, *Bold in the Spirit: Lutheran charismatic renewal in America today* (Minneapolis: Augsburg Publishing House, 1974), 49.

[198] Quoted in Manney, 'Before Duquesne', 12.

everything we had dedicated our lives to seemed to take on new light, new life and our faith in all these things was renewed'—this at a time when religious life was increasingly seen as obsolete.[199]

There were different views on the relation of *glossolalia* to Spirit baptism. Some from a pentecostal background—a prominent example was Derek Prince—taught the tongue was the initial evidence of having received.[200] Initially, Bennett and Stone asserted something very near to this. The formula to which Bennett testified was one whereby 'willingness to release the tongue to praise God in whatever words or language He chose to use was a vitally important key to receiving the fulness of the Holy Spirit.'[201] Jean Stone argued in 1961, 'For surely the unknown tongue is the initial, audible evidence of the infilling of the Holy Spirit.'[202] In contrast, some evangelical mainliners and independents maintained a position closer to higher life teaching. The description in a parish newsletter by a Church of Scotland minister of receiving the 'fulness' is telling. He described it as 'what many of God's people have experienced through the ages. Sometimes it is called a baptism of Love. Finney, Wesley and many others have known it. It is not different from what has been called "Keswick" teaching.' He added: 'I am quite sure that the fullness of the Spirit can be experienced without the gift of speaking in tongues since that is only one of the gifts of the Spirit.'[203]

In between were variations of more ambiguous positions. Broadly speaking, these rejected pentecostal teachings on tongues as inflexible and regarded baptism in the Spirit as the entry into *all* the supernatural gifts. However, ecstatic speaking was still expected as the normal first manifestation. The Ranaghans explained:

> We do not like to call this an "evidence" of the infilling of the Spirit. For certainly one can be filled by the Spirit without the tangible evidence of tongues. Yet from a powerful and expectant confrontation with the Spirit of the Lord the gift of tongues emerges again and again if not an "evidence" certainly as a "consequence" in the lives of many Christians.[204]

Praying in tongues was 'the normal and expected sign'.[205] The Lutheran pastor Larry Christenson, while rejecting the idea of initial evidence, used the acrostic PILOT to explain Spirit baptism: Power (particularly for witness); Instantaneous; Link (to Christ, along with repentance and water baptism); Objectivity (an individual will *know* they have experienced it); and Tongues, 'the objective

199 Quoted in Kody Sherman Jackson, 'Jesus, Jung and the charismatics: the Pecos Benedictines and visions of religious renewal', MA thesis, University of Texas, 2016, 84.

200 Derek Prince, 'Why the tongue?', *New Wine*, November 1969, 7–8.

201 Bennett, 'They spake', 8.

202 'Why tongues', *Trinity*, 1/1 (1961), 51–52, quote at 51.

203 Quoted in Gordon Strachan, 'Pentecostal worship in the Church of Scotland', part 2, *Liturgical Review*, November 1973, 34–47, quote at 39–40.

204 Ranaghans, *Catholic Pentecostals*, 193.

205 Ibid., 221.

manifestation'.[206] In 1964, Michael Harper argued that just as God used signs such as circumcision and baptism, so tongues were 'in the early Church the normal accompaniment of receiving the gift of the Holy Spirit, and in this sense can correctly be called the sign of this blessing'. He acknowledged that contemporary Christians might experience a 'time lag' between the blessing and reception of tongues due to 'ignorance, fear and prejudice'.[207]

The pre-eminence of tongues in early charismatic spirituality indicates the degree of influence which pentecostals had on the renewal. The Roman Catholic pioneers of The Word of God community, Ann Arbor, admitted the group was initially very 'Pentecostal'—baptism in the Spirit and tongues were centres of attention.[208] Given this emphasis, there was also a great deal of what we might call 'tongues anxiety' amongst those who had prayed for the gift but struggled to receive. Dennis Bennett received correspondence from all over the world from Christians yet to be released into the gift.[209] Alternatively, some believers who had spoken in tongues became unconvinced their experience was genuine because it lacked intense emotion.[210] The practice was often said to involve 'yielding'. For the Notre Dame New Testament scholar Josephine Massyngberde Ford, the essence of tongues was 'one's surrender to God'. At the same time, the practice was distanced from involuntary behaviour, which, as we saw in Chapter 2, had been a criticism of pentecostalism. 'One is perfectly in control of oneself and can begin and cease to speak at will', Ford added. [211] The discourse around tongues also had a psychological component. Harald Bredesen described an experience of 'tremendous catharsis and fulfilment'.[212] For Bennett, it was 'a freeing of the personality in expressing one's self more profoundly'.[213] The connection was made between tongues and mental health, a subject more openly discussed by the 1960s. 'The new movement in the churches', Michael Harper claimed, 'is spearheading a recovery of the power to lead others into mental and emotional healing'.[214] The notion of an expressive release of the unconscious—which would also be particularly evident in charismatic prayer ministry—was in tune with the rise of depth psychology in previous decades. Themes of authenticity and self-actualisation were often present in charismatic testimonies of *glossolalia*.

Leaders tended to resist the label 'tongues movement' due to its pejorative connotations and their own theological nuances. However, the secular and religious media was fascinated by tongues above all other aspects of the charismatic

[206] Larry Christenson, *Speaking in tongues and its significance for the church* (London: Fountain Trust, 1968), 53.

[207] Harper, *Power*, 36–37.

[208] 'Introduction', *Life in the Spirit*, 3rd edn., 1973, 4.

[209] See, for example, RUSCA, Dennis J. Bennett papers, box 8.

[210] Derek Prince, *Foundations* (Book 3), 273.

[211] Josephine Massyngberde Ford, *The Pentecostal experience: a new direction for American Catholics* (Paramus, NJ: Paulist Press, 1970), 8.

[212] Phillips, 'Glossolalia', 86–87.

[213] 'Speaking in Tongues', *Time*, 15 August 1960.

[214] Harper, *As at the beginning*, 110.

movement.[215] 'Like a 2-edged sword of the Psalms a strange New Testament phenomenon is cutting a wide swath through staid Christian circles across the nation today', reported the *Dallas Morning News* in 1964.[216] Comically, reporters included the details of phonetic structures ('It may sound like: Ba hai, hunta, hunta, kai ee', wrote a 1963 *Washington Post* article).[217] In a stream of official Church reports in the United States from 1960 onwards, there was some appreciation of possible benefits coming from renewal in the Holy Spirit, but a degree of scepticism or even hostility regarding tongues. A charge frequently made—and sometimes not unreasonably—was that tongues speakers exhibited spiritual elitism. Tongues, it was also claimed, might indicate or exacerbate mental instability. In the Diocese of California, the *Report of a Study Commission on Glossolalia* (1963), which had input from two psychologists, described tongues as a 'psychological phenomenon' which at worst was associated with schizophrenia. A pastoral letter by Bishop James A. Pike (who, ironically, later became a figure of controversy for his interest in Spiritualism) forbade clergy from taking part in services or meetings involving tongues speaking.[218] Non-official statements from individual church leaders could border on the vitriolic. One Episcopalian cleric described glossolalia as 'pure craziness, psychotic behaviour purposely induced for fictitious religious benefit'.[219] For Fr. George McLean, of St Joseph's Roman Catholic Church, Issaquah, Washington State, tongues were a 'liturgy of hypnotism'—and like some other critics he associated this charismatic practice with the religion of primitive societies.[220] Peter Lineham describes the atmosphere amongst the New Zealand Brethren as comparable to that of McCarthyite anti-communism.[221] In *Tongues Under Fire* (1966), the independent charismatic David Lillie defended Spirit baptism and tongues from extensive evangelical criticism in both New Zealand and Britain. He upheld the practice against all kinds of claims, including the assertion of New Zealand Brethren writer Enoch Coppin—whose criticisms also influenced Brethren assemblies in California—that 'Pentecostal brainwashing' associated with Spirit baptism resulted in the brain's 'higher' nervous system giving way to the stomach's 'lower' ganglionic nervous system, as in times of illness or hypnosis.[222]

215 For example see: Lane Smith, 'Reporter hears apparent "speaking in tongues"', *Seattle Times*, 3 December 1961, 14; Farrell, 'Outburst of tongues'.

216 'Speaking in tongues: a point of dissension', *Dallas Morning News*, 28 June 1964, 26.

217 Barbara Hogan, 'A Christian controversy: glossolalia', *Washington Post*, 22 September 1963, 5–6, quote at 5.

218 James A. Pike, 'Pastoral letter regarding speaking in tongues', *Pastoral Psychology*, 15 (May 1964), 56–61, at 57.

219 Hogan, 'A Christian controversy', 5–6.

220 RUSCA, Dennis J. Bennett papers, box 1, vol. 1: George McLean, 'Priest discounts Seattle's "tongues" vogue', *The Progress*, 18 October 1968.

221 Lineham, 'Tongues', 44.

222 David Lillie, *Tongues under fire* (London: Fountain Trust, 1966), 17.

However, given their reservations about the 'tongues movement' label, charismatic responses could be paradoxical. Some early leaders were not averse to exploiting publicity opportunities by demonstrating tongues speaking to a fascinated media. Harald Bredesen and Jean Stone on different occasions spoke in tongues on television in California, on the *Paul Coates Show*.[223] Furthermore, outside criticism of tongues could solidify the significance of the phenomenon as an identity marker for charismatics. One informed observer described prayer groups in southern California in the early 1960s as having 'some of the characteristics of a secret society' such was the threat of 'ridicule or censure'.[224] The risks to reputation were sometimes very real. Individuals, parishes, and even dioceses were often anonymised in letters to the editor in *Trinity* magazine.[225] One participant at a Sunday morning gathering of students in Palmerston North recalled that by 1969 it consisted largely of Baptists, Methodists, and Presbyterians who had been 'put out' of their churches for tongues speaking.[226] The 1968 study by Gerlach and Hine concluded that for some, 'persecution psychology' was an accurate perception of 'real opposition'.[227] The theme of persecution, which was another point of identification with the primitive church of the Book of Acts, was firmly established in *Trinity* following Bennett's resignation in southern California. Its first issue asked readers to consider if the 'pioneers of faith' always faced challenges because they upset 'the equilibrium of established order'?[228] A later editorial expressed the same sense of victimhood:

> We live in a day when the cleansing, purifying Spirit of God is sweeping through His Church with a mighty rushing wind and tongues of fire, separating the chaff from the wheat, burning away the dross, and calling a people to consecration and holiness. Let us, then, rise up in this age of the Spirit and stand with the martyrs in our fight for the Truth.[229]

A shared experience of hostility, or a collective fear of it, strengthened bonds within the charismatic outgroup.

* * *

'Liberals, conservatives, Protestants, and Catholics are being drawn together by the phenomenon of speaking in tongues', the Reformed theologian Robert Glenn Gromacki wrote in *The Modern Tongues Movement* (1967). 'This *may* supply the inner unity that the ecumenical movement could not do organizationally. It is an

[223] Jean Stone, *The acts of the little green apples* (New Kensington: Whitaker House, 1973), ch. 6.
[224] Kelsey, 'Tongues', 12.
[225] See for example 'Epistles to the editor', *Trinity*, 1/2 (1961–2), 55–56.
[226] Ken Harrison interview. [227] Gerlach and Hine, 'Five factors', 36.
[228] 'Why tongues', *Trinity*, 1/1 (1961), 51–3, quote at 52. [229] Editorial, *Trinity*, 1/4 (1966), 1.

Fig. 3.2 Archbishop Bill Burnett and independent pentecostal Cecil Cousen.

Fig. 3.3 Kevin Ranaghan.

Fig. 3.4 Merv and Merla Watson leading worship.

Fig. 3.5 Martha Bringewatt, of Fulton, Missouri, raises arms in worship at the 1977 Kansas City Conference.

Fig. 3.6 Edward England of Hodder & Stoughton.

Fig. 3.7 Brother Andrew at a Fountain Trust conference in Derbyshire, England.

Fig. 3.8 Jeanne Harper leading worship, using *Sounds of Living Water.*

inner unity based upon experience, not doctrine.'[230] Gromacki may have had an axe to grind about the experiential dimension, but he was right in his assertion that a search for empowerment—a reconnection with authentic, New Testament Christianity—was a defining feature of the emergence of charismatic renewal. The context was the experience or perception of crisis in the long Sixties. As we have seen, stories and testimonies were integral to the formation of the charismatic imagination, and these collectively pointed towards a sense of inhabiting a larger eschatological moment: 'I will pour out my Spirit on all people'. We will now look more closely at the role of mediation in the formation of the charismatic imaginary.

[230] Robert Glenn Gromacki, *The modern tongues movement* (Philadelphia: Presbyterian and Reformed Publishing, 1967), 142.

4
Mediation

> ...all of you who live in Jerusalem, let me explain this to you; listen carefully to what I say
>
> Acts 2:14

In August 1965, David MacGregor wrote to Jean Stone of the Blessed Trinity Society (BTS) in Van Nuys, California. MacGregor was the Managing Director of the G. H. Bennett bookshop in Palmerston North, New Zealand (Fig. 4.1). Over the previous year, Christian students at nearby Massey University had been experiencing Spirit baptism, partly through the ministry of the Anglican chaplain and curate at All Saint's church, Ray Muller. MacGregor, a parishioner of Muller's, had been filled. 'I am interested', he told Stone, 'in obtaining, from any sources, information about what is happening within the American churches and elsewhere'.[1] Such an appetite for Spirit-filled media was characteristic of charismatic renewal. The G. H. Bennett bookshop was a hub connecting a flourishing charismatic scene in Palmerston North with a translocal subculture. At different points over the 1960s and 1970s, it was a literature agent for Britain's Fountain Trust, it imported media for Christian Advance Ministries, a New Zealand service group, was an agent for the American *New Wine* magazine, and was a distributor for all materials associated with the Catholic Charismatic Renewal Service Committee (CCRSC) in the United States.[2] Through this bookshop, then, media produced by charismatic service agencies travelled through the Anglo-world.

This chapter addresses the role of these agencies and the translocal movement of media, people, and ideas through bookshops, conferences, and countless prayer groups and communities. As we saw in Chapter 1, charismatic renewal was an exemplar of what David calls mediation *as* religion.[3] Indeed, it was distinctively so. Charismatic texts, sounds and images, and rapidly changing technologies, including tape cassette and video, were understood to work symbiotically with the Spirit, extending Her ministry and imparting anointing. Service agencies

[1] DAHL, Jean Stone and Rick Willans papers, box 5, David S. Macgregor to Jean Stone Willans, 20 August 1965. On MacGregor and Muller, see LPL, Michael Harper papers, 1967/32, Ray Muller to Michael Harper, Maundy Thursday 1967, 5.

[2] LPL, Michael Harper papers, 1967/32, R. J. Muller newsletter, 7 June 1967, 2. UNDA, James E. Byrne papers, Service committee correspondence 1970–1973, Kevin Ranaghan, 'The Ranaghans' trip to New Zealand and Australia', 5.

[3] David Morgan, 'Mediation or mediatisation: the history of media in the study of religion', *Culture and Religion*, 12/2 (2011), 137–52, at 140 and 151.

Age of the Spirit: Charismatic Renewal, the Anglo-World, and Global Christianity, 1945–1980. John Maiden, Oxford University Press. © John Maiden 2023. DOI: 10.1093/oso/9780198847496.003.0004

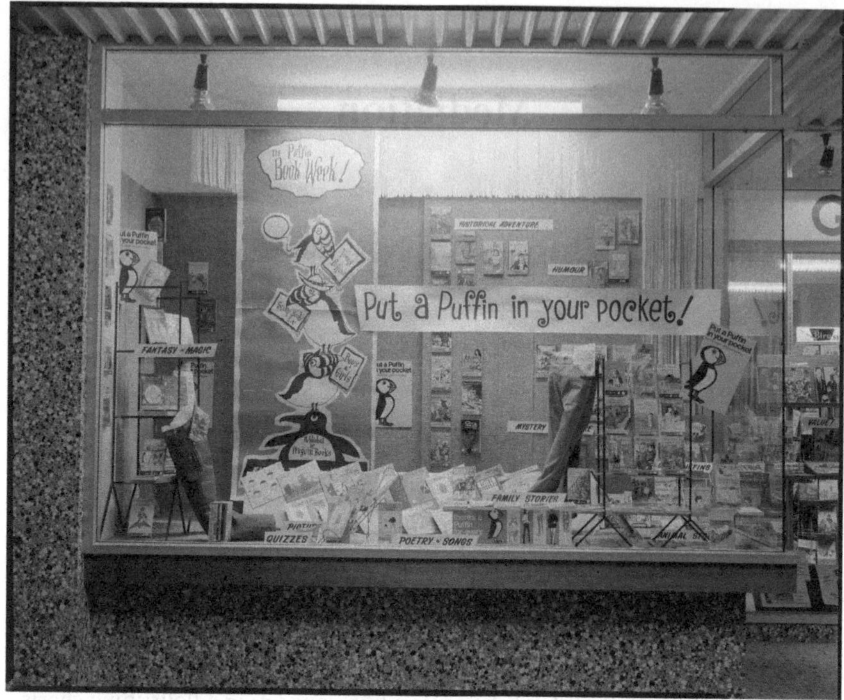

Fig. 4.1 The shop window of G. H. Bennett bookshop, Palmerston North in 1965. The display of products by British company Puffin Books is another example of media flows in the Anglo-world.

produced the homogenising and heterogenising flows which shaped the Spiritscape of charismatic renewal. As they constructed the charismatic imagined community, however, they also fostered pluralities and contestations.

Mediation: 'Now! Have Your Own Tape Cassette Ministry!'

In 1971 a writer in the *Oklahoma City Times* tried to capture the essence of the '"neo-Pentecostal" or "charismatic renewal" movement'. She described a phenomenon with 'no organizational set-up, headquarters or "leaders"', but added 'It does have personalities – men and women "baptized with the Holy Spirit" – who spend much of their time lecturing, teaching and writing books.'[4] The characterisation was astute. Charismatic renewal lacked structures and cohered instead around individuals—'personalities'—and media. Stories, as we saw in the previous chapter, constructed a translocal imaginary. Before Dennis Bennett arrived in

[4] Gail Driskill, '"Charismatic renewal" making gains', *Oklahoma City Times*, 6 February 1971.

England in 1965, he had already 'created a good impression', claimed Michael Harper (who had played the American's tape so many times he 'almost knew it by heart').[5] When Harper and his wife Jeanne visited Adelaide, Australia, in 1967, they gave their testimony at a Methodist chapel—and returning some years later they found 'the same tape was still circulating having been heard by innumerable groups who had never set eyes on us.' Harper spoke of a charismatic 'testimony technique' or 'testimony theology'.[6] These articulations of encountering the Spirit reproduced the desire for these experiences and expectations of what they should entail.

There was also a hunger for Bible teaching. Some of those who experienced baptism in the Spirit became disorientated as they now read the Bible with fresh eyes and its supernatural dimensions—and the possibility of the continuation of the charismatic gifts—came into focus. In Palmerston North, Ken Harrison, a Methodist who had also attended Brethren camps in his youth, found the Bible 'came alive' when he was 'filled' at Massey University in 1968. He and various friends discarded their Scofield reference bibles (he remembers hearing Derek Prince say, 'The Bible is inspired, the writing down the side isn't').[7] More widely, many Catholics reported reading the Bible seriously for the first time. 'One of the most universally experienced consequences of the baptism in the Holy Spirit', the Ranaghans claimed in *Catholic Pentecostals*, 'is the spontaneous turning to the word of God'.[8] The renewal produced new relationships with Scripture. The familiar became strange for some, and the strange, familiar for others. Teachers of the Word were much in demand.

Media has been the arsenal of historic revivalist movements. The magazines of service agencies—titles such as *Trinity*, *Renewal*, *New Wine*, and *New Covenant*—were shapers of charismatic subculture. Their content expressed the liquidity of the renewal, drawing on writers and news across various traditions, often with considerable cross-pollination, including between Protestant and Catholic and independent and mainline. They also pointed towards the coherence of the renewal, for example, in their recommendations for literature—with names such as David Wilkerson, Jean Stone, Nicky Cruz, Graham Pulkingham, Basilea Schlink, Michael Harper, Arthur Wallis, David Sherrill, Bob Mumford, Robert Frost, David du Plessis, and Kevin Ranaghan ubiquitous in advertisements. The magazines produced a sense of charismatic renewal as a 'big tent'. Service agencies were also responsible for intensive translocal flows of non-print media: the magnetic audiotape, both reel-to-reel and then cassette tape, and videotape. The

[5] Michael Harper, *None can guess* (London: Hodder & Stoughton, 1971).

[6] Michael Harper, *Charismatic crisis: the charismatic renewal past, present and future* (Sydney: Anglican Renewal Ministries Australia, 1980), 5.

[7] Interview with Ken Harrison (Auckland, 9 August 2019). The Scofield Bible is an annotated version of the Scriptures, popularised in the early twentieth century, associated with dispensationalism.

[8] Kevin and Dorothy Ranaghan, *Catholic Pentecostals* (New York: Paulist Press, 1969), 239.

cassette tape had a particularly important role. Various studies attest to its significance in other late twentieth-century religious contexts, from Haitian religious ritual to Islamic piety in Egypt.[9] Karen Richman and Terry Rey argue, 'the simple audiocassette tape recorder' is 'one of the most effective mechanisms in the establishment and maintenance of transnational religious communities'.[10] In scholarship of the long Sixties a theme has been the transnational mobilities of ideas, practices, and creativity resulting from innovations in audio and video.[11] Charismatics inhabited this same technological and sensory world.

Ray Muller started a charismatic tape library for New Zealand in 1966, convinced that 'the possibilities of this sort of ministry [were] infinite.'[12] Although after entering the market in the early 1950s, reel-to-reel technology was not particularly successful in domestic settings, charismatic groups utilised it often for recording, duplication, and listening. In the early 1960s, Michael Harper's London flat was described as a 'hive of activity' as 'Tape-recorders whirled around in the drawing room.'[13] From 1963 the cassette tape grew in popularity. The Fountain Trust hailed the technology a 'revolution', as cassettes were easier to use, smaller, lighter, and—importantly—cheaper to post both nationally and internationally.[14] 'Now! Have your own tape cassette ministry!', the American service agency Logos International Fellowship announced in 1971. Magazines offered deals enabling readers to purchase package deals consisting of a cassette player and the tapes of speakers such as Nicky Cruz, Judson Cornwall, and Dennis Bennett.[15] Teaching and testimony tape libraries such as the Inspirational Tape Library in Phoenix, Arizona, and the Cassette Lending Library in Victoria, Australia, further nourished a charismatic media ecosystem—the former had over 2,500 recordings available by 1967 and offered a plan allowing members to receive one each week.[16] When it came, the portable cassette copier was deemed a 'breakthrough' for expanding charismatic witness.[17] At Melodyland Christian Centre, Anaheim, by the 1970s, a hundred tapes were made immediately available

[9] Charles Hirschkind, *The ethical soundscape: cassette sermons and Islamic counterpublics* (New York: Columbia University Press, 2006).

[10] Karen Richman and Terry Rey, 'Congregating by cassette: recording and participation in transnational Haitian religious ritual', *International Journal of Cultural Studies*, 12/2 (2009), 149–66, at 151.

[11] Anne E. Gorsuch and Diane P. Koenker, 'The socialist 1960s in global perspective' in Koenker and Gorsuch (eds.), *The socialist Sixties: crossing borders in the Second World* (Bloomington: Indiana University Press, 2013), 1–24.

[12] Quoted in Dale Williamson, 'An uncomfortable engagement: the charismatic renewal in the New Zealand Anglican Church, 1965–85', PhD thesis, University of Otago, 2007, 121.

[13] Harper, *None can guess*, 60.

[14] RUSCA, Dennis J. Bennett papers, box 1 (scrapbooks), vol. 2, Fountain Trust Newsletter, 38 (February 1971).

[15] Advert, 'Now! Have your own tape cassette ministry!', *Logos Journal*, September–October 1971, 23; Advert, 'Now: extend your ministry outreach', *New Wine*, August 1971, 31.

[16] 'Tape libraries', *Charismatic Communion*, no. 2 (March 1967), 2.

[17] Advert, 'The cassette copier breakthrough', *Logos Journal*, May–June 1972, 9.

at the end of a service for attendees to take home.[18] The CCRSC in the United States described this aspect of their ministry as a 'tape apostolate'.[19] Production and dissemination of tapes was regarded as a conduit for the expansion of the Spirit's work.

Moving pictures had long been utilised by evangelicals and pentecostals for public performance, for example in Oral Roberts' ministry. Increased ownership of television sets and related audio-visual technologies opened new possibilities to exploit. In the early 1970s, video tape was seized upon by some service agencies, notably Christian Growth Ministries (CGM) in Fort Lauderdale. Its magazine *New Wine* declared in 1972 that colour video signalled the Church 'entering a new era in Bible teaching'. CGM's Video Ministries Inc. was established to film teaching sessions. Couldthis allow the Holy Spirit to get 'the most of the time and energy expended' by speakers 'in the light of modern communication and technology available to them?'[20] In previous decades, radio and gramophone had brought in a new phase in the domestication of Christianity. The charismatic renewal coincided with a further stage of technological advancement—of cassette and video. Along with television broadcasting—discussed in Chapter 6—these technologies supported the primary pattern of charismatic ministry: the home prayer group meeting.

'The Spirit of God Poured Forth': The Blessed Trinity Society and Protestant Mainline Renewal

We now turn to individual service agencies and their emphases. The pioneer agency was the Blessed Trinity Society. As we saw in the previous chapter, its driving force, Jean Stone, had been a parishioner of Dennis Bennett's at the time of his controversy. Despite only having a short existence, the BTS and its magazine *Trinity* were seminal in the development of Protestant mainline charismatic renewal in North America and beyond, in particular Britain. They evinced a strong sense of the eschatological moment: 'God has sent TRINITY in this 11th hour', the BTS magazine declared, 'as a Laser beam to pierce the theological anamorphosis which has obscured the simplicity of the Gospel. This is God's time, our time and your time.'[21]

The roots of the BTS were a small prayer and Bible study group, the Blessed Trinity Society of Prayer, established around 1959 by St Mark's parishioners. Stone was the Directress. She had recently come into an experience of

18 Ralph Wilkerson, *Satellites of the Spirit* (Anaheim: Melodyland, 1978), 83.

19 SiS, minutes of the Catholic Charismatic Renewal Services Committee, Memo from George Martin, 16 July 1970.

20 'Entering a new era in Bible teaching', *New Wine*, January 1972, 12–13.

21 'The inside story of Trinity', *Trinity*, 3/2 (1964), 34–37.

Pentecost, explaining 'My life now contains a peace and a joy and a power that I was not previously endued with, and I am now cognizant of the fact that the Holy Ghost has been *with* me but He had not been *in* me. He had not *filled* me as the Bible said He will do.'[22] In the wake of the Bennett controversy, Stone developed links with Harald Bredesen, the pastor of Mount Vernon Dutch Reformed Church, New York City, and the BTS became a non-profit organisation, with her the Executive Secretary. The backgrounds of its board of directors displayed a range of mid-century experiential pieties: Bredesen (Chairman) and William T. Sherwood had both experienced Spirit baptism through Camps Farthest Out; Dr William Standish Reed was an Episcopalian medical doctor and advocate of healing ministry; and these were joined by the pentecostal David du Plessis. The BTS was a cottage industry with global aspirations. Prayer meetings and media operations were run from Stone's home, although later a chapel was purchased for regular public meetings.[23] The group was marked by a desire for the renewal of the churches through radical discipleship, creedal orthodoxy, and evangelistic commitment, all driven by an awakening to the Spirit. Stone wrote in *What has Happened to the Holy Spirit?* of the 'powerful, pulsating, vigorous Person of the Godhead, who is able to breathe upon illiterate fishermen and transform them into forceful evangelists capable of bringing Christianity to a pagan world'.[24] The message of salvation and fullness of the Spirit had to be communicated 'to the world' and 'through every media possible'.[25]

Stone travelled widely throughout California and other parts of the United States, speaking at charismatic prayer groups and pentecostal assemblies. With Bredesen and others she ran interdenominational 'Christian Advance' meetings—events 'patterned to reach the people of the historic churches' in various cities, particularly on the West coast.[26] Stone's reputation became such that clergy and laity from California, other states, and even foreign nations came to Van Nuys to be 'filled'. Even if the number of visitors was nowhere near the scale of the Azusa Street revival, there were obvious parallels. It was, for example, following a visit by Ken Pagard, a pastor in the San Joaquin Valley, that charismatic renewal entered the American Baptist Convention.[27] In 1962 the visitors included two foreign individuals at opposite ends of the Anglican spectrum, Fr. Bill Wood, the Anglo-Catholic warden of the London Healing Mission (who inducted Stone into the

[22] DAHL, Jean Stone and Rick Willans papers, box 1, file 11, Jean Stone, *What is happening today in the Episcopal Church?* (pamphlet).

[23] Morton T. Kelsey, 'Tongues in the traditional churches', *Trinity*, 3/4 (1964), 11–36.

[24] DAHL, Jean Stone and Rick Willans papers, box 1, file 11, *What has happened to the Trinity?* (pamphlet).

[25] DAHL, Jean Stone and Rick Willans papers, box 1, file 1, Board of directors' minutes, 5 July 1961.

[26] Jean Stone, 'By my Spirit, saith the Lord', *Trinity*, 2/2 (1962–3), 52–53.

[27] Albert Schenkel, 'New wine and Baptist wineskins: American and Southern Baptist denominational responses to the charismatic renewal, 1960–80', in Edith Blumhofer, Russell P. Spittler, and Grant A. Wacker (eds.), *Pentecostal currents in American Protestantism* (Urbana: University of Illinois Press, 1999), 152–67.

Order of Saint Luke during his stay) and the England-based, Anglican evangelical Philip E. Hughes.[28] The next year, the Revd. George T. Pattison, who was until recently the Dean of St Andrew's Cathedral in Prince Rupert, Canada, moved into 'a home for displaced parsons' leased by the BTS.[29] Van Nuys thus became the first Anglo-world hub for charismatic renewal. In 1964, Michael Harper invited Stone to speak in England and Scotland. BTS media reached Australia and New Zealand. When Ray Muller set up his tape library for New Zealand in 1966, he adopted the name 'Christian Advance Ministries'; and much of its early catalogue was made up of BTS recordings.[30]

Trinity was printed on expensive paper and displayed a stylish aesthetic. It was 'Interdenominational in scope but with an Episcopal "flavour"'.[31] Every issue included testimonies from mainline clergy and laity of their experience of Spirit baptism. There were reports on the spread of the outpouring, notably in universities: 'The Yale Story', 'Awakening at Stanford', and 'Awakening at Wheaton' were amongst the eye-catching headlines.[32] Some developments in other countries, particularly Britain, were described. 'The eyes of the world', *Trinity* argued, 'are focussed upon the identical sign that was seen and heard on the Day of Pentecost over nineteen hundred years ago, when the multitudes heard those from the upper room speaking with tongues and magnifying God.'[33] The BTS had a vital role in narrating a globalising vision of charismatic renewal.

The magazine shaped the identity of the movement. There was no doubt as to the eschatological significance of the developments underway. 'We are living in a day when the Spirit of God is being poured fourth upon all flesh', Stone asserted.[34] After the Bennett controversy, for a brief time Stone attended a pentecostal church and might easily have lost interest in her own denomination. However, she returned to Episcopalianism and her focus became the renewal of the historic Churches.[35] The BTS proposed a formula of local, non-separatist, and ecumenical charismatic fellowships, existing parallel to denominational commitment. An early piece argued:

> In contrast to the ecumenical efforts of men, the Holy Spirit is busy at this moment calling together a most diversified assembly of Christians, but He is not calling them into ecclesiastical union. Rather, He calls them together for a season of prayer, a time of fellowship, during which they gather power to witness to

[28] 'By my Spirit, saith the Lord', *Trinity*, 1/4 (1962), 32–3.

[29] George T. Pattison, 'An Anglican dean and the Holy Spirit, *Trinity*, 3/1 (1963), 2–5.

[30] JKTL, Cecil T. Marshall papers, ANG178, series 1, item 15, Christian Advance Ministries tape library catalogue.

[31] Board of directors' minutes, 5 July 1961.

[32] 'The Yale Story', *Trinity*, 2/2 (1962–3), 2–16; Revd. J. David Biglow, 'Awakening at Stanford', *Trinity*, 2/4 (1963), 22.

[33] 'The eyes of the world', *Trinity*, 2/4 (1963), 38.

[34] Stone, *What has happened*, 2.

[35] Jean Stone Willans, *The acts of the green apples* (New Kensington: Whitaker House, 1973).

> Jesus Christ. They then return to their own denominations and tell others of the saving grace which lies in the Lord Jesus and of the blessings which come from following Him.[36]

It was Stone and Bredesen who in 1963 advocated the label 'charismatic renewal'—rather than neo-pentecostalism—to describe the current work of God. They were sensitive to mainline theologies of Christian initiation. The primitive model, it was argued, was for the Christian to experience the fullness of the Spirit in the context of initiation. There were, Stone and Bredesen pointed out, some exceptions in the New Testament, such as in Samaria in Acts 8, where laying on of hands was used because of a 'deficient initial experience'. This apostolic model, they explained, had been lost by the Church, so that 'the exceptional situation in Samaria has become the common one today, and needs to be remedied in like manner so that Christians may know in experience what was meant to be theirs from the beginning of their lives.'[37] The renewal was framed as a rediscovery of the third Person of the Trinity in the churches.

Stone's marriage was dissolved in 1966—later, she claimed, due to her husband's adultery and drinking habits—and *Trinity* ran into serious financial troubles and folded.[38] As Chapter 7 will explain, Stone remarried and relocated to Hong Kong as a missionary. However, the mainline-friendly approach articulated by the BTS had a considerable impact. In the United States, the FGBMFI, CFO, and other existing pan-denominational organisations continued to offer support to mainline charismatics; and later the Logos International Fellowship, discussed in Chapter 6, was particularly sensitive to denominational loyalties. Various denominational service agencies began slowly to appear with a similar ethos. Furthermore, as we shall now see, the agenda of the BTS—a 'stay in' attitude to denominations and openness to both sacramental and evangelical Protestantism—had an afterlife outside of the United States.

The Fountain Trust and Old Commonwealth Mainline Networks

Trinity had moved rapidly around Britain's inchoate charismatic networks. Its ethos informed the mainline Protestants who established the Fountain Trust in 1964. The FT also exploited old Commonwealth networks to foster renewal in Australia, New Zealand, and South Africa, supporting several likeminded service

[36] 'The Holy Spirit and the ecumenical movement', *Trinity*, 1/2 (1961–2), 50–60, at 50.

[37] Jean Stone and Harold Bredesen, 'The charismatic renewal in the historical churches', *Trinity*, 3/1 (1963), 28–35, at 33.

[38] See Stone Willans, *The acts*, epilogue.

agencies which emerged between 1966 and 1973. Whereas *Trinity* was the product of Anglo-Catholic Episcopalianism, the FT had its origins at the heart of post-war Greater British Anglican neo-evangelicalism: the Revd. John R. W. Stott's All Souls, Langham Place, London. As described previously, one of Stott's curates, Michael Harper, had a higher life experience of the Spirit in 1962. Harper spoke in tongues the following year and resigned from All Souls in 1964 to set up the FT. Though he continued to admire Stott greatly, their correspondence indicates intense theological disagreement. A solid evangelical, Harper informed Stott he was as convinced of the baptism in the Spirit 'as a basic doctrine' as he was of justification by faith.[39] Stott meanwhile became 'even more convinced that the "Pentecostal" position is not scriptural', a view which he expressed at the Islington Clerical Conference, the annual gathering of evangelical clergy, the same year.[40] While Harper parted ways with Stott, the Rector had a continued influence on his former curate. Harper's emphasis on denominational loyalty—a key conviction of his organisation—paralleled Stott's own message which he would assert in public disagreements with British evangelical separatists such as Martyn Lloyd-Jones. Harper's organisation, furthermore, maintained the same kind of uncompromising Biblicism which Stott demanded. 'Everything must be brought to the touchstone of the Scriptures, which must obviously be more thoroughly and carefully read than ever before', Harper argued.[41] Like Stott, from the mid-1960s Harper (albeit driven by eschatological considerations) was remarkably open to encounters with Christians, including Roman Catholics, to whom evangelicals had traditionally been hostile. Like Stott's brand of neo-evangelicalism, also, during the 1970s the Fountain Trust proved surprisingly open to irenic theological engagement. Stott, paradoxically, and indirectly, therefore influenced the FT's brand of charismatic renewal in its inception and direction. It is not surprising, as later chapters show, that card-carrying charismatics and conservative evangelicals later found common ground again.

The Fountain Trust adopted a mode similar to the BTS, organising regular meetings and conferences, sponsoring tours by foreign speakers, publishing a magazine—*Renewal*—from 1966, producing its own booklets, pamphlets, and recordings, and selling a wide range of literature, largely of British and American charismatic authors and higher life works by Andrew Murray, Watchman Nee, A. W. Tozer, and others. In 1965 the distribution of books was separated from the other activities of the organisation with the formation of Gateway Outreach, run by Noel and Hilary Doubleday.[42] In 1971, as we saw in the opening vignette of

[39] LPL, John R. W. Stott papers, 5/22, Michael Harper to John Stott, 9 August 1964, 209; Harper to Stott, 21 August 1964, 217.

[40] LPL, John R. W. Stott papers, 5/22, John Stott to Michael Harper, 28 August 1964, 216.

[41] Michael Harper, *As at the beginning* (Atlanta: Society of Stephen, 1994), 120.

[42] DGC, Fountain Trust Papers, Fountain Trust Committee Minutes, 29 September 1964, 26 April 1966, 15 June 1965.

Chapter 1, the FT began to host large international conferences and so fostered a translocal network of likeminded organisations and individuals.

Although all its trustees were Anglican, the vision, as with the BTS, was for the pan-denominational rediscovery of the Holy Spirit and New Testament Christianity. The first edition of *Renewal* announced: 'The armoury of the spiritual gifts – which played such an important part in the early days of the Church – is again being redistributed by the Spirit within the Body of Christ.' It added: 'The Acts of the Apostles reads like a thriller. Why should the acts of the modern apostles read like a government white-paper?'[43] The influence of charismatics from the West coast of America was evident. Stone, du Plessis, and Bennett were each invited to visit in 1965 and Harper entered into regular correspondence with key leaders such as Larry Christenson and Frank Maguire. The Americans shared recommendations of literature and advice for ministry with the less experienced Englishman. Maguire, the Rector of a suburban parish in the Los Angeles area (two of whose parishioners had in fact led Dennis Bennett into Spirit baptism) became an airmail mentor, offering advice on issues encountered in California which the British might expect to face, such as prophecies of healing or claims of anointing for this purpose which did not result in the desired outcome.[44] The Americans were a moderating influence on the FT from its beginning.

Given the evangelical stable from which most FT speakers and authors came, it is not surprising they located their piety and eschatology within a longer history of revivalism.[45] The early vision of the Trust displayed strong continuities with the expectations of empowered evangelicals in the 1950s. In its initial mission statement, of 1965, the first aim was 'To pray and work for revival', which sat above the second, 'To minister concerning the Holy Spirit and the gifts of the Spirit'. The circle around Harper included older men such as Bill Grant, Eric Houfe, and Charles Clarke, each predisposed towards the idea of a latter rain outpouring.[46] Harper's eschatology in *As at the Beginning* (1965) also appears based on a latter rain understanding of history: 'from time to time, increasing with frequency, the gifts of the Spirit were reappearing throughout the period from the Reformation to the present day', he argued.[47] A 1969 editorial in *Renewal* asserted that just as God had removed the reproach on his people at Pentecost, so:

> We live in the days of another outpouring, and again the reproach is being taken away. It is coming when some speak in terms of the death of God. So God is

[43] 'Editorial', *Renewal*, 1/1 (January 1966), 2.

[44] LPL, Michael Harper papers, 1963/10, Frank Maguire to Michael Harper, 31 October 1963, 11.

[45] One example of this is Harper, *As at the beginning*. The book is replete with references to evangelicals such as John Wesley, Charles Finney, and Dwight Moody.

[46] Bill Grant, 'The Middle East and the Second Coming', *Renewal*, 10 (August/September 1967), 15; Charles Clarke, 'Quest', *Renewal*, 1/5 (October/November 1966), 14–15.

[47] Harper, *As at the beginning*, 20.

> vindicating Himself as His people are filled with the Holy Spirit and the signs and wonders are again being performed in the name of Jesus. Jesus still saves, heals, fills and sets His people free. What a glorious day to be alive in![48]

There were affinities with aspects of Arthur Wallis' restorationist eschatological outlook; indeed he made an important contribution to the FT as a speaker at conferences and writer in *Renewal* magazine.

Expectation of revival—and excitement when it seemed evident 'elsewhere'—shaped the Trust's global imaginary. The Harpers began to travel extensively, not only to North America (where 750 issues of the first issue of *Renewal* were sent), but also to countries in the old Commonwealth.[49] Jeanne Harper, a gifted, trained pianist, often led worship, and spoke on topics such as counselling. *Renewal* dedicated space to reports on signs of revival elsewhere—a 'round the world' column in the first issue set the tone, covering Kenya, New Zealand, New Guinea, South Africa, and Germany.[50] The magazine was also a travelogue for the Harpers. An article, 'American diary', in spring 1966 described visits to Dennis Bennett in Seattle, Mennonite charismatics east of Vancouver, Larry Christenson in San Pedro, various Episcopalians in Texas and Trinity Church, Wheaton (regarded by some as the real birthplace of Episcopalian renewal), James Brown's Presbyterian congregation in Philadelphia, and to the Baptist theologian Howard Ervin's church in Atlantic Highlands, New Jersey.[51] This kind of charismatic pilgrimage to flagship American ministries was soon replicated by many others. For British charismatics able to travel, and for the many more who could not afford to, *Renewal* produced a cosmopolitan sense of participation in a wider movement of the Spirit.

The elements of latter rain (though he rarely used the term) eschatology in Harper's thinking contributed initially to a close affinity with pentecostalism. Harper described the charismatic movement as the 'second wind' of work of God which began at Azusa Street. As we saw in the previous chapter, the Trust partnered with FGBMFI for the 'spiritual airlift' to London in 1965. Nevertheless, as Harper and others negotiated the realities of their ecclesiological and social contexts, they became increasingly cautious in their relations to pentecostalism. Warnings came from American colleagues. Frank Maguire told him frankly in 1963, 'NEVER, NEVER, NEVER' allow pentecostals to minister at gatherings where 'sensitive' mainliners were present (David du Plessis, Maguire said, was an exception to the rule).[52] After the FGBMFI conference Harper developed his

48 Editorial, 'Removing reproach', *Renewal*, 22 (August/September 1969), 7.

49 DGC, Fountain Trust papers, Fountain Trust committee minutes 29 September 1964–26 April 1966, 18 February 1966.

50 'Round the world', *Renewal*, 1/1 (January 1966), 11–14.

51 Michael and Jeanne Harper, 'American diary', *Renewal*, 1/3 (May–June 1966), 12–14.

52 LPL, Michael Harper papers, 1963/10, Frank McGuire to Harper, 10 September 1963, 9.

own reservations, perceiving a flamboyant style and a tendency to exaggerate (what Dennis Bennett described as the 'whoop-de-do' of the regional and international conventions).[53] Harper also became wary of independent pentecostal teachings on exorcism. Maguire had warned him of extremes encountered in California—individuals who 'detected demons in almost everyone'.[54] While *Renewal* initially promoted Derek Prince and Maxwell Whyte, a concern about excesses in their theology and practice of spiritual warfare meant Harper soon gave them a wide berth.[55] The FT leadership was convinced they should not offer platforms which might 'close the door into the churches'.[56] In a 1969 *Renewal* editorial, Harper spoke of the 'confusion between reformation, renewal and revival'. The charismatic renewal was not itself revival, Harper said, but a movement *within* the churches to establish Spirit-filled communities. Renewal would be 'part of the great outpouring, but only one facet of the whole'.[57] While something approximating to the hope of the latter rain remained evident, the opening-up of eschatological breathing space enhanced the Trust's ability to work within the denominations.

In the mid-1960s there was interchange with leading independents such as Arthur Wallis, Campbell McAlpine, and Cecil Cousen, who each became members of the advisory group from 1969. The involvement of these restorationist fellow travellers underlines intra-charismatic unity in the 1960s. However, ecclesiological and theological tensions with independents were never far from the surface. The Trust's leadership was critical of the 'Jesus only' sacramental theology of the non-denominational fellowship in South Chard, and the perfectionism of churches influenced by G. W. North and others.[58] Where there were signs of separatism locally, Harper found himself in discussion with frustrated local clergy, sometimes concerned about losing their young people.[59] A 1968 *Renewal* editorial appears to include a thinly veiled criticism of North's network; that the quest for Christian perfection could easily become a '"holier-than-thou" mentality' and '"true church"' separatist orientation, the kind which led to 'the bold assertions of tiny sects, each claiming the truth'.[60] The FT was sensitive to any 'anti-church' tendency.[61] The likes of Wallis, McAlpine, and Cousen were pragmatic in their dealings with the Trust, determined to maintain charismatic unity despite

[53] LPL, Michael Harper papers, 1967/1, Dennis Bennett to Harper, 10 January 1967, 1–2.
[54] LPL, Michael Harper papers, 1964/28, Frank McGuire to Harper, 1 April 1964, 2.
[55] DGC, Fountain Trust papers, committee meetings 1966–69, notes of discussion with Noel Doubleday of Gateway Outreach, 14 February 1967.
[56] DGC, Fountain Trust papers, committee meetings 1966–69.
[57] Michael Harper, 'Editorial: ministry of encouragement', *Renewal*, 19 (February–March 1969), 2–3.
[58] DGC, Fountain Trust papers, committee meetings 1966–69. See also p. 61 in this volume.
[59] LPL, Michael Harper papers, 1968/36, Revd. David E. Wills to Michael Harper, 30 May 1968, 2.
[60] 'Editorial: Looking for purity', *Renewal*, 14 (1968), 2–3, at 3.
[61] See LPL, Michael Harper papers, 1967/30, Harper to the Revd. Norman Meeten, 12 January 1967, 6–7.

ecclesiological variances. However, as the next chapter shows, differences became increasingly evident.[62]

The Trust's early stress on worldwide revival was a stimulus to exploit Commonwealth pathways, particularly through Anglican networks.[63] The Trust's literature was often appreciated. In New Zealand, Cecil T. Marshall, the Rector of Eltham, wrote Harper in 1967 that *Renewal* was balanced and could 'allay fears of eccentricity'.[64] From Australia, a Baptist informed Harper that pentecostal literature was generally unpopular, but the Fountain Trust was 'another thing'.[65] The Harpers looked for kindred individuals and groups abroad and supported their endeavours. The second issue of *Renewal* included a report by David MacGregor, the bookseller mentioned at the beginning of the chapter, and a New Zealand 'special issue' followed.[66] Service agencies appeared in New Zealand, Australia, and South Africa which developed close affinities or were modelled on the FT. In 1966, *Logos* magazine was established in Christchurch, with both mainline and independent pentecostal involvement. Its first editorial, by David W. Edmonds, a Methodist, asserted: 'We have been hearing through magazine and tape recordings of people baptised in the Holy Spirit in denominational churches in different parts of the world.' *Logos* could now witness to God's work in New Zealand. 'It can't happen here! Well it has!', he added.[67] There were parallels between *Logos* and the glossy look of *Trinity*, and initially, like *Renewal*, the New Zealand publication's explicit aim was to witness the Spirit to the historic churches. Harper's testimony was published in the first issue, other *Renewal* articles were republished, and the two magazines cross-advertised.[68]

Harper developed a good relationship with Ray Muller of the Christian Advance Ministries tape library, who shared his commitment to denominational renewal. A *Renewal* article by Muller, 'I have no Intention of Leaving the Church', triggered one of the early debates between mainliners and independents in the British magazine. Muller argued that the 'new experience of the blessings of Pentecost' was largely 'within the historic churches and not outside'.[69] In response, a letter from David Lillie asserted he did not believe that God's Spirit 'was any more willing today to be accommodated to the old wine-skins of our many and varied church organisations than it was 50 or 1900 years ago, however much we

62 DGC, Fountain Trust papers, Advisory Council minutes, 13 April 1972.

63 While Harper had no connections with British Israelitism, some in the orbit of the FT did, and these contributed also to transnational networks. See p. 68 in this volume.

64 LPL, Michael Harper papers, 1967/30, Revd. C. T. Marshall to Harper, n.d., 1.

65 LPL, Michael Harper papers, 1967/14, David Evans to Harper, 11 May 1967, 3.

66 *Renewal*, 1/4 (August/September 1966).

67 David W. Edmonds, 'Editorial', *Logos*, 1/1 (August 1966), 1.

68 Michael Harper, 'Testimony', *Logos*, 1/1 (August 1966), 4–5; Advert, *Renewal*, 1/2 (March–April 1966), 11.

69 Ray Muller, 'I have no intention of leaving the church', *Renewal*, 1/4 (August–September 1966), 7–9.

might have hoped that it would be otherwise'.[70] *Logos*, we shall see, later relocated to New South Wales and moved decisively in a restorationist direction. In 1971 Muller and his wife spent a year in England working for the Fountain Trust and on their return he established, as its Director, a new service agency—continuing the name Christian Advance Ministries (CAM)—which was firmly mainline orientated.[71] CAM ran a summer school for clergy and laity from 1973, and by 1977 over 1,300 attended. The clergy present were overwhelmingly Anglican and Roman Catholic. Alongside Catholic charismatic materials from the United States, CAM drew on Fountain Trust media.

The Harpers sought contacts and opportunities to disseminate FT literature in Australia. By 1967 the Trust's media was sold at bookshops in Adelaide, Brisbane, and Toowoomba. The Harpers began to visit the country and New Zealand in 1967.[72] In 1971, Alan Langstaff, a Methodist minister from the Sydney suburbs, attended the Trust's Guildford conference. On his return he was released by the Methodist Church to establish the Temple Trust, an agency which he envisioned as 'similar to that of the Fountain Trust in England'. Its magazine was called *Vision*.[73] FT tapes were advertised in *Vision* and fittingly, on Easter Sunday 1974, the Revd. Tom Smail, a Scottish Presbyterian who was by then General Secretary of the Fountain Trust, did the honours of opening the organisation's new offices and a Charismatic Information Centre in Waverley.[74] 'Temple' referred to the body of Christ, and the Trust described itself as 'an interdenominational organisation dedicated to work in co-operation with Christians in all denominations, for the restoration and renewal of the whole Church'.[75] It also developed links with various ministries in the United States, including the independent charismatic Melodyland in Anaheim. The organisation's language of restoration *and* renewal was used advisedly. It reflected the liquid quality of charismatic subculture in Australia in the mid-1970s. The breadth of Langstaff's vision was underlined when they looked towards television ministry later in the decade.

In South Africa during 1968, a service agency known as Christian Interdenominational Fellowship (CIF) was established by mainliners, mostly Methodist, in Nigel, Transvaal. Its magazine, *Gift*, was edited by the Revd. D. A. Scott. CIF was established for mainline Christians who desired 'charismatic fellowship where it is not provided elsewhere'. The vision was ecumenical—'spiritual fellowship across doctrinal and ecclesiastical boundaries'—and evangelical—'where the teaching of the Bible would be central'. Links were established

[70] D. G. Lillie, 'Renewal in historic Churches', *Renewal*, 1/5 (October–November 1966), 7–8.

[71] Dale Williamson, 'An uncomfortable engagement: the charismatic renewal in the New Zealand Anglican Church, 1965–85', PhD, University of Otago, 2007, 151–90.

[72] LPL, Michael Harper papers, 1967/14, David Evans to Harper, 11 May 1967, 3.

[73] 'The birth of the Temple Trust', *Vision*, 30 (January–February 1979), 22–25.

[74] Alan Langstaff, 'New offices opened for the Temple Trust and Charismatic Information Centre', *Vision*, May–June 1974, 9.

[75] Alan Langstaff, 'The Temple Trust: what is it?', *Vision*, 1 (January–February 1974), 18–19.

with the FT. 'We praise God for this news of yet another area of the world opening up to this move of God', Harper announced in *Renewal* (the front cover with pleasant images of Table Mountain, the botanical gardens in Pietermaritzburg, and downtown Pretoria), which also began to advertise the magazine.[76] The next year CIF organised for Harper to visit the country, a tour described in detail in *Renewal*.[77] In 1971, following a controversy involving the leadership of the organisation, Derek Crumpton, the former Methodist who now led an independent ministry in East London, took over its running as a non-profit and ceased to publish *Gift*, starting *New Vision* magazine as a replacement in 1976.

Harper seems initially to have considered exercising some translocal authority over the direction of renewal in the old Commonwealth. He attempted to intervene as he recognised problems abroad already encountered in Britain. In New Zealand, the influence of independents prompted him to warn against the dangers of 'come-outism', re-baptism, and extremes in exorcism (Derek Prince's international ministry was popular in the country). Harper in 1967 wrote an 'encyclical' to 'the brethren of the churches in New Zealand'. Adopting a Pauline style, the epistle carried the warning: 'SEE WHAT LARGE LETTERS I AM WRITING TO YOU WITH MY OWN HAND. IT IS THOSE WHO WANT TO MAKE A GOOD SHOW IN THE FLESH THAT WOULD COMPEL YOU TO BE EXORCISED.' He warned that independents had 'taken the initiative in the charismatic renewal in New Zealand'.[78] As *Logos* magazine looked set to be dominated by independents, Harper urged the formation of a national organisation for mainline renewal. Similarly, he wrote to Australian leaders, offering cautionary tales on charismatic pitfalls, urging balance.[79] By the time Christian Advance Ministries, the Temple Trust, and Christian Interdenominational Fellowship were established, Harper and the FT had settled on a non-paternalistic approach. The strategy was instead to cultivate relational ties with likeminded groups rather than set up FT branches. As Harper explained to a New South Wales cleric in 1971, 'We feel that it is much better for national groups to be formed or local groups of their own accord, rather than stimulated from a distance.'[80] However, the FT international conference, which Ray Muller, Alan Langstaff, and Derek Crumpton all attended in 1971, provided an opportunity for mutual exchange and building friendships. For the American ministries involved, too, at Guildford that year, 'Greater Britain' was conveniently gathered. The Fountain Trust oiled the wheels of translocal mainline charismatic expressions.

[76] Michael Harper, 'And now – South Africa', *Renewal*, October–November 1968, 1–2, at 1.
[77] Michael Harper, 'South African scene', *Renewal*, 25 (February–March 1970), 34–35.
[78] LPL, Michael Harper papers, 1967/32, 'Encyclical', n.d., 25.
[79] LPL, Michael Harper papers, 1967/14, Dave Evans to Harper, 15 March 1967, 1–2.
[80] LPL, Michael Harper papers, 1971/57, Harper to Doug Peters, 29 December 1971, 4.

A 'New Word': Independent Charismatic Networks

The charismatic world of the 1960s blurred the lines between 'renewal' and 'restoration'. The charismatic prayer group often had an ambiguous ecclesiological status, with the lines between interdenominational group, a 'church within a church', or the believer's fellowship (or 'house church') sometimes unclear or shifting over time. Those most committed to a particular ecclesiological agenda could still acknowledge that the Holy Spirit would blow where She will. In Britain, the independent pentecostal Cecil Cousen believed home groups represented 'the move of God's people all over the world who are beginning afresh to seek God for revival, to restore spiritual fellowship, to give opportunity for the full development of the body of Christ in action, especially in the manifestation of the charismatic gifts'. Cousen supported the idea of groups meeting at non-church times so that mainliners could 'bring renewal to their churches' on a Sunday.[81] However, notwithstanding this liquidity, from the late 1960s some service agencies moved towards—or were specifically established to represent—a distinctively independent, restorationist identity. We begin with the American service agency Christian Growth Ministries (CGM) to explore these translocal independent networks.

CGM had its background in the mid-1960s soup of Spirit-filled initiatives in the United States. *Trinity* magazine found its way into the hands of Eldon D. Purvis, a Floridian stockbroker and nominal Episcopalian. He was prompted to seek out charismatic believers and came under the influence of two local female Bible teachers. After a conversion experience, and baptism in the Spirit at a FGBMFI event in Miami, Purvis established a Bible meeting in his home which grew and multiplied. In 1965, Purvis and others started The Committee of Forty, which organised 'Holy Spirit Teaching Missions' to mainline Christians in the United States, the Caribbean, and Britain. Its media enterprise, the Fresh Bread Tape Library, loaned out books, over 1,500 tapes, and portable tape recorders. The Committee of Forty sponsored Purvis' service agency, the Holy Spirit Teaching Mission (HSTM), which circulated media and organised seminars.[82] HSTM also offered regular teaching holidays, mostly attended by American charismatics, in Montego Bay, Jamaica. Their link with the island was the sugar plantation owner and Custos of the parish of St James, Sir Francis Moncrieff Kerr-Jarrett. Along with other British landowners, Kerr-Jarrett had been busy developing tourist resorts and simultaneously attempting to limit the spread and free movement of Rastafari; and in this climate, in April 1963 three Rastafari, along with two policemen and three civilians, were killed during an incident at Montego Bay.

[81] Cecil Cousen, 'The house group, the local church and the Christian', *Renewal*, 34 (September 1971), 26–28, at 28.

[82] 'Birth of a mission', *New Wine*, April 1970, 12–16; S. David Moore, *The shepherding movement: controversy and charismatic ecclesiology* (London: T&T Clark, 2003), 22–32.

Kerr-Jarrett had previously drawn on other spiritual resources to bolster the status quo on the island. He became involved in Moral Re-Armament (MRA, formerly the Oxford Group) in the 1950s, allegedly to convert—and divide—Rastafari through MRA teaching.[83] In 1967, Kerr-Jarrett first hosted HSTM on the island, another group likely to reinforce conservatism, only now in a post-colonial setting. In Kerr-Jarrett's own words it was necessary to 'revert to the simplicity of the early church and regain the will to be guided by the Holy Spirit and to experience spiritual healing, in order to conquer the Anti-Christ'. The permanent property and funding which Kerr-Jarrett offered HSTM was a means of supporting charismatic mission, including amongst those involved in resistance movements, on the island. It was an idyllic base for HSTM training and leadership retreats.[84]

In 1969 *New Wine* magazine, the mouthpiece of HSTM, was established. This had a wide appeal amongst prayer groups and included mainliners such as Dennis Bennett and Harald Bredesen amongst its contributing editors. Several gifted Bible teachers became associated with HSTM: Don Basham, a Disciples of Christ minister who was Spirit baptised at Camps Farthest Out in 1953; Bob Mumford, who came from an Assemblies of God background, but who had recently studied at Episcopal Reformed Seminary; Derek Prince, the British-born, Seattle-based independent pentecostal; and Charles Simpson, a Southern Baptist pastor based in Mobile, Alabama. In 1974, these were joined by the Canadian independent pentecostal Ern Baxter—and they became known collectively as the 'Fort Lauderdale Five'.[85] Purvis was accused of moral indiscretion and in 1970 resigned from HSTM. A period of uncertainty followed, but soon after Basham, Mumford, Prince, and Simpson determined it was the Spirit's will that they become accountable in ministry to each other. They were increasingly involved in HSTM, joining its board of directors, and writing regularly in *New Wine*. In 1972, the name changed to Christian Growth Ministries, a title reflecting the leaders' emphasis on Bible teaching and discipleship. An editorial of *New Wine* spoke of the 'magnitude of the demand for teaching', claiming that God had 'sovereignly brought the men, ministries and equipment here in Ft Lauderdale to establish a "spiritual kitchen" from which He can provide for the needs of His people'.[86] There was a view that the prayer groups appearing throughout the country needed solid food. Under Purvis, the HSTM had already placed great emphasis on the trans-denominational house meeting and a conviction that 'America can be saved though homes'.[87] The point of HSTM was to equip the 'Charismatic Fellowship Meeting' through its magazine, tape library, leadership courses, seminars and workshops, 24-hour

[83] See Horace G. Campbell, 'Coral gardens 1963: the Rastafari and Jamaican independence', *Social and Economic Studies*, 63/1 (2014), online

[84] 'Birth of a mission', at 14. [85] Moore, *Shepherding*, 22–32.

[86] W. Haythorn-Thwaite, Editorial, *New Wine*, 4/3 (March 1972), 2

[87] Eldon Purvis, 'The co-ordinator's report', *New Wine*, 1/1 (June 1969), 4.

prayer ministry, and an aspiration for 'Christian TV for everyone'.[88] The teaching courses at Montego Bay provided additional leadership training for home group leaders. After Purvis' departure, the accent on a restored, New Testament church became sharper.

The restorationism of Basham, Mumford, Prince, and Simpson (and later Baxter) was not based on a single, well-defined eschatological schema. Prince was a pre-millennialist and assumed Israel was central in God's end time plans, while Baxter had what approximated to a post-millennial perspective.[89] What the five had in common—and this message was loud and clear in *New Wine*—was a shared conviction that the Church was maturing, becoming a beacon of light, a kind of the avant-garde of the kingdom of God, in a darkening world of political corruption, permissive society, and economic recession. The foundation for this victorious church would be the restored Ephesians 4 ministries of apostles, prophets, evangelists, pastors, and teachers. Importantly, although they were accused of having an anti-denominational agenda (and, paradoxically, plans to set up a single charismatic denomination), CGM and *New Wine* actively supported the work of denominational charismatics throughout the 1970s. However, there was also a growing scepticism of what might ultimately be achieved inside denominational structures.[90] Don Basham informed *New Wine* readers as early as 1969 that reports of the charismatic revival successfully fusing with the 'existing forms and structures of the church' were relatively few 'compared with the thousands of small groups and house churches which have sprung up, not actually outside but clearly alongside the institutional church'. God was able to 'reshape and strengthen' old wineskins where necessary, but 'when and where necessary, can provide entirely new wineskins to hold the new wine'.[91] Derek Prince was the most critical of denominations, asserting that the Church's 'deliverance and restoration' from the Babylonian captivity was unfinished and taking place in these days.[92] The Fort Lauderdale people became intent on establishing a network of fellowships, consisting of converted, Spirit filled believers, within and alongside the existing denominations, just as earlier pietistic movements had.[93]

The teaching of HSTM and CGM could divide charismatics, as we have seen in Fountain Trust responses to Prince. He, along with Basham and the Canadian H. A. Maxwell Whyte, presented radical views on the supernatural world in *New Wine*. In 1970, the Canadian informed readers that *all* those healed by Jesus in the

[88] See front cover diagram, *New Wine*, April 1970.

[89] S. David Moore, '"Discerning the times": the victorious eschatology of the shepherding movement', in Peter Althouse and Robby Waddell (eds.), *Perspectives in Pentecostal eschatology: world without end* (Cambridge: James Clarke and Co., 2010), 273–92.

[90] Moore, *Shepherding*, 180–83.

[91] Don Basham, 'Revival with a difference', *New Wine*, October 1969, 2.

[92] Derek Prince, 'Restoration through fasting', *New Wine*, July 1970, 13–16.

[93] Moore concludes this decisively in *Shepherding*, 180–83.

gospels were oppressed by the devil.[94] Teaching on re-baptism by full immersion drew the ire of some mainline charismatics.[95] From 1972, teaching on authority—part of a restorationist vision of God's kingdom 'government'—was increasingly apparent, presented by Mumford in *New Wine* as a 'new word' from God. A biblical principle of 'covering', argued Simpson in October 1972, required that submission be at the centre of discipleship, not only within the church, but also the family and civil government.[96] Between 1974 and 1976 national conferences for male 'shepherds', which involved also Catholic charismatics from South Bend and Ann Arbor, were conducted. This alliance again blurred the lines between mainline and independent charismatics. Teaching on authority and the leadership of Simpson, Mumford, and others in these shepherding networks were important dimensions of the work of CGM as a service agency. As we shall see in the next chapter, it also placed CGM at the centre of a storm of controversy in the 1970s.

HSTM was aware of ministries with similar emphases elsewhere. One unlikely early translocal connection was between Fort Lauderdale and the village of South Chard in Somerset, England. Here, as we saw in Chapter 3, a fellowship led by ex-Brethren Sid and Mill Purse had in the 1950s emerged as a centre for independent charismatics. The spiritual 'twinning' between South Chard and Fort Lauderdale was significant. Although the Purses' ministry was not strictly speaking a service agency, as a base of creativity and teaching it influenced HSTM while it found its feet as a restorationist-oriented outfit. 'Uncle' Sid, Harry Greenwood, a converted sailor-turned evangelist, the singing group The Four Kingsmen, and others ministered in Florida and other US states, and Montego Bay.[97] Greenwood became a contributing editor of HSTM's magazine and one of the first authors to be published by New Wine Press.[98] South Chard emphasis on healing and demonology sat well alongside the teachings of Basham and Prince. HSTM teaching events in Florida and Monegro Bay attracted Christians from Britain, Ireland, and Canada.[99] Soon other British restorationists were drawn into the orbit of Fort Lauderdale. Arthur Wallis was speaking in Florida by 1971 and writing in *New Wine*.[100] This independent charismatic exchange laid the foundations for later transatlantic restorationist flows.

As Chapter 3 mentioned, the makings of a British restorationist circle were evident at the Herne Bay conference of 1965. Solid networks, however, took time to emerge. A magazine, *Fullness*, edited by Graham Perrins, was established in

[94] H. A. Maxwell Whyte, 'Oppressed by the Devil', *New Wine*, July 1970, 30.
[95] 'Forum: water baptism', *New Wine*, May 1973, 28–31.
[96] Charles Simpson, 'Covering of the Lord', *New Wine*, October 1972, 24–27, quote at 25.
[97] Eldon Purvis, 'The co-ordinator's report', *New Wine*, October 1969, 4, 18.
[98] Eldon Purvis, 'The co-ordinator's report', *New Wine*, June 1969, 4.
[99] See, e.g., Bob Feller, 'Report on International Holy Spirit Teaching Mission event in Florida', *New Wine*, October 1969, 22.
[100] 'Points of interest', *New Wine*, October 1971, 2; Arthur Wallis, 'When faith would fail', *New Wine*, October 1971, 12–13; Arthur Wallis, 'Pathway to power', *New Wine*, February 1972, 24.

1970, with teaching on apostleship and anti-denominationalism. Another magazine, *Restoration*, appeared five years later, produced in Bradford by a media outfit known as Harvestime. This was overseen by Bryn Jones, a Welshman known for having a strong, charismatic personality and who had led an independent congregation in the city since 1969. As differences of style, personality, and theology opened divisions in British restorationism, Jones and Arthur Wallis became the leading figures of a cluster which included apostles such as Terry Virgo in Brighton and Barney Coombs in Basingstoke. *Restoration* carried their teachings, while annual conventions—the Lakes Bible Week in 1975, which became the Dales Bible Week from 1976 (and to which was added the Downs Bible week from 1979)—became their platform. *Restoration* initially situated itself in a wider move of God. Jones made it clear that the Spirit was working in both the denominations and the house churches.[101] However, as various prayer groups aligned themselves with an apostle, the British magazine, like *New Wine*, increasingly offered distinctive teaching on the kingdom of God and the restored Church, discipleship and authority in the congregation, and marriage and family.

Two of the CGM 'five', Ern Baxter and Bob Mumford, developed a relationship with the *Restoration* apostles. Although the potential for a thoroughgoing optimistic eschatology had long existed in Wallis' teaching, Baxter's message of a triumphant Church was eagerly consumed everywhere in the British scene. He and Mumford began to visit as headline speakers (Baxter each year 1975–78 and Mumford 1976–78) at Bible weeks. A series of talks by Baxter at the 1975 Lakes Bible week, 'The King and his Army', was particularly influential. This spoke of a Church which like King David was after God's heart, and which would replace a defunct Church that was, according to an Old Testament parallel with King Saul's leadership, based on human thinking and strength. Baxter's popularity was such that he embarked on a 24-date tour of the United Kingdom in 1977 and became an associate editor for *Restoration*. He told British charismatics 'we need to know that we have been mandated... not simply to get people converted. We are to recover the earth for God – every city, every country and nation – until "the kingdom of the world has become the kingdom of our Lord and of His Christ".'[102] In the same issue, the British independent David Matthew argued: 'The old man of godless society is cracking up as God's new man flexes his muscles ready for the takeover. And as we rise together, glowing with the life and vigour of God himself, a sinking world will exclaim, "Behold, the Man"...'.[103] Within the *Restoration* milieu there was some eschatological vagueness, described retrospectively by Matthew as 'amillennialism with postmillennialist leanings'.[104] Overall, they

[101] Bryn Jones, 'Editorial', *Restoration*, 1/4 (September–October 1975), 1.
[102] Ern Baxter, 'Taking the nations', *Restoration*, November–December 1977, 19–20.
[103] Matthew, 'Behold', 8.
[104] David Matthew, 'Restorationism in British Church life: an insider's view' (online).

increasingly took inspiration from Ern Baxter's teaching on the kingdom but drew also from the mid-century neo-Puritan resurgence in Britain which had been superintended by the Welsh preacher Martyn Lloyd-Jones, whose preaching on Ephesians and revivalism tended to suggest a hopeful future for the Church.[105] British independents such as Peter Parris and Terry Virgo had been influenced by Lloyd-Jones' preaching. It is notable that Iain Murray's 1971 study *The Puritan Hope* was recommended reading to leaders being trained in Bradford.[106]

In 1976, a proposal came from Fort Lauderdale. It was suggested that to heal the divisions between British apostles, each would submit to Wallis who in turn would come under the covering of an American.[107] This was not agreed, even though Bryn Jones was initially favourably inclined. In the same year, during a visit to Britain Ern Baxter appeared to support Jones and Wallis. This helped consolidate their position in the restorationist scene. However, despite the influence of Baxter and Mumford's teaching, according to Andrew Walker, a sociologist of British restorationism, Jones came to the view that Britain should not become 'merely the satellite of American interest'.[108] There was a hint of spiritual nationalism but likely the view reflected a difference of ecclesiological emphasis. Compared to CGM, which had very close links with Roman Catholic charismatics, the *Restorationist* milieu was more overtly sceptical of old wineskin denominations. 'God never intended that we should spin around without purpose on a "renewal" roundabout until Jesus comes again', asserted an article in the first edition of *Restoration*.[109] The British restorationist variety was more separatist than its American counterpart.

Another speaker at the 1978 Dales Bible week was a New Zealander, Howard J. Carter. He was Director of the Logos Foundation, a service agency which produced the magazine *Restore*.[110] The publication had its roots in the tensions between mainline and independent charismatics in the New Zealand scene. In 1969, the Christchurch-based magazine *Logos* took a sharp change in direction

105 William K. Kay, 'Martyn Lloyd-Jones's influence on pentecostalism and neo-pentecostalism in the UK', *Journal of Pentecostal Theology*, 22 (2013), 275–94.

106 Matthew, 'Restorationism'; on *The Puritan hope*, see James Martin Scott, 'The theology of the so-called "new church" movement: an analysis of the eschatology', MA thesis, Brunel University, 1997. Murray was a close ally of Lloyd-Jones.

107 Andrew Walker, *Restoring the Kingdom: the radical Christianity of the house church movement* (Guildford: Eagle, 1998), 99–100.

108 Ibid., 101.

109 'From "renewal" to "restoration": clichés or Scripture?', *Restoration*, 1/1 (March–April 1975), 5.

110 On Carter, see Mark Hutchinson, 'Reframing Howard Carter: alternative "routes" for the emergence of the Australasian Charismatic renewal', in Cristina Rocha, Mark Hutchinson, and Kathleen Openshaw (eds.), *Australian Pentecostal and Charismatic movements: arguments from the margins* (Leiden: Brill 2020), 25–52.

under the editorship of Paul Collins, who relocated the base of operations to the Christian Faith Centre, Sydney. While some denominational Christians, such as the New Zealanders Owen Woodfield and David Balfour, remained on the editorial board of the new magazine, the growing influence of independent pentecostals, in particular those of a Latter Rain background, such as Trevor Chandler, Kevin Connor, and Rob Wheeler, was clearly evident.[111] *Restore* developed links with King's Temple, Seattle, whose founder E. Charlotte Baker, a Canadian with Latter Rain pedigree, became an American editorial representative. Connections with CGM in Fort Lauderdale were also strong. Bob Mumford was invited to visit Australia and New Zealand in Christmas 1969, speaking at the Faith Bible School (Assemblies of God) Tauranga convention, and in 1974 Baxter came to the Christian Faith Centre.[112] Under Carter's directorship, the Logos Foundation headquarters moved to the Blue Mountain Christian Centre in Hazelbrook, New South Wales. This became the setting for a residential leadership course for ministers, a Home Ministry correspondence-style training course (which during that decade was taken by around two thousand people in Australia and New Zealand), a convention centre, and Restore Ministries, who produced the magazine as well as tapes and literature. The leadership of Restore Ministries was based upon a relational commitment, similar to that made by the Fort Lauderdale leaders, between the Australian and New Zealand restorationists, Carter, Collins, David Jackson, Hal Oxley, Trevor Chandler, Bob Midgely, and Bill Hawkins.[113] The relationship with Fort Lauderdale was significant: Carter, who shepherded various Australasian leaders, was submitted to the translocal covering of Baxter.[114] This connection was cemented in 1977, when *New Wine* asked readers in Australia and New Zealand to subscribe instead to *Restore*, promising that their articles would be offered to Carter and his team to be published locally.[115]

From the late 1960s, independent charismatic agencies aimed at supporting the 'church in the home' had expanded. Overlaps with mainliners remained, but as the restorationists enlarged their infrastructure and resources, signs of strains between the two groups appeared. As we have seen in the case of British restorationism, not all roads led to Fort Lauderdale. However, the translocality of independent networks, built simultaneously upon convictions about the local church and the universal significance of the eschatological moment, was an important feature.

[111] Wheeler, for example, gave teaching on the feast of tabernacles. See 'The feast of tabernacles', *Logos*, 3/3 (1969), 2–3, 19, quote at 19.

[112] Bob Mumford, 'The whole Christ', *Logos*, 4/1 (1970), 2–3, 10; Advert, *Logos*, 3/2 (September 1969), 22

[113] 'Echoes of the Spirit', *New Wine*, September 1975, 23.

[114] Howard Carter, 'A personal letter', *Restore*, March 1979, 2; Moore, *Shepherding*, 147.

[115] JKTL, Cecil T. Marshall papers, ANG178, series 1, item 2, 'Importance notice'.

'God Has Called and Anointed Us': The South Bend–Ann Arbor Cockpit and Varieties of Catholic Charismatic Renewal

By 1973, Cardinal Léon Joseph Suenens was the leading patron for charismatic renewal in the Roman Catholic hierarchy. From Belgium he was aware the location of power in this movement was in the United States. According to one recollection, he once instructed American leaders not to be 'self-conscious about the role that the Lord has placed [you] in'. Just as Europe's religious orders had evangelised North America, so now the reverse was true and even more so: American Catholic charismatics were having worldwide influence.[116] Since 1967 the cockpit for the translocal mediation of Catholic charismatic renewal was the small, upper Midwest university cities of South Bend and Ann Arbor. The pilots for this operation had been involved in Cursillo networks. They were distinctive in their intellectual weight; for example, in Ann Arbor Steve Clark was a former Fulbright Scholar who had undertaken doctoral studies at Yale and would produce *Confirmation and "Baptism in the Holy Spirit"* (1969); and Fr. Edward O'Connor, who wrote *The Catholic Pentecostal Movement* (1971), was a professor of theology at Notre Dame. Their texts, along with the Ranaghans' *Catholic Pentecostals*, made a powerful contribution to the renewal.

The energies for Catholic charismatic ministry in the United States came from three communities: The Word of God (1970) in Ann Arbor, and True House (1971) and the People of Praise (1971) in South Bend. What became Charismatic Renewal Services (CRS) began with the decision in 1969 to establish a communications centre, including a print and tape ministry, in South Bend. The communities here were responsible for organising the annual international conferences which took place at Notre Dame annually from 1967. In 1970 this was attended by 1,500 and three years later the figure was around 22,000.[117] The other branch of CRS was in Ann Arbor, where The Word of God (TWOG) organised conferences for leaders of prayer groups nationwide, produced a pastoral newsletter which in 1971 became *New Covenant* (it increased its subscribers from 1,000 to 11,000 in the next year), and ran Word of Life publishing.[118] TWOG created the *Life in the Spirit*, a course which initiated Christians into charismatic spirituality. It sold 70,000 copies by early 1975.[119] CRS became a non-profit corporation in 1971. Its commitment to distribution of media was total. The steering committee for CRS

[116] 'The Great Catholic Charismatic Explosion', *Logos Journal*, 7/2 (March–April 1977), 6–14, quote at 7.

[117] Valentina Ciciliot, 'The origins of the Catholic Charismatic Renewal in the United States: early developments in Indiana and Michigan and the reactions of the ecclesiastical Authorities', *Studies in World Christianity*, 25/3 (2019), 250–73, at 258

[118] Editorial, *New Covenant*, 1/12 June 1972, inside cover.

[119] Mary Ann Jahr, 'An ecumenical Christian community: the word of God, Ann Arbor, Michigan', *New Covenant*, 4/8 (February 1975), 4–8. On *Life in the Spirit* see this book, 143.

asserted in 1974 a holy ambition: 'to move forward aggressively in sales and service to the charismatic renewal and to the church as a whole'.[120] By 1977, CRS brought in an estimated revenue of between two and three million dollars.[121]

In 1970, a Catholic Charismatic Renewal Services Committee (CCRSC), later known as the National Service Committee, had also been established. This had oversight of the CRS—becoming its board of directors the following year. At the meeting of incorporation in February 1971, the CCRSC consisted of Jim Byrne (South Bend), Clark (Ann Arbor), Bert Ghezzi (Grand Haven), Fr. George Kosicki (Detroit), Ralph Martin (Ann Arbor), O'Connor (South Bend), and Kevin Ranaghan (South Bend).[122] It sought to liaise with the American hierarchy and in 1971 appointed Joseph McKinney, Auxiliary Bishop of Grand Rapids, as episcopal adviser.[123] The influence of the CCRSC on the direction of renewal was marked. It controlled, as we have seen, a vast media operation. As CCRSC expanded and integrated leadership from other parts of the country, CRS was restructured to include two representatives from the CCRSC, TWOG, and People of Praise. These changes meant the CCRSC and CRS still overlapped, and the Ann Arbor and South Bend personnel maintained a significant stake in both.[124] The CCRSC determined who spoke at international and national gatherings and published their addresses and prophecies in *New Wine*, underlining the sense that these conferences were authoritative. At one meeting of the Committee, it was commented that the group of men had a role which was 'more than a mere liaison and less than a corporate philosopher king'.[125] There was a sense of responsibility for the entire direction of renewal amongst Catholics; and with the tools and the leadership experience at their disposal the Committee was aware of an 'intrinsic authority'.[126] As Catholic prayer groups increased in number, the Committee sought to cultivate stability and pastoral responsibility in local gatherings; there were concerns, for example, about groups which they regarded as 'wild' and which allowed 'no outside teaching'.[127] Importantly, although the CCRSC was committed to advancing renewal within the Catholic Church, its orientation was largely Catholic-ecumenical.[128] This was a reflection of the model operated by People of Praise and TWOG, who were both open to all denominations. *New Covenant* was strongly ecumenical (Larry Christenson, David du Plessis, and Michael Harper were contributing editors) drawing on contributions from a whole range of charismatic voices, including denominational leaders and the radical

[120] SiS, CCRSC minutes, Steering committee of the CRS board of directors,18 June 1974.

[121] Kody Sherman Jackson, 'Jesus, Jung and the charismatics: the Pecos Benedictines and visions of religious renewal', MA thesis, University of Texas, 2016, 140.

[122] SiS, CCRSC minutes, 5 February 1971.

[123] SiS, CCRSC minutes, 16 August 1971.

[124] On the structure of the CRS, see Cindy Conniff, 'Charismatic renewal services', *New Covenant*, 4/9 (March 1975), 24–27.

[125] SiS, CCRSC minutes, Memo from George Martin, 16 July 1970.

[126] SiS, CCRSC minutes, 21 June 1971.

[127] SiS, CCRSC minutes, 16 August 1971.

[128] 'Service committee issues ecumenical statement', *New Covenant*, 3/6 (January 1974), 19–20.

independents at Fort Lauderdale. The latter were particularly influential amongst the Catholics. Derek Prince and Don Basham popularised deliverance ministry during a visit to Ann Arbor in 1970; and a commonality in shepherding practices emerged, particularly concerning 'covenanted' relationships and traditional ideas of gender and family life.[129] The influence was two-way: Derek Prince believed that Catholic communities were teaching Protestants to forsake individualism.[130] TWOG's *Life in the Spirit* course was used widely by Protestants also. The South Bend/Ann Arbor approach was replicated widely.

The CCRSC was increasingly aware of their international influence. Closest to home, in 1972 when proposals appeared for a Canadian conference the Americans took a keen interest in checking whether the leadership and direction were sound.[131] Further afield, the popularity of its media established an informal translocal authority. Correspondents from Australia described *New Covenant* as 'sharper than a two-edged sword'; claiming 'hardly a day has passed in recent weeks when we have not heard of yet another religious being deeply moved by *New Covenant*'.[132] When Kevin Ranaghan visited Australia for CRS in 1973, he found Catholics in Perth had 'a library of just about every tape that we have ever put out'.[133] Formal relationships were established with distribution centres in London and Brisbane. Reel-to-reel master tapes were sent from South Bend to be recorded and distributed locally, and *New Covenant* was delivered in bulk by air freight.[134] These flows of media increased demands for visits by authors; for example, Ralph Martin visited England in 1972 and the Ranaghans, as we have seen, toured Australia and New Zealand the following year. Where they found kindred spirits with similar values, close and lasting connections were established. In the early 1970s, the CCRSC believed Australia was the most promising non-American location for renewal. They developed a relationship with Brian Smith, the lay leader of the lively Catholic-ecumenical Friday night meeting in Bardon, Brisbane. Smith was regarded as a 'stable' and pastorally responsible leader and was invited to write in *New Covenant*. His standing with the CCRSC made him an obvious choice to chair a National Advisory Group for Australian renewal, set up in 1973. The growing web of relations between CCRSC and Catholic leaders around the world had led to the formation of an International Communications Office, run by Ralph Martin of TWOG, in 1972. This was intended as a mechanism for maintaining global links, keeping track of developments abroad, and

[129] Jahr, 'Ecumenical'.

[130] Derek Prince, 'The church of the seventies', *New Covenant*, 4/3 (September 1974), 10–11.

[131] SiS, CCRSC minutes, 25 April 1972.

[132] Letter from Joan Lewis and Brian Smith, *New Covenant*, 2/5 (November 1972), 21.

[133] UNDA, James E. Byrne papers, Service Committee correspondence 1970–1973, Kevin and Dorothy Ranaghan, 'The Ranaghans' trip to New Zealand and Australia'.

[134] Ibid.

disseminating media. As Chapter 6 describes, it would also become an instrument for the integration of charismatic renewal with the Curia.[135]

Some were critical of the influence wielded by the CCRSC. One priest in Pennsylvania, for example, made comparisons between the American committee and the Curia (indeed, Ann Arbor was often referred to as 'the charismatic Vatican').[136] In 1973, the CCRSC was hit by the resignation of Fr. O'Connor over the influence of the covenant communities and the danger he perceived that prayer group leaders read *New Covenant* as if it had 'something approaching infallibility'. Josephine Massyngberde Ford, another professor of theology at Notre Dame, came into disagreement with members of the CCRSC, whom she described as an 'oligarchy' imposing 'one pattern of leadership'—that of South Bend and Ann Arbor—on Catholic charismatic groups. She believed that the CCRSC was establishing a network of charismatic communities with a 'fully established para-ecclesial structure' and a 'corpus of "tradition"' derived from pentecostal theology, including emphasis on personal salvation, *glossolalia*, deliverance, and a tendency to exclude those not living to prescribed standards.[137] These criticisms are explored in the next chapter. For some, the concentration of power in the CCRSC—and by extension Ann Arbor and South Bend—risked a distortion of the Spirit's work in the Catholic Church.

An influential Catholic alternative, however, was 'the world's first Pentecostal monastery' in Pecos, New Mexico. Our Lady of Guadalupe had faced bankruptcy in the late 1960s, a demise which presented an opportunity for charismatic monks at Benet Lake monastery, Wisconsin. In 1969, having experienced tensions with brothers who were unconvinced by their charismatic piety, they relocated to Pecos to establish a charismatic retreat centre, led by David Geraets, O.S.B. They established a highly successful programme of retreats, a newsletter *The Pecos Benedictine* which soon had 60,000 readers, and Dove Publications, which by 1977 had sent out over a million pamphlets.[138] Charismatic renewal, it was argued, was 'nothing less than a renewal in mysticism—the direct experience of God's personal presence in the life of His people'.[139] Readers of the newsletter found a holistic approach to spirituality which integrated teaching on the charismatic gifts with articles on diet, exercise, and creative practices—including controversial approaches such as eurhythmy, a movement-centred approach to experiencing the Spirit which had past links with Rudolf Steiner and anthroposophy.[140] The New Mexico service agency was not set up in opposition to the CCRSC—indeed

[135] SiS, CCRSC minutes, 25 April 1972. [136] Cited in Ciciliot, 'Origins', 256.

[137] Josephine Massyngberde Ford, 'Neo-pentecostalism with the churches', *The Ecumenist*, 13/3 (1975), 33–36, quote at 33. For 'oligarchy' description, see Josephine Massyngberde Ford, *Which way for Catholic Pentecostals* (New York: Harper & Row, 1976), viii.

[138] Jackson, 'Jesus', 28–29. [139] Ibid., 101. [140] Ibid., 28–29, 257–58.

they were to be offered representation on the Advisory Committee—but the renewal ethos which radiated from Pecos appeared more liberal.[141]

As Catholic Charismatic renewal spread in the 1970s beyond the United States, national organising committees and newsletters or magazines were established. *New Covenant*, *Life in the Spirit*, and the Notre Dame conference ensured the translocal dominance of South Bend and Ann Arbor; however, not all were fully convinced by their approach. The flavour of renewal evident in *Day of Renewal* (later *Goodnews*), published in England from 1972, was rooted in Catholic spirituality and psychological approaches to inner healing. It said almost nothing about shepherding and submission, gender roles, or deliverance. Fr. Ian Petit O.S.B., a leading priest figure in the English renewal, had a charismatic experience while staying at the Pecos monastery.[142] While there were occasional reports of visits to South Bend and Ann Arbor, the newsletter consisted largely of talks given at conferences in different parts of England.[143] Speakers included English charismatics who did not fit the CCRSC mould, such as Fr. Simon Tugwell, an Oxford-based Dominican who was less certain of the influences coming from the United States; and those with expertise in psychological approaches, including Dr. Bernard Gilsenan and depth psychologist Dr. Frank Lake.[144] The keynote speaker at the first national conference for Catholic charismatic renewal in England in 1974 was Carol Marie Bandini, of New York City, who spoke on interpersonal relationships. *Day of Renewal* reported 'The combination of someone "spirit-filled", and an authority in her field of psychotherapy was powerful.'[145] Indeed, a distinctive of Catholic renewal in England was a greater openness to female leadership; in 1974, three out of six members of the newly formed National Service Committee were women: Sister Bernarde of the Holy Cross Convent and two laity, Lisa Reynolds and Jill Bray. While media from the upper Midwest had an important role in cultivating initial awareness of Catholic renewal, the case of England indicates also local and national distinctiveness.

'Jets and Cassettes': Translocal Fellowship in the Spirit

Service agencies and their flows of media and people sustained the charismatic imaginary. International hubs of renewal were often small cities, towns, and

141 Ibid., 225. 142 'Harrogate Day of Renewal', *Day of Renewal*, November 1972, 5.

143 Mark White, 'Reflections on a visit to Ann Arbor's "Word of God" community', *Goodnews*, December 1975, 8.

144 See for example, Peter Hocken, 'Prayer groups, Christian community and world transformation', *Day of Renewal*, March 1973, 1–3; Dr Berard Gilsenan, 'Psychology and religion', *Day of Renewal*, July 1973; *Goodnews*, February–March 1977, 10. On Tugwell's views, see Peter Hocken, 'Baptism in the Holy Spirit: a spiritual and theological journey', in Eric Nelson Newberg and Lois E. Olena (eds.) *Children of the calling: essays in honor of Stanley M. Burgess and Ruth V. Burgess* (Eugene: Wipf & Stock, 2014), 298–310.

145 'Report on the Fruit of the Spirit conference', *Day of Renewal*, November 1974, 3–4, at 4.

villages in which agencies were based: for example, South Bend, Ann Arbor, Pecos, and Fort Lauderdale in the United States; Bradford and Chard in England; and Hazelbrook in New South Wales. Together, the various networks, relationships, and media, which moved across mainline, independent, and pentecostal expressions, constructed the charismatic Spiritscape. Harnessing deterritorialising media technologies and new and affordable air routes, service agencies shaped eschatological imaginations, spiritual practices, and patterns of ministry. They also created the pluralities within the larger whole: a 'Spiritscape of Spiritscapes' which included orientations towards 'renewal' or 'restoration', contrasting conservative and liberal charismatic articulations, and reterritorialized local and national expressions.

The translocalism of charismatic renewal was also at the more fundamental level of Spirited bonds of impartation, feeling, and relationality. The significance of media and its interrelationship with the senses and experience means that Birgit Meyer's notion of aesthetic formation—'the affective power of images, sounds, and texts over their beholders'—lends itself to the charismatic renewal of the long Sixties and after.[146] Magazines, for example, did not only impart knowledge. Brian Casebow, a Scottish Presbyterian minister, described how in 1962, after a Sunday evening service 'reading TRINITY in my study quite alone when on a sudden impulse I went down on my knees and immediately the experience was mine'.[147] *New Wine* offered a spiritual techne, the 'Anointed prayer page', to be touched for 'Deliverance for your needs, family, infirmities and bondage'.[148] The sound of cassettes in prayer groups (sometimes actually described as 'Tape-fellowship' meetings) compressed space and time: 'may God bless you richly, as His Holy Spirit speaks to you' read the strapline of the Blessed Trinity Society tapes catalogue.[149] The immediacy of cassette recordings mediated experiences. One New Zealand clergyman in a letter to Michael Harper in England described how when listening to a recording at a prayer meeting, the participants 'felt the presence of the Lord and a mild anointing'.[150] Video added a new sensory impact and was celebrated as a unique medium for impartation of anointing. The filming of teaching sessions by Christian Growth Ministries apparently meant 'the benediction is only the beginning' before the Spirit continued to work as they were distributed more widely.[151] One article in *New Wine* described video cassette

[146] Birgit Meyer, 'Introduction: from imagined communities to aesthetic formations: religious mediations, sensational forms, and styles of binding', in Meyer, *Aesthetic formations: media, religion, and the senses* (New York: Palgrave Macmillan, 2009), 1–28, at 6.

[147] Revd. Brian C. Casebow, 'The joy of His presence', *Trinity*, 2/2 (1962–63), 40–41.

[148] 'Anointed prayer page', *New Wine*, November 1969, 24.

[149] DAHL, Jean Stone and Rick Willans papers, box 1, file 11, Trinity Tapes, 1. On 'tape-fellowship' see JKTL, Cecil T. Marshall papers, ANG178, 1/15, Marshall to Ray Muller, 10 June 1966.

[150] LPL, Michael Harper papers, 1967/32, Ray Muller to Harper, 30 August 1967, 19–21.

[151] 'Entering a new era', 12–13.

players as 'electronic Philips' to 'meet the Ethiopian eunuchs who desperately wait in the desert'.[152] Spiritual power was moving across borders.

Conferences were portals for experiences of spiritual power. Printed texts and audio recordings paved the way for visits by international speakers. Their teachings could seem to clarify or validate experiences and practices already occurring locally. In New Zealand, a former Massey University student recalled listening to Don Basham's teaching on deliverance and thinking, 'we had been doing that kind of thing without knowing what it was.'[153] The translocal nexus of service agencies allowed charismatics to fetishise ministries which might impart an anointing or message for a particular *moment*. 'Praise the Lord for both of you, for your wonderful ministry', wrote the Australian David Balfour to Michael Harper in 1967, 'the time was so right for your visit and you helped so much to clarify things.'[154] International speakers allowed conference goers to tap into what God was doing elsewhere. When Ann Arbor's Ralph Martin visited Brisbane early in 1975, an observer described palpable excitement as he stepped up to the microphone and 'Now the expectation became a reality':

> Was it going to be another "Juan Ortez" – "Bob Mumford" or perhaps a Derek Prince type teaching on "Romans". No! Ralph Martin was here to give of himself and speak about us and what we must be moving on to as God's Spirit moves throughout the world.[155]

The impact of Ern Baxter on British restorationists in 1975 was such that decades later Terry Virgo recalled how the Canadian 'showed us' that God was raising an army. 'The power of the Holy Spirit was on him', Virgo claimed. The tapes 'went buzzing around the nation' and 'everyone was saying "have you heard Ern Baxter on the King and his army"'.[156] International visits promised spiritual breakthroughs and prophetic insights.

'The present generation of Christians stands at the end of nearly two thousand years of the Church's existence. Two millennia of fragmentation. But now we have radio, television, tape recorders, telephones, motorways and jets. For the first time ever, the saints of God are able to know each other on a worldwide scale.'[157] The enthusiasm of this British house church leader testified to a wider charismatic assumption, held explicitly or implicitly, that the eschatological moment was

[152] Donald Widmark, 'A concept whose time has come…', *New Wine*, January 1972, 24.

[153] Ken Harrison interview.

[154] LPL, Michael Harper papers, 1967/2, Revd. David Balfour to Harper, 26 September 1967, 2.

[155] Ray Stewart, 'Ralph Martin in Brisbane', *National News* (Australia), 3/2 (February 1975), 8–9, at 8.

[156] Terry Virgo, 'The Story so Far', Stoneleigh Bible Week. https://www.youtube.com/watch?v=nd79zP1VIuQ (accessed 26 March 2020).

[157] Matthew, 'Behold', 8.

being served providentially by technological developments. These words bring out another vital dimension: the possibility of *knowing* those from elsewhere. As we will see again in Chapter 6, bonds of affection were formed not only by the aesthetics of media but by travel and personal communication (particularly airmail in the early years of renewal). What charismatic renewal lacked in structures, it made up for in relationality. As the Spirit moved throughout the world a fellowship in the Spirit was being established.

5
Body

> All the believers were one in heart and mind. No one claimed that any of their possessions was their own, but they shared everything they had.
>
> Acts 4:32

On the streets of Belfast in 1971, the Revd. Cecil Kerr encountered a group of young American men from Houston, Texas. The Church of Ireland chaplain of Queen's University had bumped into members of Church of the Redeemer. 'Redeemer' was an Episcopalian congregation committed to bringing a Spirit-filled, communitarian model of mission, social engagement, worship, and ministry to the wider Church. Kerr was intrigued by their conversation. He decided to visit Houston, where he met the Rector, Graham Pulkingham (Fig. 5.1), and forthwith invited him to speak in Northern Ireland. The result was the formation of an early morning small group for students, which became a prayer meeting attracting both Protestants and Catholics. Kerr and his wife Myrtle subsequently felt a prophetic call to establish a community for renewal, intercession, and reconciliation. The Christian Renewal Centre was established in Rostrevor in 1974 involving Anglican, Presbyterian, Methodist, and Roman Catholic participants, some of whom were committed to living together for a year or more. From this setting both the North and South of Ireland were visible. It was contested country. Later, in 1979, at nearby Warrenpoint, eighteen British soldiers were killed in a Provisional Irish Republican Army ambush. The ministry of the Centre included local prayer meetings (one such gathering, in a bombed-out hotel, was apparently once visited by an army patrol mystified to find Protestants and Catholics worshipping together) and a wider ministry of reconciliation on the island.[1]

The story of Kerr and his ministry offers a way in to a discussion of the gathered expressions of charismatic renewal. Prayer groups, in the words of one American Catholic, were the 'building blocks – the "living stones" – of the charismatic renewal'.[2] As we have already seen, these often displayed a significant

[1] Cecil Kerr, 'A beacon of hope in Ireland', *New Covenant*, 7/5 (November 1977), 10–12.

[2] Bert Ghezzi, 'Prayer groups: source of spiritual renewal', *New Covenant*, 5/8 (February 1976), 4–7, at 6.

Age of the Spirit: Charismatic Renewal, the Anglo-World, and Global Christianity, 1945–1980. John Maiden, Oxford University Press. © John Maiden 2023. DOI: 10.1093/oso/9780198847496.003.0005

Fig. 5.1 The Revd. Graham Pulkingham, in full flow.

pan-denominational breaking down of barriers. From the late 1960s, furthermore, there appeared increasingly communal expressions of charismatic renewal. The Christian Renewal Centre was a particularly radical example—but there were many others, responding to a whole variety of local situations. Charismatics sought to display authentic Christian love and community during a time of religious and cultural crises. This chapter shifts emphasis from flows towards *forms*. As individuals experienced Spirit baptism and tapped into charismatic subculture, it examines the question what forms did 'New Testament Christianity' take on the ground? As we consider this we will adopt, as many charismatics did, the Apostle Paul's multi-variant metaphor of the Church as body. The renewal involved experimentation with the functioning of this body, for example, lay roles, exercise of authority, spiritual gifts, gender roles, and practices of worship and creativity. The new Pentecost outpouring of the Spirit on all people had profound ecclesiological implications. Disagreements over Christian initiation and different approaches to renewal—mainline, independent, and pentecostal—came more sharply into focus. In examining these charismatic forms, we continue to do so from a translocal perspective. Christ's body, after all, was imagined as local and global.

'The Body Is Not the New Church Buildings Going Up All Over Suburbia': Prayer Groups

'Daily around the world we witness a remarkable work of God in the central function and chief instrument of the charismatic renewal: the prayer meeting.' Since the beginning of the renewal, Jim Cavnar asserted, these groups had 'been spontaneously adopted as the natural vehicle'.[3] We have already come across them in various guises: rural cottage meetings in New Zealand, a group in a Transvaal mining town, suburban prayer fellowships in South California and Florida, university groups at Yale, Notre Dame, Cambridge, and Massey. The common environment for prayer groups, however, was suburbia. This reflected changing patterns of population distribution and church planting and construction.[4] For Charles P. Schmitt, writing in *New Wine*, prayer groups were the new wineskins in which Spirit-filled Christians could minister to each other.[5] Meeting on a weekday, these gatherings often had an indeterminate ecclesiological status—although in the early years of renewal this ambiguity did not seem to matter. Some prayer groups remained committed to the renewal of denominations, others evolved into independent fellowships of various kinds, while still others 'blew up' or disintegrated before there was a chance to decide. What they had in common was a claim of primitive Christian authenticity. 'The Body is not the new church buildings going up all over Suburbia', argued a writer in *Trinity*.[6] Prayer groups were seen as the antithesis of the pristine new buildings of the church boom and Berton's 'comfortable pew'. The distinctive devotional, epistemological, relational, and sensorial dimensions of charismatic prayer meetings opened a new mode of everyday Christianity.

As has been found more broadly within so-called 'pentecostal' varieties of Christianity the 'biblical *locus classicus*' of charismatic prayer groups was the Christianity of the Book of Acts.[7] There was also frequent reference to the Epistles, not least 1 Corinthians 14:26–33 and the Apostle Paul's instruction 'When you come together, each one has a hymn, or a word of instruction, a revelation, a tongue or an interpretation.' In an early description of a prayer group, Dennis Bennett spoke of an 'ancient type of prayer meeting' of the 1 Corinthians 14 type. They were marked by informality and flexibility to the Spirit's leading (though Bennett also emphasised that those attending could

[3] Jim Cavnar, 'Worship in prayer meetings', *New Covenant*, 2/5 (November 1972), 10–12, 29, at 10.

[4] Bill J. Leonard, 'Dangerous and promising times: American religion in the post-war years', in Stephen Stein (ed.), *The Cambridge history of religions in America* (Cambridge: Cambridge University Press, 2009), 16.

[5] Charles P. Schmitt, 'New wine in new wineskins', *New Wine*, 1/1 (June 1969), 1, 5–6, 14–15, at 6.

[6] 'The Holy Spirit and the ecumenical movement', *Trinity*, 1/2 (1961–62), 50–51, at 50.

[7] Edmund J. Rybarczyk, 'New churches: pentecostals and the Bible', in John Riches (ed.), *The new Cambridge history of the Bible* (Cambridge: Cambridge University Press, 2015), 591.

equally delight still in the 'highly-structured and formal' services of Sunday worship).[8] 'How beautifully all the pieces fall together!', argued another writer, when a gathering was 'pliable and flexible to HIS MIND as revealed through His various members'.[9] About a decade later, Kevin Ranaghan described how the 'shockingly different' aspect of prayer meetings, in comparison with other Catholic meetings and sodalities, was that they were 'a voluntary grouping of people who came together to praise God, spontaneously and out loud'.[10] Spontaneous responses to the Spirit's presence, freedom, and power were a primary characteristic.

Of course, consciously unprompted worship still negotiates its own underlying ritual structures over time. While the sequences of prayer meetings varied from group to group, the following main components were normally present. The first was praise. 'Praise the Lord'—or 'PTL'—was a catchphrase or 'pass code' often associated with prayer meetings.[11] 'More than a slogan, it is the heart of the activity of the prayer group', argued the Ranaghans.[12] A joyful atmosphere was cultivated by singing. An article 'How to Start a Home Prayer Group' explained 'we know of no better way to start a meeting of believers than to swing into thanksgiving and praise in song and in prose with every believer present participating.'[13] Praise led God's people into his presence. Initially, music consisted of existing hymns and gospel songs but over time, as we shall see in the next chapter, new repertoires appeared. The role of leading worship—or music ministry—began to emerge, not only to discern what might be sung, but because it was necessary that someone had 'specific responsibility to start songs at a singable pitch'.[14]

Meetings were interspersed with times of prayer and intercession, testimony, and operation in the spiritual gifts. The latter often involved the practice of silence: 'waiting on God'. Despite the preference for spontaneity, it was also held that body ministry in the supernatural gifts required this be in balance with order. 'The only rule of the house is that there be order and everyone speak in turn', was a description of one prayer meeting.[15] A Church of Scotland minister spoke of 'orderly freedom in the interpersonal ministry of visions, prophecy, words of knowledge and speaking in tongues and interpretation'.[16] Frequent reminders

[8] DAHL, David du Plessis papers, box 99, folder 11, Dennis Bennett, 'When Episcopalians start speaking in tongues', pamphlet.

[9] Schmitt, 'New wine', 14.

[10] Kevin Ranaghan, *The Lord, the Spirit and the Church* (Ann Arbor: Word of Life, 1973), 20.

[11] John O'Neill, 'Charismatic renewal and its spirituality', *The Furrow*, 25/11 (November 1974), 599–603.

[12] Kevin and Dorothy Ranaghan, *Catholic Pentecostals* (New York: Paulist Press, 1969), 233.

[13] George and Harriet Gillies, 'How to start a home prayer group', *New Wine*, 2/3 (April 1971), 12–15, at 13.

[14] John Pippenger, 'Music at prayer meetings', *New Covenant*, 2/2 (August 1972), 17.

[15] Ranaghans, *Catholic Pentecostals*, 233.

[16] Quoted in Gordon Strachan, 'Pentecostal worship in the Church of Scotland', part 2, *Liturgical Review*, November 1973, 34–47, at 42.

of the necessity of order and edification sometimes reflected anti-pentecostal stereotypes and criticism; however, they were also a practical, preventative measure to avoid a spiral into a spiritual free-for-all. In the case of *glossolalia*, Dennis Bennett stipulated a public tongue should occur without 'emotional build-up' and would not be 'gibberish' but 'clearly recognizable as a language and inspiring to the hearers, even though not directly understandable'. From this should follow interpretation by another, often in 'flowing and beautiful English, beyond the ordinary ability of the person speaking'. Another person might confirm they had received the same interpretation.[17] In 1968, Michael Harper observed a trend of groups speaking in tongues in concert, without interpretation. This, he argued, disobeyed Paul's command in 1 Corinthians 14:26 that '*all* things' be done for congregational edification.[18] Where prophecy was concerned (both 'words from the Lord' and tongue interpretations), the impartation of extra-biblical divine revelation often came in the language of the King James Version. The phrase 'Thus saith the Lord' could lend authority to spontaneous utterances.[19] Some frowned upon this, either because, as Michael Harper complained, it implied 'inerrancy', or as the Catholic Jim Cavnar argued, 'biblically sounding phrases, even from current translations, don't really speak to the average American.'[20] Prayer meetings opened new spaces for interpersonal sharing. With these opportunities for mutual exchange, some warned also of potential pitfalls. The prayer meeting was not a place to share 'one's psychological problems', Cavnar instructed.[21]

Prayer meetings were typically imbued with Scripture. This included, as we see in the next chapter, the singing of biblical texts. There was often emphasis on formal teaching, sometimes provided by a lay participant, or occasionally a member of the clergy, but often through audio ministry. As described already, the reel-to-reel or cassette player was the essential material object of everyday charismatic ritual. Given the novelty of their radical new perspective on the supernatural in the New Testament, for charismatics knowledgeable and authoritative teaching were at a premium. During Friday night prayer meetings at Massey University in the late 1960s, worship was followed by a teaching tape which provided instruction and inspiration for body ministry. A participant recalled students being 'hungry for the word of God' and taking notes; tapes were 'like gold... being a student was secondary'.[22] 'Tape fellowship' was translocal, with the voices of du Plessis, Bennett, Mumford, Prince, Ranaghan, Harper, and others heard widely in small groups. In cases of less formal Bible study formats there was a diversity of approaches. In Auckland, some groups engaged

17 Bennett, 'When Episcopalians start speaking in tongues'.
18 Michael Harper, *Walk in the Spirit*, rev. edn. (Eastbourne: Kingsway 1983), 71–2.
19 Ibid.
20 Jim Cavnar, 'Sharing at prayer meetings', *New Covenant*, 2/6 (December 1972), 6–8, at 7.
21 Ibid. 22 Interview with Ken Harrison.

in 'disciplined and thoughtful study, with commentaries and alternative translations' while others appeared to use verses 'culled almost at random, with a claimed relevance to the present situation'.[23] The sharing of Bible verses was a common practice, sometimes through the ritual of 'praying for a text'.[24] A result of this was often a tendency towards the atomisation of biblical verses. Engagement with Scripture, furthermore, was rarely a purely cerebral activity, as teaching was followed by participation in a time of ministry in the supernatural gifts, putatively modelled on the New Testament.

Prayer groups were settings of embodiment and relationality. They could break social and religious mores. The moment of 'receiving' the Spirit through the laying on of hands is an example; the Brisbane Catholic Brian Smith recalled of the early 1970s, 'Australian men, certainly at that time, did not lay hands on people unless it was a football match or funeral!'[25] The experiences and vulnerabilities which came with body ministry, combined with the imagined parallels between the early Church and relaxed home atmosphere, cultivated environments of warmth and camaraderie. These were fostered also in the cordial domestic ritual of tea, coffee, and biscuits. The religious practices and social dynamics of prayer meetings risked producing a sense of spiritual elitism, or at least the perception of such. Catholic charismatics in Brisbane, for example, warned against their ecumenical prayer groups becoming exclusive. They should not be 'SMOTs' ('Secret Meetings of the Saints') but open to all.[26] Where there were cliques or an inclination towards secretiveness, this could reflect genuine concerns to avoid the prejudices of other Christians, especially where individuals feared being 'put out' of their churches. Whatever the motivation, prayer groups were often marked by their intensity of fellowship.

The Body Charismatic: Variations in Prayer Meetings

There was significant variety in prayer groups. Many were ecumenical, even if they reflected the denominational character of their leaders or hosts. A Saturday night prayer meeting in All Saints, Palmerston North, for example, was based upon the Anglican Collect, Epistle and Gospel, and included prayers for the parish and clergy; however, Presbyterians, Methodists, and Roman Catholics were made

[23] JKTL, ANG 016/1/1, John Morton, 'What has happened', Commission on the Charismatic Renewal, September 1973, 3.

[24] J. Massyngberde Ford, *The Pentecostal experience: a new direction for American Catholics* (Paramus, NJ: Paulist Press, 1970), 32.

[25] Brian Smith, *Streams of living water: autobiography of a charismatic leader* (Melbourne: Comsoda Communications, 2000).

[26] N. Hayter, 'Home prayer meetings', *Newsletter (for the Catholic Charismatic Renewal)*, December 1973, 3–4.

welcome.[27] Catholic groups often drew in Protestants while maintaining aspects of their denominational distinctiveness. This could pose dilemmas. 'How do I react when my Catholic prayer group does something I don't do?', asked one Ann Arbor Lutheran. 'What do I do when confronted with a Hail Mary, the sign of the cross, a Catholic Eucharist?' The right question to ask, he argued, was not whether one agreed with the practice but 'Is it a reasonable thing for Christians to be doing?'[28] Exposure to other Christian traditions could foster an attitude of generous orthodoxy amongst fellow believers, with a common characteristic of shared commitment to Christ and the presence of the Spirit. 'The real Church is the Christians themselves, the "ecclesia," the "called-out ones", the people chosen of God', argued *Trinity*. Indeed, the author suggested, arguments over dogma might be 'evidence of unspirituality'.[29]

'We now see Catholics, evangelicals and fundamentalists sitting around the Word in a common experience of salvation to praise our Father with one voice in unity and love', wrote Kevin Ranaghan.[30] Where it occurred, the coming together of Protestant and Roman Catholic could be linked with social and religious factors. Local population movement which came with suburbanisation reduced the likelihood of Protestants and Catholics living separate lives. In New Zealand by 1970, over half of marriages in the Catholic Church were mixed—in the diocese of Wellington the figure was 66 per cent.[31] In the analysis of one historian 'Compared with the pre-war years, as a social group Australian Catholics had fewer defining social characteristics.'[32] The Second Vatican Council was a landmark for greater possibilities of interaction. Even in Sydney, where evangelical Anglican anti-Catholicism was traditionally manifest, Cardinal Gilroy in 1966 was present at the enthronement of Archbishop Marcus Loane.[33] Many evangelicals were at best ambivalent about Vatican II; however, the language of 'apostasy' and the notion of Catholicism as a product of Satanic inspiration was in decline.[34] In emerging contexts of Protestant and Catholic interaction—but even, as we have seen in the case of the island of Ireland, places of heightened sectarianism—the charismatic prayer group was a remarkable development in grassroots ecumenicity. Indeed, it was arguably the most significant since the Reformation.

The question of intercommunion—the most powerful symbol of Christian unity—raised a significant dilemma for some groups. Some Catholic-ecumenical

[27] JKTL, C. T. Marshall papers, ANG178, Series 1/15, item 15, Ray Muller to Marshall, 20 June 1966.
[28] Steve Peterson, 'Building bridges: Protestants in Catholic prayer groups', *New Covenant*, 5/7 (January 1976), 16–19, at 18, 19.
[29] 'The Holy Spirit', 50.
[30] In Kevin and Dorothy Ranaghan (eds.), *As the Spirit leads us* (New York: Paulist Press, 1971), 116.
[31] 'More mixed marriages, NZ reports', *Catholic Weekly*, 23 April 1970, 12.
[32] David Hilliard, 'The religious crisis of the 1960s: the experience of the Australian Churches', *Journal of Religious History*, 21 (1997), 209–27, at 215.
[33] Ibid., 216.
[34] John Maiden, 'Evangelicals and Rome', in Andrew Atherstone and Mark Hutchinson (eds.), *The Routledge research companion to the history of evangelicalism* (London: Routledge, 2019), 93–109.

groups adopted the practice. For example, in Silver Springs, Maryland, in the early 1970s one group enjoyed an unrestricted communion at Mass in advance of their meeting.[35] In 1972, an incident at the annual Notre Dame conference brought this issue into sharp relief. At the final worship session there was a request that Protestants should not partake in communion. The moment reverberated widely. 'In prayer groups across the country it raises a larger issue', an editorial in *New Wine* admitted. 'How are we to be ecumenical and Catholic at the same time?'[36] In Silver Springs after the announcement, the Mass was restricted. The decision was described as 'painful' and one which younger Catholic participants found it difficult to come to terms with—and which prompted some Protestants to leave the group.[37] In the north of Ireland it was said that the 'pain of separation at the Lord's table' had become 'more than words for many charismatic groups'. 'If an official breakthrough is to come on the intercommunion question it is most likely to be for groups such as these', one observer argued.[38] The sense of grief articulated by some, even if they agreed in principle with the teaching of the Church, demonstrated the commonality which had developed on the ground.

This is not to say that Catholics were not the dominant presence in many groups. A 1972 survey of 130 American Catholic prayer groups found that 64 were over 90 per cent Catholic in membership and a further 29 between 70 and 90 per cent.[39] Some Catholic groups—those less influenced by People of Praise and The Word of God—were not ecumenically minded, and more inclined towards clerical leadership and the sacraments, perhaps with Eucharist and confession available after prayer meetings.[40] A survey of Roman Catholic groups in New Zealand in the mid-1970s displayed a range of ecclesiological stances. In Christchurch (where by 1974 there were fourteen suburban prayer meetings), a group in North Beach had been 'strongly influenced by classical Pentecostalism' and had 'difficulty relating' to the Church. In contrast, a group at St Andrew's Hill consisted only of Catholic women and had no interaction with Protestants. Across the Cook Strait in Wellington, a prayer meeting in Hutt Valley was strongly ecumenical and had strained links with the local Church leadership. But, in central Wellington, several groups, consisting mainly of students and young people, were characterised by their 'entrenched conservatism, and their total embracing of traditionalist Tridentine spirituality'.[41] Catholic prayer groups varied in their theological, ecumenical, and demographic character.

[35] 'Intercommunion: a local situation', *New Covenant*, 2/9 (March 1973), 14, 17.

[36] 'From the editor', *New Covenant*, 2/2 (August 1972), inside cover.

[37] 'Intercommunion'.

[38] Jerome McCarthy, 'The charismatic renewal and reconciliation in Northern Ireland', *One in Christ*, 10/1 (1974), 31–43, at 39.

[39] J. Massyngberde Ford, *Which way for Catholic Pentecostals?* (New York: Harper & Row, 1976), 66.

[40] Ibid., 67.

[41] JMKL, ANG 016/1/2, Allen G. Neil, 'The origins, development and present extent of the Charismatic Renewal in the Church in New Zealand', Provincial Commission on the Charismatic Renewal, 1973, quotes at 24, 27.

By the 1970s charismatic renewal was producing larger local expressions of the body of Christ. In Toronto, the Catacombs prayer meeting began in the home of musicians Merv and Merla Watson, and by 1971 had 800 or more attending its three-hour Thursday night worship gatherings.[42] Some gatherings brought together multiple prayer groups; this for example, was how the large 'Dynamis' monthly Friday night meeting in Cleveland, Ohio, where 'several hundred believing Christians, mostly Spirit-baptized, [came] together to worship, pray and praise God', emerged.[43] Larger local gatherings could display ecumenical cooperation. In Christchurch in the mid-1970s, a bimonthly 'Group 70' meeting at the Roman Catholic Cathedral drew together Catholic and Anglican prayer groups. Intercommunion was practised openly.[44] In Buffalo, New York State, a Sunday night prayer meeting at Tommy Reid's pentecostal assembly was joined by a local Roman Catholic group. This more than doubled its size (to nearly 400), but produced interesting tensions, theological and social, for example as some frowned upon Catholics smoking or women wearing slacks to church.[45] The leadership dynamics of larger meetings were necessarily different to smaller gatherings. There was a greater emphasis on 'anointed' leaders and coordination of body ministry; for example, the triaging of prophetic words and other individual contributions to check their relevance to the wider group. Larger meetings offered unique experiences of communal praise, sometimes accompanied by larger musical groups. The Catacombs meeting included an hour or more of singing, drew on gifted classically trained musicians and included the use of a five-manual Casavant organ.[46] These could be powerful occasions of 'Singing in the Spirit'. In the *Toronto Star* this practice at the Catacombs was described vividly: 'They stand in silence, some with tears in their eyes, and then, as Merla chants softly in a strange language, a growing whisper sweeps up and you realize that dozens around you are "praying in tongues".'[47] Individual tongues were joining together to produce a highly pitched, otherworldly sound which was often described as harp-like or angelic. Here and elsewhere, spectacles of worship could draw large crowds.

Roman Catholics adopted new structures to maintain local unity and leadership of the renewal, using the mechanism, promoted in South Bend and Ann Arbor, of local service or core groups. An example was in Brisbane, where in the early 1970s a Friday night prayer meeting was begun in the parish of St Mary Magdalene, Bardon. The meeting came to be regarded as a 'kind of Mother

[42] Ewen H. Butler, *Canadian winds of the Spirit Canadian winds of the Spirit: holiness, pentecostal and charismatic currents* (Lexington: Emoth Press, 2018), 125–33.
[43] John D. Beckett, 'Cleveland's west side story', *New Wine*, February 1974, 14–15, at 15.
[44] Neil, 'The origins', 25.
[45] Tommy Reid (with Doug Brendel), *The exploding Church* (Plainfield, NJ: Logos, 1979), 90.
[46] Butler, *Canadian winds*, 130.
[47] "Fervent teenagers say: isn't Jesus wonderful?", *Toronto Star*, 19 February 1972, 85.

Community' for Catholic renewal in Brisbane.[48] Archbishop Francis Roberts Rush requested the service group oversee the unity of renewal as it expanded in the city.[49] They stipulated that any new prayer meetings obtain the permission of a local parish priest and take care to prevent circulation of unauthorised literature not 'in accordance with the teaching of our Mother the Church'.[50] A similar structure was proposed to the Catholics in Auckland following a visit by Kevin Ranaghan in 1973. Here, a main meeting was held in the hall of St Patrick's Cathedral and one of the core group, Fr. John McAlpine was appointed liaison with the diocese.[51] The model could maintain denominational loyalty and bring coherence to local renewal. It brought also, however, a concentration of authority.

Protestants also experimented with local unity. A well-known example in the United States was Seattle, where with the support of Dennis Bennett a prayer cell of church leaders was established from 1968. This soon included mainline Protestants, Assemblies of God (AoG) leaders, independent pentecostals, and Roman Catholics, who in 1971 organised a larger event for their churches. 'What an inspiration to see Protestants and Catholics lifting their hands, singing, and praising God together', were the sentiments of one observer. The leaders began to see themselves as members of 'one church' and some went as far as to think in terms of a city-wide eldership.[52] In Brisbane a Charismatic Minister's Fellowship became a place for interchange.[53] The AoG minister Gerald Rowland of the city's Glad Tidings Tabernacle, articulated this unity by arguing Protestants and Catholics 'need to break down the walls of isolation and come together for conversations in the spirit of Christian love'.[54] A corollary of this prizing of unity, one particularly associated with Christian Growth Ministries and *New Wine*, was the concept of the 'city-wide church'. Examples include in Kentucky, where leaders met as the 'elders in Louisville' and a pan-Christian gathering began to attract 1,400 attendees.[55] The idea that the body of Christ was co-extensive with locality rather than denominational identity was strongly advocated by Derek Prince.[56] Such teaching on trans-denominational cooperation ('the church in Seattle', 'the church in Brisbane') between prayer groups and individual mainline, independent, and pentecostal congregations, was seen as a return to a

[48] Vince and Norma Kearney, 'Brief history of CCR Bardon', in *The little church on the hill: memories of early years of Bardon Catholic Charismatic Renewal* (Self-published, n.d.).

[49] *Newsletter (for the Catholic Charismatic Renewal)*, June 1973, p. 11.

[50] Ibid., May 1973, p. 17.

[51] Neil, 'The origins', 18.

[52] Jim Hamann, 'One city one church', *New Wine*, February 1974, 25–27.

[53] 'Brisbane's first Holy Spirit seminar', *Charismatic Contact*, 2/3 (1973), n.p.

[54] Gerald Rowland, 'Catholic-Protestant relationships within the charismatic renewal', *The Evangel*, 31/11 (November 1976), 10–11. On broader tensions in the AoG in Australia, see Shane Clifton, *Pentecostal churches in transition: analysing the developing ecclesiology of the Assemblies of God in Australia* (Leiden: Brill, 2009), 143–45.

[55] Frank S. Longino, 'City government – can it work?', *New Wine*, June 1974, 15–18.

[56] Derek Prince, 'Local church: God's view vs man's view', *New Wine*, May 1973, 14–18.

New Testament model. However, there was also a more radical expression of primitivism; one which rejected existing church structures entirely.

Zacchaeus Come Down: The Restorationist Tendency

Since the earliest phase of the renewal, some within denominations—both mainline and pentecostal—found they had little choice *but* independency. Jimmy Moore, a Southern Baptist, was left without a pulpit following his baptism in the Spirit. He described feeling like a Zacchaeus in a tree 'with the limb being cut off'; but as he started to minister in local prayer groups, he came to realise that Christ was saying 'Sir, come down for I must dwell in your *house* today.'[57] Others rejected denominationalism on principle. As the Spirit moved through Episcopalian parishes in southern California from the late 1950s, the Revd. Frank Maguire in Monterey Park observed the emergence of separatist 'New Testament churches' in homes.[58] In Britain, Michael Harper and others became conscious of anti-denominationalism creeping into prayer groups and some attempts 'to re-create the apostolic church without apostles'.[59] Spirit baptism could have far-reaching ecclesiological consequences.

The experience of the Spirit could be akin to a 'conversion', in the sense of a thoroughgoing reorientation in the practice and understanding of the faith. A thorny issue was Christian initiation. An individual's charismatic experience could be so transformative that they doubted the integrity of their infant baptism. In other cases, interaction with credobaptist pentecostals or evangelicals produced a questioning of the theology of baptismal rites. An early example was that of the Revd. George Forrester and St Paul's Anglican, Bromley, south-east England. In January 1964, the Assemblies of God magazine *Redemption Tidings* mentioned an 'unusual meeting in Bromley'; a 'united Baptism service' in a local AoG church, where Forrester preached and candidates were all from St Paul's.[60] Later that year, Forrester resigned from the Church of England over infant baptism; preaching itinerantly in Full Gospel churches until his induction as pastor of the AoG congregation in Deal, Kent, in 1967.[61] Re-baptism had the potential to become divisive wherever the renewal made inroads. The issue was prevalent in Jesus People congregations, where a New Testament sensibility prompted spontaneous baptismal rites, perhaps in 'authentic' outdoor settings. In Durban, the Invisible Church, an independent hippie followship, once baptised over thirty-five denominational Christians on a beach without planning—the only requirement being

[57] Jimmy Moore, 'The church in your house', *New Wine*, January 1973, 16–19, quote at 19.
[58] LPL, Michael Harper papers, 1965/36, Frank Maguire to Harper, 3 March 1965, 1.
[59] LPL, Michael Harper papers, 1964/28, Frank Maguire to Harper, 11 November 1964, 7.
[60] 'Unusual meeting at Bromley', *Redemption Tidings*, 29 January 1964, 18.
[61] 'Induction of George Forrester', *Redemption Tidings*, 10 February 1967, 17.

that Jesus was confessed as Lord.[62] Amongst mainline charismatics one of those to oppose re-baptism was Dennis Bennett. Writing in his Seattle church newsletter in 1973 (the article was republished in *New Covenant*), Bennett spoke of re-baptism as a 'real hot issue'. 'If a person is persuaded to be "rebaptized" as a believer', he argued, 'he or she calls into question their whole church background, and the faith of their parents, their minister, and the whole validity of the Christian tradition in which they were raised.' Whether an individual's decision followed immediately from their baptism in the Spirit, or, as Bennett perceived, came during a moment of spiritual dryness subsequent to this elevated experience, re-baptism could 'destroy their witness to their denomination'.[63] Other mainline leaders expressed the same concern, and with an even sharper criticism if their co-denominationalists were re-baptised in 'Jesus' name' (rather than according to a Trinitarian formula), the practice prevalent amongst independent charismatics with a Latter Rain influence.

The re-baptism controversy was one amongst a cluster of ecclesiological tensions. As we have seen already, the fundamental status of a prayer group could become ambiguous. This was increasingly the case in the early 1970s, when there was a bubbling up of teaching on the Ephesians 4 offices of apostle, prophet, evangelist, pastor, and teacher. Some were convinced that this required a breaking down of the distinction between lay shepherds or elders (often the leader of a home fellowship) and professional clergy. With these teachings also came emphases on discipling relationships and spiritual submission or 'covering'. Derek Prince was uncompromising on the matter: charismatics needed to move on from the 'noise and shaking of the preliminary stages [of the renewal]' and 'find bone coming to bone' in order 'to find their place in the Body'.[64] This teaching was not inherently anti-denominational—networks of covering and submission could superimpose, rather than replace, existing structures of church authority. However, these discipleship teachings came amidst a growing output of literature on believer's fellowship and the problems of denominationalism. Charles Simpson argued portentously in *New Wine* in 1972, 'Personally, I believe that we are moving beyond the era of the prayer groups and into the era of the Church.'[65]

As we saw in Chapter 4, Christian Growth Ministries and *New Wine* became geared towards equipping believers' fellowships and the realisation of God's kingdom government. This reflected the changing ecclesiological situations of the 'Fort Lauderdale' men. In Alabama and Mississippi, an association of house churches, the Gulf Coast Fellowship, was established in 1972; with their most influential 'shepherds' under the covering of Charles Simpson, the Southern

[62] APCSA, Interview with Dave Lipawsky conducted by Glen Thompson, 25 May 1994.
[63] Dennis Bennett, 'An open letter on rebaptism', *New Covenant*, 3/9 (April 1974), 36–37, quote at 36. Article originally published in *St Luke's Newsletter*, 13 July 1973.
[64] Derek Prince, 'Can these bones live?', *New Wine*, January 1973, 5–10, at 10.
[65] 'Home prayer meetings', *New Wine*, October 1972, 20.

Baptist. He and others initially continued attending their traditional congregations on Sunday; however, by 1975, their home fellowships essentially functioned together as a church, gathering for a large monthly meeting.[66] In Florida, Mumford and Prince had oversight over mid-week house churches which by the mid-decade were morphing into formalised non-denominational congregations.[67] Teaching on submission through 'shepherding' was another outflow of these experiments. This had a wider impact with the organic emergence of local, regional, and even national networks of shepherds. At ground level, shepherds included prayer group leaders and others (such as youth leaders) who were accountable to another shepherd, and so on. The practice was relational—Simpson referred to it as an 'unfolding genealogy'. At the top of some of these translocal shepherding networks were CGM men.[68] To repeat, shepherding networks also involved some denominational Christians—including clergy. However, at the 1975 National Men's Shepherds Conference (overseen by CGM along with the Lutheran Larry Christenson and upper Midwest Catholics Steve Clark, Ralph Martin, Paul DeCelles, and Kevin Ranaghan), of the 4,600 shepherds present, two thirds were independent charismatics.[69] Shepherding was the backbone of many emerging independent charismatic expressions.

Often participating in these 'new paradigm' congregations were the Jesus People. A multitude of fellowships led by or catering for hippies appeared in the United States. In the Washington DC area in the early 1970s, two young Roman Catholics, Larry Tomczak and C. J. Mahaney, began to lead a mid-week prayer meeting, 'Take and Give', which soon attracted 2,000 every Tuesday night. To their frustration many converts were not settling into local churches; and in response they founded Gathering of Believers, a church which wandered around local schools and community centres and later became Covenant Life Church.[70] Various leading figures in Jesus People fellowships, such as Lonnie Frisbee (Calvary Chapel, Cosa Mesa), Scott Ross (Love Inn, New York), and Oliver Heath (Harvest House commune, San Francisco), came under the covering of senior shepherds, including Fort Lauderdale men.[71] Other independent groups emerged from Jesus People circles. In 1973, Kenn Gulliksen, a pastor at Calvary Chapel, established a home group in Cosa Mesa, California. Other likeminded groups soon appeared alongside them (hosts included the musicians Larry Norman and Pat Boone). By 1975, these met together as the Vineyard Christian Fellowship of Beverly Hills, and other church plants followed in California and elsewhere. They became known for intimate worship; and even had musicians

[66] S. David Moore, *The shepherding movement: controversy and charismatic ecclesiology* (London: T&T Clark, 2003), 59–60.

[67] Ibid., 139. [68] Quoted in Ibid., 60. [69] Ibid., 126.

[70] 'Keeping their eyes on the cross', *Washington Times*, 23 December 2002.

[71] Larry Eskridge, *God's forever family: the Jesus People movement in America* (New York: Oxford University Press, 2013), 249–50.

such as Bob Dylan, T. Bone Burnett of Rolling Thunder Revue, and Bernie Leaden, the founder of the Eagles, involved at different times. Although fellowships met together as larger congregations, Gulliksen continued to rely on mid-week home groups as a central aspect of their life.[72] The Vineyard (like Calvary Chapel) was to become a significant international movement in the 1980s; at its embryonic stage, like many other Jesus People expressions, it was a laboratory for restorationism.

In Britain, the ex-Brethren, Baptist, and independent pentecostal leaders who had gathered around Arthur Wallis from the 1960s also sought a restored Church based on the Ephesians 4 ministries. Prophesy influenced their experimentation; and these utterances situated British restorationism in a local or national context while also placing its mission in a global eschatological frame. One prophecy, for instance, warned British restorationists not to see their work as '*exclusive*', but rather to exemplify 'I am working among many... all over the earth.'[73] Amongst these groups, submission and leadership were also prominent themes—though the language of 'discipleship' and 'yoking' was often preferred to 'shepherding'.[74] Increasingly, the expectation was that local independent leaders would be 'covered', 'committed', or 'related'. Apostolic leadership was being recognised; as one leader put it in 1975, 'some of us are learning to invite foundational men into our local situations'.[75] John Noble in the south-east of England and Bryn Jones in Yorkshire were amongst the earliest apostolic figures, planting churches and taking responsibility for existing prayer groups, home fellowships, independent congregations, and Baptist churches. These networks, which often appeared to offer a charismatic Christianity unstrained by tradition, were able to attract some mainline Christians to join them.

There was no single pattern in the emergence of these British apostolic networks. The journey of Barney Coombs, a policeman turned church leader, is one example. Basingstoke Baptist church had a congregation of around 300 when in 1974 Coombs struck 'a severe blow to traditionalism' by abolishing their normal mid-week meeting. House fellowships—each subdividing as it reached twenty-five people—were formed. The leader of each group undertook their pastoring and even rites of passage. On Sundays, fellowship leaders met with Coombs and his elders, and once every month all members (of what was now Basingstoke Community Churches) met for an 'All Saints' worship gathering. Coombs was attracted to the city-wide church model advocated by Derek Prince and others. Charismatics from local traditional churches were invited to All Saints gatherings,

[72] Thomas W. Higgins, 'Kenn Gulliksen, John Wimber, and the founding of the Vineyard Movement', *Pneuma*, 34 (2012), 208–28.

[73] Dave Emmett, 'An examination of the development of a distinctive Restorationist doctrine during the years 1975–1985 and the extent of its application in the city of Manchester in recent years', (online), 7.

[74] 'Viewpoint', *Restoration* 1/1 (March–April 1975), 9–11.

[75] 'Viewpoint', *Restoration* 1/4 (September–October 1975), 16–17.

intended as an 'oasis for many who are thirsting for God's Spirit'. The leaders of 'the Church in Basingstoke', including charismatic Anglican, Catholic, Methodist, and Pentecostal clergy, met monthly. Coombs' church, which left the Baptist Union around 1977, became the Salt and Light apostolic network.[76] The Basingstoke experiment is a reminder of the fluid boundaries between mainline and independent renewal. However, the contrast between these charismatics—and the dichotomous language of 'renewal' and 'restorationism'—grew more quickly in Britain than in the United States, in part because British independents grew more explicit, sooner in their emphasis on apostleship.

In New Zealand, ex-Brethren and Baptists were similarly influential. One early independent charismatic congregation, the Palmerston North Christian Centre (PNCC), was formed after the secession of Awapuni Baptist Church from the Baptist Union in 1965. It was largely made up of Baptists and ex-Brethren, and by 1974 growth was such that it moved to a theatre.[77] In New Zealand and Australia, however, Latter Rain emphases had a more decisive impact on ecclesiological developments. In New Zealand, the independent New Life Churches (a network which PNCC joined as an affiliate) were a key grouping. Some New Life pastors, like Peter Morrow in Christchurch, encouraged Spirit-filled mainliners to return to their churches. However, most local congregations were marked by their sectarianism—Rob Wheeler in 1965 gave thanks that mainliners and pentecostals were stepping out of the 'historic' church into 'house meetings, cottage groups and so-called "Independent" groups, where Denominationalism is not recognised or desired, and where the Spirit of the Lord can continue to restore His Truths and Gifts to His People'.[78]

Latter Rain teaching also had a profound impact on the AoG in New Zealand. Queen Street, Auckland, rapidly became the largest AoG church in the country in the 1970s, gathering for multiple meetings each Sunday at the Town Hall (with seating for well over one thousand). Latter Rain practices, such as dancing in worship and singing Scripture songs, were evident; and its pastor, Neville Johnson, while maintaining his denominational accreditation, operated as an autonomous, visionary leader.[79] Similar characteristics appeared within the Australian AoG. Bob Midgely, Johnson's predecessor at Queen Street, influenced young leaders in Queensland, including Andrew Evans, the pastor of Klemzig AoG in Adelaide, and David Cartledge. The latter took on Calvary Temple, Townsville, an AoG congregation of sixty which met in a wooden hut, in 1970. He invited Midgely to preach the next year on topics such as worship and deliverance.

[76] Barney Coombs, 'It all fits together', *Restoration*, 1/2 (May–June 1975), 18–19.

[77] Brett Knowles, *The history of a New Zealand Pentecostal movement: the New Life Churches of New Zealand from 1946–1979* (Lampeter: Edwin Mellen Press, 2000), 155–57.

[78] Rob Wheeler, 'Will God revive the historic churches?', *Bible Deliverance*, April 1965, 13–15.

[79] Paul B. Harrison, 'An analytical study of the Latter Rain teachings and practices of New Zealand pentecostalism (1950–2000)', MA thesis, University of Auckland, 2009, 85–103.

Significant growth followed, including from mainliners unwelcome in their congregations. Cartledge defied the attempts of the AoG national executive to prohibit charismatic influences (dancing in worship was a particular bugbear).[80] He became editor of *Charismatic Contact*, which drew a readership of AoG and mainline Christians. Another Latter Rain influence was Frank Houston, who arrived from his large, flourishing AoG congregation in Lower Hutt, New Zealand, in 1977. Planting a church in Sydney, Houston became an advocate of strong leadership in the hands of an 'apostolic' leader and eldership.[81] During the 1970s—in which the number of New Zealand-born living in the country doubled—Latter Rain influence on the Australian Assemblies was greater than in any classical Pentecostal denomination in any other English-speaking country.[82] Outside the AoG, another product of Latter Rain influence was the highly-attended Christian Outreach Centre in Brisbane, planted in 1974 and discussed in the final chapter. In Australia, experimentation in the 'restored church' produced various prototype charismatic mega-churches which were to have a regional and global influence.

'Not Just a Parish with Renewal Downstairs': Congregational Renewal

In the early 1970s, in Morwell, the state of Victoria, the Revd. Ron Foulkes, recently baptised in the Spirit, began to explore 'exciting new vistas of spiritual opportunity'. He arrived at St Luke's Methodist Church in 1971 and soon a sizeable number of his young people had joined him in the experience of the Spirit. Through their energies, a Thursday night Bible study (Life-in-Depth), an evangelistic motorcycle club, a Sunday night meeting—held in the church's coffee house—with 'Praise, sharing and the ministry of the gifts of the Spirit', and a residential home for vulnerable young people known as the Zoe Community were established.[83] If one trajectory of prayer groups in the 1970s was towards independent fellowships, another looked towards the integration of their newly discovered 'New Testament' patterns of worship, body ministry, and leadership into their local mainline churches.

It is difficult to overestimate the significance of Church of the Redeemer, close to downtown Houston, as a contemporaneous exemplar of congregational renewal. The rector, Graham Pulkingham, had read *The Cross and the Switchblade* and was then baptised in the Spirit in 1963 after travelling to New York City to

[80] Clifton, *Pentecostal churches*, 140–51. [81] Ibid., 155–57.

[82] Alison Green, 'New Zealand migrants to Australia: social construction of migrant identity', PhD thesis, Bond University, 2007, 124.

[83] Ron Foulkes, 'Breakthrough among Methodists', *Charismatic Contact*, 2/3 (1973), n.p.

meet the book's protagonist, David Wilkerson. The spirituality and mission of his congregation was transformed. In 1963, there were about 600 confirmed communicants, mostly inactive; by 1971, 1,400 were on the church roll and over 90 per cent of those were actively involved. Over the same period, annual giving rose from 40,000 to 220,000. The emergence of 'households', as we shall see, placed a communitarian ethos at the heart of the parish. The five-fold gifts were recognised amongst the laity and decisions were often made collectively, in the guiding light of prophecy. A range of ministries were established: a coffee house, medical clinic, street mission, work with addicts, and Fisherman's Inc., which offered resources to the wider Church.[84] Sunday worship maintained an Anglo-Catholic, Eucharist-centred format, but offered liturgical space for healing, prophecy, and singing in tongues. They were marked also by acts of affection. One visitor remarked on 'the rather unconventional manner of a physical embrace – without respect to age or sex' and a Kiss of Peace which involved leaving one's seat and 'hugging friends and strangers alike'.[85] The church developed a reputation for excellence and innovation in music. As we shall see, Redeemer represented how a renewed congregation, permeated by the Spirit, might look, in the United States and well beyond.

The Church received publicity through a CBS documentary called *Following the Spirit* (1971) and Pulkingham's book *Gathered for Power* (1972). Pulkingham was also travelling widely in the Anglo-world, moving to Britain in 1972. The Church was additionally promoted through the cheerleading of Michael Harper, who visited Houston in 1965 and 1972 and then published *A New Way of Living* (1973), a journalistic account of the parish. Harper was attracted to what he witnessed on several levels. He saw solutions to the crises perceived to be facing British Christianity: 'declining manpower, shortage of money, poor deployment of resources and structural inadequacies'.[86] There was an answer to another problem he identified in the wider charismatic movement: that it was increasing in number, yet 'amorphous' and lacking a 'corporate dynamic'.[87] Harper's conservative evangelical background attuned him to a 'Bible loving' church, but which had 'escaped from the trap of "Bible worship"'—rather it was the Lord who 'speaks to and directs His people'.[88] Redeemer's approach spread through mainline congregations in the charismatic world. In Britain, *Renewal* described it in 1971 as 'probably the most go-ahead and successful charismatic church in the United States'.[89] It had a lasting impact on the inner-city Anglo-Catholic parish of St Paul's, Auckland. The priest, Fr. Kenneth Prebble, had been influenced by Dennis Bennett's visit in 1966, and three years later went to his church in Seattle, and then south to Texas, and Church of the Redeemer. After his witnessing the Houston parish, and following visits by Pulkingham to New Zealand in 1971 and 1972—as

[84] Michael Harper, *A new way of living* (London: Hodder & Stoughton, 1973), 25–41.
[85] Ibid., 132. [86] Ibid., 45. [87] Ibid., 50. [88] Ibid., 67.
[89] 'Not just lovey dovey', *Renewal*, 33 (June/July 1971), 15–16, quote at 15.

well as a longer visit by his colleague Bill Farra—St Paul's introduced spontaneous prayers in the Eucharistic service, the Kiss of Peace (with hugs, of course), the integration of folk liturgies, and shared leadership.[90]

A similar, overlapping model of congregational renewal, also Anglican, was found in York, England. Whilst Church of the Redeemer was particularly appealing to Anglo-Catholics and offered hope to parishes in socially 'challenging' environments, David Watson's ministry, at St Cuthbert's and then St Michael-le-Belfrey, provided a thoroughgoing conservative evangelical version, suited to students and a middle-class environment (Watson was the product of the Iwerne Camps, the elitist ministry for boys in England's top public schools which produced evangelical stalwarts such as John Stott and Dick Lucas). He had an experience of the Spirit and later spoke in tongues as a curate in Cambridge in the early 1960s. Watson was a gifted evangelist and St Cuthbert's, which was earmarked for closure by the Church Redundancy Commission, grew rapidly as he introduced family orientated worship, guest services, and university missions.[91] While the preaching of the Word remained central, the context for charismatic expressions moved from mid-week to Sunday meetings, where spontaneity and praise became features. Shared leadership was introduced through the appointment of elders. St Cuthbert's was outgrown and developed a reputation as a success story, with the British Broadcasting Corporation filming a Sunday meeting in 1972. The next year, Watson was invited to move to St Michael-le-Belfrey, close to the historic York Minster. Here he incorporated new music, dance (through the influence of Toronto's Merv and Merla Watson), and drama. The introduction of households, home 'area' groups, and a coffee house followed.[92] Through 'renewal weeks' for visitors and the sending out of ministry teams of gifted members of his congregation nationally and internationally, the church's formulae of Word, creative praise, evangelism, and corporate life spread. The integration of renewal and liturgy was made easier in Anglican and Episcopalian churches because of the flexibility which came with contemporary liturgical experimentations (Series III in the Church of England). Non-Anglicans, too, were influenced by York's example. Murray Robertson, the minister of Spreydon Baptist Church, Christchurch, was impacted by Watson during his 1973 mission to New Zealand. Robertson saw a glimpse of how evangelical congregational life might be renewed without incorporation of the kind of Latter Rain pentecostalism which was influential in the country. Spreydon adapted Watson's approach and became a model for other Baptist charismatic congregations.[93]

[90] Neil, 'The origins'; Don Battley, *No way back* (Auckland: Castle Publishing, 2020).

[91] See John Maiden, 'Watson, David Christopher Knight (1933–1984)', *ODNB* (online).

[92] David Watson, *You are my God* (London: Hodder & Stoughton, 1983), 74–106.

[93] Michael Reid, 'But by my Spirit: a history of the charismatic renewal in Christchurch, 1960–1985', PhD thesis, University of Canterbury (2003), 71, 314.

Alongside these Houston and York flagships were other mainline experimentations. A 1974 Lutheran national leaders' conference in the United States included discussion topics like incorporating the spiritual gifts and music in worship, developing an eldership structure, and evangelism and mission.[94] In Roman Catholic parishes, some charismatic priests promoted prayer groups; in southern California, for example, most were run by clergy, with meetings often held in the church.[95] However, in the main, Catholic congregational renewal was based on the lay organisational model whereby a group of individuals—either a prayer group or local 'community'—leavened the overall life and witness of the parish. Those parishes which went further stood out. St Patrick's, Providence, Rhode Island, became synonymous with renewal in the early 1970s, particularly following its decision to re-open the parish school (where parents and children were required to take the *Life in the Spirit* discipleship course) and the formation of a pastoral team which included lay members.[96] The motor for this transformation was a 500-strong Catholic community, many of whom lived in households modelled on Church of the Redeemer.

'Fellowship in Depth': Communities

The practice of community life entered a nadir in the 1920s. As Timothy Miller says of the United States, the fear of communism meant that existing groups adopted a 'low-profile communitarianism' before the communal 'explosion' of the 1960s.[97] However, the idea of intentional communities for the laity quietly gained traction within the churches before the wider resurgence of interest in the common life. A prominent example was the Iona Community in Scotland, established in 1938 by George MacLeod. The publication in English of Dietrich Bonhoeffer's *Life Together* (1954) proved inspirational for some. One group in the United States, which subsequently joined the New Left, involved students at the University of Texas, Austin. The Christian Faith-and-Life Community (whose founder, a Presbyterian university chaplain, W. Jack Lewis, had also visited Iona) established a covenant of common living to ease 'social and spiritual alienation'.[98] A similar search for authenticity—inspired by early Church primitivism—was

94 DAHL, David du Plessis papers, box 10, file 83, 'Lutheran Charismatic Renewal, National Leaders' Conference, 1974', leaflet.

95 Kody Sherman Jackson, 'Jesus, Jung and the charismatics: the Pecos Benedictines and visions of religious renewal', MA thesis, University of Texas (2016), 234

96 'Sixth international conference', *New Covenant*, 2/1 (July 1971), 1–5.

97 Timothy Miller, 'Religious communes in America: an overview', in Timothy Miller (ed.), *Spiritual and visionary communities: out to save the world* (London: Routledge, 2016), 197.

98 Doug Rossinow, '"The break-through to new life": Christianity and the emergence of the New Left in Austin, Texas, 1956–64', *American Quarterly*, 46/3 (1994), 309–40, at 319.

evident in the development of charismatic communities. They were sometimes a natural extension of the spirituality and fellowship of prayer groups, but they also held the promise of resolving perceived weaknesses of them. In Brisbane, Brian Smith, who founded what became the Catholic-ecumenical Emmanuel Covenant Community, identified a frustrating 'revolving door syndrome' in prayer groups.[99] Community experimentations within the body charismatic offered the promise of solidity and commitment.

Charismatic communities were shaped by a range of overlapping impulses. The early examples were primarily efforts to address pastoral and therapeutic concerns through the experience of love and spiritual growth. In Britain in 1968, the Fountain Trust announced an intention to begin a community 'where those who need it will find re-creation in faith, power and vision'.[100] Two years later, the Barnabas Fellowship in Whatcombe, Dorset, opened its doors, offering guests the experience of an extended Christian family'. Other communities offered similarly intensive pastoral care. In the early 1970s in the Georgian environs of a mansion at Lytchett Minster, Lord Thomas and Lady Faith Lees, with the assistance of the Americans Jean and Elmer Darnell, began to welcome people to live amongst them. It was an unlikely partnership. Tom Lees, his wife said, was something of a P. G. Wodehouse character and the Darnells were ministers in the Foursquare Church (Jean was for a time assistant pastor at the Angelus Temple). What later became the Post Green community was influenced by the Lees' experience of Anglican community at Lee Abbey. This was, in fact, another example of connections between charismatic renewal and the Oxford Group. Since 1946, Lee Abbey had introduced, through the influence of its first Warden, John de Pemberton, and chaplain Jack Winslow, Group practices (based on a 'house party' model) to provide spiritual refreshment, guidance by the Spirit, and spiritual unity. In the Devon coastal setting, Christians came together across boundaries; the Abbey was as likely to welcome the evangelical Universities and Colleges Christian Fellowship as it was the Anglo-Catholic Mirfield Fathers. The model was one of empowering the laity—the 'quickening of their faith' as Winslow put it—for service in church and world.[101] Post Green developed similar accents on teaching, refreshment, and empowerment, running youth camps and weekend retreats. A similar initiative was the 'un-denominational' Orama community, in Karaka Bay on the Great Barrier Island, New Zealand, founded by Neville and Dorothy Winger in 1963 as a place for 'seekers'—including addicts, the mentally ill, and those facing marital strife. By 1977, there were fifty residents, some attending rehab, others at Bible school or taking time

[99] Smith, *Streams*, 34.
[100] 'Fountain Trust: a new community', *Renewal*, February/March 1968, 11.
[101] Donald G. Bloesch, *Centers of Christian renewal* (Philadelphia: United Church Free Press, 1964), 35.

out from ministry, and others involved in the production of books and tapes.[102] Amongst Catholics, an example of a pastoral and therapeutic community was the Benedictine monastery at Pecos, New Mexico, under the leadership of David Geraets. In a relaxed atmosphere (the monks wore t-shirts and jeans), where men and women lived alongside each other, ecumenical retreats offered Jungian depth psychology for the 'inner healing' of past hurts.[103] Charismatic communities offered spiritual growth and healing.

Another impulse was mission. Here, again, the most influential model was Church of the Redeemer, and its communitarian blend of evangelism and social action. Harper's book described the Houston parish as 'a fairly typical "no go" area, where normally no viable church structures are possible' and praised Pulkingham for stopping a steady flow of Christians to the suburbs. Might a similar approach halt the decline of urban Christianity in Britain, Harper wondered? In Houston, middle-class families and singles established households near the church. These specifically cared for locals with vulnerabilities—drug addicts, the elderly, single mothers, and disabled people. The church community, Harper claimed, modelled reconciliation by 'working out the tensions and problems of racial integration' (one household was situated next to the local headquarters of the Black Panthers).[104] With each household living by its own common rule, they shared possessions and money to maximise social action and evangelistic witness. In Chula Vista, the Baptist pastor Kenneth Pagard replicated Redeemer's household approach to enable the vulnerable to 'live in an atmosphere of Christian love'.[105] Reba Place Fellowship, a community in Evanston, Illinois, which had pre-charismatic roots amongst Anabaptist-influenced students at Goshen College, came into the renewal through Pulkingham's influence. They bought up buildings in a three-block area of the city for their households, sharing a common purse based on welfare standards.[106]

Local adaptions of charismatic incarnationalism inspired by Pulkingham and Houston also appeared abroad. In the Haymarket and Surry Hills areas of Sydney, the St Francis Community, under the leadership of Alex Reichel, channelled the influence of the 'Three Francises'—Francis of Assisi, Francis de Sales, and Francis Xavier—to address issues of inner-city poverty and addiction.[107] In 1971, Charles Waldegrave, an Anglican who had been involved in the awakening at Massey University, established a community intended as a 'family for oppressed people' in

[102] 'Fellowship life', *Panorama*, December 1977, 12.

[103] Kody Sherman Jackson, 'Jesus, Jung and the charismatics: the Pecos Benedictines and visions of religious renewal', MA thesis, University of Texas (2016), 103–13, 169–72.

[104] Harper, *A new way*, 132.

[105] RUSCA, Dennis J. Bennett papers, Box 1, Scrapbook vol. 3, '"Don't quit churches", Pentecostals urged', *Minneapolis Star*, 12 August 1972.

[106] 'Reba Place fellowship', *New Covenant*, 5/1 (July 1975), 6–9.

[107] Mark Hutchinson, 'Reichel, Alex', ADPCM.

Hamilton, with a particular aim to promote racial harmony with Māori youth.[108] In East London, Cape Province, the Caring Centre, established by Derek Crumpton, worked closely with addicts and prostitutes. In 1975, Crumpton had met a Redeemer leader while visiting Post Green in England and immediately headed to Texas to find out more. On his return to South Africa, he encouraged families to move close to the Centre and the core group lived in extended households.[109] At the invitation of the Bishop of Coventry, Pulkingham and fifteen other adults and young people had moved to England in 1972, establishing themselves on a council estate. Next year, the Community of Celebration moved to Yeldall Manor, a former convent west of London. They then established an Episcopalian ministry and international community on the Isle of Cumbrae, in the west of Scotland; while another split off to settle at Post Green—which by now had taken on the Redeemer household model.[110] The collective life modelled by the Houston Episcopalians had utopian qualities appealing to young people and hippies. At least one visitor to the Isle of Cumbrae observed parallels with communism.[111] In Northamptonshire, England, a community formed out of Bugbrooke Baptist Church in 1973 was also influenced by Houston. It became known for work with young people, hippies, prostitutes, and bikers, a common bank account, its renouncing of possessions, and self-sufficiency—including pig farming.[112] There was a radical communitarian strand of charismatic renewal.

A third impulse for community living was discipleship. Roman Catholic communities became prominent advocates of long-term commitment and submission to authority. The Word of God, Ann Arbor, exemplified this. Community life, of course, was deeply rooted in the Catholic tradition; and Steve Clark and Ralph Martin, who led TWOG, had also been influenced by the discipleship methods of Cursillo. Once baptised in the Spirit they became advocates for the working out of charismatic life in the context of intentional community.[113] Another influence on TWOG, counter-intuitively, was socialism, and specifically the work of Douglas Hyde, a former Methodist and member of the Communist Party of Britain and news editor for the London *Daily Worker*, who converted to Catholicism. *Dedication and Leadership: Learning from the Communists* (1966), published by Notre Dame University, was a study of 'Communist successes and Catholic

[108] Charles and Kasia Waldegrave, 'Troubled youths and a household', *New Covenant*, 4/10 (June 1974), 12–13.

[109] Dot Mitchell, *He said yes! The story of Derek A. Crumpton* (Self-published, 2018), 221–37.

[110] 'Celebration revisited', *Renewal*, 65 (October/November 1976), 5–6.

[111] RUSCA, Dennis J. Bennett papers, box 5, Fred Hacker (Belfast) to Dennis Bennett, 19 August 1976.

[112] William K. Kay, *Apostolic networks in Britain: new ways of being church* (Milton Keynes: Paternoster Press, 2007), 151–57.

[113] Jim Manney, 'Before Duquesne: sources of the renewal', *New Covenant*, 2/8 (February 1973), 12–17.

weaknesses'. Hyde described the dedication of communists and the role of small groups in ideological formation; remarking that in contrast, 'a man may decide to become a Catholic without its ever occurring to him that the pattern of life will be transformed, that the whole of every waking day will be different because of the set of beliefs he has accepted.'[114] The book was sold through Charismatic Renewal Services and became recommended reading for community leaders.[115] Clark spoke of learning from socialist strategy, describing parallels with the attempts of the early Christians to 'gradually build their own social order while gradually working for a transformed society'.[116] This approach of building radical new societies within the existing society was seen by Clark as preferable to the Constantinian model, and as an appropriate response to de-Christianisation.[117] One chorus sang at TWOG, 'You are my God', included the line 'You give marvellous comrades to me, the faithful who dwell in this land.'[118] The priority of the Church, Clark argued in *Building Christian Communities* (1972), was to 'make it possible for a person to live a Christian life'.[119] To this end, shepherding practices were to become a key practice at TWOG.

By 1970 the core of TWOG agreed to covenant to each other. Two years later over 500 had made the commitment.[120] The community was ecumenical and by 1974 only 55 per cent were Catholic. Most continued their involvement in existing churches on Sundays but gathered in two sub-communities on Thursday nights for lively, free worship. The majority were part of households (again, based on the Houston model), either residential or non-residential, where 'mutual submission, honesty and sharing of each other's lives' found expression.[121] Joining the covenant community was not a straightforward process. Candidates were first required to spend one to two years in a 'under-way' commitment. A mechanism for initiation was the *Life in the Spirit* course, mentioned in Chapter 4, which worked through a charismatic catechumen. By 1973, this led participants through the basics of salvation, prayed for their deliverance from evil spirits, guided them into the baptism in the Spirit and yielding to tongues, and taught the reorientation of the whole self towards Christ and community. 'Normal Church life is not enough', the *Manual* explained.[122] This course was followed by another, *Foundations in*

114 Douglas Hyde, *Dedication and leadership* (Notre Dame: University of Notre Dame Press, 1966), at 5 and 39.

115 Manney, 'Before Duquesne'.

116 Steve Clark, 'Social action: strategy and priorities', *New Covenant*, 2/5 (November 1972), 7–9.

117 Steve Clark, 'The de-Christianizing of western society', *New Covenant*, 4/10 (June 1974), 18–20.

118 Bob Sutton, 'The Word of God', *New Wine*, September 1974, 9–11, at 11.

119 Steve Clark, *Building Christian communities: strategy for renewing the Church* (Notre Dame: Ave Maria Press, 1972), 20.

120 'National news', *New Covenant*, 2/6 (December 1972), 24.

121 Sutton, 'Word of God'.

122 *The Life in the Spirit seminars: team manual* (Notre Dame: Catholic Renewal Services, 1973), 160.

Christian Living.[123] The TWOG model was one of costly commitment within a highly organised community regime.

Not all Catholic covenant communities in the United States followed the TWOG approach. Some, like True House (1971), which largely attracted Notre Dame students, were not ecumenical. However, TWOG and the People of Praise (1971), led by Kevin Ranaghan in South Bend, which ran along similar lines, were the primary model for Catholic-led communities across North America. By 1972, for example, on the campus of Oral Roberts University, pentecostals, mainline Protestants, and Roman Catholics (there were about 100 Catholic students that year) built community life on campus whilst participating in their denominations on Sundays. The Methodist chaplain, the Revd. Bob Stamps, attended Ann Arbor conferences, and regarded TWOG (as well as Church of the Redeemer) as a sister group.[124] Through the extensive travels of Clark, Martin, and Ranaghan, both TWOG and People of Praise developed global connections. It was partly through their influence that in Brisbane the Emmanuel Covenant Community was set up in 1975, a group which five years later had 300 fully 'covenanted' members. Emmanuel similarly practised headship and submission to male eldership, looking to TWOG for innovations such as a community house for single men. The Brisbane group, through the wider ministry of Brian Smith, helped in the establishment of communities in Perth (Bethel), Canberra, Melbourne, and Adelaide (Hephzibah), Sydney and Melbourne (Disciples of Jesus).[125] With the popularity of TWOG's *Life in the Spirit*, too, the distinctive emphases on discipleship and gender travelled widely. In 1976, TWOG and People of Praise took the lead in establishing an Association of Communities, which cemented their influence both in North America and internationally.

Behind the formation of this 'community of communities' lay another impulse for corporate life in the 1970s: eschatology. Some communities were moving onto a spiritual warfare footing for a battle for a soul of their nations—the struggle against 'secular humanism'. The pioneers of the Ann Arbor model and the Fort Lauderdale teachers shared the view that God was preparing the Church for a coming storm. In 1974, Steve Clark argued communities were necessary 'to survive in an increasingly hostile environment'.[126] Around this time, as the next chapter describes, various prophecies warned of a coming conflict. This prompted a 'circling of the wagons' in many communities. Dorothy Ranaghan, of People of Praise, said awareness of spiritual warfare was 'all pervasive'.[127] Derek Prince in

[123] Thomas Csordas, *Language, charismatic and creativity: the ritual life of a religious movement* (Berkeley: University of California Press, 1997), 81.

[124] Bob Stamps, 'God's work at Oral Roberts University', *New Covenant*, 1/11 (May 1972), 10, 11–28.

[125] Adrian Commadeur, *The Spirit in the Church: exploring Catholic charismatic renewal* (Melbourne: Comsoda Communications, 1992), 78.

[126] 'Forum: community', *New Wine*, 6/8 (1974), 28–32, at 28.

[127] Quoted in Jackson, 'Jesus', 200.

New Covenant urged a community phase in the renewal, involving covenant commitment. 'We're going to have to do it because of the intense pressure of evil and violence and lawlessness: we won't survive if we don't', he warned.[128] Fort Lauderdale teachings informed the thinking of Howard Carter and the Logos Foundation in New South Wales, where a covenant community in the Blue Mountains was established for the imagined coming confrontation. Here, too, a high level of commitment was required—taking the covenant was preceded by a 42-lesson course. The 'government' of the community, which stretched across a 40-mile distance, ostensibly was based upon an Old Testament model, with the basic unit of individual families, the 'Household of the fathers' (an idea taken from 2 Samuel 2:1–3) of four to five families, the 'tribe' of no more than sixty, and the 'nation' which was the whole community.[129] This reflected Carter's growing interest in Christian reconstructionism—the idea that society might be run along the lines of Old Testament law. He wrote in *New Wine* at the end of the 1970s that in the 'political confrontation' between Christianity and humanism—a 'war to the death'—covenant communities would be the means through which creation was reconciled to God's purposes.[130] The Australian community included another feature popular amongst groups of similar orientation: Christian schooling. The Mountains Christian Academy used Accelerated Christian Education (ACE), a curriculum developed in the United States as an alternative to the 'secular humanist' provision.[131] The British house church network Salt and Light, led by Barney Coombs, also used ACE. The educational philosophy associated with these churches was one of a 'battle for the minds of children'—a war against secular humanism where victory was ultimately assured.[132] This reflected the larger eschatological mindset shaping many charismatic communities.

'God Is Looking for a Man': Authority, Gender, and Abuse

Within the body charismatic a widely discussed issue was authority. Various entangled concerns were involved; including the need to establish pastoral oversight within different charismatic ecclesial expressions, the desire to replicate primitive models of leadership, and the ambition to create a Godly 'kingdom' in societies where presumed Christian values appeared enveloped by a secular darkness, particularly where gender, sexuality, and family were concerned.

128 Derek Prince, 'The church of the seventies', *New Covenant*, 4/3 (September 1974), 10–11.
129 Howard Carter, 'News and happenings', *Restore*, March 1979, 17–21.
130 Howard Carter, 'Conflict of the ages', *New Wine*, 11/3 (March 1979), 28.
131 Carter, 'News and happenings', 20.
132 Helen Everett, *Faith schools, tolerance and diversity: exploring the influence of education on students' attitudes of tolerance* (London: Palgrave Macmillan, 2010), 110.

Alongside the democratisation of the ministry of spiritual gifts within the body, a *modus operandi* of charismatic renewal was endorsement of lay leadership roles. At a basic level, prayer groups required leaders. Across the charismatic spectrum the question of eldership—or 'shepherds'—came under the spotlight. The breaking down of the clerical and lay distinctions could reflect a pragmatism (e.g. in relation to capacity and resources) as well as conviction that spiritual authority did not only rest with professionals. In those Protestant mainline traditions where eldership was largely absent, congregational renewal frequently included experimentation with this pattern of leadership. In the Australian Anglican parish of St Paul's, Fairy Meadow, for instance, the Revd. Charles Widdowson appointed elders to help spread the load of the expanding ministry of the church. He considered himself 'the presiding elder, and not the rector—the man who is expected to do everything'.[133] In England, David Watson introduced elders to support his ministry in York, having them commissioned by the local bishop to bring the scheme under the authority of the Church.[134] In some Catholic charismatic communities, most prominently TWOG, layers of 'coordinators'—a term used instead of elder—provided the architecture of leadership.[135]

Partly due to the influence of local expressions of pentecostalism, such as the Foursquare Church, during the early phase of charismatic renewal women were often involved in leadership. In Van Nuys, Jean Stone found that prayer groups provided opportunities for ministry otherwise unavailable. She explained, 'Being a woman I could not be a priest; being married I could not be a nun. My husband did not have a call to the mission field, so that possibility was out. I thought that I had failed to discover God's purpose for my life in time for me to fulfil it, and that there could never be a deep satisfaction until I came face to face with the Lord.'[136] Stone spoke widely in pentecostal assemblies in southern California, where she likely found justification for her own ministry.[137] Another example of female authority was Merla Watson's role at the Catacombs, Toronto, where the leadership was egalitarian in practice.[138] In Potomac, Maryland, prayer meetings at Our Lady of Mercy Church were initiated by Judith Tydings, a religious studies teacher, who with Edith Difato co-founded the Catholic-ecumenical Mother of God community. In some cases, renewal cultivated female leadership in contexts which were largely traditionalist.

[133] Charles Widdowson, 'A church transformed', *Vision*, May–June 1975, 7–8, 12, at 11. There are many similar examples; e.g. Tom Walker, *Open to God: a parish in renewal* (Bramcote: Grove Books, 1975), 18–19.

[134] Watson, *You are my God*, 158.

[135] Csordas, *Language*, 81–82.

[136] DAHL, Jean Stone and Richard J. Willans papers, box 1, file 11, Jean Stone, 'What is happening today in the Episcopal Church?'; Jean Stone Willans, *The acts of the little green apples* (New Kensington: Whitaker House, 1973), Act 1.

[137] DAHL, Jean Stone and Richard J. Willans papers, box 1, file 9, Jean Stone, Appointment Book (1962).

[138] See Bruce Douville, 'The uncomfortable pew: Christianity, the New Left and the Hip Counterculture in Toronto, 1976–1975', PhD dissertation, York University (2011), 447–51.

These, however, were outweighed by examples of gendered conservatism. Pastoral responsibilities were normally male. This was the expectation of Christian Growth Ministries, restorationist leaders such as Arthur Wallis and Howard Carter, the non-denominational ministry of Melodyland in Southern California, and the TWOG and People of Praise communities. Derek Prince was unequivocal: citing Proverbs 31 he argued 'the highest achievement for a woman is to be a successful wife and mother.'[139] TWOG developed a model where alongside the male coordinators, female 'handmaids' assisted in work involving women. This approach was copied elsewhere. In the Emmanuel Community, Brisbane, one handmaid described her role as 'basically an extension of the [male] Coordinator [elder]', helping him to enable 'the women grow into all that God wants them to be'.[140] Conservative evangelicalism remained largely complementarian in the 1970s, and charismatics in these circles usually maintained traditional views on gender. Even in more flexible congregations, such as David Watson's Anglican church in York—where the 'area groups' (small groups) were sometimes led by women (including his wife, Anne)—the elders of the church were all-male. One official denominational report of the congregation described it as follows: 'male-administered, female-attended, mother-and-family and student orientated... It is directed by men, women being excluded from the eldership, but playing a leading role through prophecy.'[141] Anne Watson was in fact required by the elders to temporarily step down from church leadership, not only of area groups but in ministries such as worship and children's work, for a time, because some elders believed her 'too strong and dogmatic'. Her husband believed this was 'doubtless due to her having spiritual maturity and vision beyond that of most of the elders'. It may also not have been coincidental that some in the church were in contact with a non-denominational group in Northern Ireland with links to Fort Lauderdale.[142] The congregation in York had operated on a principle common amongst charismatic groups: eldership was male, but it was biblical and womanly to be a prophetess. For most charismatic women this glass ceiling could not be broken.

The divine order of God applied in the home, too. An influential book which rejected the 'feminisation' of society was Larry Christenson's *The Christian family* (1970). The Lutheran's teaching was popular amongst independents as well as mainliners (the Fountain Trust published his book in Britain). Decrying what he called 'petticoat rule', Christenson argued 'Scripture knows nothing of a 50–50 "democratic marriage". God's order is 100–100. The wife is 100% a wife, the husband 100% a husband.'[143] The architects of discipleship, prolific in magazines

[139] 'Forum: six questions that puzzle me', *New Wine*, February 1972, 8–16, at 10.
[140] Quoted in Smith, *Streams*, 63.
[141] Archbishops' Council on Evangelism report, quoted in Watson, *You are my God*, 152.
[142] Watson, *You are my God*, 164.
[143] Larry Christenson, *The Christian family* (Ada: Bethany Fellowship, 1974), 33.

such as *New Wine, New Covenant, Restore,* and *Restoration,* were normally the keenest advocates of Godly 'government' in family life. Derek Prince pulled no punches:

> It is about time that Christian men started acting like men. Leadership was never intended to be in the hands of ladies. I do not say this to criticize ladies, because it is the men's fault. I am firmly convinced that American men have abdicated from their three main responsibilities – as husbands, fathers and spiritual leaders. God is looking for a man.[144]

The woman should be subordinate to the man, who would protect and love her as Christ loved the Church. Robust teaching on the topic came from Ann Arbor, later articulated in Ralph Martin's *Husbands, Wives, Parents, Children* (1978) and Steve Clark's *Man and Woman in Christ* (1980). Clark, a celibate man, produced a book over 700 pages in length, combining biblical exegesis with social science critique. While calling for 'complementarity' and mutual service in marriage, he demanded 'a restoration of sexual division of labor in the midst of technological society'. Commitments to home and children would mean a woman ideally not taking a job which involved 'significantly more managerial responsibility, prestige, or remuneration than that of her husband'.[145] The restoration of 'manly personality' of aggressiveness (zeal, of course) and courage in church and family was required.[146] Similar views were to be found in Britain's *Restoration* magazine. A special issue on the theme of marriage in 1976 included articles by David and Pat Tomlinson. The former compared women to 'china', suggesting that their vulnerability and 'physical and emotional "weakness" draws out the manliness from a man'.[147] The latter reminded wives that sex was not a 'passport to sleep'.[148] God was building an alternative society from the ground up and discipleship began in the home. This required the end of what Ralph Martin saw as a trend towards American homes being run by children.[149] Books and articles appeared on restoring God's government to parent–child relationships. Insubordination had to be crushed. Christenson regarded the hypothetical question 'But what if my parents command something wrong?' as 'precocious inquisitiveness'. 'Such a question should perish on the lips of a Christian child', he asserted.[150] Punishment should be unequivocal and immediate. The 'rod' was 'the first response, not the last resort'.[151]

[144] Derek Prince, 'Praying for the government', *New Wine,* March 1970, 5–11, at 11.
[145] Steve Clark, *Man and woman in Christ* (Ann Arbor: Servant Books, 1980), quotes at 604, 660.
[146] Ibid., 638.
[147] David Tomlinson, 'Share my umbrella', *Restoration,* 2/1 (March–April 1976), 5–10, at 9.
[148] Pat Tomlinson, 'Submitted or submerged?', *Restoration,* 2/1 (March–April 1976), 15–18.
[149] Ralph Martin, *Husbands, wives, parents, children: foundations for the Christian family* (Ann Arbor: Servant Books, 1978).
[150] Christenson, *Christian family,* 98. [151] Ibid., 103.

The question of discipleship—or shepherding—was the most controversial. When the American sociologist R. Stephen Warner in 1976 attended a talk by Bob Mumford in California, he heard a 'masterly combination of soft sell and hard doctrine' on the topic. Warner described how Mumford said 'ree LAY shun ship', for emphasis. '"You say 'he's talking about *authority*!'" Mumford said, feigning shock. "Well you're right. I am", he answered in a mock sinister voice. "But you can't have community without authority."'[152] Shepherding won strong advocates abroad. In Australia, Howard Carter expressed his own role to his under-shepherds thus: 'I have sought to reproduce myself in those of the men committed to me.'[153] In England, Ron Trudinger of the 'Church in Basingstoke' asserted: 'The leader, in his watching over and caring for the members deals directly with single men. He and his wife deal with single girls... *Every* man needs another man with delegated authority as a shepherd over his personal life. Every leader, then, himself needs a leader – a voice from God, we may say.'[154] Although British restorationists were generally more cautious about shepherding, which as we shall see was developing something of a toxic reputation by the mid-1970s, their underlying commitments to radical, relational discipleship in the structures of Godly government were still evident. Bryn Jones cited the English Puritan minister Richard Baxter and his desire to catechise each individual in his parish.[155] Dave Tomlinson described the house group leader as a 'joint of supply' who must ensure that teaching 'doesn't stop in the person's head, but filters through to his everyday life'.[156] His compatriot, Arthur Wallis, when asked whether it was right to 'interfere' in intimate aspects of another person's life, gave an ambiguous answer: 'The only time you should touch intimate areas in other people's lives is when those areas need touching.'[157] Teachings on shepherding and discipleship had the potential to be put into practice in abusive ways.

At a local level, the notion of whole life discipleship, perhaps combined with a gendered understanding of authority, resulted in significant accusations of coercion of individual autonomy through spiritual, emotional, psychological, sexual, or physical abuse. In 1975 'whistle blower' type allegations about the True House community in South Bend (which had been closed a few years earlier) produced what the *New York Times* described as 'the first major controversy... of the Catholic Pentecostal movement'. Allegations included the practice of 'break-through ministry', with one testimony describing an individual awoken in the night and taken to a 'darkened room' for questioning about sinful behaviour

[152] Quoted in R. Stephen Warner, *New wine in old wineskins* (Berkeley: University of California Press, 1988), 240.

[153] Howard Carter, 'Editorial', *Restore*, March 1979, 2.

[154] Quoted in James Martin Scott, 'The theology of the so-called "New Church" movement: an analysis of the eschatology', MA thesis, Brunel University (1997), 43.

[155] 'Viewpoint', *Restoration*, 1/1 (1975), 13–15.

[156] David Tomlinson, 'The House Church', *Restoration*, November–December 1978, 6–9, at 8.

[157] 'Viewpoint', *Restoration*, 1/1 (1975), 13–15, at 14.

requiring confession. Prayer for 'healing of memories' and exorcism might follow, or even the burning of personal objects.[158] The following year J. Massyngberde Ford published *Which Way for Catholic Pentecostals?*, which criticised a culture of male-dominated submission.[159] Alarming stories were soon rife. Some leaders were left in a conflicted position. Barney Coombs, for example, was appalled by stories of abuse but also urged Christians not to 'throw out the baby with the bath water' on the principle of submission. Coombs was clear that some Christians had been 'bulldozed, dominated or submerged', but he was nevertheless concerned that Christians with a 'strong independent spirit' might use these allegations to reject a biblical teaching on discipleship.[160] In later decades, other reports or accusations emerged. One, by nine members of TWOG, concerning its environment from 1970, praised aspects of community life ('experience of God's presence' and 'God's love made practical') but also reported cult-like patterns.[161] The exercise of control in the community could have a detrimental effect specifically on men, too, who were apparently treated as 'over-aged teen-agers, required to submit their courtship, schedule, finances, and intimate details of their other personal lives to another who was assigned to them'.[162] As later chapters explain, the shepherding controversy had a profound impact on charismatic renewal, and with lasting legacies.

* * *

Charismatic experimentation with the body of Christ went beyond the established boundaries of church life and practice. The 'liquid' quality of the renewal was evident in its movement into domestic settings, its building new forms of intentional community, the establishment of alternative, relational structures of authority, and the transcending of denominational boundaries. If baptism of the Spirit was a gateway into authentic Christianity, the body charismatic was meant to provide ongoing, collective, and embodied experiences of the everyday 'reality' of the same Spirit. These were grounded local contexts, but experimentations with the body charismatic frequently had a translocal dimension in their exchange of experience, knowledge, and affections. Media, we have seen, fostered this

[158] 'Catholic Pentecostals charged with unauthorized exorcisms', *New York Times*, 10 August 1975, 38.

[159] Ford, *Which way for Catholic Pentecostals?*, 9–12.

[160] Barney Coombs, 'Viewpoint', *Restoration* 2/1 (1976), 20.

[161] The Word of God Covenant Community, 1970–1991 (A Branch of the Sword of the Spirit, 1982–1991), 25. https://www.scribd.com/document/98731671/Critique-of-Life-and-Development-of-the-Word-of-God-1991-by-Clark-Maney-Noetzel (accessed 23 April 2020). This online version says on the cover page 'created by an unofficial nine person study group signed by three of the authors, Muriel Maney, Peter Clark and Jo Noetzel'. Other reports on Catholic communities include, Adrian J. Reimers (a former member of People of Praise in South Bend), 'Charismatic covenant community: a failed promise', *Cultic Studies Journal*, 3/1 (1986), 28–42; David Crumm, 'The rise and fall of the Word of God covenant community', *Detroit Free Press Magazine*, 20 September 1992, 8–19.

[162] The Word of God Covenant Community, 1970–1991 (A Branch of the Sword of the Spirit, 1982–1991), 20.

translocalism, facilitating the movement of patterns of practice, gathering, and leadership from place to place. Relationally, regimes of authority and influence could connect individuals or groups at great distance.

A cartoon which did the rounds in the 1970s showed a clergyman behind a pulpit, saying to his congregation: 'I don't know who it was interrupted our worship last Sunday with the words "Praise the Lord", but in future will he kindly remember that this is the House of God and not do that again.'[163] Experimentation produced tensions. In some cases, clergy, both mainline and pentecostal, felt undermined. In 1964, for example, the Revd. Frank Maguire reported from southern California home prayer meetings which contained 'cultists' determined to establish their own little churches, and who weakened the role of clergy by celebrating communion themselves.[164] The potential for disunity was significant. In many congregations, the zealousness of those practising the supernatural gifts, or the opposition of those who were sceptical, produced painful secessions. These divided not only churches, but families. It is worth pausing to consider how difficult all this was to negotiate. In some Protestant denominations there were parallels with controversies over the 'romantic' turn towards sacramentalism in the nineteenth century. Where the worship of mainline congregations moved in the direction of renewal, inevitably some of their members were left behind. Richard Hare, the English Anglican Bishop of Pontefract, observed such 'signs of strain':

> You can see them in parish after parish, where one section of the congregation has been renewed in the Spirit, but by no means everyone. The apprehensive, threatened look when you reach the Peace; the regulars, and the regular abstainers, when it comes to a time of free prayer; sadly, the refugees scattered abroad among other congregations in the town.[165]

Pentecostal denominations, too, were drawn into controversy; and divisions here could be as acute as those resulting from the Latter Rain and healing evangelist movements decades earlier. Wherever the renewal spread, it reshaped and contested existing ecclesial patterns and practices.

[163] Richard Hare, 'Freedom and the growth of worship', *Renewal*, 70 (August/September 1977), 16–18.
[164] LPL, Michael Harper papers, 1964/28, Frank Maguire to Harper, 1 April 1964.
[165] Hare, 'Freedom', 17.

6
Imagination

> . . . I have made you a light
> Acts 13:47

Gwen Savage, from Dublin, listened to the music filling the football stadium at Notre Dame. 'It's magnificent. Beautiful. I feel really close to God', she told a journalist. The 1974 international conference on the Catholic charismatic renewal was a spectacle (Fig. 6.1). A Friday night healing service with Fr. Francis MacNutt was followed by reports of divine interventions around the stadium. People 'with poor vision could see clearly without glasses; people with deafness listened to the ticking of their watches'. As the sun set the next evening, 700 white-robed priests moved in procession across the football pitch. Eucharist was led by Cardinal Suenens, as 300 ushers and priests distributed the communion high into the stands. Then, a moment of symbolic power: candles were lit, one by one, around the stadium. Fr. George Kosicki, of Detroit, instructed the crowd, 'take them home with you. Take them home around the country, around the world.' On the Sunday, following talks by Suenens and the non-denominational charismatic Robert Frost, Ralph Martin unpacked the previous night's symbolism.[1] Three 'pentecostal rivers'—classical, neo-pentecostal, and Catholic—were coming together at an unprecedented time for the Church. 'The darkness is growing darker . . . and the light must grow brighter.'[2]

The charismatic imagination concerned what God was doing in the world. In the mid-1970s, the renewal reached 'full flow' in the volume and intensity of translocal exchanges; music, books, and 'pilgrims' of the Spirit. With this compression of time and space the collective imaginary was increasingly focused. Many began to see a Church, united and empowered, ready to be a light in the world, even as the 'darkness' of moral change, violent conflict, economic volatility, and political corruption appeared ready to envelop it. The charismatic imagination challenged secularising and permissive trends and addressed religious and ethnic divisions in the power of the Spirit. However, despite a sense of forward motion—that God was working through a worldwide community of the Spirit, to some kind of larger eschatological climax—the juggernaut of charismatic renewal was also beginning to shudder, with some of its components starting to loosen and

[1] 'The 1974 Notre Dame conference: a turning point', *New Covenant*, 4/3 (August 1974), 4–6.
[2] Ralph Martin, 'God is restoring his people', ibid., 3–6.

Age of the Spirit: Charismatic Renewal, the Anglo-World, and Global Christianity, 1945–1980. John Maiden, Oxford University Press. © John Maiden 2023. DOI: 10.1093/oso/9780198847496.003.0006

Fig. 6.1 Notre Dame conference, 1974.

spin off. By the end of the decade, differences seemed as pronounced as commonalities in the charismatic imaginary. This chapter examines the symmetries and asymmetries in the Spiritscape of charismatic renewal at its high point in the Anglo-world.

The 1970s: Growth

'We live in a time where there is a return to Jesus', declared Fr. Ian Petit in a 1972 edition of the *Catholic Herald*. To the Englishman, charismatic renewal was part of wider cultural turn, evident in *Jesus Christ Superstar* and *Godspell*, towards Jesus.[3] There was some substance to this claim. In the United States the success of the Oral Roberts variety show-style television specials attracted bone fide stars of music and film (Johnny Cash, Jerry Lewis, Pat Boone, and Mahalia Jackson were among the guests) and by 1972 broadcast on more than four hundred stations.[4] As the influence of the Jesus People movement grew, and external interest in the 'scandal' of tongues speaking faded, a Christocentric dimension of renewal was increasingly prominent. This, as one Australian Uniting Church pastor put it, was observable in 'the cultural and spiritual expressions of the movement – the

[3] Ian Petit OSB, 'What is this charismatic renewal', *Catholic Herald*, 27 October 1972, 4.

[4] David Harrell, *Oral Roberts: an American life* (Bloomington: Indiana University Press, 1985), 151–52, 270.

bumper sticker, T-shirts, banners and prayers of "charismatic" Christians'.[5] The optics of large set-piece conferences indicated success. One such event, the Conference on Charismatic Renewal in the Churches in Kansas City, 1977, even received greetings from President Jimmy Carter. Confidence abounded and charismatics appeared ready to do battle for the souls of nations.

The impact of renewal, of course, varied. In England, Catholic charismatic growth was far less marked than North America or Australasia. 'Are you just a little tired of hearing, repeatedly if not constantly, of the "amazing" growth of the Charismatic Renewal in the US, in Australia and New Zealand, and more recently in Ireland? Do you wonder sometimes of the Spirit has chosen not to blow quite so strongly around here, or do you simply dismiss slower growth as the result of British reserve', asked a *Day of Renewal* newsletter in 1975.[6] A few years later, a proposal to hold a Catholic charismatic conference in London's Wembley concert arena came to nothing. However, the overall picture across the Anglo-world was one of charismatic growth. In the United States by 1974 there were an estimated 1,800 Roman Catholic prayer groups, 1,000–1,500 Episcopal prayer groups (10 per cent of the clergy), and 500–600 American Baptists pastors; though the largest single group were non-denominational Christians.[7] In New Zealand, one clergyman observed a 'groundswell' of mainline involvement.[8] In Auckland, by 1974 approximately 40–50 per cent of Anglican clergy were involved in or 'open' to the renewal, and a third of parishes had laity baptised in the Spirit; while large charismatic Baptist congregations, like Hamilton Central, Spreydon, and Te Buke, also emerged.[9] In Australia, mainline and independent numbers continued to grow, as did various 'charismaticised' Assemblies of God congregations. It was a mixed picture, but overall, in the eyes of participants—particularly those attending large conferences—the Spirit was moving.

Geographies of the Spirit and Power Pilgrimage

There was a mental map of charismatic geography; of flagship Spirit-filled congregations, communities, and ministries. This was illustrated in the itinerary of Brisbane's Brian Smith, who like Gwen Savage attended the 1974 Notre Dame conference. His tour included Melodyland, Anaheim, The Word of God (TWOG), Ann Arbor, H.O.P.E., New Jersey, and the St Patrick's church, Providence, Rhode

[5] Pastor M. Moonie, 'The place of charismatic renewal within the UCA', *Renewing*, 6 (1977), 16–26.

[6] Editorial, 'The Spirit blows where it will', *Day of Renewal* (London), January 1975.

[7] The mainline figures came from a survey of denominational groups in *New Covenant*. See Cindy Conniff, 'Moving on', *New Covenant*, 4/3 (September 1974), 23–25.

[8] JKTL, ANG178, Cecil T. Marshall papers, Series 1, item 6, Marshall to Rollin Hill, 5 February 1976.

[9] JKTL, ANG 016/1/2, Allen G. Neil, 'The origins, development and present extent of the Charismatic Renewal in the Church in New Zealand', Provincial Commission on the Charismatic Renewal, 1973, 61–81.

Island.[10] On the way home he stopped in Ireland, visiting an ecumenical meeting in Dublin, before heading to Belfast, where he met the Revd. Cecil Kerr of the Rostrevor community. He visited the Revd. Ian Paisley's church in the hope of witnessing to him. Perhaps fortunately, he found the building was closed. Smith spoke at the Clonard Street Redemptorist Monastery on the peace line, where he found Protestants attending a Monday night prayer meeting. On leaving Ireland, he visited the Post Green community in England, before flying home via Jerusalem (Pastor Ralph Wilkerson in Melodyland felt the Lord wanted Smith to visit the holy city and gave him a cheque to extend his travels).[11] That year, Smith clocked up significant air miles witnessing the work of the Spirit.

Many rank-and-file clergy, religious, and middle-class laity also engaged in charismatic pilgrimage. From 1973, the Revd. Allan Alcock (St Luke's Anglican church, Clovelly) of the Temple Trust organised tours to the United States. By 1975, they offered three itineraries. The longest was a six-week 'World Charismatic Tour', stopping in Bangkok, Israel, Rome, Germany (to visit the Mary Sisters at Darmstadt), England (to attend a Fountain Trust conference), and then Los Angeles (Melodyland) and San Francisco, with a trip also over the border to Mexico.[12] For Australians and New Zealanders with sufficient funds, an unofficial pilgrimage route emerged, taking in, at least, Israel, England, and the United States, often timed to coincide with the Notre Dame conference or Melodyland's Charismatic Clinic, or from 1974 a World Conference on the Holy Spirit in Jerusalem. From the British Isles and mainland Europe, people toured through the United States and Canada, following well-travelled charismatic routes, seeking experiences described in service agency magazines.

It was normal for charismatics to combine this power pilgrimage and holiday making. A visit to Melodyland, for instance, invariably took in Disney's secular alternative.[13] However, charismatic travel was done with intentionality. When Mary Miscamble, a Brisbane lay Catholic, visited South Bend's True House community in 1973, she was struck by the experience of community love. 'If one wanted proof of the validity of Charismatic Renewal', she wrote, 'then here was the place to see it'.[14] Mark White, an English lay Catholic who visited TWOG felt, 'This is how it was always meant to be.'[15] New methods were brought home. When Brian Smith visited Post Green, he met a couple from New South Wales doing six months of worldwide travel to learn about community households.[16]

[10] Brian Smith, 'Let God arise', *Newsletter (for the Catholic Charismatic Renewal)*, 2/8 (1974), 18–19.

[11] Letter from Brian Smith, ibid., 2–3.

[12] 'Temple Trust news', *Vision*, January–February 1975, 17–18.

[13] Alan Langstaff, 'Temple Trust tour', *Vision*, September–October 1974, 11–14.

[14] Marie Miscamble, 'Impressions', *Newsletter (for the Catholic Charismatic Renewal)*, July 1973, 2–6.

[15] Mark White, 'Reflections on a visit to Ann Arbor's "Word of God" community', *Goodnews*, December 1975, 8.

[16] Smith, 'Let God arise'.

In York, the demand to visit St Michael-le-Belfrey was so high that the church explored opening a guest house.[17] From April 1977, David Watson's 'renewal weeks' allowed visitors to experience the church and attend seminars on community life, creative arts, and evangelism. These attracted 1,500 from the British Isles and abroad over five years (in Wales, it was joked that charismatics were distinguished by the letters B.Y.—been to York—rather than B.A.).[18] Testimonies of travel spoke to a sense of consistency in the Spirit's work. After Auckland's David Balfour visited Britain in 1976, he wrote Dennis Bennett that his experience of St Michael-le-Belfrey was like that of St Luke's, Seattle and St Paul's, Auckland. There was, Balfour confirmed, 'One and the same Lord and one and the same Spirit'.[19]

The United States was the most popular power pilgrimage destination. Before Allan Alcock first visited from Australia, he drew up a spiritual bucket list, including St Luke's, Seattle, Melodyland, Church of the Redeemer, Houston, and Teen Challenge in New York City.[20] The numbers such places attracted were notable. Melodyland, named after the 3,700-seat theatre where it was based, from 1969, held Charismatic Clinics to explore supernatural gifts from 1967. By August 1973, these drew 5,000 visitors annually from the United States and abroad, with 350 church leaders attending a pastoral institute beforehand. A School of the Bible for laity and a School of Theology for ministerial candidates was presided over by J. Rodman Williams and an international Board which included Michael Harper and Alan Langstaff.[21] David Wilkerson's Teen Challenge exerted a magnetic pull over visitors during the 1970s. For Catholics, but also some Protestants, the reputation of People of Praise and TWOG communities (as well as their proximity to the Notre Dame conference) made them popular destinations. In 1974 alone, the Ann Arbor community claimed around 2,000 international visitors. This was said to confirm the prophecy upon which the group's name was based, that they would offer 'my word now to the whole face of the earth'.[22] Imagined geographies were made up of places where God was at work, or speaking a 'new word', as the Spirit moved.

'All over the World the Spirit Is Moving': Portals for the Imagination

We now look in turn at three 'portals'—music, books, and television/film—which transported the imaginations of charismatics. New songs and arrangements, for

[17] *Newsletter*, St Michael-le-Belfrey with St Cuthbert's, York, May 1976.
[18] Teddy Saunders and Hugh Sansom, *David Watson* (London: Hodder & Stoughton, 1992), 181.
[19] DAHL, Dennis J. Bennet papers, box 8, David Balfour to Bennett, 16 November 1976.
[20] DAHL, Dennis J. Bennet papers, box 8, Jim Glennon to Bennett, 17 July 1972.
[21] Richard Quebedeaux, *The new charismatics* (New York: Doubleday, 1976), 105–06, 122–23.
[22] Mary Ann Jahr, 'An ecumenical Christian community: The Word of God, Ann Arbor, Michigan', *New Covenant*, 4/8 (February 1975), 4–8.

example by Ralph Carmichael and youth-orientated bands such as Campus Crusade's New Folk, influenced by folk and popular styles, were a feature of post-war evangelicalism.[23] However, by the 1970s charismatics were at the driving wheel of Christian musical creativity and industry. 'In the fresh move of God we are enjoying throughout the world today there is renewed interest and emphasis upon praise', argued Judson Cornwall.[24] Praise and worship fostered local creativity while expanding the global horizons of songwriters, musicians, and worshippers. Charismatic music—praise and worship albums, songbooks, and sing-along recordings—facilitated the making of these global imaginaries. The compilers of *Sound of Living Waters: Songs of Renewal* (1974), the American Betty Pulkingham and the Fountain Trust's Jeanne Harper, expressed this through the evocative words: 'From the coasts of England, from the islands of New Zealand, from the expansive shores of America, the songs roll in as a powerful tide of praise to the Saviour.'[25] This creative outpouring was often framed eschatologically. Pastor Neville Johnson, of the AoG in Auckland, claimed in the liner notes for David and Dale Garrett's *Prepare Ye the Way* (1972) that the 'coming forth of anointed music' was part of an outpouring of the Holy Spirit preceding the Second Coming. This could 'come forth in your home having a marked effect on yourself and your family', he said.[26]

In the early 1970s, praise and worship still included the older hymns and choruses which were the mainstay of charismatic meetings the previous decade. At the Catholic-ecumenical prayer meeting in Barden, Brisbane, for instance, the usual thirty minutes of singing might include 'How Great Thou Art', 'To God be the Glory', and 'He Lives'.[27] However, alongside these traditional compositions, there had been for a number of years a groundswell of new creativity. Some of the earliest new songs were gospel style. The Southern gospel of Bill Gaither described personal encounters with God. Britain, too, produced new gospel music. From north-east Scotland, the kilted Cameron Family and Roy Turner had a transatlantic audience, appearing on Pat Robertson's *The 700 Club* in 1967 and through the popularity of the album *Songs of the Holy Spirit* (1968), and with choruses like 'I'm getting ready in the Latter Rain' and 'All over the World the Spirit is Moving'. Another group, The Four Kingsmen, linked with the independent fellowship in Chard, England, blended gospel with an electric Beatlesesque style. They were introduced to America by the Holy Spirit Teaching Mission in the late 1960s.

For many, the soundtrack of charismatic renewal was the folk song. Initially, these combined a simple tune—suitable for both piano and guitar, short, and

[23] Larry Eskridge, *God's forever family: the Jesus People movement in America* (New York: Oxford University Press, 2013), 210–12.

[24] E. Judson Cornwall quoted in album sleeve of David and Dale Garrett, *Prepare ye the way*, 1972, Anchor Recordings, vinyl LP.

[25] Betty Pulkingham and Jeanne Harper, *Sound of living waters: songs of renewal* (1974).

[26] David and Dale Garrett, *Prepare ye the way*.

[27] Philip Audemard, 'Bardon: a puzzle for the Protestant evangelical', *The Fraternal*, 168 (1973), 40–44.

intended for worshipful repetition—with lyrics verbatim or derived from Scripture, often the Psalms or Revelation. New Zealand punched well above its weight in the production, collection, and popularisation of Scripture songs. The team largely responsible were Dave and Dale Garrett, a Wellington Brethren couple who had relocated to Neville Johnson's Queen Street congregation in Auckland. Their use of Scripture—usually the King James Version—was an indicator of the influence of the Latter Rain movement. Their 1968 *Scripture in Song* album was followed by the publication of *Songs of Praise* (1971) and multiple albums and songbooks. The Garretts were unlikely pioneers. Neither were musicians and their 1968 album was recorded in four hours and sounded fairly basic. This, however, was somewhat deceptive, as several choruses had a mesmeric quality and their simplicity made them ideal for the prayer group setting.[28]

The Garretts' songbooks were popular in Australia, where at Calvary Temple AoG, Townsville, David Cartledge literally locked the old pentecostal hymnbooks away as he introduced them.[29] The appeal of the Scripture in Song corpus travelled much further. 'This is the Day', which was derived from a Fijian folk tune, became a theme song for the renewal worldwide, featuring in the film of the first World Conference on the Holy Spirit in 1974. The Garretts performed in the United States in the mid-1970s. In Britain, where they were distributed by Anchor recordings (run by Arthur Wallis' brother, Peter), they were amongst the first charismatic 'new songs' to be heard. This prompted a move away from the historic hymns and *Youth Praise* songs which were the mainstay of charismatic praise and worship in the 1960s. *Arise Shine* (1977), the worship album of the Dales Bible Week, published by Bryn Jones' Harvestime, included the Garretts' 'For His Name is Exalted', 'His Name is Higher than any Other', and 'Hallelujah for the Lord God Almighty'.[30] Scripture in Song was not only a vehicle for New Zealand songwriters and arrangers, it was also a global sorting house for charismatic choruses. The provenance of the 218 songs in the Garretts' 1971 songbook indicates extensive transnational exchange, particularly between New Zealand, from where 58 of the songs came, and the United States, where 83 originated.[31] Scripture songs from the United States included 'Great is the Lord and Greatly to be Praised' by Robert Ewing of Waco and 'Thou Art Worthy' by pentecostal songwriter Pauline Mills. British songs found their way into the Garretts' songbooks in the mid-1970s.[32] David Fellingham, a musician who attended an Anglican church in Brighton, England, was inspired by the Garretts' work, and his 'Alleluia! The Lord Reigns'

[28] David Santistevan, 'David Garrett on worship music in the 60s, Scripture in Song and being led by the Holy Spirit' (interview), https://www.davidsantistevan.com/58/ (accessed 21 May 2021).

[29] Shane Clifton, *Pentecostal churches in transition: analysing the developing ecclesiology of the Assemblies of God in Australia* (Leiden: Brill, 2009), 140–51.

[30] Various artists, *Arise shine! Worship from the Dales Bible Week 1977*, 1977, Harvestime, cassette.

[31] Brett Knowles, '"From the ends of the earth we hear songs": music as an indicator of New Zealand Pentecostal spirituality and theology', *Australian Pentecostal Studies*, 5/6 (2002), online.

[32] Ibid.

was picked up by them during a British tour and published by Scripture in Song.[33] Fellingham, a worship leader at the Downs Bible Week, joined a vanguard of British worship leaders disseminated by Thankyou Music (later Kingsway Music) in its *Songs of Fellowship* songbook from 1979.

Scripture featured heavily in another sub-stream of worship, recognisable for its musical dexterity and synergies with dance and other creative practices: folk art. Amongst the pioneers were Merv and Merla Watson, the leaders at Toronto's Catacombs.[34] Here the performance of worship was a spectacle, described in the *Toronto Star* as 'a mixture of the old-time revival meeting, a modern hootenanny and a classical concert'. They even drew on choral influences and used a pipe organ.[35] The Watsons played the Fountain Trust's 1971 Guildford conference and headlined an arts festival and symposium at Post Green, attended by 3,000 delegates, the next year.[36] In albums such as *Hidden Manna* (1975) they adopted more fully a Hebraic, klezmer style which could be heard in 'Hear my Prayer' on their *Sounds of Fresh Waters* (1970).[37] Along with the work of Messianic Jewish duo Lamb, these sounds complemented the eschatological interest of many charismatics with Israel.

Catholic communities were another source of folk art. The Word of God's music group was the most influential. Although sometimes criticised for being subdued (percussion was usually limited to tambourine), their music included guitar, flute, cello, and a choir. The albums and songbook compilations placed worship in a community context. 'These songs are a part of our daily life in The Word of God' read the sleeve of *New Life* (1972).[38] The album began with the opening line of Karen Barrie's composition 'Psalm 89', a favourite in Ann Arbor: 'I have made a covenant with my chosen, given my servant my word.'[39] TWOG releases incorporated new compositions and existing works, including post-Vatican II choruses like Sr. Suzanne Toolan's 'I am the Bread of Life' (1966). Their own songs used the Psalms, or ranged Scripture more widely, for example in 'A Voice Cries Out in the Wilderness' (Isaiah 40) and 'Consider the Lilies' (Matthew 6) on *You Are My God* (1973).[40] *New Covenant* recommended the

[33] Moir, *Missing jewel.* David Fellingham, 'Alleluia! The Lord reigns', *Call to war*, 1981, Scripture in Song, various formats.

[34] See this book, p. 59.

[35] Bruce Douville, 'The uncomfortable pew: Christianity, the New Left and the Hip Counterculture in Toronto, 1976–1975', PhD dissertation, York University (2011).

[36] Faith Lees (with Jeanne Hinton), *Love is our home: the beginnings of the Post Green community* (London: Hodder & Stoughton, 1978), 206.

[37] Merv and Merla Watson, *Hidden manna*, 1975, Catacombs Productions, vinyl LP.

[38] The Word of God, *New life*, 1972, The Word of God, vinyl LP.

[39] Karen Barrie, 'Psalm 89', The Word of God, *New life*, 1972, The Word of God, vinyl LP.

[40] Billy Kangas, 'John Wimber and the Vineyard influence on Charismatic Catholic worship', in Lester Ruth (ed.), *Essays on the history of contemporary praise and worship* (Eugene: Wipf & Stock, 2020), 34–54.

music for prayer meetings 'large or small'.[41] Their profile was raised by the international conferences at Notre Dame; and they led worship at a key occasion for global charismatic renewal, described below, the Rome conference of 1975.

Another folk art contribution came from Church of the Redeemer, Houston. Its coffee house group The Keyhole, who released albums such as *The Way In* (1968) and *Hallelujah, Jesus is Lord* (1969), were influenced by the folk revival. From this circle emerged the Fisherfolk, a collective of travelling groups of musicians, dancers, and other artists. In 1973, Fisherfolk musicians joined the Revd. Graham Pulkingham and others to form the Community of Celebration in England, as described in the previous chapter. Meanwhile another Fisherfolk team, along with The Keyhole, travelled extensively in the United States. The enterprise required a significant organisational structure. In Houston, The Fishermen Inc. and NET distribution served a growing demand for anything associated with Church of the Redeemer, while in Britain income from Fisherfolk distribution and royalties supported the Community of Celebration.[42] As with TWOG, an attraction was the authentic communitarianism evident in the Fisherfolk's song writing and performance.[43] Betty Pulkingham and others believed folk art should enrich community and parish life.[44] This purpose shaped their most unique works, the expansive sacramental album *Celebrate the Feast* (1975)—which included Pulkingham's 'King of Glory' mass setting—and *God's People Give Thanks* (1977).[45] Both were live recordings of eucharistic celebrations, with use of the English liturgy, at St John's College Chapel, Oxford. The inclusive, participatory approach had historic parallels with church gallery music, although some choruses were akin to Scripture in Song or the evangelistic works of the Jesus People (a version of 'The Joy of the Lord' included a chorus entirely of laughing as an expression of this joy).[46]

Merv and Merla and the Fisherfolk were influential in Britain. Folk art was introduced to St Michael-le-Belfrey through the Watsons, who brought seventy musicians, singers, and dancers to York in 1972. The Canadians persuaded David Watson (no relation, and he admitted to having not so much as swayed since his

41 Advert, *New Covenant*, 3/4 (October 1973), 25.

42 'Music department', *Glad Tidings*, 1/3 (June 1974), 1–2; 'Sales department', 1/4 (July/August 1974), 1–3.

43 Philip Bradshaw, *Following the Spirit: seeing Christian faith through community eyes* (Ropley: John Hunt, 2010), ch 10.

44 Betty Pulkingham discusses the difference between 'folk art' and 'fine art' in *Sing God a simple song: exploring worship in music for the eighties* (New York: HarperCollins, 1986), 84–87.

45 The Fisherfolk, *Celebrate the feast*, 1975, Celebration Records, vinyl LP; Church of the Redeemer Choir, *God's people give thanks*, 1977, Celebration Records, vinyl LP.

46 James H. S. Steven, '"Worship in the Spirit": a sociological analysis and theological appraisal of charismatic worship in the Church of England', PhD thesis, King's College London (1999), 36. Alliene Vale, 'The joy of the Lord', The Fisherfolk, *Worship with the Fisherfolk*, 1978, Celebration Record, vinyl LP.

pre-conversion, ballroom dancing days) of the experience of God's presence through worship. In the vicinity of York Minster, a tourist hot spot, the church began to perform 'vivacious Israeli dances' to signify that God was amongst them.[47] The Fisherfolk visited York regularly and cemented folk art practices (featuring on an Easter Day programme of the BBC's *Songs of Praise* in 1975). However, the relationship between the Fisherfolk and Britain was one of cross-fertilisation. As much was clear with the influence of English musical and liturgical styles and the cooperation between Pulkingham and Jeanne Harper in the editing of songbooks. It is also important to note that these song-writing and worship compilations featured women, such as Mimi Farra of the Fisherfolk, heavily. Existing songbooks were male dominated. *English Praise* was put together by an entirely male committee and only four of its 120 items were by women.[48] In *Sound of Living Waters*, by contrast, 31 out of the 133 items were by women. Freedom of the Spirit ushered in a new phase of women's hymnody.[49] Britain again provided a connecting link between North America and Australasia. David Watson took Merv and Merla on an eight-week tour of New Zealand in 1973, where their influence led St Paul's, Auckland (where Graham Pulkingham had visited the year before) to introduce dancing.[50] Edward Prebble, the vicar's son, joined the Community of Celebration in England and featured, with his wife Sherrell, on the Fisherfolk and Post Green Community album, *Be Like Your Father* (1979). The Church of the Redeemer believed they had received a prophetic call to prioritise their ministry efforts in the English-speaking world, rather than mission fields such as Latin America.[51] They were a catalyst for translocal musical creativity in the Anglo-world.

'Why should the devil have all the good music?' enquired Larry Norman on his album *Only Visiting This Planet*.[52] The Jesus People wanted to claim it back. This stream of charismatic music was eclectic. Larry Eskridge describes the music of Calvary Chapel as 'all over the map: folk, light pop, soft rock and country'. Lyrically, there were Scripture songs, evangelistic choruses, and more intimate and expressive works.[53] The sounds percolated into the wider charismatic worship scene. While Jesus musicians were found across the United States, their creative centre was the Los Angeles area. The likes of Norman played shows at Hollywood Presbyterian and the Palladium venue. Jack Hayford's Church on the Way, in Van Nuys, became a source of congregational songs and the home of Pat Boone, the

47 David Watson, *You are my God* (London: Hodder & Stoughton, 1983), 131, 135.

48 Janet Wootton, *This is our song: women's hymn-writing* (Eugene: Wipf & Stock, 2010), 177.

49 Ibid., 191.

50 Dale Williamson, 'An uncomfortable engagement: the charismatic renewal in the New Zealand Anglican Church, 1965–85', PhD thesis, University of Otago (2007), 217.

51 Philip Bradshaw, 'Community of Celebration', *Glad Tidings*, 1/5 (September 1974), 3–5.

52 Larry Norman, 'Why should the Devil have all the good music?', *Only visiting this planet*, 1972, MGM, vinyl LP.

53 Eskridge, *God's forever family*, 219.

Jesus People patron, and musical composers Jimmy and Carol Owens. Calvary Chapel, Costa Mesa, with *The Everlastin' Living Jesus Music Concert* (1971), released into the world musicians like Love Song, Mustard Seed Faith, and Karen Lafferty, through Maranatha! Music. The commercial hub, though, was Waco, Texas, the home of Light Records, a division of Lexicon music; and Myrrh Records, a subsidiary of the evangelical giant Word Records.[54] This musical counterculture was given the thumbs up by Billy Graham in 1971. It drew strength also from celebrity, through passing engagements with spiritually searching artists such as Bob Dylan and Bruce Cockburn. Country musicians Johnny Cash and Kris Kristofferson were on the bill with Jesus People artists at the final concert of Campus Crusade's Explo'72.[55] Jesus People music was to prove the most commercially viable charismatic music; indeed, it laid the groundwork for Contemporary Christian Music.

Beyond the United States, Jesus People music was popularised through three musicals in the vein of *Hair* (1967) and *Jesus Christ Superstar* (1970): *Come Together* (1972), *Lonesome Stone* (1973), and *If My People* (1974). In Britain, an American group, The Sheep, financed by a British businessman, composed and performed *Lonesome Stone*, a portrayal of 'the search of thousands of today's youth surrounded by the darkness of materialism, dead religions, sex, new gurus, astrology and mind expanding and bending drugs'.[56] This provided momentum for the setting up, in 1974, of the Greenbelt Festival. This annual event shaped Christian counterculture in the British Isles by providing a creative outlet for Jesus musicians as well as a wider array of bands, including, later, the Dublin band U2 (influenced by Larry Norman), who performed in 1981. There were tours. Andraé Crouch, a former Teen Challenge worker whose pioneering contemporary gospel talent had been honed in the Church of God in Christ, was one of a few African American Jesus music artists and became popular in Australia and Britain. His Grammy Award-winning *Live in London* (1978) album ('tonight we are not going to have a concert... we are going to have church') was recorded at London's Hammersmith Odeon and Manchester's Free Trade Hall.[57] Crouch, Karen Lafferty, Keith Green, and Jack Hayford contributed to the staple chorus diet of congregations who used *Scripture in Song* and *Songs of Fellowship* for praise and worship.

The translocality of charismatic renewal was evident in praise and worship at churches and conferences. In the 1970s, worship at Christ Church, Kenilworth,

[54] Ibid., 210–28.

[55] Don Cusic, *Encyclopedia of contemporary Christian music: pop, rock and worship* (Santa Barbara: Greenwood Press, 2010), 179.

[56] Advertising leaflet, quoted in Tony Cummings, 'The Sheep: '70s Jesus freaks who pioneered the Lonesome Stone Rock Opera', https://www.crossrhythms.co.uk/articles/music/The_Sheep_70s_Jesus_freaks_who_pioneered_the_Lonesome_Stone_rock_opera/50944/p1/ (accessed 21 June 2021).

[57] Andraé Crouch, *Live in London*, 1978, Light Records, vinyl double LP.

saw for the first time American, rather than English, influences on South African Anglican worship. Later a songbook *Praise the Lord* was introduced as a local version of transatlantic songbooks like *Sounds of Living Water*. Although most of the material was from overseas there were local arrangements by musicians Tony Westwood and Chris Dare, developed for Christ Church's 'Parish Praise' services, where groups such as the Fisherfolk had inspired experimentation. The book was used trans-denominationally in South Africa in the 1980s.[58] A Christian Advance Ministries conference in New Zealand in 1977 included a majority of songs from that country (from Spreydon Baptist Church, Scripture in Song, and St Paul's, Auckland), along with choruses from the TWOG, the American Jesus People songwriter John Fischer, and Jim and Jean Strathdee, of the United Methodist Church in California.[59] Within a relatively short period of time, charismatic gatherings were drawing on an extensive translocal repertoire of songs.

Broad characteristics and trends were found in this song-writing and music. Singing in the Spirit was as likely to be heard in Cathedral celebrations as at Bible Week tent gatherings, with worship records including live tracks of the phenomenon. The emphasis on the presence of God demonstrated the diffusion of the Latter Rain movement into the charismatic bloodstream. Similarly, expectation of an encounter with God's presence was evident in the singing of Davidic Psalms, and references to the 'sacrifice of praise' and the Tabernacle as a space of dancing, singing, and instrumentation, which God inhabited. This Davidic orientation was not limited to independent charismatics. David had danced before the Lord with all his might, reasoned David Watson in York.[60] The worthiness, character, and acts of God were a steady theme.[61] The 1970s saw increased focus on Christology and with this came an inflection on the kingdom of God and the 'church victorious' eschatology now emanating powerfully from restorationist circles. The chorus of English songwriter Dave Richards' 'For I'm Building a People of Power' (1977) expressed this:

Build your Church, Lord
Make us strong, Lord
Join our hearts, Lord, through your Son
Make us one Lord
In your Body
In the Kingdom of your Son.[62]

[58] Andrew-John Bethke, 'Contemporary musical expression in Anglican churches in the Diocese of Cape Town: developments since the liturgical, theological and social revolutions of the twentieth century', PhD thesis, University of Cape Town (2012), 109–11.

[59] JKTL, ANG178, Cecil T. Marshall papers, series 1, item 9, Revd. A. G. Neil to Marshall, 23 January 1978.

[60] Watson, *You are my God*, 131.

[61] Knowles, '"From the ends"'.

[62] Dave Richards, 'For I'm Building a People of Power', 1977, Kingsway's Thankyou music.

As charismatics sung lyrics from across the Anglo-world, the collective sense of participation in a global community of the Spirit was reinforced.

Books were another portal for the imagination. In 1974, Dennis Bennett received a letter from the minister of a United Church congregation on Vancouver Island. It described the impact of *Nine C'clock in the Morning* (1970). Bennett's testimony had been passed between congregants in a plain brown wrapper (a strategy adopted to avoid a 'riot') on twenty-four-hour loan. Word travelled and a waiting list for the illicit text grew. A small group expanded and became a prayer and praise meeting. This was soon ecumenical and began running *Life in the Spirit* courses.[63] As this minor example illustrates, the rise of the religious paperback best-seller was another important factor in the translocalism and expansion of charismatic renewal. Some of the groundwork had been done by the growth of the Christian bookstore movement of the 1950s—which was 'Evangelicalism's miracle of the mid-century' according to *Christian Life*.[64] In the United States during the 1970s, overall religious book sales rose dramatically compared to general industry growth: 112 per cent compared to 70 per cent between 1972 and 1977.[65] The establishment of the Evangelical Christian Publishers Association (ECPA) in 1974 was a signal of a flourishing market. Initially, books such as Bennett's were often sold 'under the counter'; however, soon the Christian book market opened up.[66] America became home of a charismatic publishing complex. Alongside Logos International—Bennett's publisher—were Robert Walker's Creation House in Illinois and Servant Publishing in Ann Arbor. Established Christian booksellers like Ave Maria Press, Paulist Press, and Fleming H. Revell also spotted a market opportunity. Outside of the United States the main publisher of charismatic literature was Hodder & Stoughton, a company with offices in London, Toronto, Sydney, and Auckland. They had historic evangelical pedigree; however, by the mid-twentieth century they largely relied on secular authors like W. E. Johns (of Biggles fame) and spy novelist John Le Carré. Through the efforts of Hodder's religious editor, Edward England (who also brought the New International Version of the Bible to Britain), the company published a string of charismatic books, including Michael Harper's *A New Way of Living* (1973), Colin Urquhart's *When the Spirit Comes* (1974), and Jackie Pullinger's *Chasing the Dragon* (1980).

Logos International was the prolific publisher of the charismatic renewal. It was established in the mid-1960s by Dan Malachuk; an independent pentecostal and FGBMFI committee member who perceived a gap in the market for a publisher of

[63] RUSCA, Dennis J. Bennett papers, box 5, T. W. Ridewoord to Dennis Bennett, 5 December 1974.

[64] 'Christian bookstores come of age', *Christian Life*, October 1955, 25.

[65] Erin A. Smith, *What would Jesus read? Popular religious books and everyday life in twentieth-century America* (Chapel Hill: University of North Carolina Press, 2015), 207.

[66] Dan Malachuk, 'Publishing: getting out the charismatic word', *Logos Journal*, January–February 1981, 62–64.

pentecostal literature acceptable to mainline Christians. By 1978, Logos International had produced over 250 titles. These and the magazine *Logos Journal*, published from 1971, sought to represent the width of the charismatic spectrum. The magazine absorbed *The Herald of Faith-Harvest Time*, which had merged publications edited by independent, Latter Rain influenced pentecostal Joseph D. Mattsson-Boze and Mennonite pastor-turned-healing figure, Gerald Derstine.[67] Malachuk boasted of the editorial department whose advisers included 'Methodists, Episcopalians, Catholics, Pentecostals—in fact, every major historic church is represented'.[68] *Logos Journal* encapsulated its vision of the scope of charismatic renewal by adopting the inclusive, pan-denominational strapline 'The magazine of New Testament Christianity'.

A survey of Logos International publications indicates changing interest trends. Following early successes such as *Run Baby Run* (1968), the story of Nicky Cruz (the gang leader in *The Cross and the Switchblade*), and Bennett's work, Logos International made its name through 'charismatic witness books'.[69] Other examples were Merlin Carothers' *Prison to Praise* (1970), an autobiographical story of armed robbery, military service, conversion, Spirit baptism, and ministry as a Methodist chaplain; Arthur Katz's *Ben Israel: Odyssey of a Modern Jew* (1970), the conversion narrative of a Brooklyn-born, atheist Jew who founded the Ben Israel Fellowship community in Minnesota; and Fr. Joseph E. Orsini's testimony, *Hear my Confession* (1971). While retrospective criticism is perhaps unfair, in its response to a growing demand in the market for dramatic testimonies, Logos International sometimes lacked discernment. Some authors were later found out. In the wake of *The Exorcist*, Mike Warnke's *The Satan Seller* (1972) had claimed to tell the story of a man's involvement as a Satanist priest; however, after a high-profile career, including featuring on *The Oprah Winfrey Show*, Warnke was the subject of an exposé.[70] Michael Esses' *Michael, Michael, why do you Hate Me?* (1973) told the story of the conversion of a Rabbi to whom the risen Jesus had shown his wounds. Esses was later appointed to the Faculty of Melodyland School of Theology; however, his ex-wife later alleged the story was significantly fabricated.[71] Testimony books were the mainstay of Logos International's output in the 1970s, with a flood of publications; but later allegations meant that confidence in narratives of transformation by the Spirit was somewhat undermined.

[67] For example, see Gerald Derstine, 'Harvest Time news', *Logos Journal*, November–December 1971, 57.

[68] Dan Malachuk, 'Editorial: Dear reader', *Logos Journal*, March–April 1972, 5.

[69] 'International news', *Logos Journal*, September–October 1971, 56–57.

[70] Don Cusic, 'Warnke, Mike', in Cusic, *Encyclopedia*, 458–59; Mike Hertenstein and Jon Trott, *Selling Satan: the evangelical media and the Mike Warnke scandal* (Chicago: Cornerstone Press, 1993), 159–60.

[71] Betty Esses DeBlase, *Survivor of a tarnished ministry: the true story of Michael and Betty Esses* (Orange: Truth Publishers, 1983).

Logos International also published teaching texts, such as Baptist theologian Howard M. Ervin's scholarly *These are not Drunken, as ye Suppose* (1968). Popular works on entering the Spirit-filled life followed, like Robert Frost's *Aglow with the Spirit* (1971); and then books on wider topics, such as spiritual warfare (e.g. the American version of Michael Harper's *Spiritual Warfare* in 1970), worship (e.g. Judson Cornwall's *Let us Praise* in 1973), and community living (e.g. Harper's *A New Way of Living* in 1973). Inner healing was an increasingly popular subject. Logos International republished Agnes Sanford's *The Healing Light* in 1972, with many titles following, such as Jamie Buckingham's *Risky Living: Keys to Inner Healing* (1975) and Conrad W. Baars' *Feeling and Healing your Emotions* (1979). Baars was a Catholic doctor and advocate for the integration of spirituality and psychiatry. One issue often discussed in publications on 'inner healing' was sexuality and gender. Baars, for example, wrote about a transsexual whom he claimed experienced a reversal of their gender identity and became 'free of…homosexual thoughts for two years, and was looking forward to marriage'.[72] Books by Kent Philpott, including *The Third Sex? Six Homosexuals tell their Story* (1975), contributed to the rise of the so-called 'ex-gay' movement. The compiler was a founder of Love in Action, Los Angeles, one of the first American charismatic ministries (others included EXIT, the 'Ex-Gay Intervention Team'—later Exodus—at Melodyland) claiming healing of homosexuality through therapeutic prayer. According to one of those who testified in *The third sex*, John Evans ('Ted' in the book), who later rejected the agenda of Love in Action, he and three others in 1979 asked that publication of *The Third Sex* cease. 'We cannot with good Christian conscience allow these falsifications to continue', they asserted, adding 'none of us have ever changed and become heterosexual and are living at this time, satisfying Christian lives with our mates, following our natural homosexual orientation.'[73] Evans came to be regarded by some as the first 'ex-ex-gay'.

Logos International began to publish therapeutic literature addressing everyday issues. Marriage became a popular topic, with titles on resolving relationship difficulties including Harold Page Williams' *X-rated Marriages* (1977). There was a growing cultural appetite for self-improvement, and books followed on finances, health, and weight loss. Joan Cavanaugh and Pat Forsyth's *More of Jesus, Less of Me* (1976) and Patricia Kreml's *Slim for Him: Biblical Devotions on Diet* (1979) arguably presented the Spirit as a kind of divine dietician, a perspective which attracted readers in what *Bookstore Journal* observed was a growing Christian market in physical fitness.[74] From the mid-decade, Logos International

[72] Conrad W. Baars, *Feeling and healing your emotions* (Plainfield: Logos International, 1979), 258.

[73] John Evans, 'The history of Love in Action', https://exgaywatch.com/2005/08/co-founder-sick/, accessed 21 May 2021.

[74] R. Marie Griffith, *Born again bodies: flesh and spirit in American Christianity* (Berkeley: University of California Press, 2004), 172.

published advocates of the abundant life. Lester Sumrall, in *Miracles don't just Happen* (1979), argued 'the thing which turns God on to a miracle is a man's faith'. Jim Bakker's autobiography *Move that Mountain* (1976) gave another nod to Word of Faith teaching. Later books by the Seoul mega-church pastor Paul Yonggi Cho, such as *Solving Life's Problems* (1980), offered similar emphases, albeit developed in a Korean context of poverty and war rather than post-war American materialism.[75] The steady stream of Logos International titles displayed the expansion and diversification of the charismatic market.

A further portal was television. In North America, just as Fr. Charles E. Coughlin, Aimee Semple McPherson, and Billy Graham had seized upon radio, so charismatics innovated with television broadcasting. The Holy Spirit Teaching Mission were involved, if only initially, in plans for what in 1975 launched as World Harvest Florida Television in South Florida (this was later purchased by Trinity Broadcasting Network).[76] The pioneer of charismatic broadcasting, though, was the Southern Baptist future presidential candidate Pat Robertson. His Christian Broadcasting Network (CBN) by 1977 ran at a $20 million budget. Robertson's biography *Shout it from the Rooftops* (1976) was published by Logos International and CBN raised the profile of Logos authors on shows such as *The 700 Club*. Its wide appeal meant CBN built bridges between charismatic renewal and 'born again' American Christianity. The evangelists of Word of Faith were particularly drawn to the opportunities of television. Significant players included Trinity Broadcasting Network, which operated in southern California, and from 1974, Jim and Tammy Bakker's PTL (Praise the Lord) Network Inc., which was based in Charlotte, where they eventually built a headquarters designed to resemble colonial Williamsburg, known as Heritage Village. There was also the FGBMFI's *The Good News* show, which by 1978 was shown on 120 stations throughout the United States.[77] For some it was clear that television was the future. 'Television and radio are like master keys', claimed Logos' Dan Malachuk in 1977.[78] There was a potentially enormous audience and advocates for the medium claimed broadcasting might build a bulwark against non-Christian values. As Jamie Buckingham put it, broadcasting could conquer 'a domain formerly held by the "prince of the power of the air"'.[79] There were, however, subtler reasons why television was ideally suited to charismatics. The domestic, suburban technology reached into the settings where charismatic spirituality had already flourished. There was also ecumenical potential in

[75] Lester Sumrall (with J. Stephen Conn), *Miracles don't just happen* (Plainfield: Logos International, 1979), 19.

[76] Tom Monroe, 'Birth of a TELEvision', *New Wine*, August 1970, 11.

[77] Kenny Waters, 'Full Gospel Business Men: fulfilling a vision', *Logos Journal*, January–February 1978, 15–19.

[78] Dan Malachuk, Editorial, *Logos Journal*, May–June 1977, 1.

[79] Jamie Buckingham, 'Forecast: reconciliation', *Logos Journal*, May–June 1977, 9.

television. Programmes need not make denominational distinctions and could reach a diverse Christian audience with what Buckingham called 'a Gospel of unifying love'.[80]

Television was impactful beyond the United States. Shows such as PTL were broadcast north of the border, where there was also a steady supply of Canadian broadcasting. The most influential Canadian programme, established in 1977, was *100 Huntley Street*. With roots in Pentecostal Assemblies of Canada (PAOC) broadcasting, it was the outcome of David Mainse's vision of an ecumenical ministry.[81] The former PAOC pastor invited ordained ministers such as the Anglican Al Reimers and Roman Catholic priest Bob MacDougall onto the show's staff. Appropriately, David du Plessis, whose ecumenism had inspired Mainse, was amongst the first guests. In Australia, American television ministries influenced a change in the direction of the Temple Trust. Alan and Dorothy Langstaff had grown interested in Christian broadcasting following a visit to the States in 1975. They intended to establish an 'Australian orientated' programme linked with an existing broadcaster with global reach, probably CBN. However, the Langstaffs were then asked by PTL to consider heading up a planned expansion into their country (they were invited to meet Jim Bakker, and the televangelist's full diary meant that they first encountered him in front of a camera and live audience, where he asked them directly: 'Is it time for Christian television in Australia?').[82] Establishing the apparatus for broadcasting became central to the Temple Trust's ministry strategy.[83] For the Langstaffs, Mainse, and others, television was the future for the Spirit's activity.

Imaginaries in Action: Reconciliation, Repentance, and the 'Devil's Pentecost'

Charismatics imaged the Spirit at work amongst the nations. Canadian charismatics (along with evangelicals) adopted the historic language of the country as God's 'dominion from sea to sea': a phrase used by Robert N. Thompson, the Albertan former leader of the Social Credit party, on the first episode of *100 Huntley Street*.[84] In Australia, 'Great Southland of the Holy Spirit'—the title given by Portuguese explorer Pedro de Quirós—was appropriated by Protestants and Catholics. The Spirit could have particular plans and purposes for individual nations.

[80] Ibid.

[81] Quoted in: Ewen H. Butler, *Canadian winds of the Spirit: holiness, pentecostal and charismatic currents* (Lexington: Emeth Press, 2018), 105.

[82] 'New challenges', *Vision*, May–June 1979, 34–39.

[83] 'Temple Trust update', *Vision*, January–February 1979, 43.

[84] Butler, *Canadian*, 105.

However, such expressions of national identity often developed in relation to an imagining of the Spirit's global activity. Conferences were sites of interface between national and cosmopolitan identities. Larger events were displays of collective strength often deemed symbolic of the growth of Spirit's work in a nation. The Temple Trust, for example, described its second National Charismatic Conference as a 'Day of recognition' of the contribution of the renewal to the life of the Australian Churches. However, the phrase used to designate this success—a 'coming of age'—aped the prophetic language used by the Fountain Trust to describe the advance of the movement in Britain at its 1971 Guildford conference, which Alan Langstaff had attended.[85] Conferences were portals, too, connecting local charismatics to a wider world of renewal. The Fountain Trust's 1973 follow-up to the Guildford conference, 'Gathered for Power', included a showing of *Following the Spirit*, the CBS film about the Church of the Redeemer, the worship music of the Fisherfolk, and talks by Graham Pulkingham. The delegates' programme described a conference with a 'strong Texan flavour'.[86] Conferences were platforms for both national and international leaderships. The Christian Advance Ministries summer schools in New Zealand always included a handful of international names; for example, in 1976, Tom Smail, the Director of the Fountain Trust, Ken Pagard, the California-based Baptist, and the Australian layman Brian Smith. Charismatic conferences, as we saw in Chapter 4, often seemed to fetishize the work of the Spirit 'elsewhere'. Speakers from abroad were described in ways which denoted a special authority. When Anglicans in Victoria, British Columbia, brought over Colin Urquhart from England, he was described as 'a great teacher', 'a man under authority', 'used mightily to bring God's Word to us, by the power of the Holy Spirit, to enlighten our minds'.[87] International healing ministries, such as those of Francis MacNutt, Kathryn Kuhlman, and Anne White, brought intense expectation. The United States also had its share of visiting speakers. The 1977 Kansas City conference included Archbishop Bill Burnett and Britain's Michael Harper and Tom Smail in the programme. A cohort of speakers, healers, and worship groups were in a perpetual state of transnational motion between conferences in the 1970s. The common designation of 'international' in conference titles said much about charismatics' eschatological and cosmopolitan orientations.

National leaderships were sometimes required to respond to criticism about the influence of outsiders. A 1973 article in the leading English Catholic charismatic newsletter addressed both the pitfalls of assuming a 'monolithic' international movement and the English tendency 'towards the insular'. English Catholics should have the confidence to offer to the world what the Spirit was doing

[85] Alan Langstaff, 'The day of recognition', *Vision*, March–April 1973, 3.
[86] DAHL, David du Plessis papers, box 109, file 3, Michael Harper, 'Letter of welcome', *Gathered for power*, conference programme.
[87] RUSCA, Dennis J. Bennett papers, box 8, Newsletter, Anglican Renewal Centre (Victoria), November 1976.

'through our own tradition and temperament'; however, equally they should avoid being 'cagey about receiving', not least because the English scene lagged behind others in terms of numbers and leadership.[88] In a similar vein, a *Vision* editorial acknowledged that Australians received most of their teaching from abroad and recognised that some were unsure about 'our apparent dependence upon overseas speakers and authors'. Readers were reminded that the limited capacity of Australian charismatics necessitated some reliance on foreign ministries; however, it was agreed there were dangers of 'simply seeking to copy what God had done in some other place'. The metaphor of snowflakes was used to describe the global work of the Spirit. Just as these were each different but essentially alike, so the 'creative Spirit' wished to produce 'unique works [. . .] in every place—although basically the same'.[89] We will now see how this kind of imagining of the global-local dynamic of the Spirit's work was evident in relation to three themes: reconciliation, repentance, and the so-called 'Devil's pentecost'.

'Jesus' people come together, let your light shine!' was the opening of Jimmy and Carol Owens' 'musical experience of love' *Come Together* (1972).[90] The cover, which portrayed a child, wolf, lion, sheep, and other animals, resembled one of Quaker Edward Hicks' 'peaceable kingdom' portraits. The musical was written as an expression of the life of Church on the Way, Jack Hayford's charismaticised Foursquare congregation in Van Nuys. The album, which featured the vocals of Pat Boone, consisted largely of lyrics taken from Scripture. It was performed throughout North America from 1972, with a special broadcast from the Los Angeles Forum. The next year, Jean Darnell, the Foursquare minister by now residing at Post Green, invited the Owens to bring their musical to Britain. A core group of performers joined British musicians and singers, while local troupes presented the musical at hundreds of venues around the country.[91] A few years later, after a tape of the Los Angeles film was brought to South Africa (by someone returning from Post Green), a group toured throughout the country.[92] 'Come Together' was not merely a performance, it was a participatory ritual which included breaks in which those gathered formed small groups for sharing and prayer.[93] It expressed a desire that God's people reconcile, to shine a light of unity in fractured, dark times.

The Spirit of reconciliation working in the world became a charismatic trope. How far might the Spirit go in breaking denominational and ethnic barriers?

[88] 'International leader's conference', *Day of Renewal*, July 1973, 2.
[89] Alan Langstaff, Editorial, *Vision*, November–December 1974, 2.
[90] Jimmy and Carol Owens (featuring Pat Boone), 'Come together', on *Come together*, 1972, Light Record, vinyl LP.
[91] Jimmy and Carol Owens, *Restoring a nation's foundations: prayer strategies and action plans* (Los Angeles: Foursquare, 2007), 133.
[92] See comments in https://khanya.wordpress.com/charismatic-renewal/charismatic-renewal-people/, accessed 13 July 2020.
[93] Album sleeve, *Come together*.

From the late 1960s, the Troubles on the island of Ireland were a reminder of a historic, sectarian animosity between two groups involved in charismatic renewal. By 1972 news that 'the Spirit is breaking down old walls' filtered into charismatic magazines.[94] The island became a test case for reconciliatory power. Pat Boone and others performed 'Come Together' the day after a British soldier was shot near the Belfast venue in September 1973. After each of the 1,200 people were searched on entry to the auditorium, the performance was one of the few—and perhaps the first—large, public interfaith gatherings involving Protestants and Catholics in the city since the resurgence of violence. The lyrics of redemption and forgiveness, 'Freely Freely, you have received; Freely, Freely, give', obtained a powerful resonance. Prayer—another portal for the charismatic imagination—occurred behind the scenes, with Christians in the United States and even a prayer group in Israel, amongst those interceding.[95] On Pentecost Sunday earlier that year, as Chapter 3 mentioned, there had been a worldwide day of prayer for the country as charismatics from North and South took a pilgrimage to the Hill of Slane under a banner 'We are one in the Spirit'.[96] The decision to begin annual ecumenical conferences for the whole of the island from 1974 was a significant step. At the second conference, the Scottish Presbyterian Tom Smail asserted: 'The Holy Spirit is directing our steps to new ways of living together, especially in Ireland. Perhaps because the bad days are coming when we will really need one another.'[97] The American charismatic press published articles on reconciliation through prayer groups. Although most groups in the North were segregated because of the risks involved, the Spirit was still said to be moving. 'Security forces have not been able to do what the Lord has done. He is working to heal his own people but this will not happen immediately. Eventually his love will convict the IRA and the Ian Paisleyites also', read one interview with a County Antrim Protestant minister in a *Logos Journal* article.[98] The Revd. Cecil Kerr reported in *New Covenant*: 'God's Spirit is beginning to reconcile the warring factions' even as the 'frequent whir of helicopters are constant reminders that we are not far from the area where some of the worst violence of the past years has occurred'.[99] Charismatics were often hopeful for reconciliation in this political and military quagmire.

Reconciliation was a prominent theme at conferences. In Britain, Michael Harper had established a friendship with Bob Balkham, the lay Catholic leader of the Gustave Weigel Society (a transatlantic ecumenical organisation founded in

[94] Ray Reynolds, 'Report from Ireland – the Spirit is breaking down old walls', *New Covenant*, 2/1 (July 1972), 22–23.

[95] Jimmy and Carol Owens, *Restoring*, xii.

[96] Jerome McCarthy, 'The charismatic renewal and reconciliation in Northern Ireland', *One in Christ*, 10/1 (1974), 31–43.

[97] Barbara O'Reilly, 'Logos report 2: Ireland', *Logos Journal*, January–February 1976, 55–58, at 55.

[98] Ibid., 56.

[99] Cecil Kerr, 'A beacon of hope in Ireland', *New Covenant*, 7/5 (November 1977), 10–12.

Washington DC in the mid-1960s). Balkham had found his way to England, following his baptism in the Spirit, after being persuaded by fellow ecumenist Lady Bronwen Astor (whose recently deceased husband, William, was in 1963 caught up in the Profumo affair) to move to the country and establish a community near Godalming.[100] Harper and Balkham organised two International Ecumenical Charismatic Conferences in 1972 and 1973. Before this, the Fountain Trust's 1971 conference (which Balkham helped prepare) disorientated some conservative evangelicals. David Watson found it challenged his 'anti-Rome' attitude and cultivated an 'altogether new love towards many non-evangelicals'.[101] The international conferences at Nottingham (1973) and Westminster (1975) each increased their numbers of Catholic delegates.[102] In Australia, the Temple Trust in 1977 organised both its own national conference and that of the Catholic Charismatic renewal. At the Trust's conference, Tommy Tyson, the American Methodist, and Fr. Francis MacNutt 'confessed the sins and wrong attitudes that existed... between Catholics and Protestants going back even as far as the Spanish Inquisition'. In the audience, Protestant clergy joined in twos with Catholic priests.[103] In 1979, the fourth National Catholic Charismatic Conference was abandoned to support the Temple Trust conference; with the different denominational streams combining for collective gatherings.[104] This public commitment to ecumenicity was partly inspired by the United States, where at the 1977 Kansas City conference different charismatic streams met separately but also came together for worship in the football stadium. In New Zealand, 'Kansas City' was described as 'a stepping-stone for all Christianity, which has been divided since the Reformation'.[105] Conferences were spectacles of oneness in the Spirit.

What about racial reconciliation? African American involvement was very limited in the renewal, with charismatic magazines often deafeningly silent on racial injustice. In Britain, post-war migrants from the Caribbean and West Africa had in the post-war years transported existing pentecostal and holiness traditions with them; and numbers attending these churches were rapidly augmented by Black mainline Christians who on arrival in their new country had experienced a

[100] Kristina Cooper, private collection, 'Notes of conversation between Kristina Cooper and Lady Bronwyn Astor'.

[101] Watson, *You are my God*, 98–99.

[102] Connie Ho Yan Au, *Grassroots unity in the charismatic renewal* (Eugene: Wipf & Stock, 2011), 45.

[103] 'New challenges', *Vision*, May–June 1979, 35–39, quote at 35. There was a precedent for this kind of moment: at a regional Catholic charismatic conference in the south-eastern United States, Bill Beatty and Fr. Mike Scanlan, following a prophecy on the 'scandal of division' in the Church, asked forgiveness of Bob Mumford and Vinson Synan, the pentecostal, before washing their feet ('Two thousand people dropped to their knees in awe and wonder at the power of the Lord in their midst', reported *New Covenant*). See 'Southeastern regional conference', *New Covenant*, 4/7 (January 1975), 17.

[104] JKTL, Cecil T. Marshall papers, ANG178, series 2, file 25, Leaflet, Second International Conference on the Holy Spirit and the Church.

[105] JKTL, Cecil T. Marshall papers, ANG178, series 3, file 15, *CAM Newsletter*, December 1977.

cold welcome in their 'mother churches'. Interaction between charismatics and these new British 'Black majority churches' was limited. Organisations such as the British Council of Churches were more proactive in developing dialogue to promote anti-racism.[106] The most prominent charismatic voice on matters of race was the future Archbishop of Cape Town, Bill Burnett. He had been a public critic of the apartheid system as General Secretary of the South African Council of Churches, during the time it produced *The Message to the People of South Africa* (1968), a document which called apartheid a 'false gospel'. When Burnett spoke at the Kansas City conference, he said of apartheid in his home country, 'We as Christians have been unfaithful to have allowed the situation that exists to happen.' 'We are under judgement', he warned.[107] In the same year he visited the British Isles. In Rostrevor, he asserted: 'If in Ireland, Protestants and Catholics were brought together in love: what a difference this would make to the world.'[108] There is little evidence, however, that Burnett was able to prompt either the Americans or British to address their own racial injustices.

In South Africa, a potential moment for charismatic engagement with racial issues was the 1977 National Renewal Conference. This was a collaboration between South African leaders like Burnett and the independent David Crumpton with the Logos International Fellowship, whose representatives included David du Plessis (whose brother, Justus, was part of the South African team) and which made a significant financial contribution. Against the backdrop of the 1976 Soweto riots, it was conceived as multi-racial. Permission was obtained from the Prime Minister, John Vorster, to hold the Johannesburg conference despite restrictions of apartheid legislation and it was televised on a state-owned television channel. The conference team, although overwhelmingly white, were agreed in principle they must involve Black and Coloured leaders, particularly Sowetans. A scholarship scheme and financial subsidies allowed 400 leaders to attend.[109] During the course of events, Fr. Francis MacNutt suggested that each 'race, culture and denominational "group"' ask for forgiveness and bless others close to them.[110] The conference was laudable in its efforts, but was spiritual reconciliation alone sufficient? The priority reflected that of Burnett and others. The Anglican was amongst those who declined to support the World Council of Churches 1970 decision to give humanitarian grants to liberation movements in

[106] On this, see John Maiden, '"Race", black majority churches and the rise of ecumenical multiculturalism in the 1970s', *Twentieth Century British History*, 30/4 (2019), 531–56.

[107] Bill Burnett, 'Become the alternative society', *Acts 29 Newsletter*, September 1977, 2–3.

[108] *CAM Newsletter*, December 1977.

[109] DAHL, David du Plessis papers, box 22, file 10, Dan Malachuk to board of trustees, 12 September 1977; box 11, file 67, Derek Crumpton to Dan Malachuk, 4 April 1977.

[110] Dot Mitchell, *He said yes! The story of Derek A. Crumpton* (Self-published, 2018), 263.

Southern Africa.[111] In December 1976 Burnett argued, 'This is the issue that we face, not only power and powerlessness politically, but much more seriously powerlessness spiritually.' Glenn Thompson argues Burnett's political position was 'carved between Afrikaner nationalist and liberationist discourses' and became 'the common thread of the charismatic movement's reconciliatory discourse of the Spirit in the late 1970s'.[112] To some South African observers, charismatic renewal was a 'mass-escapist movement'—instead of addressing racial injustice head on, the problem of apartheid was spiritualised.[113] The power of the message of reconciliation in the Spirit cannot be dismissed, nor can the commitment of leaders such as Crumpton, but practical and political solutions to address systematic evil were not usually forthcoming from charismatic circles.

A second theme of the global-local charismatic imagination was repentance in a context of eschatological crisis. An article in *New Wine* put it thus:

> You and I are vitally concerned, with THREE THINGS, as we move into the FIRST YEAR of the SEVENTIES. They are: 1) The ever increasing Signs of World-crisis; 2) The nearing Divine Intervention in human affairs; and 3) its PERSONAL EFFECT upon us all.[114]

As we saw in Chapter 4, charismatics grew concerned about moral, social, economic, and political disorder in the 1970s. Some issues varied from nation to nation, for example, in the cases of legislation and political scandals. Other matters, though, such as energy shortages, recession, inflation, and population growth appeared to indicate what the British independent Bryn Jones described as a 'deepening global crisis'.[115] High-profile prophecies, such as Ralph Martin's at the beginning of the chapter, foresaw a climactic period ahead.

It would be a caricature to suggest charismatic concerns only reflected social conservatism. The Fountain Trust, for example, had a progressive element. In a 1977 issue of *Renewal* on national repentance, Tom Smail's editorial observed 'Most Christians find it easier to denounce sexual sin' than issues like racism, materialism, or economic injustice.[116] However, more often service agencies displayed little interest in structural social problems. Community life was often presented, in Larry Christenson's words, as a 'critical intermediate step' between

[111] John W. De Gruchy, *The church struggle in South Africa: 25th anniversary edition* (Minneapolis: Fortress Press, 2005), 124–28.

[112] Glen Thompson, '"Transported away": the spirituality and piety of charismatic Christianity in South Africa (1976–1994)', *Journal of Theology for Southern Africa*, 128 (2004), 128–45.

[113] Tim Dunne, '"Nevertheless...": a variety of religious protest', *Reality*, 9/2 (1977), 14–16.

[114] Charles French, 'Present-day events and their meaning in the Bible', *New Wine*, September 1970, 12–15, at 12.

[115] Bryn Jones, 'World crisis: people want answers', *Restoration*, 1/2 (May–June 1975), 2–5, at 2.

[116] Editorial, *Renewal*, 67 (February–March 1977), 4.

the individual and the problems of society.[117] While charismatic communities could generate local activism, a certain kind of insularism tended to block wider, strategic engagement with social issues. One might have expected a worked-out vision for social justice amongst Catholics in South Bend and Ann Arbor, given the past involvement of some community members in civil rights campaigns. However, the priority was the creation of alternative societies in a darkening world. The expectation of Christ's return ordered priorities. Steve Clark argued that even the *possibility* that prophetic words on the Parousia might be correct should influence strategy. 'We would not commit ourselves to anything that does not produce short-term results', he asserted. The proper focus was the body of Christ.[118] This position, said or unsaid, was widely evident.

A paradox, as was often the case more broadly within late twentieth-century conservative Christianity, was that combating moral degradation did not fall into the 'social gospel' category which was so often dismissed. Charismatics made powerful contributions to moral crusades in the 1970s.[119] The first editorial of *New Wine* bemoaned that Americans 'seem caught up in a delusion that patriotism is a dirty word, and that any call to honour and decency must itself be considered almost indecent'. This spiritualised patriotism and citizenship urged the Spirit-filled to march to a drumbeat other than 'violence and revolution; lawlessness and rebellion'. They should 'enlist to the supernatural move of God' and remember that 'our national destiny can be fulfilled only as we fulfil our spiritual destiny.'[120] By accenting divine order in church, family, and government, magazines such as *New Wine* and *New Covenant* tended to exhibit social conservatism. Some, concerned by Supreme Court rulings on prayer in school, riots, and crime, saw Richard Nixon's election as offering hope. 'America is returning to God!', asserted Thomas R. Nickle in 1970.[121] However, having taken the oath of office on not one, but two bibles, Nixon's steep fall from grace heightened existing fears of ethical and moral decline. For Bob Mumford, this was no less than the 'Watergate of Western civilization'.[122]

In Britain, charismatics joined with evangelicals and traditionalists such as Malcolm Muggeridge and Mary Whitehouse to establish the National Festival of Light (NFOL). The campaign was inspired by Peter Hill, a house church leader, who on return from the mission field was prompted into moral activism by the

[117] Larry Christenson, 'Social action in the charismatic movement', *New Covenant*, 4/10 (1974), 44–47.

[118] Steve Clark, Social action: strategies and priorities, *New Covenant*, 2/5 (November 1972), 7–9, at 9.

[119] See Matthew Grimley, 'Anglican evangelicals and anti-permissiveness: the Nationwide Festival of Light, 1971–83', in Andrew Atherstone and John Maiden (eds.), *Evangelicalism and the Church of England in the twentieth century: reform, resistance and renewal* (Woodbridge: Boydell, 2013), 183–205.

[120] Don Basham, 'The sound of a different drummer', *New Wine*, 1/1 (1969), 2.

[121] Thomas R. Nickle, 'America is returning to God', *New Wine*, March 1970, 12–16.

[122] Bob Mumford, 'The Watergate of western civilization', *New Wine*, January 1974, 3–6.

sight of a scantily clad woman on an advertising hoarding. The Jesus People icon Arthur Blessitt and the pop star Cliff Richard took part in large outdoor events in London in 1971, in which charismatics—house church members, in particular—were heavily involved.[123] Michael Harper was amongst those concerned the NFOL paid insufficient attention to wider social problems. However, by 1976 he, also, was convinced that without action, the country would fall prey to communism: 'The moral basis of our society is at stake, and with it our future as a land fit to live in.'[124] The same public proclamation of Christian values was heard in New Zealand's 1972 Jesus Marches, described by one contemporary as 'part of the debate over the national soul'.[125] Five years later at Jesus '76 a programme of meetings in Auckland, including an event at the Alexandra Park Raceway, called for repentance against the backdrop of the Royal Commission on Abortion, Contraception and Sterilisation. The first newsletter carried the tagline 'Righteousness exalts a nation'.[126] In Australia there were similar national calls to prayer. 'Australia: a sick nation!', stated a writer in *Vision* magazine in 1974, urging intercession 'for His supernatural intervention and guidance in the affairs of the nation'.[127] Across the Anglo-world, charismatics mobilised to address moral decay.

'We are not wrestling against flesh and blood', asserted Derek Prince. 'We are on a different plane; we have different enemies, we have different weapons.'[128] Intercession—prayer which battled the spiritual powers—was seen as essential to the moral campaign. A key movement, established by Dennis G. Clark and supported by Arthur Wallis, began in 1969. Intercessors for Britain was the 'prayer arm' of NFOL and by 1970 had over a thousand participants nationwide. Although it claimed to have no political agenda other than fighting secular humanism and lawlessness, its supplications could appear rather partisan. On the Sunday before the 1970 General Election, for example, prayers were encouraged against eight 'militant atheists' in Harold Wilson's cabinet (in the same year there was also intercession that God would confuse industrial action taken by the Trades Union Congress).[129] This model of prayer was borrowed abroad, with the establishing of Intercessors for Canada and Intercessors for the United States. America was mobilised for a 'National day of humiliation, fasting and prayer' on 30 April 1974, an unofficial event which followed the failure of a resolution for the

[123] On House Church involvement, see Andrew J. Walker, *Notes from a wayward son: a miscellany*, ed. Andrew D. Kinsey (Eugene: Cascade Books, 2015), 61–62.

[124] Michael Harper, 'Let there be light', *Renewal*, 62 (April–May 1976), 10.

[125] Neil, 'The origins', 57.

[126] JKTL, Cecil T. Marshall papers, ANG178, Series 1, item 7, *Jesus '76 Monthly Newsletter*, 1 (October 1975).

[127] 'Australia: a sick nation! Whose responsibility is it?', *Vision*, 1 (January–February 1974), 7–8.

[128] Derek Prince, 'Praying for the government', *New Wine*, March 1970, 5–11, at 9.

[129] Dennis Clark, 'The fig tree', audio sermon, 1972 (online), http://denisgclark.pbworks.com/w/page/17471953/OralMaterials (accessed 21 May 2021).

same (based on Abraham Lincoln's 'Proclamation of a Day of Humiliation, Fasting and Prayer'), by Republican Senator Mark Hatfield, to reach the House floor.[130] Intercessors' groups were founded in New Zealand and Australia. Further momentum came in 1974 through another Jimmy and Carol Owens musical: *If My People*. This was described as a 'worship experience in music and intercession' in response to 'societies and governments everywhere falling apart'.[131] Along with the touring musical, album, and songbook, there was handbook on national intercession to support local performances. At Post Green the arrival of the musical was eagerly awaited as a chance to 'gather God's people and intercede for nations'.[132] During the Australian constitutional crisis of 1975, the musical was cited as part of a wider call to prayer for Christendom.[133] The text of 2 Chronicles 7:14 was a charismatic motto during the mid-1970s.

A third aspect of the charismatic imagination concerned spiritual warfare. Even Michael Harper, who was at the cautious end of the scale on the topic, was convinced there was a 'resurgence of the power of evil supernaturalism on a truly daunting scale'.[134] He spoke of a 'devil's pentecost', asserting 'We are living in days when Satan is pouring out his spirits as well as Jesus Christ the Holy Spirit.'[135] When Dennis Bennett had visited England five years earlier, Harper saw him deliver a vicar, who manifested as 'his legs shot from under him, and he lay spread-eagled and inert on the floor' (the aftermath was very English: he 'opened his eyes, blinked, got to his feet, brushed himself down and smiled blandly'). Demonic activity was not limited to the '"uncivilized" world', as Harper put it.[136] Such evil was behind moral decline ('homosexuality, drugs'), mental health crises, and a growing fascination with witchcraft and the occult.[137] It is plausible that a factor contributing to this concern over pervasive 'evil' was the background of so many charismatics leaders as participants in the mid-century cultic milieu. Derek Prince, Maxwell Whyte, Elton D. Purvis, Lady Bronwen Astor, and Robert Firebrace were just some of the charismatics in prominent positions who had had some pre-conversion involvement in alternative religions. Another, David Watson, had searched for 'some kind of spiritual reality' in his teenage years, trying Spiritualism, Theosophy, the work of Rudolf Steiner, as well as various Eastern religions. Participation in a séance left him with a 'cautionary awareness that I was dabbling in something dangerous'. He later counselled that 'every involvement with the occult...is like playing with an unexploded bomb.'[138] The flurry of charismatic texts on the occult, such as Don Basham's *Deliver us from*

[130] 'Echoes of the Spirit', *New Wine*, March 1974, 9; 'Intercessors for America', *New Covenant*, 5/9 (March 1976), 20–21.

[131] Jimmy and Carol Owens (featuring Pat Boone), *If my people (a musical experience in worship and intercession)*, 1974, Light, vinyl LP.

[132] RUSCA, Dennis J. Bennett papers, box 5, *Post Green News*, 32, 24 October 1974.

[133] Alan Langstaff, 'Prayer for our leaders', *Vision*, November–December 1975, 3.

[134] Michael Harper, *Spiritual warfare* (London: Hodder & Stoughton, 1970), 13.

[135] Ibid., 40.

[136] Ibid., 11–13.

[137] Ibid., 142–49.

[138] Watson, *You are my God*, 14–15, quote at 14.

Evil (1972) and Nicky Cruz's *Satan on the Loose* (1973), was akin to a 'Satanic panic'. The age of Aquarius, or Bob Mumford, went hand in hand with social and political instability. They came from the same source: 'a rebellious attitude'.[139] The imagination of Spirit-filled Christians in the 1970s was one prepared for spiritual combat with the forces of disunity, secular humanism, and the occult. This charismatic cosmology of the powers of good and evil, and concern for the dominion of Christ, exerted a powerful influence in the coming decades.

City of Pentecost: Jerusalem, Israel, and the Charismatic Imagination

In 1979, Alan Langstaff conjectured that pentecostalism had been birthed at the same time as Zionism; the birth of the State of Israel in 1948 had coincided with the ministries of Oral Roberts, David du Plessis, and Cursillo; that the Six Day War of 1967 occurred alongside the rise of the Jesus People and Catholic renewal; and that charismatic renewal was 'coming of age' in 1978 just as Israel was celebrating its 30th anniversary.[140] Although charismatics were not in unison in their speculations on biblical prophecy, many were broadly convinced of the eschatological significance of the State of Israel. There was a particular identification with Jerusalem, in part because it had been the site of the first Pentecost. Israel was God's 'prophetic clock', and the holy city its central dial.[141]

The predominant charismatic eschatology, in common with post-war pentecostals and conservative evangelicals, was pre-millennial and futurist. Langstaff concurred with David du Plessis and Derek Prince, who saw the 'outpouring' in relationship with Israel: the triumph of the Jewish State would be accompanied by a latter rain of blessing on the churches. In the same year Hal Lindsey's best-selling *The Late Great Planet Earth* (1970) appeared, Gordon Lindsay claimed in a special editorial for *New Wine*: 'The reason Israel is in Palestine today is that it is God's time.'[142] Amongst Logos International's titles was Willard Cantelon's prophetic trilogy: *The Day the Dollar Dies* (1973), *Money the Master of the World* (1976), and *New Money or None* (1979). The first book addressed developments in the Middle East and with a strong vein of economic nationalism (including the Trump-like claim that post-war reconstruction meant 'almost every nation on earth was standing on the doorstep of Washington'), predicting the rise of a new world government and global money system in response to economic and energy

[139] Bob Mumford, 'The great transgression', *New Wine*, October 1972, 4–9, 31; at 8.
[140] Alan Langstaff, 'A new wave's about to break', *Vision*, 30 (January–February 1979), 5–8.
[141] Stephen Spector, *Evangelicals and Israel: the story of American Christian Zionism* (Oxford: Oxford University Press, 2009), 28.
[142] Gordon Lindsay, Editorial, 'Our stand for Israel', *New Wine*, February 1970, 1.

uncertainties.[143] Cantelon criticised the United Nations' financial support for Russia and claimed world history was 'Ultimately heading towards Russia marching on Israel'.[144] Alongside these more traditional pre-millennialist interpretations, Latter Rain influences fostered a restorationist emphasis on the return to nationhood of Israel occurring in tandem with Christians' return to their 'Spiritual Jerusalem'.[145] The embrace of charismatic renewal and Messianic Judaism underlined this connection, as did the adoption of some Hebraic practices and sounds in worship. Some were hesitant about the eschatological significance of Israel; or found the message of reconciliation in the Spirit to be at odds with a straightforward identification with the State of Israel. When *New Covenant* covered Israel and prophecy, it included an article by the Catholic Beirut prayer group leader Peter Shebaya. 'A belief that Israel is a "sign of the times" cannot be seen *as in itself* a mandate to *support* Israel', he said. 'What about Christian Arabs?'[146]

This was the immediate context for a series of international conferences between 1974 and 1976 organised by the Logos International Fellowship. The eschatological logic was clear in the strapline for the first World Conference on the Holy Spirit: 'Jerusalem II'. Al West explained in *Logos Journal* that for perhaps the first time since Pentecost, thousands 'will gather in a Jerusalem upper room to celebrate not only that event but the fulfilment of prophecy, that of Joel 2, in the present generation'.[147] The upper room was Jerusalem's Congress Hall. The stage presented the luminaries of charismatic subculture—including Kathryn Kuhlman, Merv and Merla Watson, Michael Esses, Art Katz, Michael Harper, and David du Plessis. There were between four and five thousand delegates from various nations, though three thousand were American.[148] A conference documentary, *Jerusalem II* (1974), was filmed to 'bring to the world the message of Pentecost'. It was directed by Shira Lindsay (daughter of Gordon), who had in 1968 directed *Dry Bones*—a film based on the vision in the Book of Ezekiel, made up of readings from biblical prophecy, images of actors playing prophets in the desert, and contemporary footage of Israel.[149] *Jerusalem II* was similarly interspersed with worshipping Christians, the Israeli military, and a city in 'rebirth and renaissance since 1967'.[150] During a prayer for Golda Meir in the film, there were images of Megiddo, the supposed future site of the Battle of Armageddon. 'We feel that the entire stage is being rearranged... and that the curtain is to be drawn for the final acts of God', said Roy Kreider, a Mennonite missionary to Israel.[151] The film also

[143] Willard Cantelon, *The day the dollar dies* (Plainfield: Logos International Fellowship, 1973), viii; 23–24.
[144] Ibid., 112, quote at 143.
[145] See Joseph Williams, 'The pentecostalization of Christian Zionism', *Church History*, 84/1 (March 2015), 177–82.
[146] Peter Shebaya, 'An Arab perspective', *New Covenant*, 3/8 (March 1974), 10–14.
[147] Al West, 'World Conference on the Holy Spirit', *Logos Journal*, March–April 1974, 36–37.
[148] Ibid.
[149] *Dry bones* (1968). Directed by Shira Lindsay.
[150] *Jerusalem II* (1975). Directed by Shira Lindsay.
[151] Ibid.

featured prayers by Arab Christians and a message from Joseph Raya, the Coptic Archbishop of Akko, Haifa, Nazareth, and Galilee, and champion for the rights of Arab Christians (he was previously a civil rights campaigner while assistant priest in Birmingham, Alabama). Jamie Buckingham of Logos International Fellowship claimed, 'I am able to embrace Catholic, Pentecostal, Jewish, Arab, all-alike as we come together in the Spirit.'[152] This was all very well, but political agendas were hardly disguised by the language of oneness in the Spirit.

The overriding message of 'Jerusalem II'—both the conference and film—was the Spirit at work at a time of new Pentecost. The film narrator described the conference as a 'catalyst for the world's charismatics'.[153] It very deliberately juxtaposed technology and the Spirit's work. It was said that 'modern communication', such as simultaneous translations at the conference, combined with a 'deeper spiritual force' behind the scenes.[154] It included footage of Kathryn Kuhlman speaking to a German woman who had experienced a healing. The two could not understand each other, but Kuhlman asserted 'the Holy Spirit speaks a universal language and that's wonderful.'[155] This was an idealised charismatic cosmopolitanism: a breaking down of barriers between denominations, ethnicities, and nations, with media used to fulfil the purpose.

'If Bob Mumford Goes to Israel, I Shall Not Go': Asymmetries

The themes above indicate aspects of unity and coherence in the collective imagination of a diverse, complex, global-local Spiritscape. However, at the same time, long-term tensions were emerging as asymmetries. One, in fact, was playing out behind the scenes in preparation for Jerusalem II. Bob Mumford was meant to be a conference speaker; however, Kathryn Kuhlman's opposition to his 'shepherding' teaching resulted in her threatening to withdraw from a healing service at the conference. In the end Mumford was asked to stand down from the programme.[156]

The early signs of a shepherding controversy were in the United States. Paradoxically, immediately before, it had seemed the disparate strands of renewal in the country were seeking to recognise a greater unity. An informal 'eldership' of leaders across the charismatic spectrum met in Seattle in 1971; and at a gathering in Tulsa the next year, there was recognition of the commonality, despite a range of theological differences, in the group. Bob Mumford was amongst those to celebrate this unity in diversity, saying 'anyone knows that hybrid corn is better

[152] Ibid. [153] Ibid. [154] Ibid. [155] Ibid.

[156] Jamie Buckingham, *Buckingham Report*, 1/6 (25 March 1985).

eating than seed corn'.[157] However, in May 1975, allegations of controlling behaviour at the Good News Fellowship (a group with links to Christian Growth Ministries) led Pat Robertson to condemn the CGM 'shepherds', including Mumford, on *The 700 Club* programme, and warn listeners to 'flee' leaders or groups using the terms 'discipleship, shepherding, submission and covering'.[158] Robertson informed CBN staff he feared a new charismatic denomination was afoot. He ordered all tapes of 'Bob Mumford, Charles Simpson, Derek Prince, Ern Baxter, John Poole, Don Basham, or any of the lesser lights' be erased. Other leaders, including David du Plessis, Dennis Bennett, and Demos Shakarian, also expressed criticism. The first attempt to resolve the controversy was a conversation between leaders in Dan Malachuk's hotel suite at the Christian Booksellers Convention in 1975.[159] A further meeting in Minneapolis was compared by some, in another charismatic appropriation of the Acts narrative, to one of the councils at Jerusalem. Others, perhaps appropriately, referred to it more colloquially as the 'Shoot-out at the Curtis Hotel'.[160] There seemed a possibility of a complete rift amongst American charismatics.

In December, a further national meeting was held at TWOG. Here the two sides seemed to show greater willingness to 'agree to disagree' and avoid public attacks; and there was a commitment from shepherding proponents to seek to correct local misapplications of their teachings. The question-and-answer session was published in *Logos Journal* and *New Wine*.[161] In March 1976, there was another meeting of charismatic leaders which resulted in a statement from CGM leaders (the 'five' and John Poole) that their teachings had been 'essentially sound' but sometimes 'misapplied or handled in an immature way'.[162] However, despite these efforts, there were no quick fixes. 'The schism', recalled Buckingham, 'was so deep and wide that nothing short of a miracle could bring healing'. For some, trust could not be fully restored while shepherding teachings and practices continued.[163] Dennis Bennett was still warning of the dangers of abuse in 1979, writing in his parish magazine, 'The Church . . . is an upside-down pyramid. The Church does not descend from Peter and the other Apostles. They're on

157 Jamie Buckingham, 'Breakthrough in unity', *Logos Journal*, 40/5 (September–October 1972), 37–39.

158 Quoted in David S. Moore, *The shepherding movement: controversy and charismatic ecclesiology* (London: T&T Clark, 2003), 93–94.

159 Moore, *Shepherding*, 97.

160 'Logos report: what really happened at Minneapolis', *Logos Journal*, November–December 1974, 58–61.

161 DAHL, DDP, box 9, file 9, 'A statement of information'; Buckingham, 'Changing attitudes among discipleship leaders', 1; 'Discipleship forum in Ft Lauderdale', *Logos Journal* insert, March–April 1976.

162 Don Basham, 'Toward healing the rift', *New Wine*, May 1976, 20–22.

163 Buckingham, *Buckingham Report*, 2.

the bottom of the stack. It's built on them!'[164] The controversy spread beyond the United States. Bennett and others warned colleagues abroad of the dangers.[165] A talk by Michael Harper, 'A Message to the Charismatic Movement', at the 1975 Australian Temple Trust conference spoke of the dangers of legalism in the renewal. He quoted the Apostle Paul in Galatians 3:4: 'Are you so foolish? Having begun with the Spirit are you now ending with the flesh?' Alan Langstaff warned in *Vision* that shepherding teachings were being taken to extremes. 'Although the charismatic renewal movement has faced in its time many attacks from outside its rank, the greatest dangers to its healthy development are those that come from within.'[166] From its base in the Blue Mountains, the Logos Fellowship network had cultivated a network of shepherding relationships, and Howard Carter said of the controversy '"An enemy hath done this"'. While desiring 'mutual understanding' with critics he defended shepherding principles.[167] Translocal connections were spreading controversy.

The conflict can be interpreted as a by-product of the ecclesiological ambiguities inherent in the charismatic prayer group. Were they a church or a pan-denominational gathering? Another ecclesiological divergence came with increasing concern about denominationalism. We have examined the considerable overlap between mainline 'renewalists' and independent 'restorationists'. However, from the mid-1970s this blending was giving way to a separation of the new wine of the Spirit into 'old' and 'new' wineskins. As mainline churches softened their attitudes towards charismatic renewal, there was a trend towards the formation of representative denominational bodies. The Episcopal Charismatic Fellowship was a large body, established in 1973 with the support of Bishop William C. Frey of the Diocese of Colorado. This was two years after a House of Bishops Pastoral Letter described 'a growing awareness of the pentecostal power of the Holy Spirit' in the Church. The group aimed to bring together the Catholic and Evangelical wings of Episcopalianism to 'explore the theological, ecumenical and liturgical implications of the renewing presence of the Lord'.[168] A constructive relationship with the Episcopal Church developed. The presiding Bishop, John M. Allin, told the 1977 conference: 'Not too many years ago, the Church could have conveniently ignored those things which you stand for and which you represent, but it can do so no longer.'[169] Many similar groups appeared inside and outside the United States. The editor of *Renewing*, the magazine of the

[164] RUSCA, Dennis J. Bennett papers, 'Spiritual authority', *Morning Watch*, St Luke's Newsletter, November 1979, 1–2.

[165] JKTL, Cecil T. Marshall papers, ANG178, series 1, Item 1, Dennis Bennett to Ray Muller, 10 October 1975; Dennis Bennett to Marshall, 26 November 1975.

[166] Alan Langstaff, editorial, 'Submission and authority', *Vision*, May–June 1975, 3.

[167] Howard Carter, 'A personal letter', *Restore*, March 1978, 2.

[168] 'Statement of the Episcopal Charismatic Fellowship', *ECF Newsletter*, November 1973, 4.

[169] John M. Allin, 'Presiding Bishop's message to ECF conference', *Acts 29 Newsletter*, August 1977, 1.

National Fellowship for Charismatic Renewal in the newly inaugurated Uniting Church in Australia, observed in 1977: 'Renewal in the Spirit IS increasing – in all denominational structures… praise God.'[170] Another author asserted: 'the UCA needs the life and vigour of the Charismatic Renewal; the Charismatic Renewal needs the discipline and balance of other spiritualities that the whole Church can provide.'[171] As the final chapter discusses, such sentiments were increasingly common.

Transnational denominational networks appeared. Cardinal Suenens had first visited The Word of God community incognito, as 'Father Michel Dubois'—not revealing his real identity to the community until the final day.[172] Immediately, as Valentina Ciciliot points out, the Cardinal's decision to reach out to the Americans and advocate a 'policy of presence' surpassed any legitimisation offered yet by the ecclesiastical hierarchy in the United States.[173] In 1973, there was a meeting of Catholic Charismatic leaders in Grottaferrata, near Rome. This included a discussion of a 'Statement of the Theological Basis of the Catholic Charismatic Renewal', devised by Father Killian McDonnell with an international committee. The document related 'baptism in the Holy Spirit' to traditional Catholic teaching: 'The emergences of the graces of Christian initiation into conscious experience'.[174] In 1975, instead of the international conference at Notre Dame, there was a Pentecost 'pilgrimage' to Rome. About ten thousand charismatics visited the Vatican and Pope Paul VI gave a homily after a eucharist in the Basilica. Shortly after, TWOG's Ralph Martin was persuaded to relocate the 'international communication office' from Ann Arbor to Brussels. Legitimacy, as we shall see, would come at the price of a gradual loss of American control. The direction was towards Rome, where indeed the office later moved. This model of denominational integration had an impact on Michael Harper and Terry Fullam, both of whom attended the 1975 jamboree. Drawing together the resources of Anglican representatives of the Fountain Trust and the Episcopal Charismatic Fellowship, they then organised an Anglican International Conference on Spiritual Renewal in Canterbury, England, to take place immediately before the 1978 Lambeth Conference. The invitation to Anglican leaders as far away as New Zealand spoke of a need to 'pause in charismatic ecumenical endeavours to join with our bishops in seeking God's ways of renewal amongst the structures and

170 Editorial, *Renewing*, 6 (December 1977), 1–2.

171 'The place of the charismatic renewal in the UCA', *Renewing*, 6 (December 1977), 26–23, quote at 23.

172 For a description of O'Brien's involvement, see Léon Joseph Suenens, *The hidden hand of God: life of Veronica O'Brien and our common apostolate* (London: Veritas, 1994), 228–32.

173 Valentina Ciciliot, 'The origins of the Catholic Charismatic Renewal in the United States: early developments in Indiana and Michigan and the reactions of the ecclesiastical authorities', *Studies in World Christianity*, 25/3 (2019), 250–73.

174 DGC, Fountain Trust collection, box 1, 'Statement of the theological basis of the Catholic Charismatic Renewal'.

life of the Anglican family'.[175] The conference ended with a eucharistic finale at Canterbury Cathedral, where various bishops—including Archbishop Bill Burnett—danced before the altar. By the end of the decade, mainline charismatics leaders seemed less invested in pan-denominationalism.

Concurrently, the ecclesiological identity of independent charismatics was increasingly pronounced, as they endorsed the necessity of new wineskins. The south coast English Apostle, Terry Virgo, argued in *Restoration* in 1978:

> Instead of... new energy [from the charismatic movement] being welcomed into local churches, many have shut their doors to charismatic gifts, forcing people into an unscriptural situation. While remaining loyal to their churches on Sunday, many attend mid-week meetings for charismatic fellowship. Hence energies are squandered and the church fails to benefit. If these groups are without proper oversight, they become open to error, so that the whole strategy of God for the church to contain and oversee this life is frustrated.[176]

While much cordial interaction continued, some independents were obviously frustrated to see mainliners double down on denominational loyalties. Was not 'Pentecost' meant to produce 'one body'? The title on the cover of the 1977 book by British restorationist John Noble—*Forgive us our Denominations*—gave a clue as to the unequivocal response within.

A further intra-charismatic tension concerned prosperity and healing. Teachings on the abundant life, often traced to E. W. Kenyon, had always found audiences within charismatic subculture, but without becoming a dominant influence. The rise of television ministries changed this. Initially, these were digitalised versions of the evangelical 'faith mission'. However, as John Wigger shows in the case of the Jim and Tammy Bakker's PTL network, they began to find synergies with the Word of Faith movement. Kenneth Hagin, Kenneth Copeland, and others were welcomed onto PTL, and by the late 1970s the Bakkers seemed to propagate similar principles. Reminding his television audience that God, in response to a 'positive confession', had built their evangelistic media empire, Jim Bakker said to them: 'Decide on what you need. Is it a house? A solution to a problem? A healing? Money? Salvation of a loved one? Maybe you just want to lose weight... So you begin by simply speaking out what you need.'[177] In 1980, *Logos Journal*, as ever committed to holding the centre of charismatic unity, published articles by three Americans—Charles Farah, Dennis W. Roberts, an Assemblies of God minister, and Kenneth Copeland. The former two pressed hard

175 Michael Harper quoted in JKTL, Cecil T. Marshall papers, ANG 178, file 2, series 29, Letter from CAM to Anglican clergy, n.d.

176 Terry Virgo, 'The Church: God's only answer', *Restoration*, November–December 1978, 13.

177 Quoted in John Wigger, *PTL: the rise and fall of Jim and Tammy Faye Bakker's evangelical empire* (New York: Oxford University Press, 2017), 66.

against Word of Faith, with Farah critiquing the 'rapidly spreading teachings' of 'perfect health, perfect peace and perfect prosperity'.[178] The idea of the abundant life was to become increasingly influential and controversial during the 1980s.

* * *

This chapter has discussed the renewal as power pilgrimage, music, books, and conference ministries were at full flow in the 1970s. These constructed and sustained a cosmopolitan charismatic imaginary. Charismatics sought to understand, and act within, the eschatological moment. Just as testimony narratives had brought a coherence to the imagination of the new Pentecost, stories of reconciliation, repentance, and the supernatural world continued to cultivate a powerful, translocal a sense of community, even as charismatics could also articulate a sense of national consciousness. In 1977, at the Kansas City conference, articulations of the charismatic imaginary were transmitted to the community of the Spirit across the Anglo-world. The visiting Australian AoG pastor, David Cartledge, wrote of 'the Kansas City miracle' and of 'indescribable' nightly large meetings in the Arrowhead Stadium. It was 'a foretaste of things to come around the world. Its sheer size was a demonstration to the world that the dry bones are rapidly approaching the stage where they will stand up as the mighty army of the Lord.' However, at another level, the conference revealed the limits of charismatic unity and coherence. As Cartledge explained, it was seen by some as an attempt to draw a line under the shepherding controversy.[179] The model of the conference, whereby different strands—Baptist, Catholic, Episcopalian, Lutheran, Mennonite, Pentecostal, Presbyterian, Methodist, Messianic Jewish, and non-denominational—met together in the evening, but separately by day, indicated the rise of distinctive identity groupings. A conference of such ecumenical scale and ambition was not to be repeated. As the final chapter explains, by the late decade many perceived a distinctive phase of charismatic renewal to be at an end.

[178] Charles Farah, 'Forum: Faith theology: the sovereignty of men?', *Logos*, May–June 1980, 50, 52–53, quote at 50.

[179] Dave Cartledge, 'The Kansas City miracle', *Charismatic Contact*, 6/2 (1973), n.p.

7
World

> The God who made the world and everything in it is the Lord of heaven and earth and does not live in temples built by human hands.
>
> Acts 17:24

David du Plessis (Fig. 7.1) was a missionary of Pentecost, a global witness for the 'full gospel' in churches. His regular prayer letter claimed that in 1964 alone he travelled a hundred thousand miles, across ten countries. In the early 1960s he was often visiting mainland Europe and 1967 saw extensive travels beyond the West, including Kenya, Brazil, Argentina, and Peru. Du Plessis' ecumenical connections with the World Council of Churches were such that he would have been aware of news of 'Spirit-filled' developments beyond the places he was able to travel to. When du Plessis visited Anglo-world locations, fliers for his speaking appointments referred to 'The astounding move of God and the Holy Spirit in the Historic Churches'—a 'World-wide Spiritual Awakening'.[1] There was, of course, an eschatological logic behind the language which was soon to be shared by Anglo-world charismatics—of a *global* move of the Spirit.

The previous chapters have addressed the origins and emergence of a Spiritscape of charismatic renewal in North America, the British Isles, Australasia, and South Africa. However, while this distinctive subculture of media, networks, forms, and flagship ministries mapped largely onto the Anglo-world, it was from the beginning interconnected with a global nexus of charismatic, pentecostal, and holiness movements—some pre-dating 'the renewal'—in the non-English-speaking West, the communist bloc, and the Third World. Reports of worldwide spiritual resurgences shaped their imagination. Although initially there was little substantial engagement with these movements, this began to change significantly in the 1970s.

'Revival with a Difference': Imagining Global Christian Resurgence

Charismatics looked for worldwide examples of Christian resurgence and invested them with eschatological significance. For some this was evidently a revival

[1] DAHL, David du Plessis papers, box 80, file 1, Invitation, 'Inter-church Council of Men's Societies of Victoria'.

Age of the Spirit: Charismatic Renewal, the Anglo-World, and Global Christianity, 1945–1980. John Maiden, Oxford University Press. © John Maiden 2023. DOI: 10.1093/oso/9780198847496.003.0007

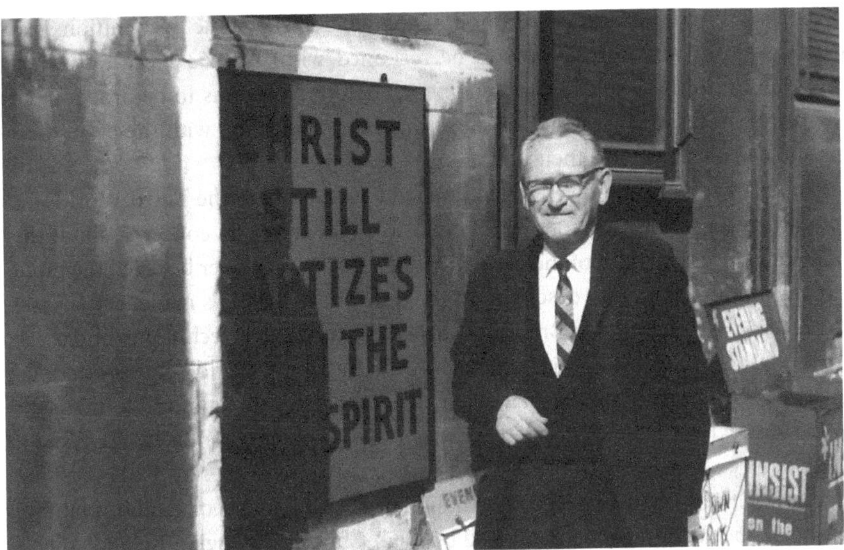

Fig. 7.1 David du Plessis outside a London church in the mid-1960s.

without precedent. In a 1969 *New Wine* editorial, Don Basham argued that historically, revivals were localised (to either a nation or continent) and based upon intellectual ascent to truth; however, what they were now witnessing was a spiritual renewal of supernatural power, and its extent was 'clearly world-wide, having spread to every continent'. 'From Ireland to Indonesia, from Argentina to Australia, from Canada to Korea, the reports come', he said, 'telling of supernatural, miracle-working revival... inspired by and infused with the Holy Spirit.'[2] Similarly, the global parameters of the new Pentecost were a frequent theme in the Catholic-ecumenical *New Covenant*. A 1971 editorial claimed, 'what we are experiencing in our life, in our country, is part of a much larger plan of God to restore the world to his Son.'[3]

As we discussed in Chapter 2, the decades after 1945 displayed a heightened expectation of revival in holiness evangelical circles, with the literature of the Worldwide Evangelization Crusade, for example, describing experiences of the supernatural on foreign soil in detail. Even beyond this eschatologically-fused, revivalistic expectation, the notion of spiritual resurgence in the Third World—what Bishop Lesslie Newbiggin had in 1952 called the 'third arm' of Christianity—had growing currency. In *Pentecostalism and Speaking in Tongues* (1964) Canon Douglas Webster of the Church Missionary Society impressed on readers the potential significance of a movement 'Among the proletarian millions of South

[2] Don Basham, Editorial, 'Revival with a difference', *New Wine*, October 1969, 2.
[3] 'I have come to cast fire on the earth', *New Covenant*, 2/7 (January 1973), 1–3, quote at 1.

America'.[4] Amongst Roman Catholics, too, there was some recognition that pentecostalism was now a force to be reckoned with. A 1963 piece by Daniel J. O'Hanlon in the Jesuit magazine *America* described lessons to be drawn from the pentecostals of Latin America, admiring their connection with the poor, their emotion in worship, and their devotion.[5]

This narrative of empowered, reanimated Christianity in the Third World was one which had synergies, too, with Anglo-world charismatic concerns about the 'religious' superficialities of the denominations. Michael Harper believed the rapid expansion of Christianity described in the Acts of the Apostles made 'embarrassing reading' for churches in Britain, with all their 'up-to-date techniques and novel methods of mass communication'. 'Only in the third world', he asserted, 'is anything comparable taking place, and it is not without significance that it is being done largely through Pentecostals'.[6] The appetite for 'New Testament Christianity' had been nourished by missionaries such as W. F. P. (Willie) Burton of the Congo Evangelistic Mission, whose accounts of church planting of indigenous congregations, inspired by High Church theologian Roland Allen's *Missionary Methods: St Paul's or Ours?* (1912), underlined the potential for small group Christianity; and proved influential, in particular, with restorationists, such as the future British house church leader Roger Forster.[7] Whilst this looking to the Third World reflected dissatisfaction with the spiritual state of their own churches, it also had other contemporary parallels, for example the tendency during the long Sixties of Western, radical left activists to look towards anti-colonial movements for inspiration and stimulus.

The worldwide move of the Spirit seemed in progress, too, in mainland Europe. Whilst language barriers limited integration between charismatic networks here and in the Anglo-world, there was some interchange between senior leaders. The Netherlands had seen post-war exchanges between pentecostal and Reformed Christians, and these were given a further boost by the visit of Tommy Osborn in 1958. A pre-war pentecostal publication, *Kracht van Omhoog* (Power from on High) was revamped as a national magazine, 'for the furthering of the message of the fulfilment of the Holy Spirit and the imminent return of Christ', and from 1960 this had a mixed mainline Reformed and pentecostal editorial team.[8] Another magazine, *Vuur* ('Fire'), had the same interdenominational approach—and already by 1964 had a Roman Catholic on its editorial team.[9] In the same year,

[4] Douglas Webster, *Pentecostalism and speaking in tongues* (London: Highway Press, 1964), 34.

[5] Daniel J. O'Hanlon, "The Pentecostals and Pope John's 'New Pentecost'", *America*, 108/18 (1963), 634–36.

[6] Michael Harper, *Walk in the Spirit*, 2nd edn. (London: Hodder & Stoughton, 1981), 9–10.

[7] William K. Kay, *Apostolic networks in Britain: new ways of being church* (Milton Keynes: Paternoster Press, 2007), 114.

[8] Paulus Nicolaas van der Laan, 'The question of spiritual unity: the Dutch Pentecostal movement in ecumenical perspective', PhD thesis, University of Birmingham (1988), 66; 199.

[9] Ibid., 271.

the Netherlands Reformed Church published a pastoral letter which was probably the first official mainline response to pentecostalism to recognise the value of the movement's contribution.[10] A businessman's group, 'Volle Evangelie Zakenlieden Nederland' (VEZA), linked with the FGBMFI, was also at work connecting Christians. David du Plessis, whose Afrikaans cultural connections gave him a particular interest in pentecostal advances in the country, visited several times. He made Britons and North Americans aware of a 'rising tide of revival' amongst both Protestants and Catholics.[11] The Fountain Trust became a node for the transfer of Dutch influences. The Trust's ethos of spiritual unity and its early concern for bringing together of pentecostal and evangelical influences was like that of *Kracht van Omhoog* and *Vuur*. Teachings by evangelists Kees Noordzij and Riemer de Graaf, who visited Britain in 1966, and by *Kracht van Omhoog* editor J. E. van der Brink, helped cultivate the early interest in spiritual warfare amongst British charismatics.[12] Corrie Ten Boom and Anne van der Bijl were two Dutch evangelicals with remarkable testimonies of commitment to Christ; the former of helping Jews and surviving the Ravensbrück concentration camp, the latter of supporting underground churches behind the Iron Curtain. They became household names in English-speaking charismatic circles. In many respects a mainline new Pentecost was more strongly evident in the Netherlands before anywhere else in the Anglo-world.

West Germany also seemed to exhibit the Spirit's work. The Lutheran pastor Arnold Bittlinger wrote to Michael Harper in 1965 of a 'new charismatic awakening'.[13] In previous years, interest in the Spirit had slowly gathered pace in the Lutheran Evangelical Church of Germany (EKD) and the Free Churches, as well as amongst some Roman Catholic clergy. The main figure to link these developments and the burgeoning renewal movement in the Anglo-world was Harper's American Lutheran friend Larry Christenson, who was fluent in German. In 1963, Bittlinger met Christenson while on a study trip to America.[14] Subsequently, Bittlinger invited Harper to speak in West Germany about the 'revival-movement' in Britain and visited along with Christenson in 1967. Bittlinger helped establish *Oekumenisches Lebenszentrum für die Einheit der Christen* (Ecumenical Life Centre for Christian Unity) at Schloss Craheim in 1968, where various national and Europe-wide conferences, attracting speakers

[10] Ibid., 179.

[11] LPL, Michael Harper papers, 1964/10, David and Anna du Plessis prayer letter, December 1964, 3.

[12] Michael Harper, 'Ministry in spiritual warfare: two Dutch evangelists visit Britain', *Renewal*, 3 (May–June 1966), 18–19; J. E. van der Brink, 'The wonder and power of Pentecost', *Renewal*, 3 (May–June 1966), 5–8.

[13] LPL, Michael Harper papers, 1964/2, Arnold Bittlinger to Michael Harper, 27 November 1965, 5.

[14] Fred W. McRae, *The history of the German Church Growth Association, 1985–2003* (Eugene: Wipf & Stock, 2014), 26.

from North America, South Africa, and Australasia, were held.[15] Christenson also came into contact with a Protestant community which had been practising the charismatic gifts long before himself, Bittlinger, or Harper: the Protestant ecumenical Sisterhood of Mary, based in Darmstadt. The group, discussed in Chapter 5, placed emphasis on reconciliation and repentance in the aftermath of the Nazi regime; but also practised spontaneous prayer and praise, moved in the supernatural gifts, and adopted a radical community life. The group had an early impact on Christenson, who invited two Sisters to relocate to San Pedro, and Harper, who even learned German in order to assist in the translation of Mother Basilea Schlink's *Ruled by the Spirit* (1969). By 1967, even before Church of the Redeemer and The Word of God (TWOG) communities arrived on the charismatic scene, the 'Mary Sisters' were convincing Harper of the value of evangelical community living.[16] Continental Western Europe did not display the dramatic signs of revival reported in the Third World but seemed to add weight to the idea of a global eschatological moment. As Michael Harper said in a survey of the Spirit's activity in Europe for *Logos Journal* in 1972: 'the Holy Spirit is not passing Europe by. He is renewing the old world as well as the new.'[17]

'To Russia, with Love': Supernaturalising the Cold War

Scholars recognise the Cold War had a strong religious dimension, with the efforts of the American 'spiritual-industrial' complex and evangelical revivalists to build a cultural bulwark against the godless forces of communism. Charismatics were conscious of the same threat. Michael Harper, although suspicious of the more belligerent theories of the '"reds-under-the-beds" lobby', saw the rise of pornography as a threat to national vitality. He warned in 1976: 'Denmark has become a fruit ripe for picking and adding to the Communist basket. Britain could follow quickly.'[18] There was, furthermore, a concern for persecuted Christians. Some readers of Watchman Nee's *The Normal Christian Life* were aware that he had been imprisoned by the Chinese government in 1956—ultimately to die in a labour camp in 1972. Cold War tensions cultivated transnational solidarity between Christians in the Anglo-world and mainland Europe, and also in those Third World contexts which appeared threatened by communist takeover. Basilea Schlink's *The World in Revolt* (1969), published by Minneapolis' Bethany House, was clear that communism was not a matter of economic policy but a

[15] LPL, Michael Harper papers, 1967/6, Arnold Bittlinger to Harper, 16 February 1967, 1. See also 'German conferences', *Renewal*, April–May 1967, 8; 'International news', *New Covenant*, 2/4 (October 1972), 23.

[16] Michael Harper, 'Editorial', *Renewal*, August–September 1967, 2–3.

[17] Michael Harper, 'A shift to Europe?', *Logos Journal*, 40/6 (November–December 1972), 32.

[18] Michael Harper, 'Let there be light', *Renewal*, 62 (April–May 1976), 10.

Weltanschauung of 'materialistic atheism'. 'Antichristianity is on the march!', she warned in 1969, even in the '"Christian world"'.[19] As we have seen, like many conservative evangelicals and pentecostals, most charismatics read 'the times'—the threat of Russia and China, and events in the Middle East—through the lenses of premillennialism. Their understanding of spiritual outpouring went side by side with prophetic speculation. This made a distinctive contribution to Christian responses to the Cold War, representing geo-political tensions in terms of spiritual warfare.

Testimonies provided a sense that the Spirit was *supernaturally* undermining communism. Again, it was a story which imprinted this on the charismatic imagination: the testimony of Anne van der Bijl. The Dutch evangelical, known as Brother Andrew, had attended the Worldwide Evangelization Crusade training college in Glasgow, where he moved in a charismatic direction after discovering a prayer group. Here he found it was 'as though every individual [...] sensed that God was very close, and in the delight of His company wanted nothing, needed nothing, except occasionally to express the joy bubbling up inside'.[20] Van der Bijl felt a calling to serve God behind the Iron Curtain, and his testimony, *God's Smuggler*, co-written by John and Elizabeth Sherrill—the co-authors of *The Cross and the Switchblade*—was a thrilling read. It recounted, for instance, passing through a checkpoint on the Romanian border, and trusting God by placing smuggled bibles in full view on the car seat. 'My heart was racing', he wrote. 'Not with the excitement of the crossing, but with the excitement of having caught such a spectacular glimpse of God at work.'[21] Van der Bijl, who was a consultant editor for *New Wine* magazine by 1970, appeared widely in the charismatic media, and was a source of information on underground churches in the Soviet Union, China, and Cuba.[22] He was critical of the communist system, arguing that the idea of dialogue between communism and Christianity was as 'unreal as Jesus and Satan sitting round a table discussing how they would solve the problems of the world'.[23] Even so, comparatively speaking his rhetoric was less strident than some evangelical language in the Cold War, with a more humane emphasis on God's love for the communist world.

Similar stories to those of Brother Andrew emerged. Chris Panos' *God's Spy*, published by Logos International, combined the spy thriller genre with the atmosphere of the Book of Acts. On one occasion, Panos claimed to have been told to 'blind' a border guard at Kiev airport just as Saul had done to the sorcerer

[19] M. Basilea Schlink, *The world in revolt* (Minneapolis: Bethany House, 1969), 5.

[20] Brother Andrew, John and Elizabeth Sherill, *God's smuggler* (New York: New American Library, 1967), 93.

[21] Ibid., 153.

[22] Brother Andrew, 'Brother Andrew on China', *Renewal*, 22 (August–September 1969), 30–39; Brother Andrew, 'Brother Andrew on Cuba', *Renewal*, 24 (December 1969–January 1970), 12–18; Brother Andrew, 'Caring enough to die', *Logos Journal*, 6/4 (July–August 1976), 4–7.

[23] Brother Andrew, 'Go – now', *Renewal*, 42 (December 1972–January 1973), 29–31, at 29.

Bar-Jesus.[24] He claimed to have received a vivid picture of Europe, in which various cities, mostly in the Soviet bloc, stood out sharply. '"Pack my bags," I said [...], "I'm going back behind the iron curtain."'[25] Studies of the long Sixties have confirmed a surprising level of exchange between West and East—music, fashion, literature and technology, as well as people. Alongside this, we see charismatic mobilities of missionaries, bibles, literature and cassettes, and spiritual practices. The transnational Spirit was regarded as undaunted by the Iron Curtain. Reports and correspondence from the communist bloc appeared in charismatic magazines. 'I do not know whether we shall see one another again on this earth', read a letter in *Renewal* from a Czechoslovakian church leader just after the Russian invasion of 1968.[26] In Britain, Noel Doubleday and Gateway Outreach, which had distributed early Fountain Trust literature, became actively involved in coordinating the circulation of its material—and also Christian Growth Ministries' *New Wine*—into Slavic countries.[27] Brother Andrew was the inspiration for much of this activity. Checkpoints need not be a barrier for the Spirit. 'Stop the negative thoughts that there are closed borders and closed countries', he said. 'They are not closed for business, for hippies or for tourists, and they are not closed for the gospel.'[28]

A Global Nexus: Engaging with the Third World

There had been, in subtle ways, interchange between the charismatic renewal and non-Western charismatics and pentecostals from the beginning. An important early influence on Anglo-world charismatics had been reports of supernatural encounters in South America, South-East Asia and Africa. 'In this enlightened, scientific age, is it possible to believe in demons?', asked *Christian Life* magazine in 1958. The answer, based on reports and photographic images of Spirit possession in Bolivia, Ecuador, and the southern Philippines, was yes.[29] Some returning missionaries came home aware of a live supernatural world. Simon Barrington-Ward, the Dean of Magdalene College, Cambridge, witnessed demonic power while working as a CMS missionary in Nigeria; he returned home and experienced the Spirit through David du Plessis, joining the Fountain Trust network.[30]

[24] Chris Panos, *God's spy* (Plainfield: Logos International, 1976), 155. [25] Ibid., 147.

[26] 'Czech pastor's letter', *Renewal*, December 1968–January 1969, 3.

[27] Jeanne Hinton, 'European gospel advance', *Renewal*, 20 (April–May 1969), 19–20; David M. Young, *Turned east: half a life for Albania* (Wrexham: Quinta Press, 2011), 113; 'Foreign outreach report', *New Wine*, January 1976, 13.

[28] Brother Andrew, 'What can we do?', *Renewal*, 33 (June–July 1971), 8–9.

[29] 'Demon power today', *Christian Life*, June 1958, 14–15; Byron W. Ross, 'Delivered', *Christian Life*, November 1959, 14–17.

[30] Graham R. Smith, *The Church militant: spiritual warfare in the Anglican charismatic renewal* (Eugene: Wipf & Stock, 2016), 78.

Similarly, aspects of Derek Prince's demonology were shaped by a period in Kenya from 1957. In the aftermath of the Mau Mau campaign he came to believe in the agency of dark forces in the life of the nation.[31]

There were stories of mainline 'Pentecosts' in Third World contexts which preceded or were simultaneous with charismatic renewal in the Anglo-world. Readers of the British Assemblies of God magazine *Pentecost* would have been aware, for example, of reports of an outbreak of tongues speaking in a Church of England Mission in Mombasa in 1958.[32] From Brazil, charismatic awakenings amongst Baptists had been reported since the early 1950s.[33] A key figure was Rosalee Appleby, a Southern Baptist missionary and church planter who served in Brazil from 1924. Appleby taught an 'advanced' version of Keswick teaching. This was condemned by the Southern Baptists' Foreign Mission Board because of its 'Pentecostal' tendency, along with the gendered criticism that they were the product of her psychological instability. A Baptist minister who later became one of Appleby's mentees, José Rego do Nascimento, of Sixth Baptist Church of Belo Horizonte, was baptised in the Spirit in 1954. Along with another Appleby mentee, Enéas Tognini, the three worked to foster interest amongst Baptists during the late 1950s.[34] In 1961, *Christian Life* reported on the outbreak of empowered evangelicalism in Brazil and the role of Appleby, Nascimento, and Tognini. Robert Walker visited the country personally to observe the movement.[35] His representation of empowered Baptists was particularly significant. He informed readers that Brazilian mainliners saw the 'current move of the Holy Spirit' as 'something akin to, but totally different from, the pentecostal doctrine'. This distinctively mainline encounter with the Spirit was reported in *Christian Life* three months before the magazine made any substantial mention of Dennis Bennett and the happenings in Van Nuys.[36] Shortly after, news of mainline renewal in South Korea was reported in the same magazine. The Episcopalian R. A. Torrey III described 4.30 a.m. prayer meetings and a situation in some indigenous Presbyterian, Methodist, and independent holiness circles where Spirit baptism and manifestations of the gifts were 'assumed to be normal, rather than [a] fringe phenomenon'.[37] For those Anglo-world Christians who looked,

[31] See Stephen Mansfield, *Derek Prince: a biography* (Baldock: Derek Prince Ministries and Authentic Media, 2005).

[32] 'Pentecostal revival in Mombasa, East Africa', *Pentecost*, 45 (September 1958), 10.

[33] 'In Brazil and the Congo', *Christian Life*, October 1950, 33; J. Edwin Orr, 'Power in United Prayer', *Christian Life*, July 1958, 15–17.

[34] João B. Chaves, '"Exporting holy fire": Southern Baptist missions, Pentecostalism and Baptist identity in Latin America', *Perspectives in Religious Studies*, 2/1 (2020), 203–14.

[35] 'Letter from the Editor', *Christian Life*, May 1961, 5–7. See also Robert Walker, 'Spiritual awakening in Brazil', *Christian Life*, August 1961, 24–27.

[36] Jean Stone, 'What is happening today in the Episcopal Church', *Christian Life*, November 1961, 38–42.

[37] R. A. Torrey III, 'Flickering light', *Christian Life*, September 1964, 29–32, 56, quote at 29.

narratives of the Spirit's activity worldwide—within and beyond pentecostalism—were readily available.

As the Anglo-world subculture of service agencies, publishing houses, and conferences appeared in the early 1960s, a geographically wider translocal charismatic nexus was also slowly being established, with flows of literature and personnel, helped along by pentecostal and holiness missionary activity. Often this involved Western efforts to replicate the renewal, although local, indigenous charismatic expressions were also identified as making a unique contribution to the whole. The common dynamics were as follows. First, early charismatics, motivated by their understanding of the eschatological moment, were drawn to foreign mission. Three leading figures of the Blessed Trinity Society (BTS) were by the mid-1960s already engaged in long- and short-term missions in South-East Asia and Latin America. The Revd. Edwin Stube, a priest in the Diocese of Montana and close collaborator of Jean Stone, in 1965 founded a non-profit mission, The Holy Way, and moved to Indonesia, where he established the Lawang Bible Training Centre, from where he ministered also in Burma and South Korea. Indonesian Protestantism had been impacted in the 1930s by the ministry of Chinese holiness revivalist John Sung and later by healing evangelists such as T. L. Osborne. When the Stubes arrived, parts of the country seemed already gripped by revivalism. Into this apparently fertile ground, the Stubes sowed distinctively charismatic patterns of ministry. They explained their strategy in a 1972 prayer letter: 'We have formed prayer groups [...] which meet in people's houses and give opportunity for Body ministry and freedom of the Holy Spirit. We believe that this ministry of prayer will lead to bigger revivals in our own area and in all Indonesia.'[38] The ministry was ecumenical. During a visit to Jakarta in 1967, they engaged with Methodists and others, establishing informal fellowships which were continued by a Mennonite pastor, Herman Tan, and his brother-in-law Pouw Liam Sien. They established the magazine *Api Menyala* ('A Blazing Fire'), 'to promote renewal and growth among the churches'.[39] Another person to enter the mission field was the former editor of *Trinity*, now Jean Stone Willans, who in 1967 moved with her husband and daughter to Taiwan to witness to Western missionaries, before relocating again to the British Crown Colony of Hong Kong.[40] Here they ran the same mid-week ecumenical prayer meetings which had been established in Van Nuys; and they soon involved Protestant and Catholic clergy and religious, missionaries, and both ex-pat and

[38] *The Holy way*, August 1972 (online), https://jspi.info/media/Eng-Mag/1970s/1972/1972-Aug(36).pdf, accessed 2 May 2021.

[39] E. B. Stube, *A fire is burning* (self-published, online), http://www.jspi.info/media/BookBlack/Eng-books/A%20Fires%20Burning%20-EB%20Stube/A%20Fire%20is%20Burning%20(UpTo-1972).pdf, accessed 25 May 2021.

[40] On Taiwan, see Judith C. P. Linn, *The Charismatic movement in Taiwan from 1945–1995: clashes, concord and cacophony* (London: Palgrave Macmillan, 2020), 89–91.

Chinese laity. Their 1971 prayer letter optimistically reported there were 'so many charismatic prayer groups here (all break-offs from this one but everyone in good fellowship) that we can no longer count them'.[41] They had a particular influence on a young English missionary, Jackie Pullinger. Through the Willans' influence, Pullinger began daily tongues speaking and began to rely on baptism in the Spirit and tongues to help addicts off heroin. The Society of Stephen—a network of homes for drug addicts—was set up. Meetings organised by the Willans were attended by up to 150 'ministers, professors, priests, and nuns' together with 'Triads and ex-junkies'.[42] Later Pullinger's story, *Chasing the Dragon* (1980), reached a new generation of readers, whose parents had been inspired by *The Cross and the Switchblade*, with the message of the Spirit's transformative power. Another BTS leader, Harald Bredesen, along with other visitors to Bogotá, Columbia, in 1967, had a role in fostering one of the earliest streams of Catholic charismatic renewal in Latin America. One of those to be influenced was Fr. Rafael García Herreros, a pioneer of the El Minuto de Dios (Minute of God) ministry in the poorer *barrios* of the city. To the existing emphases on community and social action (which were considered suspect by both the political left and right) already evident in El Minuto de Dios, was added charismatic piety.[43]

A second dynamic at work was media stimulation of translocal renewal. In Singapore, there had been a charismatic outpouring amongst revival-hungry Methodist boys at the Anglo-Chinese School in 1972.[44] This was an indigenous Singaporean moment; but it was followed by a direct instance of American influence after the Right Revd. Chiu Ban It, the Anglican Bishop of Singapore, was given Dennis Bennett's *Nine O'Clock in the Morning* during a meeting organised by the World Council of Churches in Bangkok. Spiritually fatigued, he prayed: 'If you can do this for Dennis Bennett and these other people in America, perhaps you'd be good enough to do it for me.' After experiencing Spirit baptism, he encountered a representative from World MAP, an American organisation founded by Ralph and Rose Mahoney, which played an important connecting role in translocal charismatic renewal and who encouraged the bishop to visit Bennett's congregation in Seattle. On his return he pioneered healing and prayer and praise meetings at St Andrew's Cathedral. With the help of the Revd. James Wong, of the Good Shepherd Church, a charismatic ministry began amongst Anglicans in Singapore. When John Stott visited in 1976, he described visiting a congregation where the

[41] DAHL, box 14, Jean Stone and Richard J. Willans papers, Jean and Rick Stone letter to supporters, 10 May 1971, 2.

[42] Jackie Pullinger (with Andrew Quicke), *Chasing the dragon* (London: Hodder & Stoughton, 1980), 157.

[43] Peter Hocken, *Pentecost and Parousia: charismatic renewal, Christian unity and coming glory* (Eugene: Wipf & Stock, 2013), 11–12.

[44] See Michael Poon, 'The beginnings of charismatics renewals in Singapore: an inconvenient truth, an inexpressible gift', https://acsirevivals.wordpress.com/other-revivals/acs-clock-tower-revival/, accessed 25 June 2021.

Series III liturgy was mixed with 'lively but banal choruses'. As Chapter 3 explained, Stott had been dismayed by Michael Harper's pentecostal experience, and presumably to his horror now received from Chui the laying on of hands for deliverance from backache. He observed: 'the charismatic movement has engulfed the Anglican Church', 'from Bishop downwards'.[45] Bishop Chiu also provided early leadership amongst some charismatic Catholics. The renewal in Singapore had multiple stimuli but it was a testament to the reach of Bennett's narrative.[46]

A third dynamic concerned the role of existing denominational networks. This was demonstrated in the case of Anglicanism in Kenya. The country had been influenced by the East African Revival, but pentecostals were also at work, notably through the visit of T. L. Osborne in 1957. In 1963, an interdenominational society called the Trinity Fellowship emerged under the leadership the Revd. C. R. Dawkins, at Siriba College, Maseno, the largest higher educational college in western Kenya. Those involved were committed to 'a revival of the supernatural Christianity of the New Testament'. The group was drawn to the enthusiastic teaching of John Kitts, a Pentecostal Assemblies of Canada missionary, who with his wife Sophia was also involved in the Keswick movement in Kenya. Through Commonwealth channels, the Kitts and Dawkins' son, Godfrey, and additionally Martin and Cynthia Peppiatt (the former had been a curate with Michael Harper at All Souls, Langham Place), established links with charismatics in Britain and North America. In the wake of self-governance from 1963, Kenya became a country of particular concern to the Fountain Trust. Articles appeared in *Renewal* from 1966 and Michael Harper visited the year after.[47] At a Fountain Trust conference a few years later, some reported a vision of a demonic hand over Nairobi, which during prayer was replaced by a map of Kenya being filled by the blood of Christ. The country, according to a prophecy, was to be a 'mighty nation for God in the continent of Africa'.[48] Anglican influence opened up Nairobi to a wider range of pan-denominational charismatic networks. John Kitts wrote in a prayer letter 'the eyes of the world are upon us' ahead of an International Conference for Renewal, held in the city in August 1975, where delegates joined from across the continent, Britain, and the United States.[49] The Revd. David Green of St Mark's Anglican church, Nairobi, a former 'white chaplaincy church' which now had a congregation which was 90 per cent Black African and Asian, took a key role in organising this event. It included a meeting at the Catholic Cathedral and an outdoor meeting, attended by 2,500, at Uhuru Park. The platform exhibited the ecumenical diversity of the charismatic conference circuit

[45] LPL, John R. W. Stott papers, 6/1/14, Travel Diary 1976, 62–64.
[46] James Wong, 'Renewal at the crossroads of Asia', *New Covenant*, 5/11 (May 1976), 9–11.
[47] Godfrey Dawkins, 'In Kenya – hundreds born again, the sick healed, miracles wrought', *Renewal*, 1/4 (August–September 1966), 19–24, at 23.
[48] Jeanne Hinton, 'Kenya: a mighty nation for God', *Renewal*, 27 (June–July 1970), 16–21, at 21.
[49] DAHL, David du Plessis papers, box 19, file 69, John Kitts circular letter, October 1974.

in the Anglo-world: speakers included David du Plessis and Bob Manzano (of the Bakkers' PTL network) of the United States; Don Double, the healing evangelist, and Barney Coombs, the restorationist leader of Basingstoke Baptist Church, along with fifty young people, from England; and African leaders, the Right Revd. James Mundia, Anglican Bishop of Maseno North, Kenya, and the Nigerian pentecostal Benson Idahosa. The conference placed emphasis on baptism in the Spirit, healing, and reconciliation between churches. It assisted in the formation of a distinctive identity of African charismatic renewal which was later evident again in Johannesburg in 1977.[50]

Alongside and in cooperation with Protestant initiatives, the international mobility of Roman Catholics played an important role. Prayer groups were instigated by Catholic clergy who had returned from furlough Spirit baptised. Fr. Bartley Schmitz SVD formed one of the first Catholic groups in Taiwan in 1971 after encountering the renewal in the United States. He came to believe, 'The Lord definitely has a purpose for drawing so many missionaries into the charismatic renewal, and it has to do with the heart of being a missionary.'[51] A similar pattern was repeated elsewhere. Mumbai, India, became an early centre of charismatic renewal following the return of a lay Catholic student, Minoo Engineer, and Fr. Fuster, of St Xavier's College, from the United States.[52] Catholic missionaries transported charismatic piety. In Brazil, two American Jesuits, Fr. Edward Dougherty and Fr. Harold Rahm, were implicated. The Catholic charismatic with the greatest global impact was Fr. Francis MacNutt. His visits, sometimes in cooperation with Protestant healing evangelists, stimulated charismatic renewal in Latin America; for example, during its emergence in Bolivia and Peru from 1970. He was also well known in parts of sub-Saharan Africa. In 1974, a visit to Nigeria, at the invitation of local Dominicans, was particularly influential. MacNutt reported of both continents that awareness of the spiritual world was already strong. There seemed to be an immediate response to his teaching and practice of deliverance. The rise of the Aladura churches in West Africa and independent pentecostal churches in various parts of Latin America had, he argued, filled a 'charismatic void' which had produced a 'pastoral dilemma' for Catholic leaders.[53] There was an open opportunity for renewal, he believed, if Catholics would take it.

[50] DAHL, David du Plessis papers, box 19, file 69, Prayer Circular no. 4, 23 August 1975, Nairobi International Conference for Renewal. On St Mark's Anglican Church, see 'Focus on work in Nairobi', *St Nicholas News*, November 1977.

[51] Fr. Bartley Schmitz SVD, 'You shall be my witnesses . . . to the end of the Earth', *New Covenant*, 1/12 (June 1972), 27.

[52] 'Charismatic renewal in India', *New Wine*, 3/2 (August 1973), 28 (originally published in Bombay Jesuit magazine *Our Vineyard*).

[53] Francis MacNutt, 'Report from Nigeria', *New Covenant*, 4/11 (May 1975), 8–12.

The multiplicity of flows and the uniqueness of indigenous situations of course meant every translocal encounter was different. The case of Jesus Abbey (Yesuwŏn) in the Taebaek Mountains of South Korea, exemplifies the production of distinctive charismatic expressions. The Jesus Abbey was established by the Episcopalian priest Reuben Archer Torrey III and his wife Jane, who were invited to Seoul in 1957 to re-establish the Episcopalian seminary destroyed in the war. While on leave in England, they visited Lee Abbey, the Oxford Group influenced community described in Chapter 5. After returning to South Korea in 1965, they decided to build a community of similar values in the mountainous province of Kangwŏn. Torrey shared his grandfather's beliefs regarding the baptism in the Spirit.[54] He was aware of 'primitive pentecostalism'—that is, the early century inroads which had been made into mainline denominations in Korea (sometimes in the form of 'prayer mountains')—and also of the recent growth of the Assemblies of God (AoG) in the country. As the Dean of the Anglican seminary he tried, but with little success, to introduce students to the ministry of David Yonggi Cho, the young AoG pastor whose Yoido Full Gospel Church would soon take a pre-eminent place in global pentecostalism. In 1971, however, Torrey, along with Swedish AoG missionary Mirgan Knutan, was able to witness to Catholic clergy and religious, all overseas missionaries, who had become aware of 'Catholic Pentecostalism' in the United States. Fr. Francis MacNutt was invited to Seoul. Jesus Abbey became a centre for charismatic missionaries across South-East Asia, as well as for Jesus People after they began to appear at Seoul American High School in the early 1970s.[55] When Ed Stube attended a Bible camp in 1972, he observed 'many missionaries from assorted denominations and countries... including lots of Catholics' (adding 'the Catholics have got themselves a Pentecost going here'), but noticed that few Koreans were baptised in the Spirit.[56] The latter seems to have changed as Korean Anglicans, who had been drawn into the renewal by Catholics, witnessed to the experience and ran *Life in the Spirit* courses at the Abbey.[57] Christians in the country were divided by mainline sectarianism and differences between these denominations and the expanding pentecostal churches; while there were also serious socio-economic divisions as well as geopolitical tensions between the North and South (the Abbey was close to the border, and once hosted a large contingent of South Korean soldiers searching for communist guerrillas).[58] Torrey developed a distinctive vision of *Koinonia*; indeed he saw Jesus Abbey as a 'laboratory' for community

[54] See this book, 31.

[55] R. Archer Torrey III, 'Pentecostalism in Korea', *Logos Journal*, 4/1 (January–February 1974), 56–58.

[56] *The Holy Way*, August 1972, https://jspi.info/media/Eng-Mag/1970s/1972/1972-Aug(36).pdf, accessed 2 May 2021.

[57] Deberniere Torrey, 'Yesuwŏn: an ongoing experiment in the Kangwŏndo wilderness', *Journal of Korean Religions*, 4/1 (2013), 139–67, at 144.

[58] Ibid., 148

and reconciliation.[59] 'The outpouring of the Holy Spirit of God is the only solution to the ills of Northern Ireland, or Korea, or any nation on the face of the earth', he believed.[60]

New Global Hubs: Buenos Aires and Seoul

The imagined geography of Anglo-world charismatics now included places like Anglican centres in Singapore, the Society of Stephen in Hong Kong, and Minuto de Dios in the *barrios* of Bogotá. We now discuss two further hubs, both of which revealed the liquidity between pentecostalism and charismaticism. In each case, too, these non-Western centres were significant not only nationally and regionally, but also in shaping developments in the West, particularly regarding ecclesiology and evangelism.

The *renovación* in Buenos Aires began around 1969 amongst the open Brethren in the city and soon drew in Mennonites, Baptists, and Catholics. One of those impacted was the AoG pastor Juan Carlos Ortiz. His church, *Tabernáculo de la Fe* (Tabernacle of Faith), had been planted by American missionaries following a Tommy Hicks crusade the previous decade. Ortiz' church was revitalised and grew in the context of wider renewal, later moving into a large theatre in the city. He developed links with other church leaders in Buenos Aires. Catholics even preached at the *Tabernáculo*, to the consternation of the American AoG.[61] Alongside other pastors, Ortiz became an advocate for 'one city, one church'—or, as he said metaphorically in his preaching, 'many potatoes but one *mashed* potato'. He later said of his ecclesiological journey, 'Little did I know how much I had to learn until I came together with other pastors—Baptists, Presbyterians, Plymouth Brethren, and Catholics. As a proud Pentecostal I had to become a humble elder in the church.'[62] Ortiz and others from the city travelled widely throughout Latin America, where their ministry had success in breaking barriers between Catholic and Protestant. The reputation of the wider church in Buenos Aires was underlined by Jamie Buckingham's introduction to Ortiz' book *The Call to Discipleship* (1975), published by Logos International. '"The church of Buenos Aires" has come very close to being a prototype of the New Testament church in the twentieth century', he claimed.[63]

[59] See ibid.; Joon-Sik Park, 'The legacy of Reuben Archer Torrey III', *International Bulletin of Mission Research*, 41/3 (2017), 261–71.

[60] Torrey, 'Pentecostalism', 56–58.

[61] Juan Carlos Ortiz and Martha Palau, *From jungles to the cathedrals: the captivating story of Juan Carlos Ortiz* (Miami: Editorial Vida, 2011), 325–50.

[62] Juan Carlos Ortiz, *Call to discipleship* (Plainfield: Logos International Fellowship, 1975).

[63] Jamie Buckingham, 'Introduction', ibid., xii.

The Buenos Aires experiment influenced some of the developments in charismatic ecclesiology in the English-speaking world discussed in previous chapters. In 1973, Ortiz was invited to speak in Fort Lauderdale by Don Basham, Bob Mumford, and Derek Prince. Later, Mumford recognised the effect of Ortiz on his own teaching on submission.[64] 'There will be no formation in life without submission', Ortiz (who had been influenced also by Watchman Nee) had asserted in his *Call to Discipleship*.[65] Outside of North America, others recognised the influence of his views on authority. In advance of his visit to Britain, sponsored by the Evangelical Alliance, in 1976, Michael Harper said of *Call to Discipleship*: 'I was as impressed with the book as I have been disturbed by some of its attempted expressions in this country. If the word "nurturing" had been used it might have helped.'[66] The Argentinian, both indirectly and directly, was an influence on the shepherding controversy.

Another hub was Seoul, and David (Paul) Yonggi Cho's Yoido Full Gospel Church. Cho's ministry in the aftermath of the Korean War was one which foregrounded, along with the 'fourfold gospel', a 'threefold' blessing—spiritual, material, and bodily—through prayer. The extent to which this was an incorporation of Shamanistic religion or influenced by Oral Roberts, T. L. Osborne, and others has been vigorously debated by scholars. The tent church which began in 1958 by 1973 met in a 10,000 plus seater building. Remarkable growth followed, based on a home cell-group model, where women 'deaconesses' often had responsibility for leadership. By the end of the decade the church had 100,000 members. Around 1976, Cho established Church Growth International. In a visit to Australia the next year he supported AoG pentecostals such as Dave Cartledge who were advocating the introduction of charismatic practices.[67] Various churches in Europe and North America were influenced by Cho's principles for church growth. Pastor Tommy Reid, of Full Gospel Tabernacle church in Buffalo, for example, found the concepts 'struck [him] like a bolt of lightning' and he subsequently 'got away from the "Temple mentality" that says the *church* revolves around the 11am, on Sunday mornings'. In some places this cell-group system was a systemisation of charismatic small group practices—either those authorised by church leaders or under their radar—which were already in place.[68] Seoul was added to the global itinerary of charismatic pilgrimage. After visiting from England, Alan and Eileen Vincent, of Newfrontiers, wrote a book entitled *God Can do it Here!* At the beginning of the 1980s, Dan Malachuk confirmed in *Logos Journal*, 'We believe in the cell-group

[64] S. David Moore, *The shepherding movement: controversy and charismatic ecclesiology* (London: T&T Clark, 2003), 58. Moore notes that Charles Simpson was not influenced by Ortiz.

[65] Ortiz, *Call*, 73.

[66] Michael Harper, 'Hot issue', *Renewal*, 60 (December 1975–January 1976), 8.

[67] Shane Clifton, *Pentecostal churches in transition: analysing the developing ecclesiology of the Assemblies of God in Australia* (Leiden: Brill, 2009), 143.

[68] William L. Carmichael, 'The "exploding church" of Buffalo', *Logos Journal*, January–February 1980, 15–17, at 15 and 16.

principles that have proven so successful in Dr. Cho's church.'[69] As charismatic church leaders visited Seoul, many became enthused by the possibility of revival, even in rapidly secularising contexts. Yoido Full Gospel Church was one inspiration for the coming phenomenon of the mega-church.

Integration: 'A Sort of Reverse Tower of Babel'

In the emerging post-colonialism of the 1960s and 1970s, the relationship between First and Third World Christianity was changing. Within Roman Catholicism, Western European—and specifically, Italian—dominance showed signs of weakening at Vatican II. The Anglican Church launched its initiative for 'Mutual Responsibility and Interdependence' in 1963 and set up the Anglican Consultative Council as a transnational instrument five years later. Through indigenous holiness and pentecostal movements, the nineteenth-century architecture of the 'Protestant International' was giving way to a negotiated transnationalism.[70] The global, trans-local nexus of charismatic renewal was being established just as these power relations were being rebalanced. The eschatological notion of a worldwide move of the Spirit—a 'new thing'—gave charismatics a logic on which to approach this reconfiguration of Christendom. We will now consider three examples of this integration of First and Third World Christianity, relating to Roman Catholicism, the Anglican Communion, and independent apostolic networks.

As local and national Catholic service committees were established in Third World countries in the 1970s, they invariably imported the media of Charismatic Renewal Services in the United States and TWOG community's *Life in the Spirit* (which was soon translated into Japanese, Mandarin, Korean, French, Spanish, Portuguese, Italian, Dutch, and Sesotho).[71] By 1973, *New Covenant* was sent to ninety countries—with its national and international news sections now combined in recognition of their global readership.[72] The annual conference at Notre Dame, although overwhelmingly American in participation, increasingly sought to represent a global community. In 1974, there were 2,000 international visitors (although half were Canadian), with contingents from Latin America including 350 delegates from Puerto Rico, Dominican Republic, and Mexico. The programme included teaching workshops in French and Spanish; and summaries of talks and public prophecies in plenary meetings were sometimes offered in the

[69] Daniel Malachuk, 'Growth: *Logos Journal* and church growth', *Logos Journal*, July–August 1981, 18–19, at 19.

[70] Christopher Clarke and Michael Ledger-Lomas, 'The Protestant international', in Abigail Green and Vincent Viaene (eds.), *Religious internationals in the modern age: globalization and faith communities since 1750* (Basingstoke: Palgrave Macmillan, 2012), 23–52, at 41.

[71] Ralph Martin, 'International dimensions of the Catholic Charismatic Renewal', *New Covenant*, 5/11 (May 1976), 4–7.

[72] 'News', *New Covenant*, 3/5 (December 1973), 27.

latter.[73] TWOG had a loosely linked network of communities; for example, Beirut's People of God community, established in 1976 after thirteen Lebanese visitors to Ann Arbor decided to covenant to each other.[74] As we saw in Chapter 4, by late 1972 the CCRSC had taken upon itself responsibility for 'formulating international strategy and supervising it', with Ralph Martin setting up an International Communications Office in Ann Arbor.

In 1973, following encouragement from Cardinal Suenens and Veronica O'Brien, an international leaders' conference was held in Grottaferrata, outside Rome. As well as offering an indication of the growing legitimacy of charismatics in the Catholic Church, it underlined the global character of the renewal movement, with leaders present from at least twenty-five countries and Fr. Salvador Carrillo of Mexico a keynote speaker.[75] The discussion of the 'Statement of the Theological Basis of the Catholic Charismatic Renewal', for which Carrillo was a collaborator, placed emphasis on unity in the Spirit with allowance also for regional and national expressions of renewal. Participants were told that in Latin America, 'involvement in the charismatic renewal has meant a new level of engagement in social and political programs.'[76] Some from Latin America were already considering the relationship of renewal to social action and liberation.[77] There was also a session on charismatic renewal and cross-cultural relations. The speaker, Steve Clark, spoke of learning from Mexican *cursillistas* that it was okay for two men to hug and show affection towards one another.[78] During the conference it was confirmed that the International Communication Office in Ann Arbor would continue its role as a 'clearinghouse for information' and sponsor international gatherings; however, Grottaferrata was an indicator of the role non-Western Catholics looked set to play.

Charismatic cosmopolitanism was evident on a larger scale in 1975, when the Notre Dame conference was replaced by the international pilgrimage to Rome. Although North American speakers (including the multi-lingual Fr. Francis Martin of Madonna House, Ontario) still played a prominent role, greater efforts were made to represent the international scope of the movement. The Spanish song 'Alabaré' ('I will praise') was the popular chorus of the conference. TWOG music group (who en route had led an impromptu worship time in the departure lounge at Detroit airport) led the musical worship. They had prepared by

[73] Mary Ann Jahr, 'The 1974 Notre Dame conference: a turning point', New Covenant, 4/2 (August 1974), 4–7.

[74] James J. Bulger, 'Unity in the Spirit: contribution of the charismatic renewal to ecumenism', Senior thesis, University of Notre Dame (2014), 62.

[75] DGC, Fountain Trust papers, box 1, 'List of leaders who attended First International Leaders' Conference'.

[76] DGC, Fountain Trust papers, box 1, 'Statement of the Theological Basis of the Catholic Charismatic Renewal'.

[77] DGC, Fountain Trust papers, box 1, '9 October: morning session'.

[78] DGC, Fountain Trust papers, box 1, '10 October: afternoon session'.

spending months learning songs in Spanish, French, and Italian. The Australian Fr. Paul Glynn reflected on his experience of attending, observing that charismatic renewal had once been thought of as an 'American gadget', but that 'black and brown faces and the Spanish, Italian, German and other languages at the conference clearly indicated it is no longer a US preserve.'[79] Speakers emphasised global spiritual unity: 'The world... says that nationality, tradition, and culture come first... We say that what comes first is the lordship of Jesus Christ and the power of the Holy Spirit', said Fr. Scanlan.[80] *New Covenant* reported:

> As one Saturday speaker articulated it, the distress of not being able to understand one's own brothers was diminished when one could see and understand the love and joy in their eyes. Indeed, as conference participants made and renewed international friendships, as they delighted in one another's songs and resolved to bring them back to their own prayer groups, they came away strengthened in their conviction that the Lord – in a sort of reverse Tower of Babel – was breaking own old barriers, and forming for himself one people.[81]

It is difficult to find a clearer 'insider' articulation of charismatic cosmopolitanism than this.

The 1975 Rome conference indicated a redrawing of the Catholic charismatic geography of the Spirit. Since 1974 the *Encuentros Carismatico Catolico Latino Americano* (ECCLA) had grown year on year. As Latin American renewal expanded, Puerto Rico was thought of as a bridge 'providing for a two-way flow of the gifts of the Spirit'. A Latin American communication centre had been established in Aguas Buenas, which published *Alabaré*, the adapted Spanish version of *New Covenant.* Fr. Tom Forrest, a Redemptorist priest in the American territory, believed that the 'bridge' was one over which teachings, particularly concerning ecumenism—which tended to be more strained in Latin America—travelled south, while a 'sense of freedom to celebrate the Lord, joyful and exuberant music, and insight into Christian social action' flowed north.[82] The 1978 international conference, held in Dublin instead of Notre Dame, was meant to symbolise the return of Christianity to missionary shores. Various speakers from the Third World referred to the impact of Irish missionaries on their own countries. There were 400 in attendance from Mexico alone, worship (again led by TWOG) was now in six languages, and main speakers included leaders from India, Mexico, and the Philippines. All this was indicative of the globalisation and increasing mutuality of the Catholic Church. Pentecost was again the guiding

[79] Fr. Paul Glynn, 'From Rome ... alias Pentecostals – alias Charismatics – now "the renewal"', *Newsletter (for the Catholic Charismatic Renewal)*, 3/6 (June 1975), 3–6.

[80] Bert Ghezzi, 'A joyful pilgrimage', *New Covenant*, 5/1 (July 1975), 15.

[81] Louise Bourassa, 'A joyful people', *New Covenant*, 5/1 (July 1975), 27–30.

[82] Mary Ann Jahr, 'Uniting the Americas', *New Covenant*, 4/2 (August 1974), 35–36.

motif of the charismatic imaginary. Archbishop Dermot Ryan described the gathering as 'a Pentecost in reverse'. 'The scattering of the apostles', he said, 'had become the gathering of the disciples'.[83]

As mentioned in the previous chapter, the 1975 Rome pilgrimage inspired Anglican and Episcopal observers to seek closer ties with their own denomination. The Anglican International Conference for Spiritual Renewal at Canterbury, held before the 1978 Lambeth Conference, was a recognition of the global extent of the Spirit's work in that denomination. The leaders' gathering, which was attended by delegates from the UK (110), United States (61), Canada (41), Australia (24), South Africa (21), and New Zealand (12) also included participants from Central Africa (13), Western Africa (11), Singapore (6), India (3), the Philippines (3), Malaysia (2), and Melanesia (2), as well as a contingent of seven from South America.[84] The title of the conference—specifically the choice of 'Spiritual' rather than 'Charismatic'—exhibited a desire to prioritise Anglican pneumatic movements in general over the less inclusive 'charismatic' label. At the main 'festival of praise' meeting in the Cathedral, where Archbishop Donald Coggan was in attendance, the main speaker, under the watchful eyes of a 'press corps' sent by Idi Amin, was Festo Kivengere, the exiled Bishop of Kigezi, Uganda. His spirituality, as we saw in Chapter 2, reflected the legacy of the East Africa Revival, rather than charismatic renewal.

The organiser, Michael Harper, had for some time been convinced of the need to integrate First and Third World Christianity. In 1975, he told the Australian *Charismatic Contact* magazine, 'the time is rapidly approaching when there are going to be more Christians and more healthy Christianity in the 3rd World than in our western world and the balance of power is shifting into this area away from America and away from Britain and from Europe and from Australia and countries like that.' Charismatic renewal was part of God's plan to 'bless the West through the East, through the 3rd World'.[85] This opinion was formed through the experiences of an extensive mobile ministry, but reflected also a wider recognition amongst Anglicans that the rise of autonomous churches in post-colonial nations required a rethinking of the meaning of mission. 'There is one mission in all the world', the Anglican Consultative Council had asserted in 1973: 'this one mission is shared by the world-wide Christian community.'[86] The 1978 conference reflected this ethos. Sundar Clarke, Bishop of Madras, wrote to

[83] Louise Bourassa, 'You shall be my witnesses', *New Covenant*, 8/3 (September 1978), 4–8.

[84] DGC, Fountain Trust papers, box 7, 'List of leaders attending Leaders' Conference'.

[85] 'Michael Harper views the Church', *Charismatic Contact*, 4/1 (1975), n.p.

[86] Anglican Consultative Council, quoted in Titus Presler, 'The History of Mission in the Anglican Communion', in Ian S. Markham, J. Barney Hawkins IV, Justyn Terry, and Leslie Nuñez Steffensen (eds.), *The Wiley-Blackwell companion to the Anglican Communion* (London: Wiley-Blackwell, 2013), 15–32, at 28.

Cecil Marshall in New Zealand shortly after that the Holy Spirit 'was manifesting that "In Christ there is no East and West"'.[87]

There had been discussions in advance about the desirability of 'a kind of international renewal committee for Anglicans'. Prophecies appeared to confirm God's will for this. A prophetic theme of the conference was 'love in action all over the world', inspired by the contribution of an unnamed African leader in attendance. Another prophecy read: 'I weep over my broken body. When one part of my body is in pain, the other parts do not feel the pain. Let the Holy Spirit mind the nervous system in my body.'[88] After the conference, Harper and the Americans from the Episcopal Charismatic Fellowship made plans for the new organisation. They debated names like 'Christians in Partnership', 'Love in Action', 'International Christian Ministries', and 'SHARE', before agreeing on the label 'Sharing of Ministries Abroad' (SOMA).[89] The name referred to sharing the resources of renewal with the entire body of Christ: of ministry in a 'needy world'.[90] However, while SOMA's mission was supporting churches in the global South, its *modus operandi* was mutual exchange. Anglican charismatics in the West would bring to the table teaching, practices, and resources, while Third World Anglicans could bring spiritual vitality lacking in the West. As Harper asserted a few years later: 'the Third World will need Western expertise and finance. The West needs the Third World's dedication, enthusiasm, spiritually fashioned on the anvil of poverty, suffering and persecution. SOMA is there to stand in the gap and help the mutual sharing of these resources.'[91] The leadership structure reflected a sense of interdependence: SOMA's International Board soon included Moses Tay, now Bishop of Singapore, and Sundar Clarke, who were later joined by Gresford Chitemo, Bishop of Morogoro (Tanzania), and Manasses Kuria, Archbishop of Kenya.[92] A series of major conferences followed in the 1980s, and also the sending of small teams to Third World dioceses, always with the permission of the local Bishop. As we shall see in the final chapter, the relationships established in the 1970s and cultivated in the 1980s would have profound ramifications for the politics of the Anglican Communion in the 1990s.

Global independent charismatic connections were also being established. These drew motivation from the implications of the 'kingdom now' eschatology. Some linkages overlaid existing networks cultivated by healing evangelist and Latter

[87] JKTL, Cecil T. Marshall papers, Ang 178, series 1, item 2, Bishop Sundar Clarke to Cecil and Barbara Marshall, 4 August 1978.

[88] Michael Harper, 'Introduction', in *A new Canterbury tale: the reports of the Anglican International Conference on Spiritual Renewal Held at Canterbury, July 1978* (Bramcote: Grove Books, 1978), 7–8.

[89] See deliberations in minutes of early committee meetings between November 1978 and June 1979: DGC, Fountain Trust archive, box 7, SOMA file.

[90] 'SOMA: The Sharing of Ministries Abroad', *Acts 29*, Summer 1980, 10.

[91] DGC, Fountain Trust papers, box 7, Michael Harper, 'The SOMA vision', 30 June 1983.

[92] DGC, Fountain Trust papers, box 7, Michael Harper to David Pytches, 8 November 1983.

Rain ministries. As we saw in Chapter 2, the independent pentecostal Joseph Mattsson-Boze and his *Herald of Faith* magazine provided an important continuity between the Latter Rain and charismatic renewal after it was purchased by Dan Malachuk and became *Logos Journal*.[93] Mattsson-Boze already had established international connections through his Herald of Faith mission (established 1958), and *Logos Journal* benefited from these. The hand of Mattsson-Boze on future restorationist relationships was particularly evident in East Africa, where he and Herald of Faith trained pastors had assisted in the organisation of T. L. Osborne's crusades.[94] One of these was the leader of the Voice of Salvation and Healing Church, Silas Owiti of the Luo tribe in Kenya (who had been converted after hearing a Luo family praying in the Spirit in English).[95] Mattsson-Boze and Owiti were amongst the first contributing editors of *New Wine*, alongside Bob Mumford, Harald Bredesen, Harry Greenwood, and others.[96]

The intensification of contact with Latin America resulted in Christian Growth Ministries in 1974 establishing a Foreign Outreach ministry to coordinate connections with restorationist-minded individuals and groups. The next year, a Spanish version of *New Wine*, *Vino Nuevo*, was established in Costa Rica for publication in Latin America and Spain.[97] The Costa Rican editorial team would select a particular theme, rummage through the *New Wine* back catalogue to find relevant articles for translation, and supplement these with pieces written by leaders in Latin America. Hallmark restorationist teachings—'New Birth, the Baptism in the Holy Spirit, God's Order for the Home, Spiritual Warfare, and the Kingdom of God'—were disseminated through *Vino Nuevo*.[98] An important example of independent linkages was Guatemala. Here, the independent Baptist Calvary Evangelical Churches, founded out of the Continental Missionary Crusade of Webb City, Missouri, had been active since 1940. From the mid-1960s these began to move into charismatic renewal, training up church planters at a Bible institute in Guatemala City, and later developing relations with Fort Lauderdale's HSTM/CGM. In the wake of a 7.5 Mw earthquake on 4 February 1976, CGM mobilised its supporters, using *New Wine* and a video of the devastation and reconstruction in Guatemala, to donate to the Calvary Emergency Evangelical Committee (CEMEC).[99] It seemed the Spirit was at work in Guatemala, as if 'walls of resistance to God's purposes were also levelled by the

[93] Malachuk purchased *Herald of Faith, Harvest Time*—which had previously merged Mattsson-Boze's magazine and Gerald Derstine's *Harvest Time*.

[94] See 'Joseph Mattsson-Boze: a thoroughgoing revivalist' (online) https://lrm1948.blogspot.com/2008/12/joseph-mattsson-boze-thoroughgoing.html, accessed 26 May 2021.

[95] Wilson Okonjo Adongo, 'Owiti, Silas Javan Aggrey', *Dictionary of African Christian biography*, https://dacb.org/stories/kenya/owiti-silas/, 27–28, accessed 23 June 2021; Silas Owiti, 'The Holy Spirit in Africa', *New Wine*, July 1970, 27–28.

[96] *New Wine*, 1/1 (June 1969), 3.

[97] 'Foreign outreach report', *New Wine*, July–August 1975, 23.

[98] 'Foreign outreach report', *New Wine*, February 1977, 14–15, at 14.

[99] On CGM and CEMEC, see 'Foreign outreach report: Guatemala', *New Wine*, May 1976, 17–19.

tremor' and a 'shaking'—like that which brought the dry bones together in Ezekiel 37:7—was unifying the body of Christ. It also appeared that the right-wing government was reaching out to the evangelical community.[100] In the months after the earthquake, missionaries from independent churches in the United States worked in the country, contributing to its reconstruction and planting churches. One group came from the Gospel Outreach congregations which had emerged from a collective of Jesus People communes in Northern California. These started home fellowships, later known as *El Verbo*, in middle- and upper-class circles in Guatemala City.[101] *El Verbo* retained close, reciprocal relations with Gospel Outreach. One of those converted in these home fellowships was army officer José Efraín Ríos Montt, who in 1982—immediately after requesting guidance from elders in *El Verbo*—took on leadership of a short-lived Junta regime. Gospel Outreach offered support for the Junta, even sourcing military materials from private arms dealers in North America and Israel.[102] For some American charismatics, Ríos Montt offered both an anti-communist bulwark and the potential for kingdom building in Guatemala.

'To facilitate the establishing of the kingdom of God in other nations of the world'.[103] This was the aim of Supplyline, a charity originally set up by Arthur Wallis in 1967, which in the late 1970s began to work more intensively through a partnership with Bryn Jones' Harvestime ministries in the United Kingdom. Its strategy included the dissemination of media, both British restorationist and American CGM material (by Prince and Mumford), and the provision of technology such as tape duplicators. It also ran an International Training Programme which, thanks to collections at the Dales Bible weeks, flew leaders to the UK for intensive teaching. 'Apostolic teams' began to visit overseas and there were examples of the translocal 'supply' of spiritual authority. With his wife Eileen, Alan Vincent had worked in Bombay with Gospel Literature Service since 1963. He had witnessed 'Pentecost' at a Baptist congregation in the city in 1965, and then planted various churches which had ministered also to Catholics. On his return to England, Vincent began to lead the West Herts Community Church network and in 1980 became part of Terry Virgo's apostolic team for what became Coastlands. It was from here that in 1979, Vincent, with the support of Supplyline, developed an apostolic relationship with the Indian pentecostal Y. S. John Babu, who became an independent and began to plant community churches.[104] Eileen Vincent edited the magazine *Outpouring* which offered teaching on restorationist themes for readers in India. In Nairobi, David Tomlinson and Guyana-born

[100] Ibid., 19.

[101] L. F. Turek, 'To support a "Brother in Christ": Evangelical groups and U.S.-Guatemalan relations during the Ríos Montt regime', *Diplomatic History*, 39/4 (2015), 689–719.

[102] Ibid. [103] 'Supplyline', *Restoration*, July–August 1979, n.p.

[104] Michael Bergunder, *The South Indian pentecostal movement in the twentieth century* (Grand Rapids: Eerdmans, 2008), 104; 'India', *Restoration*, July–August 1979.

apostle Harry Das had a number of churches which looked to them for leadership (Das, for example, established Christ Co-Workers' Fellowship, or CHRISCO).[105] Apostolic teams were sent also to Guyana, where Bryn Jones had previously been a missionary along with Philip Mohabir, a Guyanan who was planting independent churches in Britain.[106] While the resources of Supplyline mostly moved in a southwards direction, once arrived there was also an emphasis on working in cooperation with local leaderships.

* * *

Historians of the 1960s and 1970s are increasingly conscious of the 'globality' of these decades and cultural, intellectual, political, and economic encounters, exchanges, and reflexes between the so-called First, Second, and Third Worlds. While the Spiritscape of charismatic renewal in the Anglo-world had been bound up with its own linguistic, cultural, and political contexts; in its origins and development, it was built on the notion of a global eschatological moment and drew on existing denominational, missionary, and revivalist flows. Prophetic interpretations of the geo-political situation, particularly in relation to the communist bloc and the Middle East, were particularly important to the formation of the charismatic imaginary. Christians in the Anglo-world, furthermore, were in search of inspiration and authenticity, particularly as they assumed the progress of secularisation in their own contexts with a sense of inevitability. There are ironies here, for instance the lack of engagement in Britain between white charismatics with pentecostal, holiness, and spiritual churches from the Caribbean and West Africa, which had in effect *come to them*. However, the Third World was represented, sometimes with a strong dose of exoticism, as having massive potential in its supernaturalism, 'enthusiasm' in worship, and dedication in prayer to reanimate Christianity. Multi-directional engagement increased in frequency and intensity in the 1970s. A religious parallel can be identified in scholarship on the conservative evangelical 'global reflex' in the 1970s, particularly in relation to ideas of social justice. Although Juan Carlos Ortiz offered one of only a few 'Spirit-filled' interventions at the 1974 Lausanne Conference, a charismatic global reflex was now underway through conferences, publications, and leadership networks. The gradual integration of this wider First, Second, and Third World charismatic nexus was to have profound ramifications for global Christianity.

[105] 'Supplyline news', *Restoration*, November–December 1979, n.p.   [106] Ibid.

8
Legacy

...why do you stand here looking into the sky?
Acts 1:11

Clark Taylor was converted at a Billy Graham rally in 1959 and baptised in the Spirit through an Assemblies of God pastor eight years later. He was one of many Methodists in Queensland to have the experience around this time. After becoming involved in charismatic home groups, conflict with Methodist leaders led to him giving up training for ministry. In 1971, Taylor became assistant pastor of Brisbane Full Gospel Church, and after this the independent Christian Life Centre in the same city, led by Trevor Chandler, a New Zealander and former Baptist. After parting ways with Chandler and a season of itinerant healing evangelism ministry, Taylor returned to Brisbane to set up the Christian Outreach Centre (COC) in 1974. This started in his home but by 1977 had over 800 attending, with many coming from the mainline churches. Taylor had been influenced by the Latter Rain emphases of Chandler and others, and the positive faith confession teachings of E. W. Kenyon. In Australia, he pioneered Christian television—which he had encountered visiting the United States—with the programme *A New Way of Living*. In 1983, a 2,000-seater COC auditorium opened in Mansfield, Brisbane. During this decade congregations nationwide either began to affiliate with or were planted by the mega-church. Taylor resigned from COC in 1990. By this point 160 churches were part of the COC network, and the church was set to expand into New Zealand and Oceania but also Malaysia, Chile, and England.[1] The story of Taylor and COC illustrates how charismatic renewal changed Christianity, rather like the movement of a kaleidoscope. Taylor's journey from a mainline denomination, to an ecumenical home group and eventually to independent ministry, exhibits one trajectory of charismatic renewal as it moved out of the 1970s. Furthermore, aspects of COC's story—mainline exodus, mega-churches, 'abundant life' teaching, television ministry, and global expansion—were wider charismatic legacies.

We have seen how the Spiritscape of charismatic renewal in the Anglo-world was the product of mid-century global flows of mainline healing, Catholic apostolates, empowered evangelicalism, and pentecostal revivalism. These coalesced as an eschatological and experiential response to the geo-political, cultural, social,

[1] On Taylor, see Sam Hey, 'God in the suburbs and beyond: the emergence of an Australian megachurch and denomination', PhD thesis, Griffith University, 2010.

Age of the Spirit: Charismatic Renewal, the Anglo-World, and Global Christianity, 1945–1980. John Maiden, Oxford University Press. © John Maiden 2023. DOI: 10.1093/oso/9780198847496.003.0008

Fig. 8.1 Contemporary charismatic worship, ubiquitous raised arms.

and religious crises of the long 1960s. Charismatic identity was initially defined by the 'new Pentecost' experience of baptism in Spirit, the marker of tongues, and a radical ecumenical ethos. The charismatic imaginary—'aesthetic formation' is also an apt description given the significance of text, audio, and audio-visual media—was constructed through the kinetic, translocal exchanges of service agencies. It was a cosmopolitan fellowship of the Spirit, with its own geography of flagship ministries, communities, and conferences. It was internally diverse—a 'Spiritscape of Spiritscapes'—but unified by a distinctive, if loose, subculture. However, as we see in the case study of Clark Taylor, from the mid-1970s the charismatic renewal—what Mark Hutchinson aptly describes as a 'free-wheeling interdenominational convention movement'[2]—was subject to diversification, diffusion, and organisational and network building. In this final chapter we again 'follow the flows', looking also at the interpenetrations between the Anglo-world and a wider global charismatic nexus, assessing the trajectories and legacies of the renewal in the 1980s and beyond.

The End of an Era of the Spirit?

In 1979, Alan Langstaff announced that the Temple Trust's second International Conference on the Holy Spirit and the Church would be its last. 'A new Pentecost

[2] Mark Hutchinson, 'Alan McGregor Langstaff', *ADPCM* (online).

has indeed taken place', he asserted. The past tense was significant. From now on, Langstaff explained, the Trust would concentrate on the building of its Bible college, evangelism, and television. 'As I see it', he said, 'the era of the spirit which we have termed the "charismatic renewal" is rapidly coming to a close and God is getting the church ready for the next wave of his Spirit.'[3] The Australian was not alone in believing a moment of transition had been reached. There was no consensus on what exactly was happening, or how charismatics should respond, but others also claimed the renewal had reached a critical juncture.

Langstaff would have been aware of the Fountain Trust's deliberations in Britain. Since 1977 its Consultative Council had debated whether the renewal was 'stuck'.[4] At the end of that year, Tom Smail described a prophecy in a *Renewal* editorial which compared charismatics to the children of Israel in Exodus—looking back to times of supernatural blessing and forward to a promised land of renewal and revival. They were in the wilderness and needed to take a new step forward.[5] Smail was to resign in 1979, and then in 1980 the new director, Michael Barling, announced 'God is doing a new thing'—possibly in the direction of evangelism, reconciliation, or social action. While the renewal of the Church was far from over, Barling asserted the Fountain Trust needed to 'die', as 'in the working of God new life comes out of death.'[6] In the United States there were similar narratives of a movement which had peaked. Amongst Catholics, there had been a drop in conference attendances and the rate of subscriptions to *New Covenant* magazine.[7] In autumn 1979 a Catholic charismatic conference at the New York Yankees stadium, where it was hoped 50,000 delegates might attend, had only 15,000 bookings—and this shortly before the visit of John Paul II to the east coast. An opinion piece in *Logos Journal* asserted 'Today the storm has quieted. Everywhere people are beginning to wonder what is happening to the charismatic movement.'[8] In fact, Logos International Fellowship was struggling—its financial problems exacerbated by the failure of a new national charismatic newspaper. In 1981 they filed for bankruptcy.[9] Everywhere, it seemed, service agencies were running against challenges. Another senior figure in the global movement, Kevin Ranaghan, wondered if renewal had plateaued and if 'something

[3] Alan Langstaff, Editorial: 'It's a new day', *Vision*, 30 (January–February 1979), 1–4.

[4] DGC, Fountain Trust papers, Fountain Trust Consultative Council minutes, 8 June 1977, 2.

[5] Tom Smail, Editorial: 'Lights show red and amber', *Renewal*, 72 (December 1977–January 1978), 2–3.

[6] Michael Barling, 'Unless a grain of wheat dies', *Renewal*, 89 (October–November 1980), 2–3.

[7] Kevin Ranaghan and Michael Harper, 'Viewpoint: has the charismatic renewal peaked?', *Vision*, 31 (March–April 1979), 39–40.

[8] Harold Hostetler, 'Forum: what hath 20 years of renewal wrought?', *Logos Journal* (January–February 1980), 22–25.

[9] 'Publisher bankrupt', *The Christian Century*, 16 December 1981; Ken Waters, 'Christian journalism's finest hour? An analysis of the failure of the *National Courier* and Inspiration', *Journalism History*, 20 (1984), 55–65.

needs to happen before the renewal can move on'.[10] Just as the new Pentecost had been heralded translocally two decades earlier, so too was the narrative that it was over or on the brink of something new.

This idea was more prevalent amongst mainliners. One reason for this was numerical. The hope of Spirit-breathed revival, so prevalent in the long 1960s, had not come to fruition. Amongst those involved in the leadership of the Fountain Trust, there was a view that renewal had done little to halt the 'steady decline' of Christianity. 'How many charismatic situations have really evangelised rather than gathering the already converted from other declining parish situations', it was asked.[11] Similar concerns were evident elsewhere. Often, where charismatic congregations, mainline, and independent, had grown—and many had—observers noticed a churning of Christians already attending church, rather than conversion growth. As Kevin Ward has argued, in New Zealand charismatic and evangelical congregations were significantly more likely to grow. Spreydon Baptist, for example, trebled its membership to 486 between 1975 and 1980. However, the pastor, Murray Robertson, wrote during this time, 'We do have a real concern that far-and-away the majority of the people coming are still those coming from other churches, and we have a real need to see more growth through people coming to the Lord.'[12] By the late 1970s, across different Anglo-world contexts it was common to hear of the growth of mainline charismatic congregations and ecumenical prayer groups slowing. The tide of secularisation had not been turned. This feeling was less evident in distinctively restorationist or house church networks. Here, eschatological confidence and numerical forward momentum continued into the next decade, perhaps as their greater flexibility in relation to worship and ministry allowed continued benefit from the 'churn' of Christians seeking spiritual expression and experience.

'Charismatic Crisis': Pneumatological, Ecclesiological, and Eschatological Diversifications

When Michael Harper observed the wider scene in 1980, he spoke of a 'charismatic crisis'. The 'spiritual laissez-faire' phase of the renewal—a new brand of pan-denominationalism with parallels to evangelicalism—he said, had been in decline for several years. Charismatics had been woken from their 'dream world'.[13]

[10] Ranaghan and Harper, 'Viewpoint: has the charismatic renewal peaked?'

[11] DGC, Fountain Trust papers, Fountain Trust Consultative Council minutes, 8 June 1977, 2.

[12] Quoted, Kevin Ward, Against the odds: Murray Robertson and Spreydon Baptist Church (Auckland: Archer Press, 2016), 39; see also Kevin Ward, *Losing our religion? Changing patterns of believing and belonging in secular Western societies* (Eugene: Wipf & Stock, 2013), ch. 5.

[13] Michael Harper, *Charismatic crisis: the charismatic renewal past, present and future* (Sydney: Anglican Renewal Ministries Australia, 1980), 4.

This dawning of reality was due not only to the absence of revival and renewal, but the changing internal dynamics of the 'movement'. It was said that service agencies such as the Fountain Trust might need to 'die' because God could not be organised, and the Spirit did not work to a particular agenda; yet however persuasive this spiritual explanation might have been, changes within the wider charismatic subculture meant it was no longer *possible* to organise the wider movement through service agencies.

The baptism in the Spirit, the expected manifestation of tongues, and the release of the gifts had been at the core of charismatic renewal. However, at the end of the 1970s this cluster of characteristics was fast changing. In England, the baptism and tongues had been a source of intense controversy between conservative and charismatic evangelicals; but in 1976, two past (and intensely polite) combatants, John Stott and Michael Harper, were amongst the signatories of 'Gospel and Spirit', a joint statement by representatives of both groups. It was in many ways a pragmatic document. It said of the term 'baptism in the Spirit' that it may be 'hard to change a usage which has become very widespread, although we all agree in recognising its dangers'. There was a considered ambiguity regarding tongues; with the suggestion that they were sometimes an 'initial phenomenon' on receiving the Spirit in the Book of Acts, but the Scriptures did not allow for a claim that tongues were 'either the only, or the universal, or an indubitable evidence'.[14] A similar tendency to compromise on Spirit baptism and tongues was evident elsewhere, to the concern of some pioneers of renewal. 'The baptism in the Holy Spirit, commonly called the "charismatic experience", is not some kind of elective', Dennis Bennett warned Episcopalian renewalists in 1978.[15] A *Logos Journal* article a few years later cited a poll which indicated that 19 per cent of the United States population self-described as 'charismatic', but only 4 per cent spoke in tongues.[16] Charismatics were losing their earlier distinctiveness.

The term 'renewal', furthermore, was increasingly elastic in its usage. This allowed the formation of strategic new alliances. In the Church of England, for example, leaders representing 'three strands of renewal – catholic, evangelical and charismatic' began to meet in 1979 to find common ground to defend traditionalist positions on doctrine and male-only ordination.[17] In 1980 a decision was made to change the name of Episcopal Charismatic Fellowship to Episcopal Renewal Ministries (ERM). In American Episcopalianism, 'renewal' was increasingly a

[14] DGC, Fountain Trust papers, Evangelical-charismatic dialogue, 'Gospel and Spirit: a joint memorandum'.

[15] Dennis Bennett, 'The charismatic experience is not an elective', *Acts 29 Newsletter*, August–September 1978.

[16] Dennis Bennett, 'Is it necessary to speak in tongues?', *Logos Journal* (November/December 1980), 32, 34–39, at 32.

[17] LPL, John R. W. Stott papers, Stott/3/8/7, 'Towards a Renewed Church: A joint statement by catholic, charismatic and evangelical Anglicans', edited by Bishop Eric Kemp, Canon Michael Harper and Dr John Stott' (Draft 4), 1 March 1988, 11.

catch-all term for those co-religionists who were mission-minded, morally traditionalist, doctrinally conservative, and either Spirit-filled or respectful of those who were. When Chuck Irish, the national coordinator of ERM, described the defining features of parish renewal, he listed the conviction that Jesus Christ was Lord, personal conversion of its members, evangelism, and good works. The definition could have described most conservative evangelical and Anglo-Catholic Episcopalians.[18] Similarly, in the Uniting Church in Australia, Spirit-filled believers spoke of the need to move 'beyond charismatic renewal' in order to integrate charismatic and evangelical witness in the Church.[19] K. J. Linton, a theology lecturer at the Churches of Christ college in Glen Iris, Victoria, Australia, argued charismatic was 'a good biblical word...but inadequate to explain fully what God is doing as He renews His Church'.[20] Like some others around this time he preferred the term 'Spiritual Renewal' to express the movement of God in the Church.

The increasing flexibility of terminology was a signal of ecclesiological tensions and changes. The question of whether 'New Testament Christianity' required Spirit-filled Christians to leave their denominations had been a point of potential disagreement since the beginning of the renewal. Charismatics had often 'kicked the can down the road' on this question, preferring to find common ground in experience and eschatology. The 1977 Kansas City Conference attempted to maintain charismatic renewal as an all-embracing movement, bringing mainline, independent, and pentecostal sections together. However, it was never built upon. The Lutheran Rodney G. Lensch argued a few years later, 'the charismatic army has been fragmented.' The ecumenism of the renewal—whether in the everyday spirituality of home groups or on the charismatic conference circuit—had given way to a 'neo-denominationalism', to borrow Lensch's term, an alignment of charismatics into various mainline expressions and independent groupings.[21]

As we saw in Chapter 6, mainline charismatics had been organising into local, national, and international denominational service committees. Lensch and others believed this had fostered separation, non-communication, and preoccupation with narrow agendas.[22] Beyond the United States, too, there was a trend of mainline charismatics seeking denominational integration and legitimacy. 'Things with a charismatic label are no longer outrageous and sensational', was the view of the Fountain Trust. A 'certain degree of respectability' had been achieved.[23] Amongst Anglicans, confidence was taken from Archbishop Donald Coggan's message to the

[18] Charles M. Irish, 'What is renewal?', *Acts 29 Newsletter*, September 1981, 5.

[19] Paul Peterson quoted in Alan Williams, 'The missionary journeys of (a latter-day) Paul are to continue', *Renewing of the Holy Ghost*, 21 (September 1981), 13–15, at 15.

[20] K. J. Clinton, Editorial: 'Let the Church *be* the Church', *Renewing of the Holy Ghost*, 15 (March 1980), 2–3, at 2.

[21] Rodney G. Lensch, 'Opinion: the charismatic army has fragmented', *Logos Journal*, January–February 1981, 28–31.

[22] Ibid.

[23] DGC, Fountain Trust papers, Fountain Trust Consultative Council minutes, 8 June 1977, 2.

1978 pre-Lambeth Conference charismatic gathering; the suggestion that Christians should pray for the 'death' of the charismatic movement because it had become so much a part of the mainstream. The formation by Anglicans and Episcopalians of Sharing of Ministries Abroad (SOMA) the next year was followed by the setting up of various national bodies—under the banner Anglican Renewal Ministries—first in Englandand then in New Zealand, Canada, Australia, and South Africa. These mainline organisations did not reject ecumenism, but their formation limited some of the liquid pan-denominationalism of the previous decades.

Catholic charismatics enjoyed the greatest success building bridges with their denomination. After the 1975 Rome Conference, the International Communications Office moved from Ann Arbor to Brussels. An unintended consequence of these new Vatican connections was tensions over the radical ecumenism which Catholic-ecumenical communities, such as The Word of God (TWOG), displayed with Protestants. In *Ecumenism and charismatic renewal* (1978), Cardinal Suenens warned that even though Kansas City confirmed 'beyond all possible doubt' the Spirit was working amongst the churches, 'we must not give way to an euphoric ecumenism which, in the joy of rediscovering Christian brotherhood, would overlook the doctrinal difficulties yet to be resolved.'[24] What Valentina Ciciliot describes as the 'Catholicization' of Catholic-ecumenical renewal was underway. At the beginning of the 1980s, a split occurred in the Association of Communities which TWOG and People of Praise had pioneered. TWOG maintained an eschatologically pessimistic and separatist approach—eventually forming an international 'supracommunity' known as Sword of the Spirit; however, others followed the slightly more moderate People of Praise, and still others joined with the Emmanuel Covenant Community, Brisbane, and the Community of God's Delight, Dallas, to establish the International Brotherhood of Communities (IBOC).[25] By 1985, IBOC was seen by Bishop Paul Cordes, Suenens' replacement, as a potential 'interface' between the Church and charismatic renewal—and five years later it was recognised by the Pontifical Council for the Laity as the Catholic Fraternity of Charismatic Covenant Communities and Fellowships.[26] Brisbane's Brian Smith, baptised in the Spirit at the 'Bardon' prayer meeting nearly two decades earlier, was the first president. His appointment underlined the globalisation of Catholic charismatic renewal.

Simultaneously, there had been a greater assertion of independent charismatic ecclesiology. This was not so much a process of institutionalisation, as an

[24] Léon Joseph Suenens, *Ecumenism and charismatic renewal: theological and pastoral orientations*, Malines Document 2 (Ann Arbor: Servant Books, 1978), 45.

[25] Thomas J. Csordas, *Language, charismatic and creativity: the ritual life of a religious movement* (Berkeley: University of California Press, 1997), 13–18.

[26] Valentina Ciciliot, '"Pray aggressively for a higher goal—the unification of all Christianity": U.S. Catholic charismatics and their ecumenical relationships in the late 1960s and 1970s', *Religions*, 12/5 (2021), 353.

enhanced relationalism: what Benjamin McNair calls the emergence of the 'charismatic apostolate'.[27] In the United States and further afield, *New Wine* and the shepherding patterns of leadership promoted by Christian Growth Ministries had contributed to the rise of independent congregations. In South Africa, Derek Crumpton became an advocate for the 'restored' church. In the United Kingdom, the late 1970s began the heyday of the 'house church' networks. Bryn Jones' Harvestime enjoyed continued growth, which was consolidated by the establishment of the International Christian Leadership Programme (ICLP) in Bradford in 1980. The same year saw the birth of Terry Virgo's Coastlands (later Newfrontiers) apostolic network. By 1987 there were twenty Bible weeks in Britain which could accommodate 100,000 people.[28] While independents did not dismiss the notion of the Spirit moving in the mainline churches, there was often criticism of those charismatics committed to the denominations. 'The church is not a "pond to fish in" or a "mixed multitude", but the company of believers, born again, yielded under the Lordship of Jesus Christ and living in vital relationship with Him by the Holy Spirit', asserted David Tomlinson, the English independent, in 1978.[29] Bryn Jones, who by now was active in the United States and South Africa, saw the charismatic outpouring as a 'salutary lesson', asserting:

> already there are those who would encourage every denomination to have its self-contained charismatic work and ministry. These are multiplying rapidly, just as the early Pentecostal denominations did. At a time when we know God is moving to bring His people into oneness of heart and soul, to see further division engineered to protect denominational affiliation is abhorrent to those who are praying God to restore the Church.[30]

With this hardening of language, cooperation between mainliners and independents diminished. By 1980, Harper described how the message of the latter was often 'hyper-critical, sometimes mocking of the historic churches'.[31]

Although in earlier decades charismatic renewal was a patchwork of eschatological interpretations, these had tended to be revivalist and adventist. The key biblical reference was Joel 2:28 ('Your sons and daughters will prophesy...') and the framework was latter rain. In the next decade, the new Pentecost paradigm was giving way to a greater diversity of less compatible eschatological schemes. In

[27] Benjamin G. McNair, *Apostles today: making sense of contemporary charismatic apostolates – a historical and theological appraisal* (Eugene: Wipf & Stock, 2014).

[28] William K. Kay, 'Apostolic networks in Britain: an analytic overview', *Transformations*, 25/1 (2008), 32–41, at 37.

[29] David Tomlinson, 'The House Church', *Restoration*, November–December 1978, 6–9, at 6–7.

[30] Bryn Jones, 'Is revival sufficient?', *Restoration*, July–August 1978, 9–12.

[31] Harper, *Charismatic crisis*, 10.

Chapter 5, we observed from the mid-1970s the adoption, in independent charismatic circles particularly, of a thoroughgoing optimistic eschatology concerning the Church and the kingdom of God. The articulation of a triumphant, pure, and unified Church drew attention towards and widened the gap between independent restorationists and mainline renewalists.

There were also divisive issues *within* these milieus. Teaching on the kingdom and God's government brought dominion theology—the notion that Christians had a mandate to exercise authority in different spheres public and family life—to the fore. Amongst the Fort Lauderdale men, Bob Mumford and Ern Baxter were particularly combative on the matter. Baxter in 1979 warned:

> Those who reject the decreed dimension of God's Son-King must face His righteous judgement. Jehovah's will and government are ultimate. Men must either submit to His saving sovereign sway, or suffer the consequences of following their own counsel. All forms of humanism must inevitably be shattered by the rod of God's governmental authority.[32]

These words were in a two-part *New Wine* special issue on 'secular humanism'. There was some flirtation with Christian reconstructionism. An article by R. J. Rushdoony, the Presbyterian architect of reconstructionism, used militaristic language: 'There is a war on, and like it or not, you are in it.'[33] An article from Australia by Logos Foundation's Howard Carter referred approvingly to Rushdoony and warned charismatics to be ready: 'Not in defence, for the Kingdom God has never been on the defensive, but they shall be ready, alert and on the attack.'[34] Reconstructionism was a step too far for some who were otherwise drawn towards the notion of a victorious Church; nevertheless, there was a definite growing prominence of ideas of cultural dominion.

Another strand of teaching related to dominion was the authority of the individual Christian in 'this-worldly' matters of health and prosperity. Word of Faith had been a marginal teaching in charismatic renewal circles in the long Sixties, although the FGBMFI offered some of its advocates a platform, and the New Thought emphases of Agnes Sanford and the spiritual elitism of the Latter Rain movement permeated more widely. In *The Believer's Authority* (1966) Kenneth E. Hagin had argued, 'We are one with Christ. We are Christ. We are seated at the right hand of the Majesty on High. All things have been put under our feet.' As Michael J. McClymond explains, prosperity and health were at this stage subordinate to Hagin's larger point concerning dominion through positive

[32] Ern Baxter, 'The ultimacy of God's government: the final conquest', *New Wine*, 11/3 (March 1979), 25–28.
[33] R. J. Rushdoony, 'The world's second oldest religion', *New Wine*, 11/2 (February 1979), 4–7.
[34] Howard Carter, 'Conflict of the ages', *New Wine*, 11/3 (March 1979), 28.

confession.[35] This, as well as his teaching on authority over demons, helped Hagin to find publicity in *New Wine*. As Kate Bowler claims, 'The prosperity gospel profited from the ecumenism that propped open doors once shut.'[36] Independent, entrepreneurial Word of Faith congregations were visited by mainliners, both Protestant and Catholic. Some of these visitors remained. Networks spread, such as the Hagins' Oklahoma-based Rhema non-denominational churches and Bible schools. In South Africa, Ray McCauley, a Spirit baptised former Mr Universe competitor, visited Hagin's Bible college in Tulsa, Oklahoma, in 1978 and started a Rhema Bible Church in Johannesburg the next year. By 1985 it had moved to a 5,000-capacity auditorium, which was dedicated at its opening by Hagin Snr. The congregation grew to over 40,000 and became the largest single church in South Africa. Bolstered also by Christian broadcasting, abundant life was set to become a prominent and highly contested issue in the wider charismatic scene.

With this flux in pneumatology, ecclesiology, and eschatology, the imaginary of charismatic renewal seemed less coherent; and pan-denominational, spiritually 'laissez-faire' ways of holding the 'movement' together were less likely to work. Flux is the very nature of Appadurai's 'scapes'. The Spiritscape of charismatic renewal was becoming more diverse and began to lose the sense of unity (the '*renewal*') produced in the intensity of the eschatological moment of the long Sixties. Charismatics in the Anglo-world were also set to become integrated with a wider, expanding and evolving charismatic culture which would shape global Christianity into the twenty first century. To demonstrate these developments, we now consider a selection of key trajectories, permeations, and 'moments'.

Trajectories: Wimberism and Apostolic-Prophetic Networks

The entangled charismatic trajectories from the 1980s are often considered the 'third wave' of charismatic/pentecostal Christianity. However, we shall see, it is more helpful to identify continuities of translocal linkages and modalities, alongside discontinuities and new emphases.

The ministry of John Wimber (and the approach sometimes known as 'Wimberism') had a remarkable pan-denominational influence on charismatic ministry. Its origins could be found in reflexive engagement with the global South and in the charismatic scene in California. Like many evangelicals before him in the 1950s and 1960s, Wimber became interested in the Holy Spirit through

[35] Quoted in Michael McClymond, 'Prosperity already and not yet: an eschatological interpretation of the health and wealth emphasis in the North American Pentecostal-Charismatic Movement' in Peter Althouse and Robby Waddell, *Perspectives in Pentecostal eschatologies: world without end* (Cambridge: James Clarke, 2010), 293–314, at 307.

[36] Kate Bowler, *Blessed: a history of the American prosperity gospel* (Oxford: Oxford University Press, 2013), 77.

missionaries who reported rapid pentecostal growth in South America. He grew critical of the limitations of the Western, scientific worldview. His ministry also took direction from the experience of the Spirit in home groups linked with Calvary Chapel. In 1977, Wimber started Calvary Chapel Yorba Linda. However, his approach was radical at a time when Calvary Chapel was increasingly conservative in practice. He joined and began to oversee another network of churches born out of the renewal—Ken Gullickson's Vineyard. Wimber's own Anaheim Vineyard became known for numerical growth and supernatural ministry. In 1982, he was asked by a former missionary to Bolivia, Peter C. Wagner—once a cessationist but now attracted by the potential of pentecostalism—to teach a course 'Signs, Wonders and Church Growth' at Fuller Theological Seminary, Pasadena. Uniquely, these classes included times of Holy Spirit ministry, including Wimber's trademark time of listening for supernatural words from God. Wagner and others became full converts to the ministry of signs and wonders.[37] As Wagner became an advocate for Wimber in evangelical circles, this signs and wonders emphasis also energised existing charismatics. For some, Wimber offered the hope of what David Noder, a lay Catholic coordinator of The Lamb of God Catholic-ecumenical community in Baltimore, described as 'renewing the renewal'. In the early 1980s, the community was finding evangelistic growth difficult, and Noder was having to reach back to 'charismatic war stories' for examples of God's power. Wimber's teaching impacted the community's evangelistic and healing ministries. According to Noder, fellow leaders in the Sword in the Spirit network received prophecies about renewal in spiritual power.[38] In 1985, Wimber visited TWOG, Ann Arbor, the network's leading community, and appears to have 'initiated a renewed interest in healing prayer'. Indeed, Wimber's influence likely contributed to TWOG's decision to re-establish an open prayer meeting, a notable development given the recent tendency of the community towards insularism.[39]

Wimberism spread through existing translocal networks. From York, England, David Watson visited Fuller in 1980 and was impressed. The Anglican vicar of St Andrew's, Chorleywood, near London, also became aware of Wimber. David Pytches had been a missionary bishop of Chile, Boliva, and Peru. He was baptised in the Spirit shortly after his wife, Mary, was filled while returning from furlough in March 1971. He was then coached in the gifts of the Spirit by Kathleen Clark, another South American Missionary Society worker, who 'received' years earlier (she had been another parishioner of All Souls, Langham Place, where Michael

[37] On Wimber, see for example, Jon Bialecki, 'The third wave and the Third World: C. Peter Wagner, John Wimber, and the pedagogy of global renewal in the late twentieth century', *Pneuma*, 37 (2015), 177–200.

[38] David Noder, 'Renewing the renewal', in John Wimber and Kevin Springer (eds.), *Riding the third wave: what comes after renewal?* (London: Marshall Pickering, 1987), 135–50, at 139.

[39] Csordas, *Language*, 90.

Harper and Martin Peppiatt had been curates).[40] Pytches witnessed Anglican growth and signs and wonders in Chile (he told the story, for example, of when he reluctantly offered prayer for the healing of a baby, which to his surprise appeared to work).[41] In 1977 he returned to England. St Andrew's was already somewhat open to the Spirit, but Pytches desired to see the parish operate more fully in the supernatural. He heard of Wimber's approach through former SAMS worker Eddie Gibbs. Wimber and a large ministry team visited Pytches' and Watson's churches in 1981. His every-member-ministry was well received. Wimber had an enormous impact across the Anglo-world—he visited South Africa (from 1980), New Zealand (1985), and Australia (1987). In New Zealand, he developed a close connection with Murray Robertson of Spreydon Baptist, who experienced a 'power encounter' which left him on the floor in uncontrollable laughter. Robertson's story, and those of others from New Zealand, Britain, Canada, and the United States—as well as Jean Stone's colleague Jackie Pullinger in Hong Kong—were included in *Riding the Third Wave: What comes after Renewal?*[42] The title was telling of a reason for Wimber's appeal. Anaheim Vineyard, like various other Californian charismatic flagships before it, became a draw for international visitors.[43]

Wimber's influence had parallels with another leader from California, Dennis Bennett. The Episcopalian was acceptable to middle-class Christians in part because of a gentle style and absence of hype. The Wimber phenomenon also had much to do with eschatology. For some, he revived a sense of expectation. For one prominent British Baptist, Wimber's ministry seemed 'part of the tidal movement of the Holy Spirit which is destined to revive Christ's whole church'.[44] However, at a subtler level, the central aspect of Wimber's eschatology—of God's kingdom as 'now and not yet'—addressed unresolved tensions within the charismatic renewal. When could the Spirit be expected to act? Why did the Spirit sometimes appear *not* to act? Wimber's answer was that healings and supernatural manifestations were sovereign acts of God. This teaching was welcomed in charismatic circles uncomfortable with the 'over-realized' eschatology of Word of Faith evangelists.[45] Furthermore, Wimber's eschatology, implicitly at least, offered relief to some charismatics who had now been expecting global revival and the Parousia for two decades or more. The Spirit, Wimber taught, had been

[40] David Pytches, *Living at the edge: the autobiography of David Pytches* (Bath: Arcadia, 2002), 145. RUSCA, Dennis J. Bennett papers, South America 1978–, Arthur Lindvall to Dennis Bennett, 14 April 1971.

[41] Pytches, *Living at the edge*, 189.

[42] Murray Robertson, 'A power encounter worth laughing about', in Wimber and Springer (eds.), *Riding the third wave*, 188–97.

[43] On this see Andrew Atherstone, 'John Wimber's European impact', in Andrew Atherstone, Mark Hutchinson, and John Maiden (eds.), *Charismatic renewal in Europe and the United States since 1950* (Leiden: Brill, 2020), 215–217.

[44] Douglas McBain, 'An emptiness at the centre', *Renewal*, 112 (August–September 1984), 22–24.

[45] Stephen Hunt, 'The Anglican Wimberites', *Pneuma*, 17/1 (1995), 105–18, at 114.

active since the ministry of Jesus and the early Church. In contrast to the variations of latter rain theology which had permeated renewal, the Church had been in the 'last days' for two thousand years.[46] For Wimber, the biblical model for charismatics was not so much the Book of Acts, as Christ's inauguration of the kingdom in the gospels. Wimberism was a tonic for advent disillusionment.

The long-term impact of Wimberism is hard to gainsay. Vineyard spread internationally, but his model of ministry infused far more widely. He left a lasting impact on Pytches and many others. The Anglican's *Come Holy Spirit* (1985) argued that confirmation of the gospel through signs and wonders was 'more relevant than ever in the 1980s', and became a best-seller.[47] Pytches in fact began to advocate for Wimber's approach in the United States, teaching at Episcopal Renewal Ministries in the late 1980s.[48] In Britain, Pytches and others in 1989 established the New Wine network and festivals; and in 1993, Pytches' youth leader at St Andrew's, Mike Pilavachi, set up the youth congregation and festival Soul Survivor. By 2005, Soul Survivor festival was attracting 25,000, and smaller events were taking place in the Netherlands, Australia, South Africa, New Zealand, and the United States. Pilavachi's colleague, the teenage worship leader Matt Redman, was to become a leading international Christian songwriter. Wimber also left a mark at Holy Trinity Brompton, where he visited in 1982.[49] The Rector of 'HTB', John Collins, had been the vicar of St Mark's Gillingham when it experienced a charismatic awakening in the early 1960s.[50] HTB became one of the largest Anglican churches in England and, after launching the *Alpha* evangelistic course, one of the most internationally influential Christian congregations. In each of these contexts, and many others, the Wimber formula of worship, teaching, and the 'ministry time'—where individuals in the congregation responded to words of knowledge and prophecy by coming to the front for prayer—became the normal pattern of ministry.

Wimber and the Vineyard were implicated in another development to reshape the charismatic Spiritscape: the rise of apostolic-prophetic networks.[51] Ideas of apostolic authority had been popular amongst ex-Brethren, Baptists, and Latter Rain-type charismatics. As apostleship became popular within the renewal, it was also bound up with the controversy around shepherding. The afterlife of this was

[46] Douglas R. Erickson, 'The Kingdom of God and the Holy Spirit: eschatology and pneumatology in the Vineyard movement', PhD thesis, Marquette University (2015).

[47] David Pytches, *Come Holy Spirit* (London: Hodder & Stoughton, 1985), 1.

[48] 'What do you mean by "signs and wonders"?', *Acts 29*, February 1987, 8; 'Pytches's "power ministry"', *Acts 29*, July 1987, 1–2, at 1.

[49] See Andrew Atherstone, *Archbishop Justin Welby: the road to Canterbury* (London: Darton, Longman and Todd, 2013).

[50] See this book, 59.

[51] On these, see: John Weaver, *The new Apostolic Reformation: history of a modern charismatic movement* (Jefferson: McFarland and Co., 2016); Brad Christerson and Richard Flory, *The rise of network Christianity: how independent leaders are changing the religious landscape* (New York: Oxford University Press, 2017).

playing out in the 1980s. Derek Prince broke ranks with the CGM 'five' in 1984 and *New Wine* closed two years later. Then, in 1989, Bob Mumford offered a public apology which included the admission that some of the biblical emphases undergirding discipleship, to his own 'pain and chagrin', had 'resulted in unhealthy submission resulting in perverse and unbiblical obedience to human leaders'.[52] However, it is nevertheless probable that shepherding—despite all the concerns over its abuses—helped to prepare the ground for a further resurgence of teaching on apostles and prophets from the late 1980s.[53]

The translocal stimulation of apostolic-prophetic networks took place at two key North American nodes: the Kansas City Fellowship (KCF) and the Toronto Airport Vineyard Church (TAVC). KCF had been established in 1982 by Mike Bickle, a conservative evangelical who had reluctantly moved into charismatic ministry, in part prompted by a prophecy received at an FGBMFI event. He pastored a group of men—including Bob Jones, John Paul Jackson, and Paul Cain—known collectively as the 'Kansas City Prophets', who shared a conviction that a resurgence of prophecy was a sign of a last days' victorious church. They also taught what Cain called the 'new breed of Christians'.[54] John Wimber was drawn to KCF's prophetic emphasis partly as a result of a visit by Cain to Anaheim in 1988, when a prophetic word concerning Jeremiah 33:8 was confirmed for him by an earthquake in Pasadena on the day of his arrival, apparently at 3.38 a.m. in the morning. Cain, Bickle, and others began to work closely with Wimber, who in 1990 agreed to take them under his spiritual oversight, with KCF becoming known as the Metro Vineyard Christian Fellowship. The Wimber imprimatur helped ensure the prophets' endorsement by charismatic leaders in Britain, including Graham Cray (David Watson's replacement at St Michael-le-Belfrey), David Pytches, and Terry Virgo (now of Newfrontiers). The relationship between the Kansas City men and Wimber, however, became uneasy. By the mid-1990s, Wimber was less comfortable with the association. In 1996, Bickle's congregation withdrew from the network. However, by this time a 'Joel's Army' teaching about elite believers, and the apostolic-prophetic emphasis, had percolated even more widely.

One reason Bickle withdrew from the Vineyard concerned dramatic events in Canada. In January 1994, a revivalistic phenomenon appeared to have had broken out at the Toronto Airport Vineyard Church. The 'Toronto Blessing' became synonymous with the experience of 'soaking' in God's love, healings, slayings in the Spirit, and manifestations such as laughter, spiritual 'drunkenness', and animal noises. In fact, as Hunt and others have argued, laugher and the more

[52] Letter republished in Jamie Buckingham, 'The end of the discipleship era', *Ministries Today*, January–February 1990, 46–52.

[53] Ibid., 43.

[54] Cain quoted in Michael G. Maudlin, 'Seers in the heartland: hot on the trail of the Kansas City prophets', *Christianity Today*, 35/1 (1991), 18–22, at 21.

extraordinary aspects of the Blessing had been occasionally evident in global charismatic contexts for several years before this.[55] In fact, antecedents go back even further. Reports of early charismatic meetings sometimes contained descriptions of 'holy mirth' in the Spirit.[56] An article in *Logos Journal* in 1973 breathlessly explained, 'To know God as our heavenly Father is to be infinitely happy, to be filled with a rollocking mirth, a holy hilarity at the sheer circumstances of living for Christ.'[57] More immediately, the origins of the Toronto Blessing could be traced through various translocal linkages. Argentinian pentecostalism was influential; the TAVC pastor John Arnott had witnessed the ministry of AoG pastor whose church was known for laugher in the Spirit. The healing evangelist Benny Hinn, formerly of Merv and Merla Watson's the Toronto Catacombs, had prayed for Arnott in 1993. Another Vineyard pastor, Randy Clark, who was a speaker at the first TAVC meetings, was influenced by Rodney Howard-Browne, a South African who before his emigration to the United States taught at the Rhema Bible School. Howard-Browne was also known for promoting laughter in the Spirit.[58] As news of the Blessing spread, TAVC—like Melodyland, Church of the Redeemer, and The Word of God community in earlier decades—became another destination for global power pilgrims. The formal separation between Vineyard's board and council (which claimed a desire to focus on 'the main and plain things in Scripture') and TAVC in 1996 influenced Bickle's decision to end his association with the network of churches.

The Kansas City milieu was supportive of the Toronto revival and the spiritual energies of the Blessing charged the atmosphere in which new apostolic networks were appearing. These included those which operated under the umbrella of an organisation known as the Revival Alliance, including the former TAVC leaders John and Carol Arnott's own Partners in Harvest, Randy Clark's Global Awakening, Heidi and Roland Baker's Iris Ministries (now Iris Global), Che Ahn's Harvest International Ministries, and Bill Johnson's Bethel network. Their influence has been considerable. Bethel, for example, has links with leaders in North America, South America, Europe, and sub-Saharan Africa; and by 2010, its School of Supernatural Ministry (which has close parallels with Melodyland's Charismatic Clinic), in Redding, north California, had 1,200 participants.[59] In addition to these networks were those linked with an organisation founded by C. Peter Wagner in 1999, the International Coalition of Apostles (now the International Coalition of Apostolic Leaders); as well as outlier networks, such

[55] Stephen Hunt, 'The "Toronto Blessing": a lesson in globalized religion?', in Michael Wilkinson (ed.), *Canadian Pentecostalism: transition and transformation* (Montreal: McGill-Queen's University Press, 2009), 233–44, at 239.

[56] Peter Hocken, *Streams of renewal: the origins and early development of the charismatic movement in Great Britain* (Carlisle: Paternoster Press, 1986), 101.

[57] Philip E. Streeter, 'The laughter makers', *Logos Journal*, 3/6 (November–December 1973), 6–8, at 6.

[58] Hunt, 'The "Toronto Blessing"', 239–40.

[59] Weaver, *New Apostolic Reformation*, 109.

as Rick Joyner's MorningStar. Alongside these new apostolic networks were those which emerged in the 1970s and were subsequently impacted by the Kansas City and Toronto phenomenon. In Britain, Terry Virgo's Newfrontiers (formerly Coastlands) network was one. At a meeting of 250 leaders in 1994, a prophecy of a 'monsoon' of blessing led Virgo to introduce the song 'Singing in the Rain' ('250 men began to dance and sing. Gene Kelly never knew such joy and abandonment! Was this really 250 Englishmen?', he recalled). The Newfrontiers leaders took 'the Blessing' to British congregations, but also Cape Town, Bombay, and Bangalore. The 1990s was a breakthrough decade for apostolic-prophetic networks.

Some of those who took up apostolic ministry were former mainliners who had been involved in the charismatic renewal. The Temple Trust's Alan Langstaff, who had left Australia for the United States to develop a ministry in Christian television, later pastored an independent charismatic congregation in Minnesota and became Apostolic Overseer for Omega Team, another network of pastors. In Pretoria, South Africa, Ed Roebert led his congregation out of the Baptist Union to form the soon 5,000-strong Hatfield Christian Church. In 1989 he became the first president of the International Fellowship of Christian Churches, a network of independent congregations with a distinctively South African leadership. Also in South Africa, Derek Crumpton, the former Methodist, in 1981 established Foundation Ministries, which gathered an apostolic team from across various African nations.

In the United States, Larry Tomczak and C. J. Mahaney, two former Catholics who had led the 'Take and Give' meetings in the Washington DC area and had been involved in the shepherding movement, also moved towards apostolic ministry.[60] In 1982, they established the network People of Destiny International (PDI). This moved in a Calvinistic direction and in 1988 was renamed Sovereign Grace Ministries (SGM) (around which time Tomczak left). Along with others, like Sam Storms, a former associate pastor with Bickle in Kansas City, the New Testament theologian Wayne Grudem, and Terry Virgo (whom Mahaney introduced to the books of American Reformed pastor John Piper), Mahaney and SGM made a charismatic contribution to the neo-Reformed resurgence, particularly in North America and Britain. PDI's earlier emphases on complementarianism (which sat well in a Reformed context) and submission were maintained. On the latter, for example, regarding Jesus submitting to his Father's will (John 5:19) one SGM book asked of small-group leaders: 'Are you submitted to authority? Are you a good follower?'[61] In 2012, SGM was named amongst the defendants in a

[60] As late as 1985 Tomczak was contributing to *New Wine*. See: 'It's how you finish that counts', *New Wine*, 17/7 (July 1985), 24–27. See this book, 133.

[61] Mark Mullery, 'What makes a great leader?', in C. J. Mahenney (ed.), *Why small groups? Together toward maturity* (Gaithersburg: Sovereign Grace Ministries, 1996), 52.

class action lawsuit which asserted 'the Church covered up child molestation and sexual assaults occurring under its auspices.'[62] A 2013 article by T. F. Charlton claimed 'The combination of patriarchal gender roles, purity culture, and authoritarian clergy that characterizes Sovereign Grace's teachings on parenting, marriage, and sexuality creates an environment where women and children—especially girls—are uniquely vulnerable to abuse.'[63] The lawsuit was dismissed on procedural grounds, but the controversy did not go away and there were continued calls for an independent investigation.[64] John Weaver asserts that for some victims and critics, 'the abuses at SGM seemed directly traceable to the lingering influence of shepherding.'[65] It is difficult to confirm the truth of his analysis, but it seems plausible. A broader point, however, is incontrovertible: the rise of a charismatic, apostolic variant in the neo-Reformed world indicates the extent of the diffusion of charismatic renewal.

Another gauge of the influence of charismatic renewal was apostolic trends in the Assemblies of God. In 2001 the general presbytery of the AOGUSA agreed a position paper stating:

> The Pentecostal and charismatic movements have witnessed various excessive or misplaced theological emphases over the years. We look with grave concern on those who do not believe in congregational church government, who do not trust the maturity of local church bodies to govern themselves under Scripture and the Spirit.

The next year, a study paper by the Pentecostal Assemblies of Canada criticised the theological basis for apostolic leadership of churches.[66] These papers, produced after decades of charismatic controversy and before this, the fall out of the Latter Rain movement, were responding more immediately to growing pressures on the traditional ecclesiology of the denomination. In 2006, Bill Johnson, pastor of Bethel, took his Wimber-influenced, youth-friendly, and highly successful congregation out of the AoG. It became an apostolic network with its own international reach. The rise of a hierarchical model was also evident in Australia in the 1980s. This was partly due the influence of Frank Houston. Before moving to the country, his AoG mega-church in Little Hutt, New

[62] See https://www.sgmsurvivors.com/2012/10/18/lawsuit-text-with-address-redacted/, accessed 17 June 2021.

[63] T. F. Charlton, 'A church group, a lawsuit and a culture of abuse', https://www.bishop-accountability.org/news2013/03_04/2013_03_05_Charlton_AChurch.htm, accessed 17 June 2021.

[64] Mark Galli, 'We need an independent investigation of Sovereign Grace Ministries', 22 March 2018, https://www.christianitytoday.com/ct/2018/march-web-only/sovereign-grace-need-investigation-sgm-mahaney-denhollander.html, accessed 23 June 2021.

[65] Weaver, *New Apostolic Reformation*, 105.

[66] 'Contemporary apostles and the Pentecostal Assemblies of Canada', November 2002, https://paoc.org/docs/default-source/church-toolbox/position-papers/contemporary-apostles/contemporary-apostles-2022.pdf?sfvrsn=d97df36a_4, accessed 23 May 2021.

Zealand, was run by an eldership which he, as senior pastor, appointed. What became in 2000 the Hillsong church in Sydney, led by Brian (his son) and Bobbie Houston, advocated the same position. Described by Dave Cartledge as part of an 'Apostolic revolution', the model became widely popular in Australia. It was later revealed to the public that Frank Houston had committed sex crimes against children. It seems highly possible the system of spiritual authority which he promoted was a factor in his ability to abuse.

The hierarchical model which became so influential in Australia was in many respects a pragmatic response to the exceptional growth resulting from transfers from mainline charismatics and the adoption of the South Korean cell-church model.[67] By 2009, Hillsong claimed a congregation of 15,000.[68] In 2018, it was announced Hillsong would leave the Australian AoG (Australian Christian Churches). It by now had congregations in twenty countries and claimed a weekly attendance across this network of 130,000. Brian Houston explained, 'as Hillsong Church has continued to grow, we no longer see ourselves as an Australian Church with a global footprint, but rather a Global church with an Australian base.'[69] The global office of the Hillsong brand was now in the United States. The apostolic-prophetic revolution was a legacy of charismatic renewal which had a broad appeal.

Permeations: Praise and Worship

In 1974, it was reported by the music department of Church of the Redeemer, Houston, that it received a 'large volume of correspondence [. . .] from all over the world requesting our music'. The letters came from those who had heard Fisherfolk albums and wanted permission to put the music in songbooks for their prayer groups and church gatherings.[70] Charismatic renewal, as we saw in Chapter 6, produced a burst of creativity in worship. Recordings, songbooks, and sing-along-songbooks played an important role in the making of its subculture. In the Anglo-world, it has arguably been praise and worship, more so even than emphasis on the gifts of the Spirit, which have had the most lasting and consequential legacy of charismatic renewal. The primacy of worship was reflected in the words of the songwriter Matt Redman (of Soul Survivor, mentioned above) in 1999: 'When we get our priorities right and put the worship of God first, then

[67] Dave Cartledge, *The apostolic revolution: the restoration of the apostles and prophets in the Assemblies of God in Australia* (Sydney: Paraclete Institute, 2000); Shane Clifton, *Pentecostal churches in transition: analysing the developing ecclesiology of the Assemblies of God in Australia* (Leiden: Brill, 2009), 157–70.

[68] Clifton, *Pentecostal*, 161.

[69] Griffin Paul Jackson, 'Hillsong: "What a beautiful name" for a new denomination spanning "Oceans"', *Christianity Today*, 25 September 2018.

[70] 'Music department', *Glad Tidings*, 1/3 (June 1974), 1–2.

everything else falls into place.'[71] Praise and worship, whether as an extended, free-flowing time of continuous singing, or in the context of a traditional liturgy, became the central charismatic praxis.

Encounter with God was the emphasis. David Watson had argued, 'the aim of worship is to glorify God, and him alone, and to lead worshippers to an increased awareness of his presence with his people.'[72] It has been conventional to criticise the lyrical content of charismatic worship as 'me' focused; however, up to the late 1980s, at least, the clear, steady focus of the majority of songs was God rather than the individual Christian, with an increase also in Christ-focused songs in the 1970s (for the period 1982–1987, Brett Knowles' painstaking analysis of *Scripture in Song* found the main focuses of individual songs as follows: God, 53 per cent; Jesus, 21.40 per cent; individual Christian, 25.32 per cent).[73] Michael Harper was entitled to claim that the choruses of *Sound of Living Waters* and *Fresh Sounds* were almost all 'God-centred, and corporate rather than individual expressions of worship'.[74] This was partly due to the dominance of scriptural texts. However, as Knowles also acknowledges, songs of declaration in the late 1980s were qualitatively 'more self-assertive, emphasising the activity of the believer, rather than that of God'.[75] By the 1990s, although many new songs spoke of the character and deeds of God, the worship 'encounter' drew on a growing corpus of songs of intimacy. John and Carol Wimber suggested five phases of worship, with a goal of 'intimacy with God': call to worship; engagement (where 'the manifest presence of God is magnified and multiplied'); expressing God's love ('we move more and more into loving and intimate language'); visitation ('we should always come to worship prepared for an audience with the King'); and generosity ('the giving of substance').[76] Martyn Percy has gone as far as to describe a 'sublimated eroticism' in the lyrics of the 'third wave', saying 'their churches are to become hot, wet, passionate and open'. He saw parallels with medieval mysticism; however, the theme of intimacy in the tradition of evangelical hymn-writing is more immediately salient. It was evident in the hymns of Charles Wesley. Then, from the mid-nineteenth century, the hymnody of Fanny Crosby, Frances Ridley Havergal, and Adelaide Pollard also adopted a language of intimacy.[77] The lyrics of the Vineyard

[71] Quoted in Mike Pilavachi and Craig Borlase, *For the audience of one: the Soul Survivor guide to worship* (London: Hodder & Stoughton, 1999), 4.

[72] David Watson, *I believe in the Church* (London: Hodder & Stoughton, 1978), 192.

[73] Brett Knowles, '"From the ends of the earth we hear songs": music as an indicator of New Zealand Pentecostal spirituality and theology', *Australasian Pentecostal Studies*, 5/6 (2002), online.

[74] Michael Harper, *Three sisters* (Wheaton: Tyndale House, 1979), 63.

[75] Knowles, 'From the ends'.

[76] See John and Carol Wimber, 'Worship: intimacy with God', https://multiplyvineyard.org/wp-content/uploads/2016/08/Wimber-Intimacy-with-God-Oct-3-2012-3-56-PM.pdf, accessed 16 June 2021.

[77] C. Michael Hawn and J. H. Hobbs, '"Thy love hath broken every barrier down": the rhetoric of intimacy in nineteenth century British and American women's hymns', in Martin V. Clarke (ed.), *Music and theology in nineteenth-century Britain* (Farnham: Ashgate, 2012), 61–78.

and those from other charismatic sources echoed earlier gendered evangelical pieties. Nevertheless, even by historic standards, songs of the 1990s and 2000s, such as 'In the Secret (I want to know you)', 'Arms of Love', 'Draw me Close', and 'Come and Fill me Up', were expressive in a way which could be startlingly direct. This was perhaps because of the determination that songs should be simple and from the heart. They were expressive—and active—also in their references to embodiment (e.g. 'We Bow Down, and Confess'; 'I will Lift up my Hands'; 'Breathe'). There were new songs about the members of the Godhead, but alongside these, plenty which were *to* them.

'Almost anyone can lead songs, but it takes someone special to be able to lead *people* as they sing', argued Judson Cornwall in 1983. The importance attributed to the praise and worship encounter—and the creativity, ability to lead through the 'flow' and 'phases' of the worship set, and the skills of musical spontaneity required—resulted in the widespread popularity of the office of the 'worship leader'.[78] This role went hand in hand with a modern music industry which charismatics had largely constructed. Artists, publishers, and record companies were able to monetise and professionalise worship through the production of songbooks (compilations and those containing the music of high-profile congregations or annual conferences), worship albums (new songs, compilations, and live recordings), and from 1985, various initiatives of copyright licensing. By 1997, the Christian Copyright Licensing International administered 135,000 licences for the use of praise and worship songs by congregations in Australia, New Zealand, South Africa, the United Kingdom, Ireland, United States, and Canada.[79] The economic flows of the worship industry mapped on to the Anglo-world, as did the flagship producers of this music. In recent decades, these included Soul Survivor (worship leaders such as Matt Redman, Tim Hughes, and Vicky Beeching), Sovereign Grace Ministries (e.g. Bob Kauflin), Bethel (e.g. Brian and Jenn Johnson, Cory Asbury), and Hillsong (e.g. Darlene Zschech, Reuben Morgan, and Joel Houston). By 2012, Hillsong alone had sold over 11 million albums; and its worship leaders and sounds were prominent in its global brand.[80] The pre-eminence of such particular contemporary music ministries indicates legacies of strands of charismatic renewal: Soul Survivor of English Anglican renewal, David Pytches' experiences in Chile, and the Vineyard; Bethel and Hillsong of the Latter Rain movement; and Sovereign Grace of the independent charismatic scene. It is big business and a long way from the Community of Celebration living a 'communistic'

[78] Nelson Cowan, 'Lay-prophet-priest: the not-so-fledgling "office" of the worship leader', *Liturgy*, 32/1 (2017), 24–31.

[79] Pete Ward, 'The economies of charismatic evangelical worship', in Gordon Lynch, Jolyon Mitchell, and Anna Strhan (eds.), *Religion, media and culture: a reader* (Abingdon: Routledge, 2012), 23–30.

[80] Tanya Riches and Tom Wagner, 'The evolution of Hillsong Music: from Australian Pentecostal congregation into global brand', *Australian Journal of Communication*, 31/1 (2012), 17–36.

lifestyle on the Isle of Cumbrae. The publishers and record companies amongst the beneficiaries were not so much service agencies as profitable industries.

Charismatic praise and worship also crossed over into wider Christian circles. This had begun in the 1970s; for example, as Jesus Music artists gained in popularity (e.g. Explo '72) and the Fisherfolk became acceptable to evangelicals, even leading worship at the National Evangelical Anglican Congress in Nottingham, England, in 1975. That so much of 1970s charismatic praise and worship was drawn from Scripture—and because it made few references to pneumatic 'dogmas'—made it acceptable to non-charismatics. When *Mission Praise* was published in Britain in 1984 it included standard evangelical hymns and songs from the charismatic renewal.[81] Pan-denominational events like the Spring Harvest conferences in the United Kingdom and Baptist pastor Louis Giglio's Passion conferences in the United States were places where charismatic worship music permeated the wider church. The historic practice of singing, the American historian Mark Noll argues, has been a bonding practice for evangelicals otherwise divided by all kinds of theological debates. In the 1960s, charismatics and non-charismatics were often at loggerheads over speaking in tongues. Thirty years later, the songs of house church worship leader Graham Kendrick were standard fare on the BBC's *Songs of Praise* (indeed, in a survey by the programme in 2005 his 'Shine, Jesus Shine' was voted into the top ten of hymns and songs alongside traditional favourites such as 'How Great Thou Art' and 'Be Thou my Vision'). Fast-forward a further twenty years and it was common to hear the songs of Bethel and Hillsong in non-charismatic congregations.

As music moved beyond the charismatic milieu, so did embodied practices of praise and worship. The historian David Bebbington, a dedicated observer and notetaker of the details of church meetings, found that hand raising increased at one Baptist church in Nottingham, England, from 2 people in 1978, to 8 in 1988, to 20 at the start of 1989, and to 30 at the end of the year.[82] Many Christians felt comfortable enough to raise their hands without adopting the rest of the charismatic supernatural 'package'. To demonstrate worship with one's body became a normal practice for generations now enculturated by the expressive revolution (Fig. 8.1). As Bebbington also gleaned, the 'time' of praise of worship was increasingly common to evangelical patterns of ministry. In 1974, an article in the liturgical journal *Worship* on the charismatic 'challenge' to Roman Catholic worship, spoke of how traditional services, at their worst, were like the Swiss National Railroad: 'Trains leaving and arriving with impeccable punctuality regardless of whether or not a single passenger gets on'.[83] To Protestants and Catholics alike, charismatics offered authentic expression of worship to God.

81 Ward, 'Economies'.

82 David Bebbington, 'Evangelicals and public worship, 1965–2005', *Evangelical Quarterly*, 79/1 (2007), 3–22.

83 D. Steindl-Rast, 'Charismatic renewal: a challenge to Roman Catholic worship', *Worship*, 48/7 (1974), 382–91, at 386.

Global Moments: Lambeth 1998, Rome 2017, and Trump 2020

The contemporary praise and worship industry underlines how the Anglo-world continues to provide a distinctive sphere of translocal charismatic engagement; however, there is also much to highlight expanding and intensifying global connections. We now consider this by examining three global 'moments'. The first was the Lambeth Conference of 1998. Twenty years earlier, as we have seen, Anglicans and Episcopalians had established Sharing of Ministries Abroad (SOMA) to promote mutual exchange between charismatics across the Anglican Communion. Over the next twenty years, SOMA, led by an international leadership team of Westerners and non-Westerners, sponsored hundreds of short-term missions based on the principle of cultivating long-term relationships which represented the interdependence of the global Christian 'body' of Christ. These networks were an important context for the emergence of alliances between conservative charismatic and otherwise 'renewed' Anglicans as it became clear that the politics of sexuality would define the last Lambeth Conference of the millennium.

In June 1997, the Revd. Edward Little II of All Saints' Church, Bakersfield (who had been on the board of SOMA USA), wrote in *The Living Church* that most Anglicans lived in the developing world—with more in Nigeria than in the United States, Canada, Britain, Australia, and New Zealand combined—and these would be understood by Americans to be 'evangelicals'. From personal experience, he explained, he knew 'our third world brothers and sisters' viewed developments in the American Episcopal Church 'with increasing gravity'.[84] At the pre-Lambeth Conference renewal gathering in 1998, co-sponsored by SOMA International and Anglican Renewal Ministries (ARM), there was distress amongst African leaders over a recently published interview with American Bishop Jack Spong. This had described African Christians as 'superstitious' (a word he later described as communicating 'an unfortunate message').[85] As an act of reconciliation during the SOMA/ARM leaders' retreat, some Americans present asked publicly for the African leaders' forgiveness for the insult made against them. African leaders came forward to embrace them in response.[86] This was an important background to the subsequent vote by the bishops to endorse traditional teaching on sexuality. A report in SOMA's American magazine *Sharing USA* later claimed:

[84] The Very Revd. Edward S. Little II, 'Backward?', *The Living Church*, 15 June 1997, 4–5.

[85] Andrew Carey, 'African Christians? They're just one step up from witchcraft: what Bishop Spong had to say about his fellow Christians', *Church of England Newspaper*, 10 July 1998, 13. For Spong's response to the article see David Skidmore, 'Bishop Spong apologies to Africans', 28 July 1998, http://www.anglicannews.org/news/1998/07/bishop-spong-apologizes-for-perceived-insult-to-africans.aspx, accessed 17 August 2016.

[86] 'The Canterbury '98 conferences', *Sharing: The Newsletter of SOMA UK*, October 1998.

> Extraordinary events occurred at Lambeth. The bishops approved a resolution which reaffirmed 'the primary authority of the Scriptures'. The overwhelming majority voted for another resolution that upholds the Church's historic, orthodox teaching on sexual morality, while committing to preserve pastoral care. These resolutions demonstrated the shift of strong spiritual leadership of our beloved Anglican Communion to the developing world. SOMA began investing energy, training and people resources into these areas since our inception twenty years ago.
>
> We know that this long-term investment, from our years of building partnerships to refreshing leaders in a pre-Lambeth retreat, 'counted' at Lambeth. Many friends sowed seeds into this good soil through our organization, and it bore much fruit, good fruit.[87]

Charismatics became the transnational 'tissue' for the emergence of the Global Anglican Futures Conference (GAFCON) in 2008. A paradox is that five years after GAFCON's Jerusalem Statement announced the intention to 'reform, heal and revitalise' the Anglican Communion, Justin Welby, a charismatic with longstanding connections to Holy Trinity Brompton (in fact, he experienced the call to ordination during the visit of an American Vineyard pastor), was enthroned as *primus inter pares* of its primates. Just as many charismatic Anglicans appeared to be losing confidence in the global communion, Welby's appointment indicated the extent to which charismatic spirituality had moved from the periphery to the mainstream.

In the same year, the Argentinian Jesuit Jorge Mario Bergoglio was elected to the papacy. As Austen Ivereigh has argued, 'no pope has ever identified as closely with the Catholic Charismatic Renewal, nor been so keen to move it to front and center in the church.'[88] A second global 'moment' was the fiftieth anniversary of 'Duquesne' in 2017. In a Pentecost Vigil of Prayer at the Circus Maximus, Pope Francis stated:

> Fifty years of the Catholic Charismatic Renewal. A flood of grace of the Spirit! Why a flood of grace? Because it has no founder, no bylaws, no structure of governance. Clearly it has given rise to many expressions that, surely, are human works inspired by the Spirit, with various charisms, and all at the service of the Church. But before this flood of grace one cannot erect dikes, or put the Holy Spirit in a cage!

Not only did the Pope reiterate the view that renewal was a current of grace in the Church; he also endorsed the ecumenicity of the movement, inviting non-

[87] Edwina Thomas, 'Director's corner', *Sharing USA*, September 1998.

[88] Austen Ivereigh, 'Is Francis our first charismatic Pope?', 14 June 2019, https://www.americamagazine.org/faith/2019/06/14/francis-our-first-charismatic-pope, accessed 23 June 2021.

Catholics to the celebrations. Although the 2017 event tended to reify the standard origins account of Catholic charismatic renewal which was problematised in Chapter 2, it underlined the globality of the movement. At the same Vigil, Pope Francis read from —the Book of Acts: 'Parthians and Medes and Elamites and residents of Mesopotamia, Judea and Cappadocia, Pontus and Asia, Phrygia and Pamphylia, Egypt and the parts of Libya belonging to Cyrene, and visitors from Rome, both Jews and proselytes, Cretans and Arabians, we hear them telling in our own tongues the mighty works of God.' This message, of course, was even more powerful coming from the first non-European Pope.[89] In front of a banner reading in multiple languages 'Jesus is Lord', the Pope spoke of how representatives from 120 nations had gathered in the stadium.

A third global 'moment' concerns independent charismatics. The context was the aftermath of the campaign to re-elect Donald Trump as President of the United States in 2020. In the days after election day, when the Democrat candidate Joe Biden was poised to win the final electoral college votes, the televangelist Paula White took the stage at a prayer meeting at New Destiny Christian Centre, Orlando. White was among various leaders linked with apostolic-prophetic networks which had supported Trump. Some, four years earlier, had asserted that Trump was God's 'chosen' and would have a role like the heathen King Cyrus in the Old Testament. These often subscribed to the notion of a 'seven mountain mandate': the establishment of the kingdom of God in the spheres of religion, education, family, business, government, the arts, and media. This was the politics of dominion, with its entangled lineages of Latter Rain, independent restorationism, and Reformed reconstructionism. As the prayer vigil was streamed on Facebook Live, White prophesied: 'I hear a sound of victory, the Lord says it is done.' Her words which followed gave an insight into the American charismatic imaginary in the twenty-first century: 'For angels have even been dispatched from Africa right now…In the name of Jesus from South America, they're coming here.' There was an irony, as Bishop Talbert Swan, President of the National Association for the Advancement of Colored People (NAACP), recognised in a Tweet: 'God is sending angels from a place Trump called a sh*thole to help him get elected?'[90] It seems unlikely that President Trump rested much political hope on this prophecy; however, White's words implied that South America and Africa were places of potency for waging battle in the heavenlies. Was this a kind of angelic reverse mission, en route, by wings, from the global South? It certainly pointed to the far horizons of American charismatics.

[89] 'Pentecost Vigil of Prayer: address by His Holiness Pope Francis', https://www.vatican.va/content/francesco/en/speeches/2017/june/documents/papa-francesco_20170603_veglia-pentecoste.html, accessed 23 June 2021.

[90] See https://twitter.com/talbertswan/status/1324884932926255104.

Age of the Spirit and Era of Secularisation?

To close, we return to the three scholarly frames identified in the opening chapter: secularisation, authenticity, and cosmopolitanism. In the imagined eschatological contexts of the post-war decades, what coalesced as a Spiritscape of charismatic renewal expected the empowerment of the churches in the face of secularisation. By 1980, it was clear to some involved in the renewal for a decade or more that revival was not imminent.[91] Looking ahead to the beginning of the twenty-first century, it is fair to say that the overall trend in the Anglo-world, by some criteria, has been the continued decline of Christianity. However, in many situations, at various times, charismatic churches have grown. This was true in the 1960s and 1970s and it has remained true since. A critical perspective is important here—not all charismatic churches grew. Where they did, as was commonly the case with historic church growth in the modern period (evident, for example, in Jeffrey Cox's major study of Victorian London), there was often a correlation between growth and the dynamism and optimism of individual church leaders.[92] Being charismatic was alone not enough: but charismatic practice and belief (including the morale boosting expectations of the renewal), when combined with effective leadership and agency, could make quite the difference. As suggested above, growth was very often 'churn'. But even so, charismatic congregations, as well as numerous festivals and conferences, offered a reanimated version of Christianity. If charismatics didn't get the revival they hoped for, it is nevertheless salient to ask what condition the Western churches would have been in now *without* the renewal.

A Church of England report in 1981 asserted 'the rise of the counter-culture and of the charismatic movement were simultaneous' and that this produced 'a form of Christianised existentialism'.[93] The charismatic renewal described in this book may have had little to do directly with Sartre, Derrida, and Foucault, but it undoubtedly reflected developing notions of authenticity from the mid-century. Francesca Montemaggi's description of Christian authenticity from a Simmelian perspective offers some theoretical underpinning here. For charismatics, authenticity was to 'reconnect with Christianity' in disorientating times.[94] If this relationship with the culture offers a powerful explanation for the re-animative power of charismatic renewal, alone it is not sufficient. We have located different strands of the renewal in the tradition of historic Christian experiential impulses.

[91] Though, of course, global revival has continued to be the hope of many charismatics since the 1980s.

[92] Jeffrey Cox, *The English churches in a secular society: Lambeth, 1870–1930* (Oxford: Oxford University Press, 1982).

[93] *The charismatic movement in the Church of England* (London: CIO, 1981), 41.

[94] Francesca E. S. Montemaggi, *Authenticity and religion in a pluralistic age: a Simmelian study of Christian evangelicals and new monastics* (Lanham: Rowman & Littlefield, 2019), 1.

Revivalism, in both its (sometimes indistinguishable) empowered evangelical and pentecostal revivalist forms, was chief amongst these. In fact, some leading Catholic charismatics, even, were aware that in some sense the renewal was a process of 'evangelicalisation'. The 'spirit' of eighteenth-century evangelicalism, Bruce Hindmarsh argues, was the Holy Spirit. Drawing on a range of medieval and contemporary sources, early evangelicals believed the Spirit 'brought about the conversion of sinners and restored an experience of the immediate presence of God that was spiritually animating'.[95] Beginnings, Hindmarsh reminds us, matter. The orientation towards the practice and experience of *real* Christianity, in the power of the Holy Spirit, has remained within evangelicalism—re-emerging, for instance, in the Keswick movement, the Oxford Group, the Latter Rain movement, and in charismatic renewal. Indeed, the significant place of 'pneumatism' in evangelicalism in so many times and places may warrant it being deployed often as an 'optional' fifth characteristic to David Bebbington's evangelical quadrilateral of crucicentricism, conversionism, Biblicism, and activism. Tim Larsen has already proposed something along these lines, and this study tends to support the case.[96] Certainly, the option of a 'pentagon' might help us to understand evangelicalism as it is largely found in the global South today.

Cosmopolitanism was another feature of charismatic renewal. These days, a distinctively Anglo-world geography of the Spirit—now defined by ministries such as Bethel, Hillsong, Holy Trinity Brompton, Soul Survivor, Catch the Fire, and God TV—continues to shape and maintain the charismatic imagination and experience of 'authentic' Christianity within an increasingly secular, post-Christian arena. However, a theme running through this book has been the long-term connections between this sphere and a much wider global nexus of charismatic, holiness, and pentecostal Christianity. Global charismatic cosmopolitanism, based on translocal, mutual exchanges which emerged with the renewal, will likely play an increasingly key role in shaping the conservative Christian imagination in the Anglo-world; whether through global organisational mechanisms such as GAFCON, or techniques of revival and spiritual warfare, or through migration, 'reverse mission', and church planting. This two-way global North–South dynamic, in which charismatics remain so implicated, could define—perhaps in unpredictable ways—the story of Christianity in the Anglo-world in the twenty first century.

This, however, is speculative. In the 1960s and 1970s, the global revival desired by many Christians in the Anglo-world of North America, the British Isles, South Africa, and Australasia did not occur. The new Pentecost or 'era of the Spirit' did not result, as many hoped, in the decisive emergence of renewed, restored, or

[95] D. Bruce Hindmarsh, *The Spirit of early evangelicalism: true religion in a modern world* (New York: Oxford University Press, 2018), 268.

[96] Timothy Larsen, 'Defining and locating evangelicalism', in Timothy Larsen and Daniel J. Treier (eds.), *The Cambridge companion to evangelical theology* (Cambridge: Cambridge University Press, 2012), 1–13, at 2.

revived Church. There was no great harvest of souls in the West. Nevertheless, consider the transformation of Christian practices, embodiments, materialities, beliefs, and experiences in Anglo-world Christianity. Consider, also, the rapid movement of charismatic Christianity from the periphery to the mainstream. For the historian of religion, the period between 1945 and 1980—and beyond—still deserves the title *the age of the Spirit*.

Bibliography

Interviews

Professor Alan Guile (United Kingdom)
Ken and Raewyn Harrison (New Zealand)
Richard Hines (United States)
The Rt. Revd. David Pytches (United Kingdom)
Kevin and Dorothy Ranaghan (United States)

Existing Oral Testimonies

Wheaton College, Collection 331, Tape 1, interview with Reuben Archer Torrey III, 14 May 1986

Archival Sources

Alan Paton Centre and Struggle Archives, Pietermaritzburg (online)

Interview with Dave Philips (by Glen Thompson), 15 December 1995

David Allan Hubbard Library, Pasadena, California

David du Plessis papers
Jean Stone and Richard J. Willans papers

Donald Gee Centre, Mattersey, England

Fountain Trust papers

Lambeth Palace Library, London, England

Michael Harper papers
John R. W. Stott papers

Notre Dame University Archive, South Bend, Indiana

James E. Byrne papers
Louis Rogge Collection

Regent University Special Collections and Archive, Virginia Beach, Virginia

Dennis J. Bennett papers

Sword of the Spirit (online)

Catholic Charismatic Renewal Service Committee (CCRSC) minutes

Non-Archived Papers (currently in possession of author)

Bob Balkam, Charism and institution: 1968–1978, unpublished.
Notes of conversation between Kristina Cooper and Lady Bronwyn Astor.

Charismatic Magazines and Newsletters

Acts 29 Newsletter (United States)
Charismatic Communion (United States)
Christian Life (United States)
Day of Renewal (England)
Episcopal Charismatic Fellowship Newsletter (United States)
Full Gospel Men's Voice (United States)
Goodnews (England)
Logos (New Zealand)
Logos Journal (United States)
New Covenant (United States)
New Wine (United States)
Newsletter (for the Catholic Charismatic Renewal) (Australia)*
Panorama (New Zealand)
Renewal (United Kingdom)
Renewing (Australia)
Sharing USA
Sharing: The Newsletter of SOMA UK
Trinity (United States)
Vision (Australia)
See also:
The Holy Way, August 1972, (online), https://jspi.info/media/Eng-Mag/1970s/1972/1972-Aug(36).pdf, accessed 2 May 2021
* Also known as *Newsletter (for the Bardon Catholic Charismatic Renewal)* and *National Newsletter (Serving the Charismatic Renewal throughout Australasia and the Pacific)*

Other Magazines and Newsletters

America (United States)
Australian Church Record (Australia)
Barrier Miner (Australia)
Bible Deliverance (New Zealand)
Buckingham Report (United States)
Cambridge News (United Kingdom)
Catholic Herald (United Kingdom)
Catholic Weekly (Australia)
Christian Century (United States)
Christianity Today (United States)
Churchman (United Kingdom)
Contact (United Kingdom)

Crusade (United Kingdom)
Dallas Morning News
Detroit Free Press Magazine
Frazer's Magazine (United Kingdom)
Liturgical Review (United Kingdom)
National Catholic Reporter (United States)
New York Times
Oklahoma City Times
One in Christ (United Kingdom)
Pastoral Psychology (United States)
Pentecost (United Kingdom)
Redemption Tidings (United Kingdom)
Seattle Post-Intelligencer
Seattle Times
Spokane Daily Chronicle
St Luke's Newsletter (Seattle)
Sydney Morning Herald
The Church of England Newspaper (United Kingdom)
The Ecumenist (Canada)
The Fraternal (United Kingdom)
The Furrow (Republic of Ireland)
The Gospel Truth (New Zealand)
The Living Church (United States)
The Progress (United States)
Time (United States)
Toronto Star
Van Nuys News
Washington Post
Washington Times
Work and Worship (newssheet for All Souls, Langham Place, United Kingdom)

Albums and Songs

Barrie, Karen. 'Psalm 89', The Word of God, *New Life*, 1972, The Word of God, vinyl LP.
Church of the Redeemer Choir. *God's people give thanks*, 1977, Celebration Records, vinyl LP.
Crouch, Andraé. *Live in London*, 1978, Light Records, vinyl double LP.
Fellingham, David. 'Alleluia! The Lord reigns', *Call to War*, 1981, Scripture in Song, various formats.
Garrett, David and Dale. *Prepare ye the way*, 1972, Anchor Recordings, vinyl LP.
Norman, Larry. 'Why should the Devil have all the good music?', *Only visiting this planet*, 1972, MGM, vinyl LP.
Owens, Jimmy and Carol (featuring Pat Boone). 'Come together', *Come together*, 1972, Light Record, vinyl LP.
Richards, Dave. 'For I'm Building a People of Power', 1977, Kingsway's Thankyou music.
The Fisherfolk. *Celebrate the feast*, 1975, Celebration Records, vinyl LP.
The Word of God. *New Life*, 1972, The Word of God, vinyl LP.
Vale, Alliene, 'The joy of the Lord', The Fisherfolk, *Worship with the Fisherfolk*, 1978, Celebration Records, vinyl LP.

Various artists. *Arise shine! Worship from the Dales Bible Week 1977*, 1977, Harvestime, cassette.

Watson, Merv and Merla, *Hidden Manna*, 1975, Catacombs Productions, vinyl LP.

Primary Published Written Texts

Ahlstrom, Sydney E. 'The radical turn in theology and ethics: why it occurred in the 1960s', *The Annals of the American Academy of Political and Social Science*, 387 (1970), 1–13.

Anon. *Life and power: the "Christian cell" or group* (London: The Advisory Group for Christian Cells, 1945).

Audemard, Philip. 'Bardon: a puzzle for the Protestant evangelical', *The Fraternal*, 168 (1973), 40–44.

Baars, Conrad W. *Feeling and healing your emotions* (Plainfield: Logos International, 1979).

Battley, Don. *No way back* (Auckland: Castle Publishing, 2020).

Berton, Pierre. *The comfortable pew: a critical look at Christianity and the religious establishment in the new age* (Toronto: McLelland and Stewart, 1965).

Bloesch, Donald G. *Centers of Christian renewal* (Philadelphia: United Church Free Press, 1964).

Bonnín, Eduardo. *The how and the why* (Dallas: National Ultreya Publications, 1981).

Brother Andrew, John and Elizabeth Sherill, *God's smuggler* (New York: New American Library, 1967).

Cantelon, Willard. *The day the dollar dies* (Plainfield: Logos International Fellowship, 1973).

Carothers, Merlin R. *Prison to praise* (Plainfield: Logos International, 1970).

CFO. *CFO: What is it?* (St Paul: Association of Camps Farthest Out, 1958; 1963 edn.).

Chagnon, Ronald.*Les Charismatiques au Québec* (Montreal: Quebec/Amérique, 1979).

Christenson, Larry. *Speaking in tongues and its significance for the church* (London: Fountain Trust, 1968).

Christenson, Larry. *The Christian family* (Ada: Bethany Fellowship, 1974).

Clark, Steve. *Building Christian communities: strategy for renewing the Church* (Notre Dame: Ave Maria Press, 1972).

Clark, Steve. *Man and woman in Christ* (Ann Arbor: Servant Books, 1980).

Commadeur, Adrian. *The Spirit in the Church: exploring Catholic charismatic renewal* (Melbourne: Comsoda Communications, 1992).

Connelly, James. 'The Charismatic movement 1967–1970', in Kevin and Dorothy Ranaghan (eds.), *As the Spirit leads us* (New York: Paulist Press, 1971), 211–32.

Daniélou, Jean. *Advent* (London: Sheed and Ward, 1950).

Davison, Leslie. *Pathway to power: the charismatic movement in historical perspective* (Watchung: Charisma books, 1971).

Du Plessis, David and Bob Slosser. *A man called Mr Pentecost* (Plainfield: Logos, 1977).

Dunne, Tim. '"Nevertheless...": a variety of religious protest', *Reality*, 9/2 (1977), 14–16.

Edwards, David L. *The Honest to God debate* (London: Hymns Ancient and Modern, 1963).

Esses DeBlase, Betty. *Survivor of a tarnished ministry: the true story of Michael and Betty Esses* (Orange: Truth Publishers, 1983).

Ford, Josephine Massyngberde. *The Pentecostal experience: a new direction for American Catholics* (Paramus, NJ: Paulist Press 1970).

Ford, Josephine Massyngberde. *Which way for Catholic Pentecostals?* (New York: Harper & Row, 1976).

Foulkes, Ron. 'Breakthrough among Methodists', *Charismatic Contact*, 2/3 (1973), n.p.

Glennon, Jim. *Your healing is within you* (London: Hodder & Stoughton, 1978).

Grensted, L. W. *What is the Oxford Group?* (Oxford: Oxford University Press, 1933).

Gromacki, Robert Glenn.*The modern tongues movement* (Philadelphia: Presbyterian and Reformed Publishing, 1967).

Grubb, Norman. *Spirit of Revival: a first-hand account of the Congo revival of the 1950s* (Gerrards Cross: WEC, 1954).

Harper, Michael. *A new way of living* (London: Hodder & Stoughton, 1973).

Harper, Michael. *As at the beginning* (Atlanta: Society of Stephen, 1994).

Harper, Michael. *Charismatic crisis: the charismatic renewal past, present and future* (Sydney: Anglican Renewal Ministries Australia, 1980).

Harper, Michael. 'Introduction', in *A new Canterbury tale: the reports of the Anglican International Conference on Spiritual Renewal Held at Canterbury, July 1978* (Bramcote: Grove Books, 1978).

Harper, Michael. *None can guess* (London: Hodder & Stoughton, 1971).

Harper, Michael. *Power for the body of Christ* (London: Fountain Trust, 1969).

Harper, Michael. *Spiritual warfare* (London: Hodder & Stoughton, 1970).

Harper, Michael. *Three sisters* (Wheaton: Tyndale House, 1979).

Harper, Michael. *Walk in the Spirit*, 2nd edn. (London: Hodder & Stoughton, 1981).

Harper, Michael. *Walk in the Spirit*, rev. edn. (Eastbourne: Kingsway 1983).

Henson, Hensley. *Notes on spiritual healing* (London: Williams and Norgate, 1925).

Hertenstein, Mike and Jon Trott, *Selling Satan: the evangelical media and the Mike Warnke scandal* (Chicago: Cornerstone Press, 1993).

Hickson, James Moore. *The healing of Christ in his Church* (New York: Edwin S. Gorham, 1919).

Houdart, Sr. Marie-André. 'The International and Ecumenical Charismatic Renewal Congress', *Lumen Vitae*, 1974/1.

Hyde, Douglas. *Dedication and leadership* (Notre Dame: University of Notre Dame Press, 1966).

Irving, Edward. 'Facts connected with recent manifestations of spiritual gifts', *Fraser's Magazine*, January 1832.

Jones, Bryn. 'World crisis: people want answers', *Restoration*, 1/2 (May–June 1975), 2–5.

Jorstad, Erling. *Bold in the Spirit: Lutheran charismatic renewal in America today* (Minneapolis: Augsburg Publishing House, 1974).

King Jr., Martin Luther. *A Gift of love: sermons from strength to love and other preachings* (Boston: Beacon Press, 2012).

Landau, Rom. *God is my adventure: a book on modern mystics, masters and teachers* (London: Nicholson and Watson, 1935).

Lees, Faith (with Jeanne Hinton). *Love is our home* (London: Hodder & Stoughton, 1978).

Lillie, David. *Tongues under fire* (London: Fountain Trust, 1966).

McCarthy, Jerome. 'The charismatic renewal and reconciliation in Northern Ireland', *One in Christ*, 10/1 (1974), 31–43.

Martin, Ralph. *Husbands, wives, parents, children: foundations for the Christian family* (Ann Arbor: Servant Books, 1978).

Meyer, F. B. *Back to Bethel: separation from sin, and fellowship with God* (Chicago: Fleming R. Revell, 1901).

Miller, Keith. *A taste of new wine* (Waco: Word, 1965).

Muggeridge, Malcolm. *The thirties, 1930–1940, in Great Britain* (London: H. Hamilton, 1940).

Mullery, Mark. 'What makes a great leader?', in C. J. Mahenney (ed.), *Why small groups? Together toward maturity* (Gaithersburg: Sovereign Grace Ministries, 1996).

Murray, Andrew. *The full blessing of Pentecost: the one thing needful* (London: James Nisbet and Co., 1908).

Nee, Watchman. *The normal Christian life*, 3rd edn. (Eastbourne: Victory Press, 1963).

Noder, David. 'Renewing the renewal', in John Wimber and Kevin Springer (eds.), *Riding the third wave: what comes after renewal?* (London: Marshall Pickering, 1987), 135–50.

O'Connor, Edward D. *Pentecost and the modern world* (Notre Dame: Ave Maria Press, 1972).

O'Neill, John. 'Charismatic renewal and its spirituality', *The Furrow*, 25/11 (November 1974), 599–603.

Orchard, W. E. *The outlook for religion* (London: Cassell and Company, 1918).

Orr, J. Edwin. *Full surrender* (London: Marshall, Morgan and Scott, 1951).

Ortiz, Juan Carlos. *Call to discipleship* (Plainfield: Logos International Fellowship, 1975).

Ortiz, Juan Carlos and Martha Palau. *From jungles to the cathedrals: the captivating story of Juan Carlos Ortiz* (Miami: Editorial Vida, 2011).

Owens, Jimmy and Carol Owens. *Restoring a nation's foundations: prayer strategies and action plans* (Los Angeles: Foursquare, 2007).

Page, Charles H. 'Bureaucracy in the liberal Church', *Review of Religion*, 14/3 (July 1951), 149–50.

Panos, Chris. *God's spy* (Plainfield: Logos International, 1976).

Pilavachi, Mike and Craig Borlase, *For the audience of one: the Soul Survivor guide to worship* (London: Hodder & Stoughton, 1999).

Prince, Derek. *Pages from my life's book* (Charlotte: Derek Prince Ministries International, 1987).

Prince, Derek. *Purposes of Pentecost* (Charlotte: Derek Prince Ministries International, 1966).

Pulkingham, Betty. *Sing God a simple song: exploring worship in music for the eighties* (New York: HarperCollins, 1986).

Pulkingham, Betty and Jeanne Harper. *Sound of living waters: songs of renewal* (1974).

Pullinger, Jackie (with Andrew Quicke). *Chasing the dragon* (London: Hodder & Stoughton, 1980).

Pytches, David. *Come Holy Spirit* (London: Hodder & Stoughton, 1985).

Pytches, David. *Living at the edge: the autobiography of David Pytches* (Bath: Arcadia, 2002).

Ranaghan, Kevin. *The Lord, the Spirit and the Church* (Ann Arbor: Word of Life, 1973).

Ranaghan, Kevin and Dorothy Ranaghan (eds.). *As the Spirit leads us* (New York: Paulist Press, 1971).

Ranaghan, Kevin and Dorothy Ranaghan. *Catholic Pentecostals* (New York: Paulist Press, 1969).

Reid, Tommy (with Doug Brendel). *The exploding Church* (Plainfield: Logos, 1979).

Reimer, Al. *God's country* (Toronto: G. R. Welch, 1979).

Robertson, Murray. 'A power encounter worth laughing about', in John Wimber and Kevin Springer (eds.), *Riding the third wave: what comes after renewal?* (London: Marshall Pickering, 1987), 188–97.

Robinson, John T. *The new Reformation?* (London: SCM, 1965).

Rowland, Gerald. 'Catholic-Protestant relationships within the charismatic renewal', *The Evangel*, 31/11 (November 1976), 10–11.

Sanford, Agnes. *The healing light*, English edition (Evesham: Arthur James, 1949).

Saunders, Teddy and Hugh Sansom. *David Watson* (London: Hodder & Stoughton, 1992).
Schlink, Basilea. *Praying our way through life* (London: Marshall, Morgan and Scott, 1970).
Schlink, Basilea. *Repentance: the joy-filled life* (London: Lakeland. 1972).
Schlink, Basilea. *Ruled by the Spirit* (London: Oliphants, 1969).
Schlink, Basilea. *The world in revolt* (Minneapolis: Bethany House, 1969).
Scroggie, W. Graham. *The Baptism of the Spirit and speaking with tongues* (London: Pickering and Inglis, 1956).
Smith, Brian (with Adrian Commadeur). *Streams of living water: autobiography of a charismatic leader* (Melbourne: Comsoda Communications, 2000).
Stone Willans, Jean. *The acts of the little green apples* (New Kensington: Whitaker House, 1973).
Spiritual healing: report of the clerical and medical committee of inquiry into spiritual, faith and mental healing (London: Macmillan and Co., 1914).
Strachan, Gordan. 'Pentecostal worship in the Church of Scotland, part 1', *Liturgical Review*, November 1972, 16–27; part 2, November 1973, 34–47.
Suenens, Léon Joseph. *Ecumenism and charismatic renewal: theological and pastoral orientations*, Malines Document 2 (Ann Arbor: Servant Books, 1978).
Suenens, Léon Joseph. *Memories and hopes* (Dublin: Veritas, 1992).
Suenens, Léon Joseph. *Open the frontiers: a spiritual testimony from Cardinal Suenens* (London: Darton, Longman and Todd, 1980).
Suenens, Léon Joseph. *The hidden hand of God: life of Veronica O'Brien and our common apostolate* (London: Veritas, 1994).
Sumrall, Lester (with J. Stephen Conn). *Miracles don't just happen* (Plainfield: Logos International, 1979).
Torrey, R. A. *The baptism with the Holy Spirit* (New York: Fleming H. Reveal, 1895).
Vaughan, David. *A faith for the New Age* (London: Regency Press, 1967).
Virgo, Terry. 'The Church: God's only answer', *Restoration*, November–December 1978, 13.
Walker, Alan. *Breakthrough: rediscovering the Holy Spirit* (Nashville: Abingdon Press, 1969).
Walker, Andrew J. *Notes from a wayward son: a miscellany*, ed. Andrew D. Kinsey (Eugene: Cascade Books, 2015).
Walker, Tom. *Open to God: a parish in renewal* (Bramcote: Grove Books, 1975).
Walker, Tom. *Renew us by your Spirit* (London: Hodder & Stoughton, 1982).
Wallis, Arthur. *In the day of thy Power: the scriptural principles of revival* (London: Christian Literature Crusade, 1956).
Warfield, Benjamin. *Counterfeit miracles* (New York: Charles Scribner's Sons, 1918).
Watson, David. *I believe in the Church* (London: Hodder & Stoughton, 1978).
Watson, David. *You are my God* (London: Hodder & Stoughton, 1983).
Webster, Douglas. *Pentecostalism and speaking in tongues* (London: Highway Press, 1964).
Wilkerson, David and John Sherrill. *The Cross and the switchblade* (Old Tappan: F. H. Revell, 1963).
Wilkerson, Ralph. *Satellites of the Spirit* (Anaheim: Melodyland, 1978).
Worsfold, J. E. *A history of the charismatic movements in New Zealand* (Bradford: Puritan Press, 1974).

Secondary Published Works

Althouse, Peter. *Spirit in the last days: pentecostal eschatology in conversation with Jürgen Moltmann* (London: T&T Clark, 2003).

Anderson, Benedict. *Imagined communities: reflections on the origin and spread of nationalism* (London: Verso, 1983).

Appadurai, Arjun. *Modernity at large: cultural dimensions of globalization* (Minneapolis: University of Minnesota Press, 1996).

Armstrong, Neil. '"I insisted I was myself": clergy wives and authentic selfhood in England c. 1960–94', *Women's History Review*, 22/6 (2013), 995–1013.

Atherstone, Andrew. *Archbishop Justin Welby: the road to Canterbury* (London: Darton, Longman and Todd, 2013).

Atherstone, Andrew. 'John Wimber's European impact', in Andrew Atherstone, Mark Hutchinson, and John Maiden (eds.), *Charismatic renewal in Europe and the United States since 1950* (Leiden: Brill, 2020), 215–39.

Atherstone, Andrew, Mark Hutchinson, and John Maiden (eds.). *Charismatic renewal in Europe and the United States since 1950* (Leiden: Brill, 2020).

Atherstone, Andrew, Mark Hutchinson, and John Maiden. 'The evidence of things unseen: the transatlantic charismatic movement in the postwar period', in Andrew Atherstone, Mark Hutchinson, and John Maiden (eds.), *Charismatic renewal in Europe and the United States since 1950* (Leiden: Brill, 2020), 1–18.

Barreira, Paul and David Hilliard. 'Filled with terrific joy! The beginnings of charismatic renewal in South Australian Methodism', *Church Heritage*, 8/2 (1993), 61–83.

Bates, J. Barrington. 'Extremely beautiful, but eminently unsatisfactory: Percy Dearmer and the healing rites of the Church, 1909–1928', *Anglican and Episcopal History*, 73/2 (2004), 196–207.

Battley, D. H. 'Charismatic renewal: a view from the inside', *The Ecumenical Review*, 31/1 (January 1986), 48–56.

Baum, Gregory. 'Catholicism and secularization in Quebec', in David Lyon and Marguerite Van Die (eds.), *Church, state and modernity: Canada between Europe and America* (Toronto: University of Toronto Press, 2000), 149–65.

Bebbington, David. *Evangelicalism in modern Britain: a history from the 1730s to the 1980s* (London: Unwin Hyman, 1989).

Bebbington, David. 'Evangelicals and public worship, 1965–2005', *Evangelical Quarterly*, 79/1 (2007), 3–22.

Belich, James. *Paradise reforged: a history of the New Zealanders from the 1980s to the year 2000* (Honolulu: University of Hawai'i Press, 2001).

Belich, James. *Replenishing the earth: the settler revolution and the rise of the Angloworld* (Oxford: Oxford University Press, 2011).

Bergunder, Michael. *The South Indian pentecostal movement in the twentieth century* (Grand Rapids: Eerdmans, 2008).

Bialecki, Jon. 'The third wave and the Third World: C. Peter Wagner, John Wimber, and the pedagogy of global renewal in the late twentieth century', *Pneuma*, 37 (2015), 177–200.

Black, Alisdair. 'Pour out your Spirit: experiences of the Holy Spirit amongst Scottish Baptists in the twentieth century', in Brian R. Talbot (ed.), *A distinctive people: a thematic study of aspects of the witness of Baptists in Scotland in the twentieth century* (Milton Keynes: Paternoster Press, 2014), 166–77.

Blumhofer, Edith. *Restoring the faith: the Assemblies of God, Pentecostalism and American culture* (Urbana: University of Illinois Press, 1993).

Blumhofer, Edith L., Russell P. Spittler, and Grant A. Wacker (eds.). *Pentecostal currents in American Protestantism* (Urbana: University of Illinois Press, 1999).

Bonner, Jeremy. *Called out of darkness into marvelous light: a history of the Episcopal Diocese of Pittsburgh, 1750–2006* (Eugene: Wipf & Stock, 2009).

Boobbyer, Philip. *The spiritual vision of Frank Buchman* (University Park: Pennsylvania State University Press, 2013).

Bowler, Kate. *Blessed: a history of the American prosperity gospel* (Oxford: Oxford University Press, 2013).

Bradshaw, Philip. *Following the Spirit: seeing Christian faith through community eyes* (Ropley: John Hunt, 2010).

Brewitt-Taylor, Sam. *Christian radicalism in the Church of England and the invention of the British sixties, 1957–1970* (Oxford: Oxford University Press, 2019).

Brewitt-Taylor, Sam. 'From religion to revolution: theologies of secularisation in the British Student Christian Movement, 1963–1973', *Journal of Ecclesiastical History*, 66/4 (2015), 792–811.

Brown, Callum. *Religion and the demographic revolution: women and secularization in Canada, Ireland, UK and USA since the 1960s* (Woodbridge: Boydell Press, 2012).

Brown, Callum. *The death of Christian Britain: understanding secularisation, 1800–2000* (London: Routledge, 2001).

Bruner, Jason. 'Keswick and the East African Revival: an historiographical reappraisal', *Religion Compass*, 5/9 (2011), 477–89.

Bryant, George. 'Four leaders in the Methodist Revival Fellowship, Aldersgate Fellowship and Affirm', *Wesley Historical Journal* (New Zealand), 65 (1997), 36–37.

Butler, Ewen H. *Canadian winds of the Spirit: holiness, pentecostal and charismatic currents* (Lexington: Emoth Press, 2018).

Campbell, Colin. 'The cult, the cultic milieu and secularization', in Jeffrey Kaplan and Heléne Lööw (eds.), *The cultic milieu: oppositional subcultures in an age of globalization* (Walnut Creek: Altamira Press, 2002), 12–25.

Campbell, Horace G. 'Coral gardens 1963: the Rastafari and Jamaican independence', *Social and Economic Studies*, 63/1 (2014), online.

Carter, Lindberg. *Charismatic movements and the Lutheran tradition* (Athens: University of Georgia Press, 1983).

Cartledge, Dave. *The apostolic revolution: the restoration of the apostles and prophets in the Assemblies of God in Australia* (Sydney: Paraclete Institute, 2000).

Chapman, Alister. *Godly ambition: John Stott and the evangelical movement* (Oxford: Oxford University Press, 2011).

Chapman, Alister. 'The international context of secularization in England: the end of empire, immigration, and the decline of Christian national identity, 1945–1970', *Journal of British Studies*, 54 (2015), 163–89.

Chaves, João B. '"Exporting holy fire": Southern Baptist missions, Pentecostalism and Baptist identity in Latin America', *Perspectives in Religious Studies*, 2/1 (2020), 203–14.

Chinnici, Joseph P. 'The Catholic community at prayer, 1926–1976', in James M. O'Toole (ed.), *Habits of devotion: Catholic religious practice in twentieth-century America* (Ithaca: Cornell University Press, 2004), 9–88.

Christerson, Brad and Richard Flory. *The rise of network Christianity: how independent leaders are changing the religious landscape* (New York: Oxford University Press, 2017).

Christiansen, Samantha and Zachary Scarlett (eds.). *The Third World in the global 1960s* (New York: Berghahn Books, 2013).

Ciciliot, Valentina. '"Pray aggressively for a higher goal—the unification of all Christianity": U.S. Catholic charismatics and their ecumenical relationships in the late 1960s and 1970s', *Religions*, 12/5 (2021), 353.

Ciciliot, Valentina. 'The origins of the Catholic Charismatic Renewal in the United States: early developments in Indiana and Michigan and the reactions of the ecclesiastical authorities', *Studies in World Christianity*, 25/3 (2019), 250–73.

Clark, Miles. *Glenn Clark: his life and writings* (Nashville: Abingdon Press, 1975).

Clarke, Christopher and Michael Ledger-Lomas, 'The Protestant International', in Abigail Green and Vincent Viaene (eds.), *Religious internationals in the modern age: globalization and faith communities since 1750* (Basingstoke: Palgrave Macmillan, 2012), 23–52.

Clifford, W. J. 'The evangelical/charismatic aspect of Methodism in New Zealand', *Wesley Historical Journal* (New Zealand), 65 (1997), 11.

Clifton, Shane. *Pentecostal churches in transition: analysing the developing ecclesiology of the Assemblies of God in Australia* (Leiden: Brill, 2009).

Cook, Hera. 'From controlling emotion to expressing feelings in mid-century England', *Journal of Social History*, 47/3 (2014), 627–46.

Cowan, Nelson. 'Lay-prophet-priest: the not-so-fledgling "office" of the worship leader', *Liturgy*, 32/1 (2017), 24–31.

Cox, Jeffrey. The English churches in a secular society: Lambeth, 1870–1930 (Oxford: Oxford University Press, 1982).

Csordas, Thomas J. *Language, charismatic and creativity: the ritual life of a religious movement* (Berkeley: University of California Press, 1997).

Csordas, Thomas J. 'Modalities of transnational transcendence', in Thomas J. Csordas (ed.), *Transnational transcendence: essays on religion and globalization* (Berkeley: University of California Press, 2009), 1–30.

Curtis, Heather D. 'A sane gospel: radical Evangelicals, psychology, and Pentecostal revival in the early twentieth century', *Religion and American culture*, 21/2 (2011), 195–226.

Curtis, Heather D. 'The global character of nineteenth-century divine healing', in Candy Gunther Brown (ed.), *Global Pentecostal and Charismatic healing* (New York: Oxford University Press, 2011), 29–45.

Cusic, Don. *Encyclopedia of contemporary Christian music: pop, rock and worship* (Santa Barbara: Greenwood Press, 2010).

Damberg, Wim. 'Is there an American exceptionalism? American and German Catholics in comparison', in David Hempton and Hugh McLeod (eds.), *Secularization and religious innovation in the North Atlantic world* (Oxford: Oxford University Press, 2017), 255–70.

Davson, Kate and Nagpal Szabolcs. *Living today the Church of tomorrow: forty years of the International Ecumenical Fellowship* (Manchester: British Region of the International Ecumenical Fellowship, 2009).

Dayton, Donald W. 'Methodism and Pentecostalism', in James Kirby and William Abraham (eds.), *The Oxford handbook of Methodist studies* (Oxford: Oxford University Press, 2010), 171–87.

Dayton, Donald W. 'The rise of the Evangelical healing movement in nineteenth century America', *Pneuma*, 4/1 (1982), 1–18.

De Arteaga, William L. 'Glenn Clark's Camps Furthest Out: the schoolhouse of the charismatic renewal', *Pneuma*, 25/2 (2003), 265–88.

De Groot, Kees. 'Three types of liquid religion', *Implicit Religion*, 11/3 (2008), 277–96.

De Gruchy, John W. *The church struggle in South Africa: 25th Anniversary edition* (Minneapolis: Fortress Press, 2005).

Dorr, Donal. *Remove the heart of stone* (Indianapolis: Paulist Press, 1978).

Douville, Bruce. '"And we've got to get ourselves back to the Garden": the Jesus People movement in Toronto', Historical Papers 2006, *Canadian Society of Church History*, 5–24.

Dwyer, Rachel. 'The Swaminarayan movement', in Knut Jacobsen and P. Patap Kumar (eds.), *South Asians in the diaspora: histories and religious traditions* (Leiden: Brill, 2004), 180–99.

Eiesland, Nancy L. 'Irreconcilable differences: conflict, schism and a religious restructuring in a United Methodist Church' in Edith Blumhofer, Russell P. Spittler, and Grant A. Wacker (eds.), *Pentecostal currents in American Protestantism* (Urbana: University of Illinois Press, 1999), 168–87.

Ellis, Bill. *Raising the Devil: Satanism, new religions and the media* (Lexington: University of Kentucky Press, 2000).

Ellwood, Robert S. *The Sixties spiritual awakening: American religion moving from modern to postmodern* (New Brunswick: Rutgers University Press, 1994).

Eskridge, Larry. *God's forever family: the Jesus People movement in America* (New York: Oxford University Press, 2013).

Everett, Helen. *Faith schools, tolerance and diversity: exploring the influence of education on students' attitudes of tolerance* (London: Palgrave Macmillan, 2010).

Faithful, George. *Mothering the fatherland: a Protestant sisterhood repents for the Holocaust* (Oxford: Oxford University Press, 2014).

Farley, A. Fay. 'A spiritual healing mission remembered: James Moore Hickson's Christian healing mission at Palmerston North, New Zealand, 1923', *Journal of Religious History*, 34/1 (2010), 1–19.

Faupel, D. William. 'The New Order of the Latter Rain: restoration or renewal', in Michael Wilkinson and Peter Althouse (eds.), *Winds from the north: Canadian contributions to the Pentecostal movement* (Leiden: Brill, 2010), 247–93.

Fink, Carole, Philipp Gassert, and Detlef Junker, 'Introduction', in Carole Fink, Philipp Gassert, and Detlef Junker (eds.), *1968: the world transformed* (Cambridge: Cambridge University Press, 1998), 1–30.

Freitag, Ulrike and Achim von Oppen. *Translocality: the study of globalising processes from a Southern perspective* (Leiden: Brill, 2010).

Gerlach, Luther P. and Virginia H. Hine. 'Five factors crucial to the growth and spread of a modern religious movement', *Journal for the Scientific Study of Religion*, 7/1 (1968), 23–40.

Goodhew, David. 'Church growth and decline in South Africa's churches, 1960–91', *Journal of Religion in Africa*, 30/3 (2000), 344–69.

Gorsuch, Anne E. and Diane P. Koenker. 'The socialist 1960s in global perspective', in Diane P. Koenker and Anne E. Gorsuch (eds.), *The socialist Sixties: crossing borders in the Second World* (Bloomington: Indiana University Press, 2013), 1–24.

Green, Simon. *The passing of Protestant England: secularisation and social change, c.1920–1960* (Cambridge: Cambridge University Press, 2010).

Griffith, Maria A. 'Women's Aglow Fellowship and mainline American Protestantism', in Edith Blumhofer, Russell P. Spittler, and Grant A. Wacker (eds.), *Pentecostal currents in American Protestantism* (Urbana: University of Illinois Press, 1999), 131–51.

Griffith, R. Marie. *Born again bodies: flesh and spirit in American Christianity* (Berkeley: University of California Press, 2004).

Grimley, Matthew. 'Anglican evangelicals and anti-permissiveness: the Nationwide Festival of Light, 1971–83', in Andrew Atherstone and John Maiden (eds.), *Evangelicalism and the Church of England in the twentieth century: reform, resistance and renewal* (Woodbridge: Boydell Press, 2013), 183–205.

Grimley, Matthew. 'Law, morality, and secularization: the Church of England and the Wolfenden Report, 1954–1967', *Journal of Ecclesiastical History*, 60 (2009), 725–41.

Hanrahan, James. 'The nature and history of the Catholic Charismatic renewal in Canada', *Bilan de l'Histoire religieuse au Canada*, 50/1 (1983), 307–24.

Harrell, Jr., David E. *Oral Roberts: an American life* (Bloomington: Indiana University Press, 1985).

Harris, Alana. 'Lourdes and holistic spirituality: contemporary Catholicism, the therapeutic and religious thermalism', *Culture and Religion*, 14/1 (2013), 23–43.

Hawn, C. Michael and J. H. Hobbs. '"Thy love hath broken every barrier down": the rhetoric of intimacy in nineteenth century British and American women's hymns', in Martin V. Clarke (ed.), *Music and theology in nineteenth-century Britain* (Farnham: Ashgate, 2012), 61–78.

Hayes, Stephen. *Black charismatic Anglicans* (Pretoria: University of South Africa, 1990).

Hejzlar, Paul. *Two paradigms of divine healing: Fred F. Bosworth, Kenneth E. Hagin, Agnes Sanford and Francis MacNutt in dialogue* (Leiden: Brill, 2009).

Hexham, Irving and Karla Poewe. 'Charismatic churches in South Africa: a critique of criticisms and problems of bias', in Karla Poewe (ed.), *Charismatic Christianity as a global culture* (Columbia: University of South Carolina Press, 1994), 50–69.

Higgins, Thomas W. 'Kenn Gulliksen, John Wimber, and the founding of the Vineyard Movement', *Pneuma*, 34 (2012), 208–28.

Hill, Clifford. *Black churches: West Indian and African sects in Britain* (London: British Council of Churches, 1971).

Hilliard, David. 'Church, family and sexuality in Australia in the 1950s', *Australian Historical Studies*, 27/109 (1997), 133–46.

Hilliard, David. 'The religious crisis of the 1960s: the experience of the Australian Churches', *Journal of Religious History*, 21 (1997), 209–27.

Hindmarsh, D. Bruce. *The Spirit of early evangelicalism: true religion in a modern world* (New York: Oxford University Press, 2018).

Hirschkind, Charles. *The ethical soundscape: cassette sermons and Islamic counterpublics* (New York: Columbia University Press, 2006).

Ho Yan Au, Connie. *Grassroots unity in the charismatic renewal* (Eugene: Wipf & Stock, 2011).

Hocken, Peter. 'Baptism in the Holy Spirit: a spiritual and theological journey', in Eric Nelson Newberg and Lois E. Olena (eds.), *Children of the calling: essays in honor of Stanley M. Burgess and Ruth V. Burgess* (Eugene: Wipf & Stock, 2014), 298–310.

Hocken, Peter. *Pentecost and Parousia: charismatic renewal, Christian unity and coming glory* (Eugene: Wipf & Stock, 2013).

Hocken, Peter. *Streams of renewal: the origins and early development of the charismatic movement in Great Britain* (Carlisle: Paternoster Press, 1986).

Hocken, Peter. 'What challenges do Pentecostals pose to Catholics?', *Journal of the European Pentecostal Theological Association*, 35/1 (2015), 48–57.

Hughson, Thomas. 'Interpreting Vatican II: "A new Pentecost"', *Theological Studies*, 69 (2008), 3–37.

Hunt, Stephen. 'The Anglican Wimberites', *Pneuma*, 17/1 (1995), 105–18.

Hunt, Stephen. 'The "Toronto Blessing": a lesson in globalized religion?', in Michael Wilkinson (ed.), *Canadian Pentecostalism: transition and transformation* (Montreal: McGill-Queen's University Press, 2009), 233–44.

Hutchinson, Mark. 'Australasian charismatic movements and the "New Reformation" of the 20th century?' *Australasian Pentecostal Studies*, 19 (2017), 24–53.

Hutchinson, Mark. 'Introduction: Australian charismatic movements as a space of flows', in Cristina Rocha, Mark Hutchinson, and Kathleen Openshaw (eds.), *Australian Pentecostal and Charismatic movements: arguments from the margins* (Leiden: Brill, 2020), 1–24.

Hutchinson, Mark. 'Reframing Howard Carter: alternative "routes" for the emergence of the Australasian Charismatic renewal', in Cristina Rocha, Mark Hutchinson, and

Kathleen Openshaw (eds.), *Australian Pentecostal and Charismatic movements: arguments from the margins* (Leiden: Brill, 2020), 25–52.

Hutchinson, Mark. 'The Latter Rain movement and the phenomenon of global return', in Michael Wilkinson and Peter Althouse (eds.), *Winds from the North: Canadian contributions to the Pentecostal movement* (Leiden: Brill, 2010), 265–84.

Hutchinson, Mark. 'The Worcester circle', https://www.academia.edu/345662/The_Worcester_Circle_An_Anglo_Catholic_attempt_at_Renewal_in_the_1920s, accessed 13 January 2021.

Jakelic, Slavica. 'The sixties: secularization and the prophesies of freedom', in Charles Mathewes and Christopher McKnight Nichols (eds.), *Prophesies of godlessness: predictions of America's imminent secularization from the Puritans to postmodernity* (Oxford: Oxford University Press, 2008).

Kangas, Billy. 'John Wimber and the Vineyard influence on Charismatic Catholic worship', in Lester Ruth (ed.), *Essays on the history of contemporary praise and worship* (Eugene: Wipf & Stock, 2020), 34–54.

Kay, William K. 'Apostolic networks in Britain: an analytic overview', *Transformations*, 25/1 (2008), 32–41.

Kay, William K. *Apostolic networks in Britain: new ways of being church* (Milton Keynes: Paternoster Press, 2007).

Kay, William K. 'Martyn Lloyd-Jones's influence on pentecostalism and neo-pentecostalism in the UK', *Journal of Pentecostal Theology*, 22 (2013), 275–94.

Klassen, Pam. *Spirits of Protestantism: medicine, healing and liberal Christianity* (Berkeley: University of California Press, 2011).

Knowles, Brett. '"From the ends of the earth we hear songs": music as an indicator of New Zealand Pentecostal spirituality and theology', *Australasian Pentecostal Studies*, 5/6 (2002), online.

Knowles, Brett. *New Life: a history of the New Life Churches in New Zealand, 1942–1979* (Dunedin: Third Millennium, 1999).

Knowles, Brett. *The history of a New Zealand Pentecostal movement: the New Life Churches of New Zealand from 1946–1979* (Lampeter: Edwin Mellen Press, 2000).

Kselman, Thomas A. and Steven Avella. 'Marian piety and the Cold War in the United States', *The Catholic Historical Review*, 72/3 (1986), 403–24.

Langhamer, Claire. 'Love, self-hood and authenticity in post-war Britain', *Cultural and Social History*, 9/2 (2012), 277–97.

Larsen, Timothy. 'Defining and locating evangelicalism', in Timothy Larsen and Daniel J. Treier (eds.), *The Cambridge companion to evangelical theology* (Cambridge: Cambridge University Press, 2012), 1–13.

Leahy, Brendan. *Ecclesial movements and communities: origins, significance and issues* (Hyde Park: New City Press, 2011).

Lears, T. J. Jackson. *No place for grace: antimodernism and the transformation of American culture, 1880–1920* (New York: Pantheon, 1981).

Leonard, Bill J. 'Dangerous and promising times: American religion in the post-war years', in Stephen Stein (ed.), *The Cambridge history of religions in America* (Cambridge: Cambridge University Press, 2009).

Lephoko, Daniel Simon Billie. *Nicholas Bhekinkosi Hepworth Bhengu's lasting legacy: world's best Black soul crusader* (Cape Town: AOSIS, 2018).

Levitt, Peggy. 'Religion on the move: mapping global cultural production and consumption', in Courtney Bender, Wendy Cadge, Peggy Levitt, and David Smilde (eds.), *Religion on the edge: de-centering and re-centering the sociology of religion* (New York: Oxford University Press, 2013), 159–78.

Lindberg, Carter. *Charismatic movements and the Lutheran tradition* (Macon: Mercer University Press, 1983).

Lineham, Peter. 'Tongues must cease: the Brethren and the charismatic movement in New Zealand', *Christian Brethren Review*, 34 (1983), 1–48.

Linn, Judith C. P. *The Charismatic movement in Taiwan from 1945–1995: clashes, concord and cacophony* (London: Palgrave Macmillan, 2020).

Macdonald, Stuart. 'Death of Christian Canada? Do Canadian church statistics support Callum Brown's timing of church decline?' *Historical Papers: Canadian Society of Church History*, 2006, 135–56.

McLeod, Hugh. *The religious crisis of the 1960s* (Oxford: Oxford University Press, 2007).

McNair, Benjamin G. *Apostles today: making sense of contemporary charismatic apostolates – a historical and theological appraisal* (Eugene: Wipf & Stock, 2014).

McRae, Fred W. *The history of the German Church Growth Association, 1985–2003* (Eugene: Wipf & Stock, 2014).

Maiden, John. 'A new nonconformity: ethnicity, evangelicalism and ecumenism, c. 1952–1985', in David Bebbington and David Ceri Jones (eds.), *Evangelicalism and dissent in modern England and Wales* (London: Routledge, 2020), 176–96.

Maiden, John. 'City, portal and hub: Brisbane and Catholic Charismatic Renewal', in Cristina Rocha, Mark Hutchinson, and Kathleen Openshaw (eds.), *Australian Pentecostal and Charismatic movements: arguments from the margins* (Leiden: Brill, 2020), 69–87.

Maiden, John. 'Evangelicals and Rome', in Andrew Atherstone and Mark Hutchinson (eds.), *The Routledge research companion to the history of evangelicalism* (London: Routledge, 2019), 93–109.

Maiden, John. '"Race", black majority churches and the rise of ecumenical multiculturalism in the 1970s', *Twentieth Century British History*, 30/4 (2019), 531–56.

Maiden, John. 'Renewing the body of Christ: Sharing of Ministries Abroad (SOMA) and transnational charismatic Anglicanism, 1978–1998', *Journal of American Studies*, 51/4 (2017), 1243–66.

Maiden, John. 'The emergence of Catholic Charismatic Renewal "in a country": Australia and transnational Catholic charismatic renewal', *Studies in World Christianity*, 25/3 (2019), 274–96.

Maiden, John. 'Watson, David Christopher Knight (1933–1984)', *ODNB* (online).

Mansfield, Patti Gallagher. *As by a new Pentecost: the dramatic beginning of the Catholic Charismatic Renewal* (Phoenix: Amor Deus, 2016).

Mansfield, Stephen. *Derek Prince: a biography* (Baldock: Derek Prince Ministries and Authentic Media, 2005).

Marrow, Alfred J. *The T-group experience: an encounter among people for greater self-fulfillment* (New York: Paul S. Eriksson, 1975).

Marsden, George. *Fundamentalism and American culture: the shaping of twentieth-century evangelicalism, 1870–1925* (New York: Oxford University Press, 1980).

Marty, Martin E. *A nation of behavers* (Chicago: University of Chicago Press, 1976).

Marty, Martin E. 'The American situation in 1969', in Donald R. Cutler (ed.), *The religious situation 1969* (Boston: Beacon Press, 1969), 15–43.

Matthew, David. 'Restorationism in British Church life: an insider's view', online.

Mbaya, Henry, H. *Resistance to and acquiescence in apartheid: St Paul's Theological College, Grahamstown, 1965–92* (Stellenbosch: Sun Press 2018).

Meintel, Deirdre and Guillaume Boucher. 'Doing battle with the forces of darkness in a secularized society', in Giuseppe Giordan and Adam Possamai (eds.), *The social scientific study of exorcism in Christianity* (Cham: Springer, 2020), 111–37.

Meyer, Birgit. 'Introduction: from imagined communities to aesthetic formations: religious mediations, sensational forms, and styles of binding', in Birgit Meyer, *Aesthetic formations: media, religion, and the senses* (New York: Palgrave Macmillan, 2009), 1–28.

Meyer, Birgit. 'Mediation and immediacy: sensational forms, semiotic ideologies and the question of the medium', *Social Anthropology*, 1/19 (2011), 23–39.

Miller, David. *God at work: the history and promise of the Faith at Work Movement* (New York: Oxford University Press, 2007).

Miller, Donald E. *Reinventing American Protestantism: Christianity in a new millennium* (Berkeley: University of California Press, 1997).

Miller, Timothy. 'Religious communes in America: an overview', in Timothy Miller (ed.), *Spiritual and visionary communities: out to save the world* (London: Routledge, 2016), 191–206.

Mitchell, Dot. *He said yes! The story of Derek A. Crumpton* (Self-published, 2018).

Moir, Les. *Missing jewel: the worship movement that impacted the nations* (Eastbourne: David C. Cook, 2017).

Montemaggi, Francesca E. S. *Authenticity and religion in a pluralistic age: a Simmelian study of Christian evangelicals and new monastics* (Lanham: Rowman & Littlefield, 2019).

Moore, S. David. '"Discerning the times": the victorious eschatology of the shepherding movement', in Peter Althouse and Robby Waddell (eds.), *Perspectives in Pentecostal eschatology: world without end* (Cambridge: James Clarke and Co., 2010), 273–92.

Moore, S. David. *The shepherding movement: controversy and charismatic ecclesiology* (London: T&T Clark, 2003).

Morgan, David. 'Mediation or mediatisation: the history of media in the study of religion', *Culture and Religion*, 12/2 (2011), 137–52.

Mufuka, K. Nyamayaro. 'The Christian Church under stress in Southern Africa since 1960', *Historical Papers: Canadian Society of Church History* (1979), 1–18.

Nabhan-Warren, Kristy. "Blooming where we're planted": Mexican-descent Catholics living out *Cursillo de Cristiandad*', *U.S. Catholic Historian*, 28/4 (2010), 99–125.

Nabhan-Warren, Kristy. *The Cursillo movement in America: Catholics, Protestants and fourth day spirituality* (Chapel Hill: University of North Carolina Press, 2013).

Nabhan-Warren, Kristy '"We are the Church": the Cursillo movement and the reinvention of Catholic identities in postwar America and beyond', *U.S. Catholic Historian*, 33/1 (2015), 81–98.

Nienkirchen, Charles. 'Conflicting visions of the past: the prophetic use of history in the early American Pentecostal-Charismatic movements', in Karla Poewe (ed.), *Charismatic Christianity as a global culture* (Columbia: University of South Carolina Press, 1994).

Park, Joon-Sik. 'The legacy of Reuben Archer Torrey III', *International Bulletin of Mission Research*, 41/3 (2017), 261–71.

Parsons, Talcott and Gerald M. Platt. *The American university* (Cambridge, MA: Harvard University Press, 1973).

Pepin, David. *Cathedrals of Britain* (London: Bloomsbury, 2016).

Pike, Sarah M. *New age and neopagan religions in America* (New York: Columbia University Press, 2004).

Poewe, Karla. 'Introduction: the nature, globality and history of charismatic Christianity', in Karla Poewe (ed.), *Charismatic Christianity as a global culture* (Columbia: University of South Carolina Press, 1994), 1–29.

Porter, Mark. 'Charismatic worship and cosmopolitan movement(s)', *Liturgy*, 33/3 (2018), 4–11.

Presler, Titus. 'The history of mission in the Anglican Communion', in Ian S. Markham, J. Barney Hawkins IV, Justyn Terry, and Leslie Nuñez Steffensen (eds.), *The Wiley-Blackwell companion to the Anglican Communion* (London: Wiley-Blackwell, 2013), 15–32.

Quebedeaux, Richard. *The new charismatics* (New York: Doubleday, 1976).

Randall, Ian. 'Baptist revival and renewal in the 1960s', in Kate Cooper and Jeremy Gregory (eds.), *Revival and resurgence in Christian history* (Woodbridge: Boydell Press, 2008), 341–53.

Randall, Ian. 'Graham Scroggie and evangelical spirituality', *Scottish Bulletin of Evangelical Theology*, 18/1 (2000), 71–86.

Randall, Ian. 'Lloyd-Jones and revival', in Andrew Atherstone and David Ceri Jones (eds.), *Engaging with Martyn Lloyd-Jones* (Leicester: Inter-Varsity Press, 2011), 91–113.

Reed, David A. 'Denominational charismatics – where have they all gone? A Canadian Anglican case study', in Michael Wilkinson (ed.), *Canadian Pentecostalism: transition and transformation* (Toronto: McGill-Queen's University Press, 2009), 197–213.

Reynolds, Amber Thomas. 'Robert Walker's Christian Life magazine: a missing link between mainstream American evangelicalism and charismatic renewal', in Andrew Atherstone, Mark P. Hutchinson and John Maiden, *Transatlantic charismatic renewal c. 1950–2000* (Leiden: Brill, 2021), 37–60.

Riches, Tanya and Tom Wagner. 'The evolution of Hillsong Music: from Australian Pentecostal congregation into global brand', *Australian Journal of Communication*, 31/1 (2012), 17–36.

Richman, Karen and Terry Rey. 'Congregating by cassette: recording and participation in transnational Haitian religious ritual', *International Journal of Cultural Studies*, 12/2 (2009), 149–66.

Robinson, James. *Divine healing: the years of expansion: theological variation in the transatlantic world* (Eugene: Wipf & Stock, 2014).

Rose, Nikolas. 'Assembling the modern self', in Roy Porter (ed.), *Rewriting the self: histories from the Renaissance to the present* (London: Routledge, 1997), 224–48.

Rossinow, Doug. '"The break-through to new life": Christianity and the emergence of the New Left in Austin, Texas, 1956–64', *American Quarterly*, 46/3 (1994), 309–40.

Rossinow, Doug. *The politics of authenticity: liberalism, Christianity, and the New Left in America* (New York: Columbia University Press, 1998).

Roudometof, Victor. 'Orthodox Christianity as transnational religion: theoretical, historical and comparative considerations', *Religion, State and Society*, 43/3 (2015), 211–27.

Rybarczyk, Edmund J. 'New churches: pentecostals and the Bible', in John Riches (ed.), *The new Cambridge history of the Bible* (Cambridge: Cambridge University Press, 2015).

Saunders, Teddy and Hugh Samson. *David Watson* (London: Hodder & Stoughton, 1982).

Schenkel, Albert Fredrick. 'New wine and Baptist wineskins: American and Southern Baptist denominational responses to the charismatic renewal, 1960–80', in Edith Blumhofer, Russell P. Spittler, and Grant A. Wacker (eds.), *Pentecostal currents in American Protestantism* (Urbana: University of Illinois Press, 1999), 152–67.

Schiller, Nina Glick, Tsypylma Darieva, and Sandra Gruner-Domic. 'Defining cosmopolitan sociability in a transnational age: an introduction', *Ethnic and Racial Studies*, 34/3 (2011), 399–418.

Schofield, Barry. 'Church renewal: examples', in Geoff Waugh (ed.), *Church on fire* (Melbourne: Joint Board of Christian Education, 2012).

Shuff, Roger, *Searching for the true Church: Brethren and evangelicals in mid-twentieth-century England* (Milton Keynes: Paternoster Press, 2005).

Smith, Erin A. *What would Jesus read? Popular religious books and everyday life in twentieth-century America* (Chapel Hill: University of North Carolina Press, 2015).

Smith, Graham R. *The Church militant: spiritual warfare in the Anglican charismatic renewal* (Eugene: Wipf & Stock, 2016).

Spector, Stephen. *Evangelicals and Israel: the story of American Christian Zionism* (Oxford: Oxford University Press, 2009).

Stanford, Peter. *Bronwen Astor: her life and times* (London: HarperCollins, 2000).

Stanley, Brian. *The global diffusion of evangelicalism* (Downers Grove: Inter-Varsity Press, 2013).

Steindl-Rast, D. 'Charismatic renewal: a challenge to Roman Catholic worship', *Worship*, 48/7 (1974), 382–91.

Sutcliffe, Steven. *Children of the New Age: a history of spiritual practices* (London: Routledge, 2003).

Swartz, David R. *Facing west: American evangelicals in an age of World Christianity* (New York: Oxford University Press, 2020).

Swartz, David R. *Moral minority: the evangelical Left in the age of conservatism* (Pittsburgh: University of Pennsylvania Press, 2012).

Sweet, Leonard I. 'The 1960s: the crises of liberal Christianity and the public emergence of evangelicalism', in George Marsden (ed.), *Evangelicalism and modern America* (Grand Rapids: Eerdmans,1984), 29–45.

Swenson, Donald S. 'The Canadian Catholic Charismatic renewal', in Michael Wilkinson (ed.), *Canadian Pentecostalism: transition and transformation* (Toronto: McGill-Queen's University Press, 2009), 214–32.

Thompson, Glen. '"Transported away": the spirituality and piety of charismatic Christianity in South Africa (1976–1994)', *Journal of Theology for Southern Africa*, 128 (2004), 128–45.

Thompson, Roger C. *Religion in Australia: a history* (Melbourne: Oxford University Press, 1994).

Torrey, Deberniere. 'Yesuwŏn: an ongoing experiment in the Kangwŏndo wilderness', *Journal of Korean Religions*, 4/1 (2013), 139–67.

Turek, L. F. 'To support a "Brother in Christ": evangelical groups and U.S.-Guatemalan relations during the Ríos Montt regime', *Diplomatic History*, 39/4 (2015), 689–719.

Wacker, Grant. 'Marching to Zion: religion in a modern utopian community', *Church History*, 54/4 (1985), 496–511.

Wacker, Grant. 'Travail of a broken family: evangelical responses to Pentecostalism in America, 1906–1916', *Journal of Ecclesiastical History*, 47/3 (1996), 505–28.

Walker, Andrew. *Restoring the Kingdom: the radical Christianity of the house church movement* (Guildford: Eagle, 1998).

Walker, Andrew. '"Thoroughly modern": sociological reflections on the Charismatic movement from the end of the twentieth century', in Stephen J. Hunt, Tony Walter, and Malcolm Hamilton (eds.), *Charismatic Christianity* (Basingstoke: Macmillan, 1997), 17–42.

Ward, Kevin. *Losing our religion? Changing patterns of believing and belonging in secular Western societies* (Eugene: Wipf & Stock, 2013).

Ward, Pete. 'The economies of charismatic evangelical worship', in Gordon Lynch, Jolyon Mitchell, and Anna Strhan (eds.), *Religion, media and culture: a reader* (Abingdon: Routledge, 2012), 23–30.

Warner, R. Stephen. *New wine in old wineskins* (Berkeley: University of California Press, 1988).

Warren, Heather A. 'The shift from character to personality in mainline Protestant thought, 1935–1945', *Church History*, 67/3 (1998), 537–55.

Waters, Ken. 'Christian journalism's finest hour? An analysis of the failure of the *National Courier* and Inspiration', *Journalism History*, 20 (1984), 55–65.

Waters, Malcolm. *Globalization* (London: Routledge, 1995).

Weaver, John. *The New Apostolic Reformation: history of a modern charismatic movement* (Jefferson: McFarland and Co., 2016).

Wigger, John. *PTL: the rise and fall of Jim and Tammy Faye Bakker's evangelical empire* (New York: Oxford University Press, 2017).

Williams, Joseph. 'The pentecostalization of Christian Zionism', *Church History*, 84/1 (2015), 159–94.

Woodbridge, David. 'Watchman Nee, Chinese Christianity and the global search for the primitive Church', *Studies in World Christianity*, 22/2 (2016), 125–47.

Wuthnow, Robert and Stephen Offutt. 'Transnational religious connections', *Sociology of Religion*, 69/2 (2008), 209–32.

Vásquez, Manuel A. *More than belief: a materialist theory of religion* (Oxford: Oxford University Press, 2011).

Yeo, K. K. 'Biblical interpretation in the majority world', in Mark P. Hutchinson (ed.), *The Oxford history of Protestant dissenting traditions*, vol. 5: *The twentieth century: themes and variations in a global context* (Oxford: Oxford University Press, 2019), 131–69.

Young, David M. *Turned East: half a life for Albania* (Wrexham: Quinta Press, 2011).

Zeifle, Joshua. *David du Plessis and the Assemblies of God: the struggle for the soul of a movement* (Leiden: Brill, 2014).

Zeller, Benjamin E.'American postwar "Big Religion": reconceptualizing twentieth-century American religion using big science as a model', *Church History*, 80/2 (2011), 321–51.

Zink, Jesse. '"Anglocostalism" in Nigeria: neo-Pentecostals and obstacles to Anglican unity', *Journal of Anglican Studies*, 10/2 (2013), 231–50.

Unpublished theses

Bethke, Andrew-John. 'Contemporary musical expression in Anglican churches in the Diocese of Cape Town: developments since the liturgical, theological and social revolutions of the twentieth century', PhD thesis, University of Cape Town (2012).

Bulger, James J. 'Unity in the Spirit: contribution of the charismatic renewal to ecumenism', Senior thesis, University of Notre Dame (2014).

Douville, Bruce. 'The uncomfortable pew: Christianity, the New Left and the hip counterculture in Toronto, 1976–1975', PhD dissertation, York University (2011).

Edmondson, Christopher P. 'Modern developments in Christian community living within the Church of England since 1945, with special reference to St. Julian's, Lee Abbey and the Pilsdon community', MA thesis, Durham University (1971).

Erickson, Douglas R.'The Kingdom of God and the Holy Spirit: eschatology and pneumatology in the Vineyard movement', PhD thesis, Marquette University (2015).

Green, Alison. 'New Zealand migrants to Australia: social construction of migrant identity', PhD thesis, Bond University (2007).

Harrison, Paul B. 'An analytical study of the Latter Rain teachings and practices of New Zealand pentecostalism (1950–2000)', MA thesis, University of Auckland (2009).

Hey, Sam. 'God in the suburbs and beyond: the emergence of an Australian megachurch and denomination', PhD thesis, Griffith University (2010).

Jackson, Kody Sherman. 'Jesus, Jung and the charismatics: the Pecos Benedictines and visions of religious renewal', MA thesis, University of Texas (2016).

Ngomane, Richard M. 'Leadership mentoring and succession in charismatic churches in Bushbuckridge: a critical assessment in the light of 2 Timothy 2:1–3', PhD thesis, University of Pretoria (2013).

Reid, Michael Andrew. 'But by my Spirit: a history of the charismatic renewal in Christchurch, 1960–1985', PhD thesis, University of Canterbury (2003).

Robinson, Martin. 'The charismatic Anglican: historical and contemporary. A comparison of the life and work of Alexander Boddy (1854–1930) and Michael C. Harper', MLitt thesis, University of Birmingham (1976).

Scott, James Martin. 'The theology of the so-called "new church" movement: an analysis of the eschatology', MA thesis, Brunel University (1997).

van der Laan, Paulus Nicolaas. 'The question of spiritual unity: the Dutch Pentecostal movement in ecumenical perspective', PhD thesis, University of Birmingham (1988).

Williamson, Dale. 'An uncomfortable engagement: the charismatic renewal in the New Zealand Anglican Church, 1965–85', PhD thesis, University of Otago (2007).

Biographical Collections

Australasian Dictionary of Pentecostal and Charismatic Movements (online).

Dictionary of African Christian Biography (online).

Oxford Dictionary of National Biography (online).

Websites and Tweets

Clark, Dennis. 'The Fig Tree', audio sermon, 1972 (online), http://denisgclark.pbworks.com/w/page/17471953/OralMaterials, accessed 21 May 2021.

Cummings, Tony. 'The Sheep: '70s Jesus freaks who pioneered the Lonesome Stone Rock Opera', https://www.crossrhythms.co.uk/articles/music/The_Sheep_70s_Jesus_freaks_who_pioneered_the_Lonesome_Stone_rock_opera/50944/p1/, accessed 21 June 2021.

Denzer, Marty. 'Revd. Mr Donald Schmit'. https://catholickey.org/2014/10/10/rev-mr-donald-schmit/, accessed 7 November 2020.

Evans, John. 'The history of Love in Action', https://exgaywatch.com/2005/08/co-founder-sick/, accessed 21 May 2021.

Ivereigh, Austen. 'Is Francis our first charismatic Pope?' 14 June 2019, https://www.americamagazine.org/faith/2019/06/14/francis-our-first-charismatic-pope.

'Joseph Mattsso-Boze: a thoroughgoing revivalist', https://lrm1948.blogspot.com/2008/12/joseph-mattsson-boze-thoroughgoing.html, accessed 26 May 2021.

'Pentecost Vigil of Prayer: address by His Holiness Pope Francis', https://www.vatican.va/content/francesco/en/speeches/2017/june/documents/papa-francesco_20170603_veglia-pentecoste.html, accessed 23 June 2021.

Santistevan, David. 'David Garrett on worship music in the 60s, Scripture in Song and being led by the Holy Spirit' (interview), https://www.davidsantistevan.com/58/, accessed 21 May 2021.

Stube, E. B. *A fire is burning* (self-published), http://www.jspi.info/media/BookBlack/Eng-books/A%20Fires%20Burning%20-EB%20Stube/A%20Fire%20is%20Burning%20(UpTo- 1972).pdf, accessed 25 May 2021.

The Word of God Covenant Community, 1970–1991 (A Branch of the Sword of the Spirit, 1982–1991), https://www.scribd.com/document/98731671/Critique-of-Life-and-Development-of-the-Word-of-God-1991-by-Clark-Maney-Noetzel, accessed 23 April 2020.

Virgo, Terry. 'The story so far', Stoneleigh Bible Week, https://www.youtube.com/watch?v=nd79zP1VIuQ, accessed 26 March 2020.

Wilson Okonjo Adongo, 'Owiti, Silas Javan Aggrey', *Dictionary of African Christian Biography*, https://dacb.org/stories/kenya/owiti-silas/, accessed 23 June 2021.

Index

For the benefit of digital users, indexed terms that span two pages (e.g., 52–53) may, on occasion, appear on only one of those pages.

The manufacturer's authorised representative in the EU for product safety is Oxford University Press España S.A. of El Parque Empresarial San Fernando de Henares, Avenida de Castilla, 2 – 28830 Madrid (www.oup.es/en or product.safety@oup.com). OUP España S.A. also acts as importer into Spain of products made by the manufacturer.

Printed in the USA/Agawam, MA
November 20, 2025

896312.467